Civil Society Processes and the State

Civil Society Processes and the State

The Bharat Gyan Vigyan Samiti and the Literacy Campaigns

DENZIL SALDANHA

RAWAT PUBLICATIONS
Jaipur • New Delhi • Bangalore • Hyderabad • Guwahati

ISBN 81-316-0352-0

Published by
Prem Rawat for **Rawat Publications**
Satyam Apts, Sector 3, Jawahar Nagar, Jaipur 302 004 (India)
Phone: 0141 265 1748 / 7006 Fax: 0141 265 1748
E-mail: info@rawatbooks.com
Website: www.rawatbooks.com

New Delhi Office
4858/24, Ansari Road, Daryaganj, New Delhi 110 002
Phone: 011 2326 3290

Also at Bangalore, Hyderabad and Guwahati

Typeset by Rawat Computers, Jaipur
Printed at Chaman Enterprises, New Delhi

Contents

Part II
Major Projects

List of Tables and Illustrations

TABLES

ILLUSTRATIONS

Abbreviations and Translations

Abhivyakti	Expression
AFLP	Accelerated Female Literacy Programme
AIPSN	All India People's Science Network
ANM	Auxiliary Nurse Midwife
APPEAL	Asia-Pacific Programme of Education for All
ASF	Asia Social Forum
Bal Manch	Children's Forum
Balmelas	Children's Festivals
Bal Sansad	Children's Parliament
BERC	Basic Education Research Centre
BGVJ	Bharat Gyan Vigyan Jatha (Indian Cultural Caravan for Scientific Awareness)
BGVS	Bharat Gyan Vigyan Samiti (The Indian Scientific Awareness Committee)
Bhashans	Speeches
BJP	Bharatiya Janata Party
BJVJ	Bharat Jan Vigyan Jatha (The Indian People's Science Caravan)
CABE	Central Advisory Board on Education
CAPART	Council for Advancement of People's Action and Rural Technology
CBO	Community-Based Organization
CCA	Convergent Community Action
CE	Continuing Education
CEC	Continuing Education Centre
Charcha Mandals	Discussion Groups
CLEP	Continuing and Lifelong Education Programme
DAE	Directorate of Adult Education
DG, NLM	Director General, National Literacy Mission

Dharnas	Sit-ins
DJDB	Desh Ko Janein Desh Ko Badlein (Let's Know and Change the Country)
DPEP	District Primary Education Programme
DST	Department of Science and Technology
DWACRA	Development of Women and Children in Rural Areas
EFA	Education for All
FCRA	Foreign Contribution Regulation Act
FFLP	Farmer's Functional Literacy Project
FLAW	Functional Literacy for Adult Women
GoI	Government of India
GP	Gram Panchayat (The Village Committee, the village institution for local self-governance)
GVK	Gyan Vigyan Kendra (Centre for Scientific Awareness)
GVV	Gyan Vigyan Vidyalaya (School for Scientific Awareness)
Hamara Desh	Our Country
Hindustan Ki Betiyan	Daughters of Hindustan
ICDS	Integrated Child Development Services
ILO	International Labour Office
IMF	International Monetary Fund
IPCL	Improved Pace and Content of Learning
Jan Chetna Kendras	People's Awakening Centres
Jan Sunwais	Public Hearings
Janadhikar Kalajathas	Cultural Caravan on People's Rights
Janotsava	People's Science Festival
Jansansad	People's Parliament
Jatha	Caravan (a socio-cultural caravan for development communication)
Jeevanshala	Schooling for Life
JoL	Joy of Learning
JSA	Jan Swasthya Abhiyan (People's Health Campaign)
JSN	Jana Shiksha Nilayam
JSS	Jan Shikshan Sansthan (People's Education Institution)
JVA	Jan Vachan Andolan (People's Reading/ Library Movement)
Kalajathas	Cultural caravans
Krishi Vigyan Kendras	Centres for Agricultural Science
KSSP	Kerala Shastra Sahitya Parishad (The Kerala Science Literature Organization)
LHP	Literacy to Health Project
Lok Sampark Andolan	Movement for Contact with People

MALAR	Mahalir Association for Literacy, Awareness and Rights
Melas	Fairs
MHRD	Ministry of Human Resource Development
MKSS	Mazdoor Kisan Shakti Sangathan (Organization of Workers and Peasants Power)
MPFL	Mass Programme of Functional Literacy
NABARD	National Bank for Agriculture and Rural Development
NAEP	National Adult Education Programme
NCC	National Coordination Centre
NCEC	Nodal Continuing Education Centre
NCERT	National Council for Educational Research and Training
NCSTC	National Council for Science and Technology Communication
NDA	National Democratic Alliance
NFE	Non-Formal Education
NIHFW	National Institute of Health and Family Welfare
NIOS	National Institute of Open Schooling
NLM	National Literacy Mission
NLMA	National Literacy Mission Authority
NLRC	National Literacy Resource Centre
NREGA	National Rural Employment Guarantee Act
NRHM	National Rural Health Mission
NSS	National Service Scheme
NUEPA	National University for Educational Planning and Administration
PAC	Project Advisory Committee
Padyatras	Processions/marches
Panchayati Raj	Local Self-governance
Pathak Manch	Reading clubs
PDS	Public Distribution System
PESA	Panchayat Extension to Scheduled Areas
PHA	People's Health Assembly
PHC	Primary Health Centre
PIA	Project Implementing Agency
PL	Post-Literacy
PRA	Participatory Rural Appraisal
Prerak	Animator
PRM	Participatory Resource Mapping
PSM	People's Science Movement
PSN	People's Science Network
PUCL	People's Union for Civil Liberties

REFLECT	Regenerated Freirean Literacy through Empowering Community Techniques
RFLP	Rural Functional Literacy Project
RGNDWM	Rajiv Gandhi National Drinking Water Mission
Rozgar Adhikar Yatra	Right to Work Caravan
Saksharta Vahini	Groups of literacy activists
Samata Vigyan Utsavas	Samata science festivals
Sampark Andolans	Contact movement
SC	Scheduled Caste
SDTT	Sir Dorabji Tata Trust
SEP	Social Education Programme
SEZ	Special Economic Zone
SGSY	Swarna Jayanti Gram Swarozgar Yojana (Golden Jubilee Village Self-Employment Scheme)
SHG	Self-Help Groups
Shramik Vidyapeeths	Worker's Universities
SLM	State Literacy Mission
SLMA	State Literacy Mission Authority
SMC	School Management Committee
SRC	State Resource Centre
SSA	Sarva Shiksha Abhiyan (Campaign for Education for All)
ST	Scheduled Tribe
SVU	Samata Vigyan Utsava (Samata science festival)
TL	Total Literacy
TLC	Total Literacy Campaign
TNSF	Tamil Nadu Science Forum
UEE	Universal Elementary Education
UNDP	United Nations Development Programme
UNESCO	United Nations Educational Scientific and Cultural Organization
UNICEF	United Nations International Children's Emergency Fund
UPA	United Progressive Alliance
UT	Union Territory
Utsava	Festival
VEC	Village Education Committee
WATSAN	Integrated Drinking Water and Sanitation
WB	World Bank
WDT	Watershed Development Team
WSF	World Social Forum
WTO	World Trade Organization
ZSS	Zilla Saksharata Samiti (District Literacy Committee)

Acknowledgements

I am grateful to the Ministry of Human Resource Development, Department of Elementary Education and Literacy for inviting me to undertake this study and for sponsoring the earlier part of it from 1999 to 2003. The Sir Dorabji Tata Trust sponsored the latter part of the study and the review of the field activities of the Bharat Gyan Vigyan Samiti from 2004 to 2007. I am thankful for this support. The Tata Institute of Social Sciences facilitated my undertaking this research as part of my academic responsibilities.

Thanks are due to Urvashi Butalia who collaborated with me during the field visits and review from 2004 to 2007. Several research assistants, field investigators and secretarial staff, too many to mention individually, assisted me at different times over the last 20 years including my earlier studies on the literacy campaigns during the late 1980s and early 1990s. All of these experiences have gone into the making of this study and I am grateful to them. I am grateful to Rawat Publications for publishing this study efficiently and in quick time and to the many well-wishers who facilitated the publication.

The leadership of the Bharat Gyan Vigyan Samiti (BGVS) at the national, state and district levels and the field level activists provided unstinting support. It was refreshing to be involved in a research capacity with an organization that was as committed in its interventions, as it was honest in its critical self-assessment. The activists and the participants in the literacy campaigns have been a major source of inspiration for one's efforts for over two decades. One is aware that this study does not capture the entire scope and significance of the interventions of the BGVS. One's effort may be seen as a small contribution to the process of social transformation that has been visualized in the literacy campaigns and to highlighting the potential of social formations such as the BGVS in this process.

Denzil Saldanha

Part I

The Context and History of Campaign Interventions

1

Introduction

1. The Issues

Some explanation is called for as regards the choice of the cover page illustration of this book. It says more than it immediately and on the surface reveals. The Bharat Gyan Vigyan Samiti (BGVS) through the literacy campaigns focused neither on children nor on the aged, though it did not neglect these sections. Its primary thrust was working with the productive and relatively youthful age group of 15 to 35 years. Yet, to modify an expression, if children are parents of grandparents; then the goal of BGVS was very much working towards a just and sustainable future for present and future generations. The illustration in some ways also speaks of the need to view education, not in isolation, but as part of larger socio-economic, cultural and political processes of development that have policy implications. If mobilizations for education are viewed in this manner then they uncover the evident, even though latent, demand for learning. In sum, the messages in the illustration constitute the story in this book of predicaments and challenges faced and not always overcome, but with some clear pointers to the future.

The number of non-literates in the productive age group of 15 to 35 years had increased from 90 million in 1951 to 107 million in 1981, with a further increase to an estimated 121 million by 1991. There were 328 million non-literates in India in the age group seven years and above in 1991, even though the literacy rate for that age group had increased from 44 per cent in 1981 to 52 per cent in 1991 (Prem Chand, 2007 and 2008). While these figures represent a significant increase in literacy rate from the 5.4 per cent for the total population in 1901 and from 18 per cent for the total population and 9 per cent for females in 1951, about the time of independence, the data for 1991 suggest a persisting unjust situation. This is especially so for a country, which had most of the relevant policy documents on education but whose identified targets had been consistently bypassed, and (a nation) which was a signatory to all relevant international agreements on the subject of education as a basic right. Illiteracy in 1988 was largely concentrated in seven states of the country – Uttar Pradesh, Bihar, Madhya Pradesh, Rajasthan, Andhra Pradesh, West Bengal and Maharashtra – where more than 70 per cent of the non-literate population was residing. The foregoing was the literacy scenario that confronted the National Literacy Mission (NLM) around the time of its formation in 1988.

The NLM documents entitled *Adult Education in India*, August 2008 and *Strategies for Adult Education*, August 2009 provide an overview of the several policy and programmatic attempts that had been made since independence till 1988 towards adult education. The Social Education Programme (SEP), implemented during the First Five-Year Plan, 1951–56, was one of the earliest and accompanied the Community Development (CD) initiatives. The Gram Shikshan Mohim, started initially on a small scale in Satara district, Maharashtra in 1959, was later extended to other parts of the state with diminishing returns. One of the earliest basic education campaigns in the country, it intended to impart literacy skills within a period of four months. The Farmer's Functional Literacy Project (FFLP) was started in 1967–68 in collaboration with different government ministries related to the training and functional literacy of agriculturists. Around the time of the Green Revolution that was taking place in certain pockets of the country, the project aimed at popularizing high yielding varieties of seeds through adult education in 144 districts. The Non-Formal Education (NFE) Programme for youth was initiated at the start of the Fifth Five-Year Plan in 1975 for the age group 15 to 25 years. A programme for the Functional Literacy for Adult Women (FLAW) was started in 1975–76 in relation to the Integrated Child Development Scheme. Awareness of aspects of health, hygiene and child care was associated with literacy for non-literate adult women. The National Adult Education Programme (NAEP), launched on October 2, 1978, was the first such effort taken up on a large scale throughout the country through a project approach. It attempted to cover 100 million non-literate adults in the age group of 15 to 35 within a period of five years so as to provide them literacy, functional skills and critical awareness. The Rural Functional Literacy Project (RFLP) was closely associated with the NAEP in conducting literacy centres with instructors being paid an honorarium. This centre-based strategy consisted of a project, one in each district, of about 300 centres, each run by a paid instructor and catering to the needs of about 30 learners. The first Director General of the NLM found that the NAEP had generally failed to produce satisfactory impact primarily because of a lack of adequate planning and preparation within diverse cultural contexts and due to a neglect of creating a demand for literacy prior to intervention (Mishra in Mukherjee and Vasanta, eds., 2002: 127). The Mass Programme of Functional Literacy (MPFL) launched on May 1, 1986 attempted to involve educated youth from the National Service Scheme (NSS), the National Cadet Corp (NCC) and other students from the university system. The NLM documents mentioned above classify the various initiatives since independence into two broad approaches: the selective-intensive (targeted) approach such as the FFLP, the FLAW, MPFL and the NFE; and the mass campaign approach of which the Gram Shikshan Mohim and the literacy campaigns may be seen as examples.

Another broad classification of the history of Indian adult education is provided by Shah (1993: 4 and 36). He suggests a phase of basic literacy (1882–1947) where the approach was more traditional and religious and was largely operationalized through night schools; followed by civic literacy (1949–1966) with a life-oriented thrust and implemented through the Social Education Programme; functional literacy (1968–1977), where literacy was oriented towards conditions of work through programmes such as Farmers Education and Functional Literacy and Shramik Vidyapeeths (Worker's Universities); and lastly a developmental literacy (1978-till date) oriented towards social change to varying degrees and executed through NAEP, MPFL and the TLCs. One might notice a general trend – from a charitable and welfarist approach to literacy to a more comprehensive one that, to some degree, recognizes the social conditions that perpetuate illiteracy, passing through an intermediary phase of a more targeted and sectoral thrust.

The NLM initiated on May 5, 1988 as one of the five Technology Missions had set a target of imparting functional literacy to 80 million persons in the age group 15 to 35 years – 30 million by 1990 and another 50 million by 1995. Functional literacy, according to the NLM, implied:

> "achieving self-reliance in literacy and numeracy;
> becoming aware of the causes of their deprivation and moving towards amelioration of their condition through organization, and participation in the process of development;

> acquiring skills to improve the economic status and general well-being; imbibing the values of national integration, conservation of the environment, women's equality, observance of small family norm, etc." (Ministry of Human Resource Development, Department of Education, January 1988: 14).

The NLM was seen as

> "a Societal Mission which implies that there is a political will at all levels for the achievement of Mission goals, that a national consensus can be created for mobilization of social forces, and mechanisms can be created for active participation of the people through energization of their talent and potential with the ultimate objective of promoting a qualitative change in their living and working conditions" (ibid.: 5).

By the time of the 2001 Census – about 12 years into literacy campaigns – the figure of non-literates in the age group of 15 to 35, considering the movement of age cohorts and the increase in population, had only declined to about 100 million from the 110 million in 1981 (Prem Chand, 2008: 38). This was despite the unprecedented increase in the literacy rate by 13 per cent over the decadal period 1991 (52%) to 2001 (65%). Literacy for males in 2001 was 75 per cent while for females it was only 54 per cent. The literacy rate among adult women, 15 years and above, was even more critical at 45 per cent. There were in all 304 million non-literates in the country in the population aged seven years and above, out of whom 193 million were female. The quotations given in the previous paragraph, which indicate the basic objectives and strategy of the NLM in one of its earliest documents, are extremely important towards an understanding of the relative decline and stagnation of the literacy campaigns over the last two decades, despite its successes during the first five years. The citations also provide a perspective to view the complex relation between the NLM and the Bharat Gyan Vigyan Samiti (BGVS) during this period. Some crucial elements of a strategy of a people's movement for education and development, implicit in the document, were neglected by the NLM over the years.

The BGVS was one of the main architects in the formulation of the Total Literacy Campaign Strategy that was adopted by the NLM post-1989. This was based on the experience of conducting literacy campaigns by the Kerala Shashtra Sahitya Parishad (KSSP), one of the constituents of the BGVS, in Ernakulam district in 1988–89 and in the entire Kerala state in 1990. In one of its early leaflets relating to the literacy campaigns, the BGVS expresses its perspective on this approach:

> "The basic principles of the Ernakulam 'model', as it has come to be known, and adopted by the NLM were: mobilization using local cultural forms, motivating voluntary teachers to take up the actual task of teaching and formation of people's structures from the district to the village levels to implement and monitor the programmes. The district administration was expected to be an active facilitator for the process" (BGVS, 1990: 2).

The campaign approach to literacy acquired legitimacy at the centre, primarily among some administrative and academic circles and to a limited extent among some political parties. It was then selectively applied, initially in a few high literacy districts. The approach might be briefly described as a concerted effort involving various social resources, with a high degree of voluntary commitment to addressing the problem of illiteracy in a defined region and within a limited period of time utilizing the methodology of the Improved Pace and Content of Learning (IPCL). This pedagogical approach moved from concepts relevant to everyday life, to sentences/phrases and then to words and letters and was built into three primers with adequate tests for feedback of learning. The social sectors generally involved in this people's movement were personnel from government education departments and educational institutions, the media, some political parties, trade unions, voluntary organizations, people's movements, community groups and interested citizens. The major steps during the preparatory phase of the campaigns were planning meetings to identify individuals and organizations that could serve as resources, creating a demand for literacy through cultural mobilizations and the use of folk cultural forms, the organization of committees at the level of the districts, blocks and villages/wards, conducting a survey to identify learners and instructors, the preparation of instructional material, training programmes for instruction at various levels. This entire preparatory phase was a mobilization that lasted for about six months to be followed by the teaching-learning phase, its monitoring and evaluation lasting for about a year, but quite often longer than that. These first two phases were generally termed as the Total Literacy Campaign (TLC) Phase, which was in fact a misnomer given that the campaign was supposed to extend for the entire duration over all the phases. The post-literacy phase was expected to last for another year to strengthen the fragile literacy of the neo-literates and to cover those who had been left out. This was to be followed by a continuing education phase lasting for about five years and transacted through nodal and decentralized continuing education centres which served as educational resource and information centres linked to issues of livelihood and culture.

The NLM and the literacy campaign strategy have had a wide coverage and have been in existence for over two decades. A strategy evolved in the context of relatively high literacy, a history of social reform movements and labour class organization and struggle was, especially after 1994, implemented across the board throughout the country without much care for contextualization. The sanction of funds to districts with relatively similar proposals to implement literacy campaigns gradually became a quick fix to the problem of mass literacy. More importantly, basic pre-conditions during the preparatory phase of the campaigns, such as the generation of voluntarism within varied institutional and individual human resources, their organization and cultural mobilization came to be neglected as the campaigns gradually were caught in a bind of being both finance-driven and drawn by the needs of low literacy states. By 1998, the strategy had reached a point of relative stagnation, seeking a breakthrough in regions of mass illiteracy and underdevelopment such as in the northern regions of the country (Saldanha, 1998: 392–93).

The growing spread of the literacy campaigns may be understood from the following data: After May 1993, the trend in sanctions of literacy campaigns shifted from high literacy rate districts to low literacy rate ones within the northern Hindi-speaking belt. During 1993–94, out of the 107 projects that were sanctioned by the NLM, 53 were in the four states of Bihar, Madhya Pradesh, Rajasthan and Uttar Pradesh. By July 1994, it was reported that a total of 275 campaigns had been sanctioned in parts of or in entire districts. In 100 of these districts, projects had been approved for Post-Literacy and Continuing Education (Directorate of Adult Education, 1994). By 2000, out of the 588 then existing districts of the country, 529 had been covered by the campaigns (NLM, Annual Report 1999–2000). It was reported that about 10 million voluntary instructors had participated in the campaigns. Out of the 529 districts, 254 had already initiated the post-literacy phase of the campaigns by the year 2000 and about 40 million learners had enrolled in these post-literacy programmes. In addition, 92 districts had launched continuing education programmes after completing one or two years of post-literacy. By March 2005, a total of 596 districts were reported to have been covered by one phase or other of the literacy campaigns. In all, 140 districts were in the basic literacy phase, 172 in post-literacy and 284 were under continuing education programmes. By August 2008, it was reported that 95 districts were still in the first phase of basic literacy programmes; 120 districts were undertaking projects to cover the residual illiteracy of those who were non-enrolled, dropped out or had relapsed into illiteracy despite earlier programmes; 175 districts were in the post-literacy phase and 328 districts were carrying out continuing education programmes (NLM, August 10, 2008: 2). Some of the districts were covering overlapping project phases. These data would suggest that most of the 593 districts in the country according to the 2001 Census, if not all, were covered by one form or other of the existing adult education programmes by 2008. The NLM (August 2008: 12) reported that the literacy campaigns had spread to around 597 districts of the country.

Significant gains have been made by way of the large-scale participation of women and their enhanced status, the growing demand for primary education, the capacity of the campaigns to reach out to SCs, STs and the rural poor, a changed orientation to developmental administration in some sections of the administration, and the relative success of the popular cultural style of mobilization that set in motion a process of decentralized, coordinated participation of different sectors of society, especially during the early years of the campaign (Saldanha, 1993 and 1995). The more specific gains in literacy terms have been highly uneven and by the mid-1990s, generally the least in the low literacy districts (i.e., districts with a 1991 Census literacy rate of 45% or less), which were largely concentrated in a belt of northern states (Saldanha, 1996).

It has been difficult to arrive at an authentic picture of literacy outcomes based on official data. Such data get cumulated at various levels, with consequent distortions. They emerge from the district literacy campaigns and go up to the national level. There is a strong tendency on the part of those implementing campaigns to inflate these data to demonstrate performance in statistical terms. However, these data do provide some insights into trends and the following has been gleaned from the official sources. It was reported that 87 million non-literates had been identified through surveys within 22 states by March 1996. About 77 per cent of them numbering 67 million had been enrolled in the teaching-learning process. About 55 per cent of the enrolled, forming 43 per cent of the initially identified, were reported to have completed all the three primers during the process. However, if participation in the post-literacy centres is seen as some index of retention of literacy, then, one arrives at the disconcerting conclusion that the rate of relapse due to various factors, including delays in sanctions and breaks in the continuum of ongoing learning, could be close to 58 per cent. At a rough estimate, with some qualifications, approximately 12 per cent of the originally targeted non-literates would be able to retain a sustainable level of literacy (Directorate of Adult Education, March 1996, analysed in Saldanha, 1999). The foregoing data do provide some proxy index of learning outcomes.

Estimations based on one's own extensive surveys of diverse samples within the literacy campaigns of the states of Maharashtra and Goa suggest that 74 per cent of the non-literates identified in local surveys were enrolled and the neo-literates who were able to achieve the NLM norms in our standardized test formed 55 per cent of the enrolled and 40 per cent of the initially identified non-literates (Saldanha, 1999: 2023).

In 2008, the Ministry of Human Resource Development commissioned a study to the SNDT Women's University, Mumbai, to assess the Tenth Five-Year Plan schemes of literacy campaigns, the post-literacy and the operation restoration for districts that were stagnant and that had not been able to reach adequate levels of performance. The summary findings of the wider social impact of the literacy campaigns appear to support one's above-mentioned conclusions relating to the literacy campaigns, especially during the initial five years:

> "At the very outset, the team would like to place on record the fact that remarkable changes have taken place in the individual as well as community life of the masses. These changes were not only observed by the team but also perceived by the learners and others who constituted the respondents of this study. It was reported that enrolment in primary schools has increased to the extent that new additions to the number of illiterates in the 15 to 35 age group would be very few. The number of children born to the educated youth has reduced. The number of institutional deliveries has increased. Access to immunization and other health facilities has improved. Women have become active members of Self Help Groups and membership of these groups has proved to be a fruitful experience. They have teamed up against violence and alcohol abuse. They have started voicing their opinions in the Gramsabha. The villagers themselves felt that the 'knowledge' and 'attitude' component of the literacy programme had much to contribute to these changes" (Chakrabarti, Patil and Sudhakar, 2008: i).

As regards the literacy outcomes, the study found that the percentage of learners who obtained 50 per cent marks in reading, writing and arithmetic were 71.9 per cent, 47.8 per cent and 21.9 per cent, respectively. A cause for concern, in sheer literacy terms, was that 86.5 per cent of the learners were unable to achieve the literacy levels according to NLM norms and that only 13.5 per cent had more than 50 per cent marks in reading, writing and arithmetic and more than 70 per cent marks on the aggregate. It might, however, be noted that the survey and testing of learners was been carried out in districts that were at various phases of the campaigns, sometimes after a gap of several years, and that there was a possibility of substantial relapse into illiteracy. It is interesting to note that, based on official government data relating to learners who have completed the post-literacy primer as an index of a non-relapsable level of literacy, Mathew (April 2000: 29) came to a similar conclusion that 13.43 per cent of the 126 million surveyed non-literates would have achieved adequate literacy levels.

Major weaknesses of the NLM approach have been the rapid expansion of the programme, especially during 1994 to 1998. This has been without adequate preparation in the low literacy districts of the country where ironically the need for literacy was the greatest but where the impact of the literacy campaigns in terms of literacy outcomes was highly uneven. The literacy gains in some of these districts within low literacy states, as seen in the 2001 Census, might be largely attributed to initiatives within formal primary education and the movement of newer age cohorts within the age group of seven years and above, assuming that the possible inflation of results over space and time is evenly distributed. The literacy campaigns in these situations would surely have played a role in creating a generalized demand for elementary education.

In addition to the problems mentioned earlier, insufficient attention has been paid to adapting the campaign strategy to the specific contextual features of less developed regions where the inegalitarian structures of caste, class and patriarchy reinforce deprivation. The responses of political and administrative systems in these contexts have been inadequate. Given the high proportion of the participation of women as learners, it was expected that the literacy campaigns in their organizational, mobilizational and pedagogical strategies would have been far more gender-sensitive than they have been. The literacy campaigns have generally lacked sustainability as regards the participatory process, with respect to the literacy gains and as a process of life-long learning (i.e., over the present 'post-literacy' and 'continuing education' phases). Non-governmental organizations, other than a few exceptions like the Bharat Gyan Vigyan Samiti (BGVS), have not participated in the campaigns to the extent that was desirable. Consequently, the progressive developmental potential of the vast scale of the campaigns has been largely unfulfilled.

A study sponsored by UNESCO and coordinated by BGVS on the Impact of Post-Literacy (January, 2002) comes to the conclusion that a lack of clarity at the policy level with respect to post-literacy and continuing education had affected the continuity of the process. There were large gaps in the flow of funds and consequently in the scheduling of the different phases of the campaigns resulting in deterioration in quality and decreasing participation. While there had been widespread participation of women and persons belonging to the SCs and STs, a growing demand for education and participation in local self-governing bodies, the linkages to other development activities, the introduction to vocational skills and a creation of a rural library network had generally been inadequate. The lack of adequate interface between literacy efforts and the wider social development process within a mechanistic ordering of interrupted phases is surprising, given that as early as 1996 the report of the Education Commission, 1964–66 had prescribed that, "The essential elements of the 'follow-up' work (through the literacy programmes) should be inbuilt in the literacy programme itself. It is a mistake to think that the activities grouped under 'follow-up' procedures should be undertaken after the literacy campaign is over and adults have learnt to read and write. In the coherent whole of literacy programmes there should be elements which are necessary to make literacy enduring and useful" (Ministry of Education, 1966).

A letter from the Director General, NLM (July 24, 1998) states: "Bharat Gyan Vigyan Samiti (BGVS), a non-governmental organization financially supported by the National Literacy Mission, has been associated with the Mission in the cause of eradication of illiteracy since its establishment in 1989. The organization is engaged in the activities of generating an environment conducive to the launching of a nation-wide people's movement for literacy." One was first approached by the Ministry of Human Resource Development and the NLM to undertake this study of the BGVS through this letter. A review of documents and secondary data provided by the NLM and the national and state offices of the BGVS, apart from one's own field exposure through research in connection with the literacy campaigns, would suggest that the BGVS has been involved in several projects related to literacy and social development throughout the country and over more than two decades. The scale of operation, the persistence over time, the particular ideological thrust of this social transformation from within the social developmental sector that laid heavy emphasis on people's participation, and the sustained, though complex, critical collaboration with government over the years, suggest that a historical study of the BGVS could provide useful insights into the potential of and constraints to organized, civil society collaboration with the state in development. This interface, in the case of the BGVS, has been quite unique, given the factors that have been briefly mentioned above.

2. Questions and Objectives

An assessment of the nature and impact of the BGVS intervention is important not only for purposes of analysing its history and suggesting future directions, but also for drawing out implications for the possibilities and constraints to civil society participation in major state-initiated programmes. The literacy campaigns under the NLM have themselves been of historical significance in terms of the wide scope and multi-dimensional impact, drawing sharp attention to the nature of the relationship between education/literacy and wider development. The BGVS, for reasons mentioned above and through its major network within the non-governmental sector and its formal involvement with the NLM at the invitation of the latter, shares in the significance of this historical phase. The following issues/concerns for study have been identified initially by reviewing the experience and documentation and in participatory interaction with government and the office bearers of the BGVS:

- How much was achieved in creating a positive environment for the launching of the campaigns in the country through a series of *jathas*?
- The role played in shaping the campaign strategy in its mobilizational, organizational and pedagogic aspects; the participation of the BGVS in the preparation of primers and training materials.
- The success attained in spreading and adapting the campaign approach in different contexts, in different parts of the country.
- The role in creating support groups in different states and districts; the role of state and district BGVS committees in orienting the campaign leadership from the administrative and voluntary sectors.

- The nature of the 'creative tension' between the BGVS and the administration over the years and at different levels; the role in offering a constructive critique.
- The part played in strengthening and expanding the base of the campaigns in the low literacy states of North India.
- The efforts to develop linkages between literacy and other sectors of development.
- The nature of the impact on women's empowerment through mobilization and the interface between learning and development.
- The efforts to initiate a people's reading and library movement through low-cost publications.
- The relevance of ongoing BGVS programmes in terms of providing sustainability, linkages of literacy with development, restoration of stagnating campaigns, evolving replicable models and in restoring the people's movement character of the campaigns.

At a substantive theoretical level, certain major questions arise: What is the relation between basic educational interventions and other development programmes in a context of underdevelopment? How can quality be sustained through the campaign approach to literacy, given the vast scale of its coverage? What are the value-loaded ideological perspectives of the major actors in the campaigns? Underlying these questions is the issue of the nature of the dynamics between civil society formations and the state in the process of basic social transformation.

It is obvious from the identification of the foregoing issues that the study is not being undertaken by a non-involved person. One has drawn on one's field exposure and access to multiple sources to not only identify initial questions but also substantiate conclusions in the course of this study. It would be upto the reader to arrive at a conclusion whether the arguments presented and the positions taken have substantive justification and are convincing.

3. Conceptual Framework and Methodology

Conceptual Framework and Structure of Presentation

An outline of the structure of the study would be in order. The outline contains an implicit conceptual framework, which will be gradually elaborated through illustrations and theoretical analysis, especially in Chapters 10 and 11. One might conceive of three major, analytically distinct but interrelated and overlapping, dimensions of the social systems that constitute any adult intervention and, for that matter, any change process.

1. *The ecological and socio-economic context:* The sharp variations of ecological and socially structured contexts necessitate a contextualization of approaches, especially for interventions like that of the BGVS that have a national coverage. Societies and communities at the macro and micro levels are structured on the basis of caste, tribe, class, other identities and gender disparities and, at times, religious marginalization. These identities tend to reinforce each other in shaping access to educational opportunities. Questions related to 'where' and 'with whom' are significant for any social transformatory process, as also the relation of educational efforts to issues related to livelihood and economic survival. Micro initiatives at sub-district levels can also have influence on macro contexts of policy through mobilization, networking, research and advocacy, especially if there exists a network of field organizations with a national coverage. This dimension covers the social spatial aspect of educational interventions, which is encounted as a given structure. However, the very structure undergoes change over a process of time due to other factors and the intervention itself. The ecological and socio-economic structures provide constraints to change, yet suggest a rationale (reason for the need) for the transformatory process. The ecological base has its own human and/or natural structural principles that also demand a regional contextualization of the change process over variations in ecological regions.

2. *The socio-political process:* This aspect of the intervention concerns the modalities, the agencies involved and the mobilization of social resources towards organization and strategic action. The process may be turned as 'political' in nature in its broader sense, because it implies the exercise of power and control over the distribution of resources in a given structured situation. In the present context, it related primarily to basic education as an intellectual resource related to other social developmental opportunities. This dimension would provide answers to questions related to 'how', 'when', 'who' and 'with whom'.

3. *The socio-cultural:* This aspect may be considered as ideological in nature providing the value-loaded vision and purpose for action. Values provide depth, significance and weight to a given transformatory effort. The vision serves as an individual and collective motivating force that provides energy to a process which possibly results in a campaign/movement for change. It provides significance and a rationale (need for a reason) for concerted intervention. Ideologies for change

need to be articulated with some degree of coherence as regards the assumptions and values underlying the intervention. This dimension responds to the questions of 'why' and 'for whom' the initiative is undertaken in the first place. It contributes the relatively subjective and communicational/symbolical aspects of transformatory processes within social systems.

The literacy campaigns of the last two decades with the involvement of the BGVS and government agencies were largely rooted within the normative directives of the Constitution that promoted equity, secularism and democracy. Even the formal policy documents of the NLM, especially during the early years of the campaigns, underwrote this perspective. The process was visualized as being democratic in character, towards strengthening people's power. It was also seen as being a people's movement with the participation of various social sectors – government, the teaching-learning community and the organized and unorganized constituents of civil society. It was to be conducted at most times on a voluntary basis, i.e., with no payment for part-time services. An important premiss for collaboration would be a basic consensus on the ideological perspective and goals of the literacy campaigns. Understandably, governments, civil society organizations, agencies, corporate bodies and their trusts, academic institutions and, most importantly, community organizations and individuals would have differences in approaches at different times based on their contextual backgrounds, needs and interests. The purposes and goals of the literacy campaigns, and hence their strategic approach, needed to be constantly negotiated, sometimes in a contentious manner.

The following diagrammatic presentation illustrates the aforementioned conceptual framework for the analysis that follows and also for the structuring of the text. It has evolved over the years and was found useful for my studies on adult and basic education programmes: adult education programmes and literacy campaigns in India (Saldanha, 1989, 1995, 1998 and 1999); the approach of Regenerated Frerian Literacy through Empowering Community Techniques (REFLECT) for adult education and empowerment in Bangladesh and India which draws on the ideas of Paolo Freire and Participatory Rural Appraisal (Saldanha et al., 1999 and 2000); an earlier unpublished version of this study (Saldanha, 2003); and a study of Doosra Dashak (The Second Decade), an approach to adolescent education for leadership development in the rural areas of Rajasthan, India (Saldanha, 2007). The frame of reference will be elaborated over the succeeding chapters of this work and

ILLUSTRATION 1.1 *A Conceptual Framework*

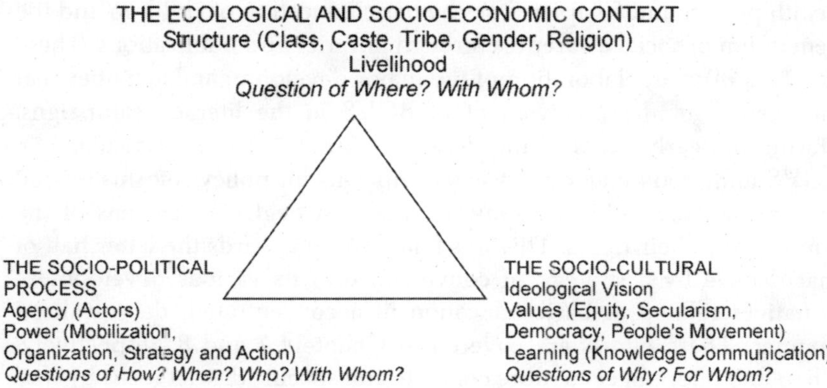

especially in the concluding Chapters 10 and 11, holding the broad parametres as relatively constant.

Part I of this study, covering Chapters 1 and 2, provides an introduction, the context and a summary narrative of the campaign interventions. Chapter 1 serves as an introduction to the overall text by presenting the literacy context and issues that confronted the NLM and the BGVS at the time of their formation in the late 1980s and later while expanding the strategic coverage to regions that demonstrated a sharp uneven development. It also provides a summary statement of one's concerns about the literacy campaign process as related to sustainable social development over the past 20 years. The methodology, sources of data, research methods and the sites visited are presented in this chapter. A general historical overview is presented in Chapter 2 in a structured manner, indicating the different phases of the BGVS process. This would help the reader to come to grips with a complex historical narrative that experienced several elaborations as well as discontinuities, as new projects were undertaken in a differentiated manner over states and districts that spanned the uneven developmental context of the country. Thus, Part I covers the contexts as well as contextual changes resulting from the historical process of a civil society formation interacting with the state in the process of conducting the literacy campaigns.

The seven chapters in Part II focus more explicitly on the process of intervention. They cover the ground in greater detail about specific projects undertaken by the BGVS while carrying out the agenda of literacy/education linked to socio-economic development: Chapter 3 on natural resource management, Chapter 4 on the mobilization of women and the organizational formation of Samata, Chapter 5 on the literacy to health project and Chapter 6 on the basic education of children and the generation of social awareness through libraries and publications. These chapters offer an elaboration of the major developmental activities that emerged from the involvement of BGVS in the literacy campaigns. During the early years of the decade of 2000–2010, in particular, the BGVS undertook major advocacy campaigns for policy reforms related to various issues affecting some of the most neglected citizens of the country and their rights. This was followed up towards the latter half of that decade by a strategy of convergence of its various development initiatives related to basic education in a concentrated, decentralized manner. These efforts are covered in Chapters 7 and 8, respectively. Chapter 9 offers an even more concrete and specific district focus by way of seven case studies that represent in some ways the limitations and potential of the BGVS strategy of education linked to development, as a civil society formation in its relation to the state.

Part III, containing the last two chapters, presents conclusions drawn from the preceding chapters. Chapter 10 presents conclusions for theory and practice and Chapter 11 suggests directions for the future, within the broad framework of structured contexts, intervention processes and the ideological/value orientations of the main actors in this 20-year-old drama. In these chapters one has drawn on the initial conceptual framework, as in this chapter. One has taken resort to a set of illustrations to facilitate one's communication of theoretical concepts, or, in some senses, falling back on the culture of visualization. This corresponds to one's understanding that there cannot be any sharp distinctions between the cultures of audio-visual communication, of orality, of the scripted universe of literacy and, for that matter, the expanding universe of electronic digital communication, even though Ong (1982) might suggest a contrary position. All said and done, social science discourse, as a communicative practice, is a secondary order, systematic and critical representation. It does not altogether transcend the primary order contexts, processes and ideological perspectives that it reflects upon, but is also embedded in them and in the multiple layered and articulated communicative practices of everyday life.

One has followed a broad thrust of moving from a general historical overview to concrete initiatives at different points of time and in different contexts. There is also a trajectory from the concrete to the abstract. Both in terms of implementation by the BGVS and the presentation of one's study, the literacy campaigns might be seen as the mainstream river into which various other related development initiatives flow in as tributaries or emerge as outlets, depending on the contextual terrain and the relation of this major civil society formation with the state and their converging and differing ideological perspectives.

Locations

As the foregoing concerns would suggest, the methodology for the study would have to be directed at the central/national level, in selected states and within selected districts. In view of the constraints as regards finances, the research needed to be modified to limit the number of field visits. However, this was compensated by one's association with the literacy campaigns over the years and by drawing on one's past and ongoing field exposure in a research, consultancy and organizational capacity as a member of NLM executive and of the NLM authority at different times, and by way of membership in different committees such as the Tenth and Eleventh Plan working groups for literacy, elementary education and the education of the adolescents.

Specific field visits for this study were made to Dhanbad district in Jharkhand, Kannyakumari district in Tamil Nadu, the Assam state, Mandi district in Himachal Pradesh, Beguserai district in Bihar, Baran district in Rajasthan, Rae Bareilly district in Uttar Pradesh, Bhind district in Madhya Pradesh and the Kerala state. In addition, earlier and later visits over two decades were undertaken in connection with the literacy campaigns and elementary education projects to the districts of Maharashtra, Goa, Andhra Pradesh, Karnataka, Orissa, Himachal Pradesh, Bihar, Rajasthan, Haryana, Madhya Pradesh, Mizoram, Meghalaya, Arunachal Pradesh and Uttar Pradesh. This field exposure to the issues of basic education in diverse contexts was of much use in analysing the secondary data on which the study largely depended.

Sources of Data and Research Methods

The historical background of the BGVS is covered largely through secondary sources and interviews and group discussions with key informants from the government, the BGVS itself and local communities. This was complemented by field visits for observations to key sites selected in consultation with the BGVS national office. The analysis and interpretation of secondary documentary sources, i.e., reports, leaflets, pamphlets, teaching/learning and training materials, publications and bulletins, constitute major sources for arriving at a historical perspective on the BGVS interventions.

The methodological approach to data analysis is largely qualitative, complemented by quantitative data drawn from secondary sources. The study has also adopted a comparative approach within a historical perspective. An attempt has been made to identify the distinctive and comparative features of the phases of the trajectory of the BGVS over the last two decades. The trajectory has been influenced by the relative concentration of its activities over different regions in a vast country, at different points of time, at varying levels – sub-district, state, national – and in interaction with shifting ideological positions of the state as a result of changing governments in power. These factors also contribute to the need for a comparative framework. There has been some degree of participatory involvement of BGVS educational activists and government personnel through interviews, group discussions and one's participation in meetings for feedback. The general body meeting of the BGVS, held in Dhanbad during February 16 and 17, 2002, served an important purpose of making a concurrent draft presentation and gaining feedback from general body members and the executive of BGVS. This has been followed up with several interactive sessions with state and district level coordinators of the BGVS and with members of its national executive and general body.

An important limitation of this study, of which one is painfully aware, is that it has been able to capture to a limited extent the richness of detail of the endeavour of persons and of specific programmes within villages/districts and states despite the case studies of processes that are presented in Chapter 9 and interspersed throughout the other chapters. This was near impossible for a single study, with a focus on an overview of social space, time and value perspectives, to draw out the historical significance of BGVS interventions. One's apologies go out to the states/districts that may not have been directly referred to. The continuously enfolding range of BGVS activities made this study an almost never-ending effort in itself. Other studies, for example, the one in which one was involved with field-level literacy activists of the BGVS (Rampal and Manimala, eds., 2002) covers Mandi (Himachal Pradesh), Begusarai (Bihar) and Durg (Chattisgarh). Mukherjee and Vasanta (eds., 2002), apart from providing general overviews and theoretical perspectives on literacy interventions, cover the states of Kerala, Andhra Pradesh, West Bengal and Chattisgarh. The edited collection by Karlekar (2004) covers different aspects of the campaigns in Ernakulam (Kerala), Nellore (Andhra Pradesh), Pudukkottai (Tamil Nadu), Ajmer (Rajasthan), Ganjam (Orissa) and Dumka (Jharkhand). There has been a more recent collection of case studies of campaign initiatives (Jena and Mathew, eds., 2008). These studies do contribute to creating an overall picture of the literacy campaigns. Other studies, including my own writings, are referred to in the text.

Another limitation of this study has been the heavy reliance on secondary data from unpublished BGVS and government sources. This would have made the study largely dependent on subjective, self-reported data and assessments by the BGVS. However, one is confident about the 'objectivity' of the analysis that has been presented on at least two counts. The data have been cross-checked through the utilization of multiple methods of data collection and several other sources, as well as relying on one's direct experience of the literacy campaigns and the BGVS interventions in relation to government. In addition, it needs to be stated that one has rarely come across an organization that has been as honest in its self-criticism with regard to the verified data that have been presented in its reports. Finally, an important limitation is that the logistics of time, space and personnel during the field trips for the study did not permit this researcher to engage in case studies of individuals who participated in the BGVS and the literacy campaign process. I have met several individuals at various levels, both government and non-government, who inspired me with their commitment and insights into field situations. This limitation has been remedied to some degree by drawing on individual case studies from other sources to bring out the human dimension of this massive enterprise.

2

The BGVS and the Literacy Campaigns

Process, Organization and Strategies

1. The Background of the Process

In 1991, about half the population of the country was educationally marginalized without access to a major enabling skill like literacy. This corresponded closely to social and economic underdevelopment, with its political implications. It was in this context that a need was felt to initiate a mass action for national regeneration – a national movement for self-reliant development with literacy as a basis and a possible starting point. As the BGVS report of 2001 states, "The crusade against illiteracy was a crusade against the conditions that maintained literacy, a crusade against disruptionists, a crusade against destabilization, a crusade against communalism, a crusade against dependence. It was seen as a second independence struggle for national integration and for self-reliance. It was a struggle to make democracy meaningful to the millions" (BGVS, 2001: 1). The BGVS' vision was one of holistic development through a people's movement, and not one of merely increasing the number of literate persons. The BGVS saw as its role "to contribute to the evolution of the district literacy organizations and to build the BGVS organization at the district and state levels in such a manner that the literacy campaign becomes the beginning of a sustainable process. Such a process should lead to post-literacy immediately and subsequently to universal elementary education, women's development, a health movement, a cultural awakening and eventually empowerment of the people. With the literacy campaigns and subsequent programmes, these processes should lead to a more democratic society where people can and do decide the course of their development" (BGVS, 1989–93: 2).

A brief background of one of the important constituents of the BGVS, i.e., the Kerala Shastra Sahitya Parishad (KSSP), would help to understand the foregoing ideological thrust of the BGVS itself (KSSP, 1984; Zachariah and Soorya Moorthy, 1994). Several people's science organizations emerged during the 1950s and 1960s. The KSSP, initiated in 1962, was one of these major formations whose objective was social transformation through the application of science and technology. Several publications were brought out in order to popularize science in keeping with its objectives of 'science for social revolution'. In the 1970s and 1980s, the organization expanded into a mass movement that devoted itself to other concerns, like elementary education, health, the environment and literacy. The KSSP had grown into a mass organization with about 75,000 members. In 1973, the KSSP adopted the theme, 'science for social revolution' and had generally been taking up a specific issue for intensive mobilization in a given year. In May 1985, the KSSP and the People's Science Movement (PSM) organized an all-India jatha (a socio-cultural caravan for development communication) in memory of thousands killed at Bhopal as a result of a major gas tragedy caused by the negligence of the state and Union Carbide. The science movements in Karnataka, Maharashtra and Andhra Pradesh had joined with the KSSP in organizing this jatha. The KSSP had been organizing such 'science through arts' jathas since 1980 with the involvement of local artists. The 1985 jatha was followed by similar programmes in Tamil Nadu with the Tamil Nadu Science Forum and the Pondicherry Science Forum, and in Gujarat with the assistance of the Gujarat Vigyan Sabha. In 1987, a state-wide health survey was carried out in Kerala to assess the health status.

By the early 1980s, other organizations for the propagation of science had also emerged in different parts of the country. About 26 of these, together with the KSSP, came together during the third anniversary of the Bhopal gas tragedy in October-November, 1987 to organize the Bharat Jan Vigyan Jatha (BJVJ) which was sponsored by the Department of Science and Technology. A 2,000 km procession converged at Bhopal from five different directions. This was a massive attempt at development communication to promote scientific awareness through a cultural caravan. It helped to expand the PSM into a national network, called the All India People's Science Network (AIPSN).

The 1987 jatha was the seed of the concept of mass mobilization for a cause like literacy. Earlier experiences with adult education, culminating with the National Adult Education Programme (NAEP) of 1978, had suggested that a demand for literacy among the people as well as a concerted response had not yet been created. While the National Literacy Mission (NLM) was formed in 1988 on the basis of learning from earlier experiences, the strategy for action was not clear. The strategy evolved as a result of interaction with different voluntary organizations and the People's Science Movement (PSM), especially the mass mobilizations of the KSSP. The KSSP, in collaboration with the district administration, had undertaken a campaign for literacy in Ernakulam district in 1988 and 1989 with the financial support of the NLM. An important element of the strategy was an environment-building campaign to generate a positive response towards literacy among the people. The *kalajathas* (cultural caravans) that formed as a part of this campaign consisted, besides displays of posters, banners, hoardings and stickers, *padyatras* (processions), street theatres and songs. Various audio-visual forms, based on the folk culture and the oral traditions of the people, were utilized to create a climate for literacy. The campaign led to a substantial rise in literacy. This was accompanied by campaigns in Kottayam district and followed by the entire Kerala state in 1989–90.

In 1989, the Ministry of Human Resource Development (MHRD), Government of India decided to adopt the Ernakulam experiment as a strategy for propagating literacy at the national level. Various PSMs were invited by the Government of India to form the Bharat Gyan Vigyan Samiti (BGVS) with the primary responsibility of placing literacy on the national agenda. The first Director General of the NLM, in an overview of the early years of the literacy campaigns, states:

> "The Department of Education, Ministry of Human Resource Development, acknowledged with all humility that the Government could not directly take up social mobilization but could create conditions which would be to conducive to such mobilization. Promoting and facilitating the formation of BGVS at the national level was one such very positive and constructive step which was initiated by the then secretary, Ministry of Education" (Mishra in Mukherjee and Vasanta, eds., 2002: 134).

The first General Council of BGVS was formed from amongst PSM activists, representatives from the MHRD, educationists, social workers, and artists from all over the country. The Council elected a 13-member Executive Committee, which functioned through a central office located in New Delhi. It is important to note that this social formation was created at the invitation of government.

Table 2.1 presents a schematic history of the initiatives of the BGVS, from 1987 to 2009. Apart from various developmental initiatives over time, one gets an overview of the concentration of these activities in particular states. This table may be read with the chronology of BGVS activities in Appendix 1. It also provides an overview for the chapters that follow. The immediate background to the formation of BGVS was the KSSP-PSM jatha of 1987 and the Ernakulam literacy campaign of 1988–89. It is possible to classify the history of BGVS into four major phases with defined characteristics:

- The period from 1989 to 1993 was characterized by mobilizations for literacy, starting from the formation of the BGVS in 1989 followed by three major jathas.
- The period from 1994 to 1997 was marked by a transition from literacy to other development initiatives and an attempt to establish a strong interface between the two. These were mainly in the areas of natural resource management, health, initiatives in basic education and the generation of social awareness through publications and the formation of saving groups on the heels of major women's mobilizations through Samata Vigyan Utsavas between 1996 to 1999. This phase was also marked by the rapid expansion of the literacy campaigns to the difficult northern belt of the country.
- The period from 1998 to 2001 might be seen as defined by a struggle to consolidate the expansion and the diversity of sectoral interventions through decentralized institutionalization, around Continuing Education Centres (CECs) and Gyan Vigyan Vidyalayas (GVVs), i.e., centres of basic education that interface with formal schooling. This was undertaken in the context of severe constraint of funds from central government sources due to ideological differences.
- The period from 2002 to the present was characterized by a double-barreled strategy. Using its mass base, the BGVS engaged in advocacy with the central government for policies related to rights issues. It also attempted to consolidate its extensive spread through a strategy of concentration in defined clusters of villages, convergence of programmes and capacity-building of village resource persons.

It is relevant to note that the marginalization of the BGVS from some of the formal literacy campaigns by the district level bureaucracies,

TABLE 2.1 *Major BGVS Initiatives Over the Years–Areawise*

Programmes and the Years Conducted	1. Andaman	2. Andhra	3. Arunachal	4. Assam	5. Bihar	6. Chandigarh	7. Chhattisgarh	8. Dadra Nagar	9. Daman	10. Delhi	11. Goa	12. Gujarat	13. Haryana	14. Himachal	15. Jammu Kashmir	16. Jharkhand	17. Karnataka	18. Kerala	19. Lakshadweep	20. Madhya Pradesh	21. Maharashtra	22. Manipur	23. Meghalaya	24. Mizoram	25. Nagaland	26. Orissa	27. Pondicherry	28. Punjab	29. Rajasthan	30. Sikkim	31. Tamil Nadu	32. Tripura	33. Uttar Pradesh	34. Uttaranchal	35. W. Bengal
THE BACKGROUND, 1987–1988																																			
KSSP, PSM Jatha, 1987		❖	❖	❖	❖	❖	❖			❖		❖	❖	❖			❖	❖		❖	❖	❖	❖		❖	❖		❖	❖		❖	❖	❖	❖	❖
Ernakulam Literacy Campaign, 1988–89																		❖																	
Kerala State Literacy Campaign, 1989–90																		❖																	
PHASE 1: MOBILIZATIONS FOR LITERACY, 1989–1993																																			
Formation of BGVS, 1989		❖		❖	❖	❖	v❖			❖		❖	❖	❖	❖	❖	❖	❖		❖	❖					❖	❖	❖	❖		❖	❖	❖	❖	❖
BGVS Jatha, 1990	❖	❖	❖	❖	❖	❖	❖	❖	❖	❖	❖	❖	❖	❖	❖	❖	❖	❖	❖	❖	❖	❖				❖	❖	❖	❖	❖	❖	❖	❖	❖	❖
BGVS Jatha, 1992		❖			❖	❖	❖						❖			❖		❖		❖						❖			❖		❖		❖	❖	
Samata Jatha, 1993		❖		❖	❖	❖	❖	❖	❖	❖	❖	❖	❖	❖	❖	❖	❖	❖	❖	❖	❖	❖	❖	❖	❖	❖	❖	❖	❖	❖	❖	❖	❖	❖	❖
PHASE 2: FROM LITERACY TO DEVELOPMENT, 1994–1997																																			
Campaign for Hamara Desh, 1993–94		❖		❖	❖									❖		❖	❖	❖			❖					❖			❖		❖	❖			
Literacy and Natural Resources																																			
Participatory Resource Mapping, 1993–97		❖		❖	❖									❖		❖	❖	❖			❖					❖			❖		❖	❖			
Integrated Drinking Water and Sanitation (WATSAN), 1993–95		❖			❖											❖	❖									❖			❖		❖				❖
Watershed Development Programme, 1995–1999		❖			❖		❖										❖	❖		❖	❖					❖					❖				❖
Desh Ko Janein Desh Ko Badlein, 1995–1998		❖		❖	❖	❖	❖			❖			❖	❖		❖	❖	❖		❖	❖					❖	❖	❖	❖		❖	❖	❖	❖	❖
Panchayat Raj, 1995…		❖		❖	❖	❖	❖			❖			❖	❖		❖	❖	❖		❖	❖					❖	❖	❖	❖		❖	❖	❖	❖	❖

Literacy to Health, 1994–1995, 1996…					❖		❖									❖	❖			❖	❖										❖		❖	❖	
Literacy and Basic Education Social Awareness																																			
Joy of Learning Campaign, 1994		❖		❖	❖	❖	❖			❖			❖	❖		❖	❖	❖		❖	❖					❖	❖	❖	❖		❖	❖	❖	❖	
Cosmic Voyage, 1995		❖		❖	❖	❖	❖			❖			❖	❖		❖	❖	❖		❖	❖					❖	❖	❖	❖		❖	❖	❖	❖	
Jeevanshala Programme, 1995–2001		❖			❖								❖																						
Jan Vachan Andolan, Libraries and Publications, 1994…		❖		❖	❖	❖	❖			❖			❖	❖		❖	❖	❖		❖	❖					❖	❖	❖	❖		❖	❖	❖	❖	
BGVS SRCs, 1995…				❖									❖	❖		❖				❖												❖			
BGVS Jatha in Uttar Pradesh , 1995					❖																								❖				❖	❖	
BGVS Jatha in Rajasthan, 1996					❖																								❖				❖	❖	
Literacy and Women's Empowerment																																			
Samata Vigyan Utsavs, 1996–1999		❖		❖	❖	❖	❖			❖			❖	❖		❖	❖	❖		❖	❖					❖	❖	❖	❖		❖	❖	❖	❖	
Samata Saving Groups, 1998…		❖		❖	❖	❖	❖					❖	❖	❖		❖	❖	❖		❖	❖					❖	❖	❖	❖		❖	❖	❖	❖	❖
Operation Restoration, 1997–1998					❖								❖			❖	❖				❖							❖					❖		
PHASE 3: CONTINUING EDUCATION FOR DEVELOPMENT WITH SCARCE RESOURCES, 1998–2001																																			
Pilot CE Centres, 1998–2001		❖		❖	❖	❖	❖						❖	❖	❖	❖	❖		❖	❖						❖	❖	❖	❖		❖	❖	❖	❖	
Gyan Vigyan Vidyalayas and Related Ed. Progs., 2000…		❖		❖	❖	❖	❖					❖	❖	❖	❖	❖	❖	❖	❖	❖	❖					❖	❖	❖	❖		❖	❖	❖	❖	
Continuing Education Programmes and Libraries, 2000…		❖		❖	❖		❖			❖			❖	❖		❖	❖	❖		❖	❖					❖	❖	❖	❖		❖		❖	❖	
National and State Health Assemblies, 2000–2008		❖		❖	❖		❖			❖		❖	❖	❖		❖	❖	❖		❖	❖					❖	❖	❖	❖		❖	❖	❖	❖	❖
PHASE 4: NATIONAL ADVOCACY FOR POLICY RELATED TO RIGHTS AND THE CONVERGENCE OF LOCAL PRACTICE, 2002…																																			
AIPSN-BGVS–World Social Forum Process, 2002–2004		❖		❖	❖					❖		❖	❖	❖		❖	❖	❖		❖	❖					❖	❖	❖	❖		❖		❖	❖	❖
Right to Food Campaign, 2002–2003		❖		❖	❖		❖			❖		❖	❖			❖				❖	❖					❖	❖	❖	❖		❖		❖		

Cont'd...

Cont'd...

Kalajatha on Peace, Unity and Sovereignty, 2003		❖		❖	❖		❖			❖		❖	❖	❖		❖	❖	❖
Gyan Vigyan Vidyalayas, 2004…				❖	❖							❖						
Activists' Education Assembly, 2004				❖	❖		❖			❖		❖	❖	❖		❖	❖	❖
Rozgar Kalajathas, 2005		❖		❖	❖		❖			❖			❖	❖		❖	❖	❖
Right to Food and Work, Mobilizations, 2005		❖		❖	❖		❖			❖		❖	❖	❖		❖	❖	❖
National Rural Employment Guarantee Act, Rallies and Conventions, 2005				❖	❖		❖			❖		❖	❖	❖		❖	❖	❖
Right to Education, 2006		❖		❖	❖					❖			❖	❖		❖	❖	❖
Indian Social Forum, 2006		❖		❖	❖		❖			❖		❖	❖	❖		❖	❖	❖
CE & Samata Convergence, 2007…		❖		❖	❖								❖	❖		❖	❖	
Jan Adhikar Kalajatha, 2007–2008		❖	❖	❖	❖					❖		❖	❖	❖		❖	❖	❖
Activists Exchange Programme, 2007		❖		❖	❖								❖	❖		❖	❖	
Education for Decentralized, Democracy and Development, 2007										❖				❖				❖
Mid-Day Meals, 2007					❖		❖			❖				❖		❖	❖	❖
National Rural Employment Guarantee Act Rallies and Conventions, 2008				❖	❖		❖			❖		❖	❖	❖		❖	❖	❖
ICDS Convention and Campaign, 2008				❖	❖		❖			❖		❖	❖	❖		❖	❖	❖
Right to Education, Mobilizations, 2008		❖		❖	❖					❖			❖	❖		❖	❖	❖

Kalajatha on Peace, Unity and Sovereignty, 2003		❖	❖						❖	❖	❖	❖		❖	❖	❖	❖	
Gyan Vigyan Vidyalayas, 2004…		❖						❖							❖	❖	
Activists' Education Assembly, 2004		❖	❖					❖	❖	❖	❖		❖	❖	❖	❖	
Rozgar Kalajathas, 2005		❖	❖					❖	❖	❖	❖		❖		❖	❖	
Right to Food and Work, Mobilizations, 2005		❖	❖					❖	❖	❖	❖		❖	❖	❖	❖	
National Rural Employment Guarantee Act, Rallies and Conventions, 2005		❖	❖					❖	❖	❖	❖		❖	❖	❖	❖	
Right to Education, 2006		❖	❖						❖		❖		❖		❖		
Indian Social Forum, 2006		❖	❖	❖	❖	❖		❖	❖	❖	❖		❖	❖	❖	❖	
CE & Samata Convergence, 2007…		❖	❖	❖				❖	❖	❖	❖		❖	❖	❖	❖	
Jan Adhikar Kalajatha, 2007–2008		❖	❖					❖	❖	❖	❖		❖	❖	❖	❖	
Activists Exchange Programme, 2007		❖	❖					❖	❖	❖	❖		❖	❖	❖	❖	
Education for Decentralized, Democracy and Development, 2007		❖	❖					❖			❖				❖		
Mid-Day Meals, 2007		❖	❖					❖	❖		❖		❖		❖	❖	
National Rural Employment Guarantee Act Rallies and Conventions, 2008		❖	❖					❖	❖	❖	❖		❖	❖	❖	❖	
ICDS Convention and Campaign, 2008		❖	❖					❖	❖	❖	❖		❖	❖	❖	❖	
Right to Education, Mobilizations, 2008		❖	v						❖		❖		❖		❖		

Source: Based on data provided by BGVS.

which began during the second phase (1994–1997) was, in some senses, consolidated at the central government level during the phase from 1998 onwards. It is also noteworthy that the first three phases depicted above, in some ways, correspond to the prescribed phases of particular district level literacy campaigns: a preparatory phase of mobilization, a literacy phase, followed by post-literacy and continuing education phases, where the linkages to broader aspects of development gain a formal legitimacy. It is not clear whether this trajectory was consciously adopted by the BGVS or emerged as a result of the socio-political spaces that were provided to it and the economic contexts that the campaigns expanded into. The history suggests that in effect this trajectory was an interplay between these two factors.

By 1994, most of the early literacy campaigns of the late 1980s and early 1990s, which were initiated in the generally high literacy rate districts, had entered the continuing education phase. This phase provided an official, governmental legitimacy for broadening out the literacy intervention in those districts to include activities related to health, gender, socio-economic survival and ecological sustainability. In contrast, during and after 1994, the literacy campaigns had spread to districts in the northern, Hindi-speaking areas of the country. These latter campaigns were in their initial literacy phase. An ideological tension related to the emphasis in the campaigns was emerging at this stage. While the government and district administrations stressed the need for coverage and meeting literacy targets to demonstrate impact, the BGVS was beginning to realize that the very condition for the possibility of fulfilling those targets meaningfully was a linkage between literacy and other developmental interventions from the very outset. We thus see an interplay of shifting socio-economic and geographical contexts, contrasting ideological perspectives and differentiated intervention strategies that mark the 1994–1997 phase of the campaigns. It might thus be said that unfortunately adult literacy, in its restricted sense of an enabling skill, was the main loser by the start of the next phase in 1998, with the state engaging in a formal literacy for the record and the primary civil society organization concentrating largely on socio-economic development in the wider sense of the term, but within the context of the literacy campaigns.

During the period 1998 to 2004, the BGVS was confronted with major differences of approach with the MHRD, the NLM and the Directorate of Adult Education at the national level and their subordinate bodies in states. This has been mentioned above. Another major conflict of ideological perspectives emerged in relation to the then central government of the National Democratic Alliance led by the Bharatiya Janata Party and its educational policies that in effect promoted sectarianism and its ideology of religious nationalism. Government funding for the BGVS projects gradually dwindled and then dried up. It was in this context that the BGVS approached the Sir Dorabji Tata Trust (SDTT) for financial assistance for sustaining its national office and the state level projects. After an initial grant to stabilize the national office, the SDTT released a three year grant for the period 2004–2007, later extended to June 30, 2008, for a project entitled 'Empowerment, Rights and Security'. The thrust of the project was to institutionalize the large-scale mobilizations through people's organizational forms like community schools, women's SHGs, libraries and publications and CECs. Capacity-building for this process of institutionalization would be provided by the national office together with regional and state level sub-centres. The components of the programme were community mobilization, Samata and SHGs, convergence of Samata with health and CECs, basic education through GVVs and libraries and publications for the Jan Vachan Andolan (JVA, People's Reading Movement). We will now continue with a description of the distinctive characteristics of the phases of the BGVS intervention from 1989 to the present.

2. Phase 1: Mobilizations for Literacy, 1989–93

The initial years of the BGVS interventions in the literacy campaigns were marked by major social mobilizations. The jathas of 1990, 1992 and 1993 may be seen in retrospect to have concentrated on three major social sectors in the interest of literacy. The 1990 jatha had a national scale and served to place literacy on the national agenda as a major socio-political priority. It provided the nucleus of what was to become the national strategy for the literacy campaigns: the focus on a district for addressing the question of adult illiteracy; socio-cultural mobilization drawing on the popular culture of orality; the creation of convergent, decentralized organizational forms for implementation from the district to the village level comprised of the administration, the voluntary sector and the teaching-learning community; and, voluntarism and a people's movement approach as the guiding principles of the campaign.

The 1992 jatha concentrated on a geographical region with low social developmental indicators – the northern Hindi-speaking belt. It was here that the concentration of illiteracy and hence the need for the literacy campaigns was the greatest, and yet the probabilities of their success were the least due to the constraints of the political economy. The 1993 Samata jatha focussed on women – the most important social sector from the perspective of the objectives of the literacy campaigns. All the three jathas served to identify and involve voluntary literacy activists, to extend the organizational presence of the BGVS to different states and districts, and to strengthen the district level organization for implementation – the District Literacy Committees. The three jathas unwittingly helped to reinforce the relatively mechanical and disarticulated strategy of a four-phased approach: preparatory mobilization; the literacy phase, which came to be called the Total Literacy Campaign (TLC) phase; and only thereafter, the post-literacy (PL) and the continuing education phases, which would serve to reinforce literacy and relate it to other development activities. This strategic option was one of the contributory factors to the relative failure of the literacy campaigns in the low literacy districts with low social developmental indicators, as may be seen from their fate during the 1994 to 1997 phase of the literacy campaigns and of BGVS interventions. In these districts, socio-economic survival was the legitimately felt priority and literacy would be accepted only if seen to be contributing to and accompanied by interventions that enhanced the quality of that survival.

The BGVS Jatha of 1990

The first initiative of the BGVS was to conduct a nation-wide kalajatha between October 2 and November 14, 1990, the international literacy year. The Executive Committee of the NLM on April 28, 1989 had approved the proposal of a kalajatha. The objective was to undertake a massive mobilization to create a demand for literacy among the people and to build people's organizations for implementation. The kalajathas that followed, apart from drawing on popular culture, attempted to relate literacy to livelihood issues and the oppressive barriers to development. The central slogan of this jatha was "science and literacy for national integration and self-reliance". One must remember that the background to the jatha was a nation that was being disrupted by casteist and communal forces.

Describing the strength of the kalajatha as a cultural mobilizational approach that communicates critical development messages, a leaflet brought out by the BGVS at the time states,

> "The Kalajatha, being extremely simple and communicative, was a novel experience to most of the villagers. As a powerful medium that packed its messages in the popular cultural idioms and forms, its message was hard hitting, linking literacy with many basic livelihood problems and even with questions of exploitation, oppression and discrimination against women. Thus, despite many odds, it managed to transform the movement into an unprecedented national mobilization, especially of the women and the rural youth" (BGVS, 1990: 2).

Writing in 1993, based on observations of the early literacy campaigns in rural Maharashtra, I arrived at the following conclusion as regards the potential of the kalajatha performances towards creating an atmosphere conducive to literacy learning:

> "The programme is generally conceived as several items, woven into a coherent whole for effective impact – scripts within a total script. It attracts a large audience of a cross-section of villagers and is able to hold them in rapt attention. The informal style, the direct and emotional appeal, the mix of humour and serious messages and, most importantly, the use of folk media that draws on the familiar culture of orality among the people and urges them to make the transition to literacy through learning, help to create a significant immediate impact. Motivation for learning and instruction, a greater resolve among the literacy activists and their local organization, flow from this generalized impact. The cultural performance provides a forum for inter-communal communication at the level of folk traditions. In addition, it provides one more occasion for dialogue and planning for the campaign" (Saldanha, 1993: 987).

As Bhola points out, the mobilizations within literacy campaigns "can provide the people with a deeply felt political experience resulting in a sense of nationhood" (Bhola, 1984: 35). However, the communicational impact of the occasional kalajatha does not get mechanically translated into the sustained communication of teaching-learning in the everyday group setting. Learners approach the instructional process with conflicting claims on their time and a set of grounded priorities emerging from the annual cycle of everyday life and the agricultural and festival seasons. Organizational factors, such as systematic monitoring, personalized contact and functionalized instruction with occasional bursts of cultural mobilization can, to some degree, resolve the objective constraints to sustain learning (Saldanha, 1993: 987).

TABLE 2.2 *Summary Status of Jathas, 1990*

	States	No. of Districts	No. of Districts with Jathas	No. of Jathas Major	No. of Jathas Minor	Total No. of Jatha Centres
1.	Kerala and Lakshadweep	15	14	15	1,400	9,510 (14)
2.	Tamil Nadu	21	21	27	–	2,570 (20)
3.	Karnataka	20	19	17	15	2,531 (19)
4.	Andhra Pradesh	23	23	21	72	5,600 (23)
5.	Maharashtra	29 (+1)	26	45	6	–
6.	Madhya Pradesh	45	42	50	–	3,800 (42)
7.	Gujarat	19	10	10	–	479 (4)
8.	Rajasthan	27	18	118	–	–
9.	Haryana	16	16	14	2	801 (8)
10.	Punjab and Chandigarh	13	13	13	–	1,028 (11)
11.	Himachal	12	12	5	–	237 (4)
12.	Uttar Pradesh	64	31	31	–	1,702 (15)
13.	Bihar	40	27	40	–	–
14.	Orissa	13	13	81	–	212 (2)
15.	West Bengal	17	17	204	12	1,169 (7)
16.	Assam	23	17	17	–	–
17.	Manipur	8	7	4	–	–
18.	Tripura	4	4	5	55	–
19.	Delhi	1	1	2	–	–
20.	Andaman and Nicobar	1	1	1	–	–
21.	Pondicherry	1	1	1	–	–
	Total	412 + Gr. Bombay	333	721	1,562	29,639 (169)

Note: Figures in parentheses indicate number of district.

Source: BGVS, Achievements Under the Bharat Gyan Vigyan Jatha and the Paidal Jatha, New Delhi, 1991: 19.

The 1990 jathas covered about 40,000 villages in 333 districts of the country. A total of 721 major jathas and 1,562 minor local jathas undertook various routes and were able to mobilize about a million volunteers for engaging in literacy. Table 2.2 shows in 14 districts of Kerala, 1,400 squads of high school students are engaged in various environment-building activities (Report of First General Council

Meeting of NLMA, February 1991: 12). Other voluntary organizations with Gandhian and Sarvodaya orientations had, in addition, organized about a 1,000 paidal jathas in the states of Uttar Pradesh, Madhya Pradesh, Bihar, Orissa and Assam. They were able to identify a number of activists willing to engage in the literacy campaigns on a voluntary basis. From the 1990 the BGVS jatha emerged as the strategy popularly called Total Literacy Campaigns (TLCs). The essential features of this strategy and the Ernakulam model adopted by the NLM were: mobilization using local cultural forms, motivating voluntary teachers and youth, and the formation of decentralized, coordinated people's structures for implementation from the district to the village levels. The district administration was expected to facilitate the entire process.

Several district literacy campaigns were initiated as a result of the 1990 jatha. Besides the entire state of Kerala and the Union Territory of Pondicherry, these were in 31 districts of Andhra Pradesh, in Bihar, Karnataka, Maharashtra, Madhya Pradesh, Orissa, Uttar Pradesh, West Bengal, and in Gujarat. The BGVS involvement in the district campaigns was varied – ranging from mobilization to strategy formulation, participation in organization, training and teaching-learning material production – depending on need.

An analytic documentation of the 1990 jatha has been carried out by Dighe and others (1991). Accordingly, the first General Body meeting of the BGVS met on December 21, 1989. It was attended by about 50 delegates from various parts of the country and evolved an action plan for the 1990 jatha. A lecture series was visualized, which would be delivered at the various kalajatha centres as well as in some of the surrounding villages. The lectures covered topics such as the world we live in, literacy for liberation, health for all, and literacy for women. Analysing the lessons learnt from the jatha, the document draws attention to the political will for literacy that was generated through approaching political parties, irrespective of their ideology. An organizational structure for implementing the literacy campaigns emerged, especially at the state level. Wherever the district administration provided support to the jatha, the outcomes were, by and large, significant. The study draws attention to the importance of the pre-jatha activities in determining the outcomes of the jatha. About 207 literacy ambassadors had been selected, who would be primarily responsible for the pre-jatha activities and the organization of the jatha. The capacities of the literacy ambassadors to mobilize persons within two or three districts was a factor that was crucial to later outcomes. The experience of the jatha suggested that the success in a number of districts could be attributed to the capacity of the literacy ambassadors to involve unions, teachers, public and private sector employees, banks and various mass organizations, in addition to individuals. The experience of the kalajathas indicated that traditional cultural forms generate the requisite social energy for a mass mobilization like the literacy campaigns. The messages and the cultural forms that were utilized demonstrated a healthy combination of centralized initiative together with decentralized creativity through adaptations. The ideological thrust of the kalajathas was such that "the problem of illiteracy was for the first time being perceived from the perspective of the poor" (Dighe et al., 1991: 84).

The Executive Committee of the NLM, in its meeting of December 14, 1990, acknowledged the significant mobilization that had been carried out by the BGVS and resolved that the BGVS activities should continue beyond December 31, 1990 – the initial contract period. In March, 1991, the NLM requested the BGVS to expand its network to state and district levels with NLM's financial support.

Messages through Folk Media

"Several folk forms have been fruitfully utilized in the literacy campaigns in Maharashtra. During the environment-building programmes in Ratnagiri district, for example, the kalajathas drew from musical forms like *lavani, povada, gondhal, jagar,* etc. Environment-building gave expression to songs from tribal traditions such as the Dhangari Lok Geet and from religious sects like the Varkaries, followers of Vithoba of Pandharpur … . The main thrust of the messages conveyed through songs, dance and discussions was literacy. However, it was reported that other issues such as mother and child care, family planning, watershed management, the problem of alcoholism and dowry, small savings and agricultural development were also conveyed.

In this district, the participants in the kalaphatak were drawn primarily from the middle classes and in particular from school teachers. However, in the TLC districts from the Marathwada region, like Latur and Nanded where the Bharat Gyan Vigyan Samiti (BGVS) has been active, one has observed a greater participation of the traditional practitioners of the folk media" (Saldanha, 1993: 981).

The BGVS Jatha of 1992

As mentioned earlier, several literacy campaigns were initiated largely in the non-Hindi-speaking states as a result of the jatha of 1990. Out of the 110 district literacy campaigns running in the country at the time, there were only three in the states of Uttar Pradesh and Bihar. While the 1990 jatha covered the northern states, its impact, in terms of sustainable organizations for literacy, was found to be generally weak. Analysing this, the BGVS attributed it to the disturbances caused by the political processes taking place at the time: the Mandal issue extending the scope of caste-based reservations and the Ram Janmabhoomi-Babri Masjid issue, also resulting in several communal conflicts. The latter was at its height on October 30, 1990 during the course of the jatha. In addition, there were few earlier established contact points by way of individuals or organizational networks that the jatha could relate to. The apathy of the middle classes and political parties was high and the messages of the jatha were unable to adequately penetrate the structures of an iniquitous society based on caste, class and gender inequity. While the enthusiasm of the non-literates as well as identified volunteers was high, the administrative support was generally weak with frequent transfers of Collectors (BGVS, 1992). A need was felt by the BGVS and the NLM to initiate campaigns in the Hindi-speaking belt of the country. The NLM requested the BGVS to undertake a second jatha with a special focus on these regions, which constituted the largest concentration of non-literates (Minutes of EC-NLMA Meeting, May 8, 1992: 20–24). The 1992 jatha covered 147 out of the then 250 districts of the Hindi states, including Orissa, by December 1992. It was successful in mobilizing and initiating an organization structure for implementation, especially in the states of Madhya Pradesh, Haryana, Uttar Pradesh, Bihar and Rajasthan.

Prior to 1992, apart from social mobilization, the BGVS was engaged in implementing a few literacy campaigns at a micro level. For example, independent BGVS literacy campaigns were established in nine mandals each of Andhra Pradesh and Assam, and in a similar number of blocks in Punjab. Programmes were initiated in a number of districts in Tamil Nadu, Karnataka, Andhra Pradesh, Madhya Pradesh (Bilaspur), Haryana (Panipat), etc., with the BGVS playing a crucial role with the respective district administrations. However, by mid-1992, the NLM suggested that the BGVS would not be ordinarily running literacy campaigns on its own. Its primary role would be "to organize, activate, nucleate and train" so as to "play a supportive role for the campaigns" (BGVS, 1993: 3). The BGVS was thus emerging from an agency for social mobilization to a nation-wide resource support organization that was accepted by the NLM as a major partner with continued representation in the NLM executive.

The messages in the kalajatha songs and in the literacy texts have been critiqued for their reinforcement of popular beliefs within a 'culture of silence' and for contributing to blaming the victim. These are for example expressions such as 'moving from darkness to light' and 'blindfolded through these roads of life', as in the text below. It must be remembered that most of the kalajatha songs were devised in workshops by grassroots activists and corresponded to the complexity of their aspirations. The songs may be seen as one small critical step within a larger ideological and mobilizational process towards organization from below:

If We Learn Ka, Kha, Ga

If we learn ka, kha, ga, my friends,
None of our problems will remain hard to crack
Letters will become sharp arrows for sure
And they will be our weapons for ever
All these days I was travelling all alone
Blindfolded through these roads of life
But today I have made friendship with these letters
And that was, my friend, a great turning point
The whole world around, suddenly turned upside down!
These endless roads are now leading me
To meaningful destinations and not to unknown destinies
Problems are there galore; the road is rocky and slippery
But with the knowledge and wisdom that letters provide
I will change the shape of this world, one day, for sure.
If we learn ka, kha, ga friends,
Then none of our problems will remain hard to crack.
(free translation by K.K. Krishna Kumar, BGVS, of a popular Hindi literacy song, widely used in the literacy campaigns in North India).

The Samata Jatha, 1993

The massive involvement of women and girl children, as learners and voluntary instructors in the literacy campaigns, could not be ignored. There was a growing demand for a greater focus on issues that concerned women and a felt need for women in leadership positions.

The Samata jatha of 1993 (discussed in greater detail in a subsequent section) was a response and the Samata Vigyan Utsavas that followed after 1996 was an attempt at consolidating the mobilization into a network. Eight kalajathas started from different centres in the country around March 8, 1993. After covering more than 20 states for about a month with about three performances every day, the jathas converged at Jhansi for a two-day convention during April 8–9, 1993. This jatha of women for education, equality and peace had reached out to over two lakh persons.

By June 1993, literacy campaigns were undertaken in about 75 districts in the Hindi-speaking states as a result of these mobilizations. The BGVS had now developed into an organizational network that was providing resource support to the literacy campaigns in most of the states. Several handbooks were brought out relating to project formulation, training, monitoring, as well as literacy primers, which were being utilized fruitfully by the districts. By 1992, the BGVS had state and district level units in 18 states/union territories, either on its own or in alliance with other people's science organizations. After 1992, the BGVS had become a major partner of the NLM and the practice of submitting

When Every Woman Learns to Read and Write

When every woman learns to read and write
Every one of them will be on their own feet
All the old sayings about women being weak
Will be thrown into the dust bins of time
Then we will unite and march along
All the way to the new era of equality
We are sure that the day when we
Break the fetters of inequality is not far away
Letters we know are the first steps, we know
We have to move further to the world around
We must know whom we elect, why we elect
We will speak aloud in the Gramsabhas
The days of silence are over now
Let us remember the old saying:
The child that doesn't cry will never get
Its share of even breast-milk for sure
(free translation by K.K. Krishna Kumar, BGVS, of a popular literacy song).

two yearly project reports was initiated. The significance of the mobilizations through the jathas of 1990, 1992, and the Samata jatha that followed in 1993, may be seen from the fact that over 200 district literacy campaigns had emerged by 1993. Literacy was placed on the national agenda and a strategy for approaching the issue through people's mobilization and voluntarism had been formulated. This was the most significant contribution of the BGVS.

3. Phase 2: From Literacy to Development, 1994–97

The campaign for Hamara Desh (Our Country) marks a transition from mobilization for literacy to taking forward these mobilizations through establishing linkages between literacy and other developmental concerns, such as popular participation in natural resource management, credit and self-help groups emerging from the Samata mobilizations of women, health, the basic education of children, publications and a library movement and interface with the Panchayati Raj bodies. Social mobilizations for literacy, such as the Uttar Pradesh jatha of 1995 and the one in Rajasthan in 1996 would continue, but the predominant characteristic of this phase of BGVS intervention would be a multi-sectoral, developmental linkage to the literacy campaigns. The BGVS was effectively, if not in a fully conscious manner, following in its own initiatives the sequencing of particular literacy campaigns – first mobilization for literacy and then establishing linkages to development through post-literacy (PL) and continuing education (CE) centres. The BGVS trajectory was also adjusting to the central tendency of most of the campaigns taken together, in that the majority were now formally moving into the PL and CE phases. As an important office bearer of the BGVS stated, the BGVS attempted to utilize all available spaces in its interventionist strategy.

This approach, while possible for already high literacy areas, such as Kerala and some of the earliest literacy campaign districts, was not feasible for low literacy regions. It was here that the structures of caste and the inequities of class and patriarchy acted as severe constraints to the introduction of 'literacy in isolation' or to a strategy of first literacy and then addressing other low social developmental indicators.

The Campaign for Hamara Desh, 1993–94

This was a campaign with a thematic focus on national unity and development conducted between August 15, 1993 and February 28, 1994.

The objective of the campaign was "spreading the message of literacy, national integration and self-reliance" (BGVS, July 1994: 16). A national workshop was organized jointly by the BGVS and the All India People's Science Network (AIPSN) during July 13–26, 1993 in which the campaign details were planned. Soon after the workshop, planning-cum-training workshops were held in most of the states during the months of August-September, 1993, followed by the district level workshops and training programmes. Mass contact programmes and *balmelas* (children's festivals) were conducted in more than 150 districts in various states (BGVS, July 1994: 17). The programme culminated with a week-long people's science festival at Hyderabad.

Hamara Desh had the active involvement of various PSMs and was undertaken through a series of activities as under:

- Balmelas that drew children and teachers together to share their experiences by living in each other's homes. Several such melas and science festivals were held at the district, state and regional levels.
- The Lok Sampark Andolan (Movement for Contact with People) was a mass contact project undertaken in several parts of the country to initiate discussion among people on issues confronting them. The volunteer instructors, the non-literates and neo-literates of the literacy campaigns were beginning to participate in these educational activities.
- Relay Cycle Yatras were held with the message of unity and progress. These started from January 1, 1994 from 14 different parts of the country and converged at Hyderabad on February 28 of the same year. Thirteen Hamara Desh relay cycle rallies were conducted during the year 1994. The relay teams came from all states to participate in this programme. The rallies evoked a "very good response throughout the country" and contributed towards "boosting the morale of the literacy activists" (BGVS, July 1994: 17). In addition to the BGVS and AIPSN activists, a large number of activists from other organizations also participated. The relay jathas comprising over 2,000 relay cyclists culminated into a massive cycle rally on February 28, 1994 and formed part of the Janotsava (People's Science Festival) that was organized by BGVS and AIPSN at Hyderabad from February 23 to 28, with support from NLM, National Council for Science and Technology

Communication (NCSTC) and the Department of Science and Technology. More than 700 delegates from various states participated in the Janotsava. The various activities organized during the Janotsava were: discussions on topics like problems and prospects of TL-PL campaign, science communication, science and technology for rural development; a national Jansansad (People's Parliament); an exhibition on PSM/BGVS activities; exhibition on rural technology; posters and exhibitions on education in India and the cultural unity in diversity of the country (BGVS, July 1994: 17). Jansansads took place at the gram panchayat, block and district levels. This was an attempt to create discussion groups and to develop alternative solutions to felt needs through popular action.

- As a result of the campaign, a number of possible areas of joint intervention by BGVS, AIPSN and other like-minded groups, such as Universal Elementary Education (UEE) programmes, Nai Talim for artisans, science communication, interventions in local area (panchayat) planning, library and cultural movements, had emerged. The state groups had begun to try and sustain the study groups formed during the mass contact project as a follow-up of the Hamara Desh campaign (BGVS, July 1994: 17).

Literacy and Natural Resources, 1993–98...

BGVS together with AIPSN had undertaken a series of interventions in the sphere of sustaining natural resources and their equitable use through community participation. Local level planning through Participatory Resource Mapping (PRM), followed by organization-building and planning for development action, was undertaken from 1993 in four blocks in each of four states. The PRM activities involved preparation of three thematic maps on terrain features, land use status and water utilization structures and other community facilities after intensive environment-building and mobilization of volunteers. The collection of data related to land, water and socio-economic status in structured data formats also formed part of the exercise. Subsequent to mapping, the key volunteers and scientific assistants undertook a combined evaluation of thematic maps and prepared a derivative map for action planning. To internalize local level action planning and implementation, the formation of user committees at hamlet, village and gram panchayat levels was also envisaged.

Related to the foregoing was the project on integrated drinking water and sanitation called WATSAN, which was continued in the four blocks of Tamil Nadu, Orissa, West Bengal and Bihar from June 1993 to July 1995. The main objective of the project was to evolve and implement a participatory planning for drinking water and sanitation. Under the project, extensive field activities were conducted, which included environment-building, orientation and training of resource persons and volunteers in PRM, organization of village communities into user committees, conducting PRM exercises, and evolving village level plans.

The Watershed Development Project was undertaken in about 25 clusters of villages, each year, for a period of three years. The aim was to achieve conservation and development of a watershed, to improve its ecological well-being and enhance its productivity and life-supporting systems through the people's participatory method. The project envisaged the protection, rational management, sustainable development and utilization of natural resources. Extensive field activities were undertaken under the project, such as the organization of sensitization camps, conduction of PRM exercises, post-PRM workshops, training in technical and managerial aspects appropriate to the location, exposure to other watershed projects, sharing experience among and between Project Implementing Agencies (PIAs), and support to the PIAs. Four regional centres were set up, one each at New Delhi, Pune, Calcutta and Palakkad. Thirty-three watersheds all over the country were delineated. Support was provided to states and the PIAs for the recruitment and development of Watershed Development Teams, including technical support and forwarding of watershed development project proposals.

Panchayati Raj was yet another project initiated by the BGVS for the maximization of people's participation in planning for their own development. Based on the Kerala people's planning experience, it was initiated in the year 1995. The project sought to strengthen the Panchayati Raj system and to extend the BGVS network along with it to the gram panchayats. A number of states organized different kinds of training programmes for elected panchayat representatives. Tours were conducted for representatives from different states for their exposure to the Kerala People's Planning Campaign. Workshops were organized to develop PL-CE-Panchayati Raj linkage material, to discuss the overall strategy of developing linkages between PL-CE programmes and Gram Panchayat Development Plans, and to prepare Panchayat Development Reports. Panchayati Raj was also strengthened through various projects, such as Literacy and Resource Literacy, Literacy to Land and Water Management, Hamara Desh, Desh Ko Janein Desh Ko Badlein and Samata Vigyan Utsava.

Desh Ko Janein Desh Ko Badlein, a campaign run between 1995 to 1998, had two major aspects – educational and developmental. The objective was to develop critical awareness and action at decentralized levels. Field investigations, the preparation of area development plans, the creation of area-based groups for development initiatives were the major phases of this project undertaken by the BGVS in collaboration with the AIPSN. The aim was to cover 10,000 gram panchayats and form study groups of about 10 to 15 members. The initial phase of this project was concluded with a series of Jansansads at the block, district and state levels, culminating in a national one at Nalanda in October 1998.

Literacy to Health, 1994–96...

The main objectives of the project were to use health education inputs as a part of the TL-PL-CE programmes, to improve child health status in a measurable manner and to intervene in women's health issues. Implemented in two phases, the first phase from March 1994 to December 1995 covered 15 districts. The focus of activities during the first phase was around health communication, participation, health survey and local planning. An extensive health education campaign was implemented in the 15 districts with a focus on 'Sampark Andolans' and kalajathas centred around core messages on health. The second phase was implemented from January 1996 onwards. The emphasis during this phase was on training of health activists, operationalization of panchayat level action plans, local level monitoring and surveillance of health status and child health. Despite various delays and obstacles, by the end of September 2000 the work progressed through different stages in 11 different districts from different states. During the implementation of the project, a number of workshops and trainings were organized for volunteers/activists and professionals with a view to capacity building. Three training manuals were produced for the activists and a set of 13 books containing health messages was published for neo-literates.

Literacy and Basic Education, Social Awareness, 1994...

BGVS had also undertaken a number of interventions in the sphere of spreading social awareness through various literacy and educational programmes. For example, the objective of the Joy of Learning (JoL) campaign, initiated in 1994, was to promote the interest of children, parents and school teachers in joyful and relevant learning. The activities consisted of a series of children's science festivals at the village, block and district levels, culminating in a seven-day festival in New Delhi in November 1994. The programmes were conducted in over 200 districts throughout the country. It was estimated that about 15 lakh children and 35,000 teachers, in addition to the general public, in the 200 districts, were exposed to the innovative teaching-learning processes of JoL. The campaign was consolidated through several activities around the time of the total solar eclipse of October 24, 1995 under the banner of the Cosmic Voyage Project.

Building on the mobilization of the JoL campaign and the Cosmic Voyage, the Jeevanshala project started in 1995 attempted to establish linkages between literacy and elementary education through intensive efforts in three blocks.

The Jan Vachan Andolan (JVA), initiated in 1994, was a country-wide campaign to encourage reading among the people, followed by an initiative for a village library movement. It was started during the course of the 1994–96 project of the BGVS. It was reported that the campaign covered a total number of 3,838 villages through the organization of *melas* (fairs) by February 1998. The campaign was accompanied by a major publication drive for good quality, relevant and low priced books. The added intention was to relate this effort to the post-literacy phase of the campaigns and to provide neo-literates with adequate reading material. More than 400 books were published under this project.

The BGVS had also initiated five State Resource Centres (SRCs) during 1995 as part of the process of institutionalizing its academic resource support to different state literacy campaigns. These were in Assam, Haryana, Himachal Pradesh, Tripura and Madhya Pradesh. The Assam unit, in coordination with the SRC in the state, had been running a seven-block, post-PL programme. Proposals had also been submitted for starting SRCs in Kerala, Andhra, Tamil Nadu, Punjab and Bihar. The SRCs have the potential of becoming major fora for the institutionalization of BGVS academic inputs through material preparation, training and strategy formulation within the states. These academic inputs had been ongoing in connection with the literacy campaigns and sporadic and specific in relation to particular projects of the BGVS.

The BGVS Jatha in Uttar Pradesh, 1995

Two states that particularly needed inputs towards stimulating mass involvement for literacy were Uttar Pradesh and Rajasthan. A jatha for the former was conducted in 1995 and for the latter in 1996. Preparatory activities for the jatha in Uttar Pradesh started in December 1994 with

> Lalita Devi resides in Bank village, Begusarai district, Bihar. She is a member of the Dalit community. She is 26 years old. Lalita is married. During her childhood she accessed formal schooling upto 10th standard. She worked as a volunteer teacher in the post-literacy programme and has recently been recruited to work as a 'Prerak' (Animator) for the village Continuing Education Centre. She is also the secretary of the Sambal Self-Help Groups.
>
> She said that initially when she joined the post-literacy programme, there was resistance from her parents-in-law to her increased mobility inside and outside the village. But today she works with total family acceptance and support. Her work, as a volunteer-instructor, extends beyond teaching women to read and write, to develop awareness on immunization, hygiene, health, women's participation in community activities and SHGs. Lalita felt that her participation in the post-literacy programme increased her self-confidence and strengthened her communication skills. She said that in the process of making others 'literate' she became 'socially literate'.
>
> Reviewing her experience of teaching literacy and numeracy skills, Lalita said that she was not happy with the content of the post-literacy primer Vikalp. She said that the primer did not respond to issues concerning women and did not reflect an understanding of the pain and sorrow they experience. She maintained the same perspective about the gender content in different training processes. Lalita's dream is to develop women's enterprise through the Sambal groups in her village.
>
> (edited from BGVS, January 2002: 132)

state and regional rehearsal camps. A total of 40 kalajathas were flagged off on February 21, 1995 within 40 districts. These teams performed at 1,600 locations and converged at a massive rally in Lucknow on February 25, 1995. A number of writers, intellectuals and artistes lent their support to the jatha. Apart from the local artistes, around 100 artists from districts of the neighbouring states of Bihar and Madhya Pradesh also participated in this project. The jatha succeeded in enthusing several struggling literacy campaigns in the state.

A number of district level training programmes were held for resource persons as a follow up to the jatha. The jatha had also received good support from the district literacy committees and the administration. However, there were a few districts where the administration was indifferent to the programme. Several exchanges between literacy activists, especially of the northern states, took place during this period.

The BGVS Jatha in Rajasthan, 1996

This jatha was reported to have covered 14 districts and about 250 gram panchayats. It reached out to about 2 lakh persons in a major mobilization for literacy during November 26 and December 7, 1996. Five kalajatha teams covered the districts of Sikar, Alwar, Dholpur, Kota, Bundi, Sawai Madhopur, Jhalawar, Baran, Jaipur, Bhilwara, Pali, Barmer and Dungarpur. In all, 75 artists participated in these jathas. One of the teams was comprised of only women.

As a result of these jathas, the BGVS was in a position to identify 13 clusters in 10 districts where work for the literacy campaigns could be undertaken in an intensive manner. A need to follow-up general mobilization with intensive cluster level work was being realized by BGVS. Both, the limited human resources and the demands of concrete institutionalization of the mobilization process required this local specific approach.

Literacy and Women's Empowerment, 1995 ...

The Samata jatha of 1993 was, after a lull, followed by the Samata Vigyan Utsavas (Samata Science Festivals) from 1996 to 1999. They consisted of mobilizations of women through melas held at various levels. These melas had corners, which provided women an opportunity for information and articulation towards solidarity and leadership building. It was reported that 3,527 village level melas were held during the period between 1994 and 1997. Several of the Self-Help Groups

(SHGs) and economic initiatives among women emerged as a result of these utsavas, especially since 1998.

Operation Restoration, 1997–98

During 1997, the BGVS put forward a proposal to the NLM for revitalizing some of the large number of stagnant literacy campaigns. About 30 senior BGVS activists from different states were identified as NLM consultants for implementing this programme. The consultants visited a number of districts and suggested several measures for restoring the campaigns. However, the reform process was unable to continue beyond a point due to resistance from the state level administration. Bihar was one of the states that took advantage of this initiative. Saharsa district was an important example of the success of these efforts. A dormant campaign was fully restored within six months, raising the enrolment to three lakh persons. Karnataka and Andhra Pradesh were other states where earnest attempts were made in collaboration with the state administration. Madhya Pradesh undertook a mass contact programme through the Jan Sampark Abhiyan (BGVS, February 1998: 20).

A critical tension had developed between the BGVS and the Department of Adult Education by 1995, within a joint membership of the NLM. Though the literacy campaigns were large scale and widespread, the majority of them were beginning to loose their potential for literacy and social transformation. The foregoing is taken note of in the minutes of the BGVS General Council (BGVS, December 1995: 7–8):

> "The BGVS General Council would like to place on record its appreciation of the voluntary work performed by hundreds of thousands of volunteers especially rural women and youth in the literacy movement. The tremendous mobilization and empowerment that this process has generated as well as the millions of people made literate in so short a time is indeed a historic achievement. The General Council would also like to record its appreciation of the very valuable and supportive role of the National Literacy Mission in this process, especially, the spirit in which the movement was guided.
>
> However, the General Council would like to express its serious concern at:

1. The indiscriminate expansion of Total Literacy Campaigns (TLCs) to districts without even minimal ground preparation, leading to an alarmingly growing number of sanctioned but stagnant districts.
2. The increasing bureaucratization of the TLCs and the failure to retain the basic spirit of the "people's movement" character of the campaigns. The concept of partnership with NGOs and involvement of people's organization is being given a go-by.
3. The erosion of the autonomous and decentralized functioning of the Zilla Saksharata Samitis (ZSS). There are growing instances of the ZSS becoming a vehicle for patronage and for corruption.
4. Increasing falsified reporting of achievements as well as undue pressures to make declarations of total literacy.

The BGV.S General Council would appeal to the NLM to reconsider the present approach to mass literacy campaign at this juncture. The time is ripe, indeed overdue, to move to a decentralized approach in the campaign where block or even a cluster of panchayats can be the basic unit and where the emerging Panchayati Raj Institutions (PRIs) can be enabled to participate and even lead these campaigns."

Problems like indiscriminate expansion, growing bureaucratization and loss of a sense of partnership are a reiteration of earlier statements made in 1994 and 1995. Together with these, new problem areas, such as growing corruption and the falsification of achievement data, are identified. There is a call for decentralization, local specificity to a block or even a group of panchayats with the possibility of PRIs playing a major role in view of the 73rd and 74th Amendments to the Indian Constitution.

4. Phase 3: Continuing Education for Development with Scarce Resources, 1998–2001

There was a clear strategy implicit in the BGVS proposal of 1997–98, later extended to 2000. The elements of this strategy were decentralization and concentration of efforts to selected villages within blocks, integration of the TL, PL and CE phases of the literacy campaigns and interlinkages with other development sectors. This strategy was formulated in the context of the phases of BGVS intervention and the external context of critical tensions with the Department of Adult Education reaching a stage of near marginalization of the BGVS. The campaigns themselves had reached a stage where there was a diversity of learning needs among the non-literates and neo-literates. While formally most of the campaigns were in the post-literacy and continuing education phases, in practice, most of them were still in a literacy phase with large concentrations of the residually non-literates. Campaigns had generally stagnated and died out in regions where there were the largest concentrations of non-literates and where the need for literacy was the greatest – the northern belt of states. It was in this context that the BGVS formulated its 1997–98 proposal.

The structural arrangement that was formally visualized by the Department of Adult Education for the Continuing Education Programme was of Continuing Education Centres (CECs) linked to a Nodal Continuing Education Centre (NCEC). A CEC would be setup for a population of 2,000–2,500 so as to cater to the needs of about 500 to 1,000 neo-literates. An NCC would be coordinating 10 to 15 CECs. Two paid workers, a Prerak and an Assistant Prerak, would manage each CEC and NCEC. At the district level, the District Literacy Committee (Zilla Saksharta Samiti) would continue to coordinate adult education activities within the district. At the state level, a State Resource Centre and the Jana Shikshan Sansthan (the earlier Shramik Vidya Peeth) would provide resource support to the CECs and NCECs. The State Literacy Mission Authority (SLMA) would be the formal sanctioning agency under the central NLMA.

The four main programmes that were visualized under the formal, government-led continuing education were the Income Generating Programme, the Quality of Life Improvement Programme, the Equivalency Programme that would attempt to equate literacy learning with formal schooling and the Individual Interest Promotion Programme. These programmes had been derived from the Asia-Pacific Programme of Education for All (APPEAL) of UNESCO. The BGVS continuing education programmes in different states operationalized changes within this formal programme to suit different contexts.

The BGVS Project of 1997–98, extended to 2000

Prior to the BGVS national proposal for 1997–98, extended to 2000, it had formulated certain guidelines on the basis of which state action plans were to be formulated. The basic approach of these guidelines was to continue seeing literacy, post-literacy and continuing education as the most important intervention. The focus, however, would be on selected villages/gram panchayats in selected districts so as to develop alternative models. It was also suggested that all the other development initiatives could be integrated to the literacy programme. The project was closely

Anati Roy is a 33-year-old woman from Rangapani Para of Srijan Gram block, Bongaigaon district, Assam. Her father, Purna Roy, was earlier a *mahajan* (moneylender). But as time passed, he fell on bad days and was overcome by poverty. Anati was the daughter of his second wife. Her father lost all his properties and had to live from begging. Often Anati had to go to bed with an empty stomach. Her father died while she was still a child. Her helpless mother had to send her to work at the village teacher's house as a domestic helper at the age of nine. She worked for them for the next 11 years of her life. Anati wanted to go to school, but such a life was denied to her.

When she was a young woman of 20, the teacher sent her back to her village. She had to again struggle with poverty. She then went to work in the Yarn Mill at Manipur. But the wages were very low, only Rs 25 per day. So she returned home after six months, but there was no one to offer her food and shelter. She, therefore, again searched for a livelihood. Anati went to Abhayapuri to work in the Weaving Mill and later to Agia of Goalpara district to work in the silk farm. While returning home from Agia, she heard about the Bongai Gaon District Literacy Committee. She heard the kalajatha songs of the literacy campaign. The song struck a chord in her heart. The song seem to tell her woeful story. There was a song that went like this, "When I was a little girl, father did not send me to school. Mother would not let me go ..." This song motivated her to once again take advantage of the literacy campaigns and learn the letters. She brought the books and quietly tried to study the books at night. In the year 2000, she collected together some of the village women Gomati Roy, Megha Roy, Janaki Roy, Monomoti Roy, Meena Roy and a few others and started a learning centre. Every evening after finishing their household tasks they used to gather at their centre. Their volunteer teacher was Monoranjan Roy of the village. He taught the women with all sincerity and devotion. Seven out of the 10 women completed the third primer.

Anati and her group were very enlightened and empowered. Anati can read and is very fond of the *Gyan Vigyan Varta* (a neo-literate fortnightly newspaper). She reads and helps others to read as well. She writes for the *Varta* and encourages others to write as well. Anati has collected some neo-literates and has formed Prochesta Self-Help Groups and keeps accounts very neatly.

They have taken her Rs 10,000 loan from the Prochesta central committee. They have successfully returned the loan. After that they

Cont'd...

Cont'd…

have taken a second loan of Rs 40,000 and have bought cows. She has helped the members to buy tin sheets for covering the roof of their houses. Anati has helped others to buy building materials. She herself has bought yarn to weave cloth. She has helped Makoni Roy to build a low-cost sanitary latrine. Anati has rebuilt her house under the scheme Indira Awas Yojana. She has helped people through various developmental schemes to install electrical hand pumps. She has bought two chairs and a bench to welcome guests.

Anati is loved by all in the village. She is the Prochesta Coordinator of Srijan gram panchayat. At present she is taking advanced training in weaving. She feels deeply indebted to the district literacy committee of Bongai Gaon. Anati's dreams have come true. Anati is now looking forward to a bright future.

(edited from BGVS, SDTT Project 2004–2008, 2008: 25).

connected to inputs in the ongoing literacy campaigns with a special focus on post-literacy, continuing education, health and other broader developmental concerns related to literacy. Sanctioned in March 1997, it was extended to September 2000. A sum of Rs 456.33 lakh was sanctioned by the NLM. However, the total amount released was only Rs 298.16 lakh with several delays in between.

The main thrust of this project for 1997–2000 was:

- To restore some of the many stagnating district literacy campaigns by involving the gram panchayats. This involved giving the campaigns a people's mobilization character and identifying motivated full-time staff.
- To work out methodologies for sustained and meaningful PL and CE. It was visualized that a strategy for CE would be operationalized through model centres with the involvement of the gram panchayats. Activities such as skill training, Jan Vachan Andolan, equivalence to formal schooling levels, and the Samata Utsavas would be linked to the CE efforts.
- To establish linkages with other development sectors. It was visualized that the linkages between literacy to other development sectors that had been brought about in a dispersed manner over the years through the series of mobilizations during the earlier phase, would be concentrated in defined areas through block level models.

The BGVS sought the 'restoration' of the many stagnant TLC districts that had got bureaucratized and had lost their people's movement character. Restoration was sought to be brought about through the creation of 'alternatives'. Some of the major characteristics of the alternative strategy implicit in the 1997–98 proposal (extended to 2000), may be noted:

1. Decentralization and concentration of efforts: The emphasis was on creating the gram panchayats within selected blocks as the units for organization for the literacy campaigns, unlike the earlier efforts of both the NLM and the BGVS of concentrating on entire districts. A total of 100 selected gram panchayats in 10 blocks, in each of the states of Uttar Pradesh, Bihar, Madhya Pradesh, Rajasthan, Haryana and Orissa, were proposed.
2. Integration of the mechanical phases (TL-PL-CE) of the literacy campaigns within a holistic approach through integrated, village level models.
3. Interlinkage between literacy and initiatives within other development sectors that had been attempted through earlier programmes, i.e., Samata and the Samata Utsavas, planning the use of natural resources through Participatory Resource Mapping, Health, the Joy of Learning and Jeevanshala, and the Jan Vachan Andolan.

It was visualized that the creation of model continuing education centres could best contribute towards the operationalization of this interlinkage. Delays in funding and the growing distance from the NLM, which was being experienced by the BGVS, called for greater self-reliance. The BGVS guidelines to the state units urge them to rely on local community support for programmes not funded by the NLM. For programmes supported by the NLM, the guidelines suggested that they should double the number of programmes within the available funding.

As visualized in the project, 47 workshops and training programmes were conducted at the national and regional levels at the initiative of the BGVS centre in collaboration with the NLM, the State Literacy Missions (SLMs), the National Literacy Resource Centre (NLRC), the Directorate of Adult Education (DAE), the State Resource Centres (SRCs), and the District Literacy Committees or the Zilla Saksharata Samitis (ZSSs) and other voluntary agencies. There were 37 other orientation workshops specially focused on the PL and CE phases

TABLE 2.3 *Training and Capacity Building Workshops for TL, PL and CE, 1997–2000*

	States	*State Level Workshops*						*District Level Workshops*						*Block Level Workshops*					
		Jan.-Dec. 1997	*Jan.-Dec. 1998*	*Jan.-Dec. 1999*	*Jan.-Mar. 2000*	*April-Sept. 2000*	*Total*	*Jan.-Dec. 1997*	*Jan.-Dec. 1998*	*Jan.-Dec. 1999*	*Jan.-Mar. 2000*	*April-Sept. 2000*	*Total*	*Jan.-Dec. 1997*	*Jan.-Dec. 1998*	*Jan.-Dec. 1999*	*Jan.-Mar. 2000*	*April-Sept. 2000*	*Total*
1.	Assam	2	29	34	7	30	102	11	26	51	5	19	112	0	56	81	7	35	179
2.	Andhra	8	38	6	3	0	55	14	76	12	3	0	105	2	64	21	4	0	91
3.	Bihar	4	17	15	3	9	48	21	98	46	11	64	240	0	388	35	258	11	692
4.	Haryana	1	16	0	0	0	17	2	37	0	0	0	39	0	11	0	0	0	11
5.	Himachal	5	32	12	8	10	67	16	13	32	12	6	79	2	37	61	2	4	106
6.	Karnataka	2	6	4	0	0	12	5	14	0	0	0	19	0	0	0	0	0	0
7.	Kerala	1	0	0	0	0	1	4	0	0	0	0	4	0	0	0	0	0	0
8.	Maharashtra	2	5	9	4	0	20	5	6	3	6	0	20	1	23	3	2	0	29
9.	MP	2	5	13	0	0	20	2	0	28	0	0	30	0	0	0	0	0	0
10.	Orissa	9	27	36	3	0	75	12	52	23	9	0	96	0	67	8	2	0	77
11.	Punjab	2	17	9	1	1	30	9	62	11	0	0	82	0	38	16	0	10	64
12.	Pondicherry	1	0	0	0	0	1	0	0	0	0	0	0	0	0	0	0	0	0
13.	Rajasthan	2	16	26	0	10	54	6	17	88	0	8	119	0	0	0	0	20	20

Cont'd...

Cont'd...

14.	Tamil Nadu	1	7	0	0	0	8	6	10	0	0	0	16	0	10	0	0	0	10
15.	Tripura	7	10	7	0	0	24	7	4	6	0	0	17	25	21	7	0	0	53
16.	UP (East)	6	12	16	0	8	42	22	19	33	0	15	89	0	19	12	0	3	34
17.	UP (West)	3	21	5	0	0	29	8	27	13	0	0	48	0	14	6	0	0	20
	Total:	58	258	192	29	68	605	150	461	346	46	112	1,115	30	748	250	275	83	1,386
	Grand Total:			605							1,115						1,386		

Source: BGVS, Project Completion Report: January 1997–September 2000, New Delhi, 2001, Annexure 1.

of the literacy campaigns. Nine other Samata workshops with the special focus on women were conducted during the project period.

At their own initiative, the BGVS state units engaged in several capacity-building workshops in 17 states to strengthen the TL, PL and CE programmes with their linkages with other sectors of development, as shown in Table 2.3. These were 605 in all at the state level, 1,115 at the district level, and 1,386 at the block level. This massive programme of training initiated by the state units amounted to a total number of 3,107 workshops. Consolidation of programmes activities required an empowerment of the literacy activists within the BGVS network and their being equipped with the requisite academic/technical skills. However, a relevant question is how far was this absorption with training for literacy activists towards enhancing the capacities of the organization for facilitating literacy for development, at the cost of organizing the beneficiaries themselves through decentralized, people's organizational forms. The honest, self-critical appraisals made by the national office bearers of the BGVS would suggest that there was a problem of lack of sustainability of interventions through the creation of local community organizations and institutions, apart from a few exceptions.

The 1997–2000 project visualized setting up of 160 Nodal Continuing Education Centres (NCECs) and 1,600 Continuing Education Centres (CECs) in different states. The CE programme at the in the national level was initial phase lack of clarity within the NLM due to about the strategy and funding pattern. There were several delays in the receipt of funds by the BGVS. In view of the constrained finances, it was decided to club two NCECs together into 80 NCEC areas, each covering a population of approximately 20,000 persons in 13 identified states. By 1999, the areas where the pilot CE programme was to be implemented had been identified and initial planning processes were initiated. These were the formation of state CE Core Groups, and academic support groups, identification of villages where pilot CE programmes would be implemented, activities to be initiated by the NCECs and the orientation of the core groups. A four-day workshop was organized at Topchanchi, Dhanbad district, for the national core group with a focus on methodologies to identify learning needs and local developmental interventions. Towards the and of the 1997–2000 project period, 60 out of the 80 pilot NCECs were established, as shown in Table 2.4:

TABLE 2.4 *BGVS Pilot Continuing Education Centres in Selected States, Districts and Gram Panchayats, 1997–2000*

	State	*District*	*GPs (Clusters) Identified for Pilot CE*
1.	Assam	Dhemaji	Samaarajan
		Darrang	Burha
		Kamrup	Pachim Mayang
		Nagaon	Dighaliati
		Morigaon	Tulushibari, Borbheli
		Dibrugarh	Rahmoria
2.	Bihar	Madhepura	Murho, Bhadaul, Bethona
		Saharsa	Ghoghanpatti, Banma, Kanp
		Begusarai	Barauni I, II and III
		Dhanbad	Ramakunda, Khesmi, Jitpur
		Darbhanga	Amta Gangdah, Kamarkalla, Badhauni
3.	Haryana	Sirsa	Bakarianwali, Chouburja, Dhukra, Guddiani Khera, Bhoria Khera
		Rohtak	Bhali, Baniyani, Dobh, Lahli, Marohdhi, Anwal, Jethpur
		Jhajjar	Gangtan, Lakaria, Dighal, Dhandhal, Karontha, Seria
4.	Himachal	Shimla	Gaini, Naldehra, Baldian, Moolkoti, Mashobra, Dhalli, Kufri, Chairi, Pagog, Chaily, Totu, Rampur Keonthal, Jalei, Thari, Kot, Anadpur, Rajhana, Pujarli, Malyana, Neen, Chamyana
		Mandi	
5.	Karnataka	Tumkur	Ganadhal, Haysala Katte, Dasudi
		Raichur	Hosursidapura, Jalahalli, Ganadalu
		Mandya	Belakavadi, B.G. Pura
		Hassan	Yalahanka, Ibbidu Hagera
6.	Madhya Pradesh Bilaspur		Jogipur, Umarnara, Jhigantpur, Ranigaon, Sildaha, Khangsare, Moharda, Padapbhara, Banabel, Barjar, Amangohan
		Durg	Pairy, Karod, Pendritarai, Kanheri, Kunwagodi
		Raipur	Nargoda, Mamoan, Matoali, Bahadurpur, Badbhait, Hazorinagar, Baisa, Ladbari, Dubar, Purvanagar, Jinagarh, Rajnagar
		Tikamgarh	Margoda, Mamoon
		Chhindwara	Kalichhapra, Junarder, Chikatvadi
7.	Maharashtra	Sangli	Bhat Shirgaon, Chikhali, Natoli, Sagaon, Kanadur, Punwat, Dholewadi, Rile, Shirala Khurd, Phupere

Cont'd...

Cont'd...

		Kolhapur	Lingnoor, Khadekewadi, Galgale, Kardyal, Mugli, Jainyal, Kapashi, Alabad, Belewadi
		Beed	Jarud, Kuntewadi, Babulkhunta, Wangi, Shivani, Ghodkarajuri, Borphadi, Mouj, Moujewadi, Samanapur, Dhekan Moha, Mochi Pimpalgaon, Imampur, Nalbandi, Imampur
8.	Punjab	Ferozpur	Mumkhera, Chuhriwala Dhana
		Faridkote	Panjgrain Kalan
		Nawan Shehar	Kravar
		Hoshiarpur	Behehur
9.	Orissa	Keonjhar	Gohira, Balarampur, Khaliabent
		Balasore	Seragarh, Barunsing, Nuagaon
		Jharsuguda	Bikampali, Palsada, Atabira
		Sundergarh	Bhedabahal, Lankahuda
		Ganjam	Gobara, Sasan
10.	Rajasthan	Baran	Kasbathana, Deveri, Natai
		Dholpur	Saddiqupur, Sighawali, Jatoli, Lohari
11.	Tamil Nadu	Dharmapuri	
		Tanjore	
		Tiruvarur	
		Nagapattinam	
		Dharmapuri	
		Kanyakumari	
12.	Tripura	West Tripura	Murabari, Bisalgarh, Rout Khola, Raghunathpur, Ghaniamera, Champamura
		North Tripura	Halflong
13.	Uttar Pradesh	Barabanki	Kasva, Adampur, Bhanamu, Sarai Ismail, Barauli Malik
		Sultanpur	Umapur Ganapatti, Trilokpur, Tala, Kushitali, Ramdaypur, Rampur Pulwari, Loharta, Bhaganpur, Amethi
		Dehradun	Gorkha Karbadi, Gardwali Karbadi
		Bijnor	Tatarpur Ishak, Dhanaura, Pratapur, Nagal, Bhagwala, Puranpur Garhi
		Aligarh	Jariti, Jatpur, Satha, Kasimpur, Ramgarh Panjipur, Rampur
		Piliphit	Ruriya, Saabepur, Parsia, Dipali, Haphijnagar Bannahi, Amara Karod, Kasimpur, Pakadiya Mangali
		Chamoli	Sagar, Gangol Gaon, Papadiyana, Alkapur, Lower Chamoli, Upper Chamoli, Paduli, Kshetrapal

Source: BGVS, Project Completion Report: January 1997–September 2000, New Delhi, 2001, Annexure 3.

The BGVS Project of 2000–2002

This project concentrated on three northern states, viz., Uttar Pradesh, Bihar and Rajasthan. The primary feature of this project was the establishment of 14 NCECs and 134 CECs, drastically reduced from what was visualized in the proposal. By July, 2001, all these centres had been established (BGVS, July 2001: 1). However, by February, 2002, only part of the first instalment had been received, which was an indication of the problems of the fund flow from the Ministry. The uncertainty of the flow of funds was severely affecting the smooth functioning of the programme. The following table provides some details of the centres:

TABLE 2.5 *Status of Continuing Education Centres, July 2001*

	State/District	*NCECs*	*No. of CECs*
1.	Rajasthan/Dholpur	Bareh Mori	11
2.	Rajasthan/Baran	Natai	9
3.	UP/Sultanpur	Kushitali	9
4.	UP/Barabanki	Chiyara	10
5.	UP/Aligarh	Jaraothi	10
6.	UP/Pilibhit	Simara Akbarganj	8
7.	UP/Bijnaur		10
8.	Uttaranchal/Chamoli	Nangal Soti	13
9.	Uttaranchal/Dehradun	Gopeshwar	6
10.	Bihar/Begusarai	Sahaspur Agragami NCEC	10
11.	Bihar/Darbhanga	Brauni–2	8
12.	Bihar/Saharsa		9
13.	Bihar/Madhepura	Gangdah	11
14.	Jharkhand/Dhanbad	Chandaur	10
		Burhi	
		Jitpur	
	Total		134

Source: BGVS, Pilot Continuing Education Programme: Interim Report, October 2000–July 2001, New Delhi, July 2001: 1.

The Continuing Education Programme, with its nodal and other education centres, provided an opportunity to the BGVS to consolidate and institutionalize its diverse range of literacy campaigns and other developmental activities. All these were to converge in a decentralized manner around these centres, visualized as sustainable pilot models that could impact on the mainstream CE programme (BGVS, Minutes of General Council, Bhubaneshwar, October 1999: 11). These activities would include aspects of natural resource management, credit and

TABLE 2.6 *Status of NCECs without NLM Support, February 2002*

	NCEC	*State/District*
1.	Paura	Bihar/Nawada
2.	Samaarajan	Assam/Dhemaji
3.	Burha	Assam/Dorang
4.	Pachim Mayung	Assam/Kamrup
5.	Dighaliati	Assam/Nagaon
6.	Tulshibari Borbheti	Assam/Morigaon
7.	Bhati-Baniyani	Haryana/Rohtak
8.	Bakarianwati	Haryana/Sirsa
9.	Gangatan	Haryana/Jhajjar
10.	Gaini	H.P./Shimla
11.	Ganadhal	Karnataka/Tunkur
12.	Hosursidapura	Karnataka/Raichur
13.	Helakavadi	Karnataka/Mandhya
14.	Yalahanka	Karnataka/Hassan
15.	Jogipur	Chhatisgarh/Bilaspur
16.	Nargoda	Chhatisgarh/Raipur
17.	Margoda	Madhya Pradesh/Tikamgarh
18.	Bhatshrigaon	Maharashtra/Sangli
19.	Lingnoor	Maharashtra/Kolhapur
20.	Jarud-Khuntewadi	Maharashtra/Beed
21.	Mumkhera	Punjab/Ferozpur
22.	Panjgrain Klan	Punjab/Faridkot
23.	Behenpur	Punjab/Hoshiarpur
24.	Bhedabahal	Orissa/Sundergarh
25.	Gohira	Orissa/Koenjhar
26.	Bikampati	Orissa/Jharsuguda
27.		Tamil Nadu/Dharampuri
28.		Tamil Nadu/Tanjore
29.		Tamil Nadu/Tiruvarur
30.		Tamil Nadu/Nagapattinam
31.	Murabari	Tripura/West Tripura
32.	Halflong	Tripura/North Tripura

Source: BGVS, General Council Meeting, Dhanbad, February, 2002.

self-help, health, basic education, the empowerment of women, skill development, rural libraries and publications.

As mentioned above, there have been some attempts at bringing about a convergence of different BGVS activities around the NCECs and their CECs. Libraries were established at all the centres. A total of 148 Self-Help Groups (SHGs) were functioning in the project areas within the jurisdiction of these centres and trainings were given to the members for maintenance of records, accounting procedures and entrepreneurship development. Panchayat Development Reports and resource mapping exercises were completed in seven gram panchayats. Some of the centres had established small-scale rural enterprises, such as soap and sattu making in Bihar, supply of food to Anganwadi centres by the SHGs in Jharkhand and stitching and embroidery in Uttar Pradesh. Farmers groups were linked with existing institutions such as the Krishi Vigyan Kendras (Centres for Agricultural Science) and sporting activities had started among the youth (BGVS, 2003–2004: 2).

The report to the General Council meeting of the BGVS on the CECs (February 2002: 3) mentions several challenges that were faced in the process of establishing the centres. Some of these were political interference as in Baran district, Rajasthan; social contradictions in Aligarh, Uttar Pradesh and Dhanbad, Jharkhand; gaps in the literacy programme in most places; problems for the SHGs with the banks; and absence of resource support agencies. In spite these several problems of institutionalizing a learning process within difficult circumstances and building the capacities of the literacy activists in the process, the BGVS was able to establish 32 other NCECs without government support. This is presented in Table 2.6. All these institutions were set up with people's contributions and in community buildings.

5. Phase 4: National Advocacy for Policy Related to Rights and the Convergence of Local Practice, 2002 to Present

In the context of the severe constraints of funding support from the Ministry of Human Resource Development, Government of India, the BGVS approached the Sir Dorabji Tata Trust (SDTT) for funding support. An initial grant for the support of the central office in 2002 was followed up by a project grant for the period 2004 to 2007, later extended to 2008. The project visualized a focus on major components that had been crucial to the ongoing activities of the BGVS: basic education, continuing education, Samata Self-Help Groups, the Jan Vanchan Andolan towards a movement for establishing publications and libraries – all supported by mobilization campaigns and advocacy activities. The project attempted to consolidate the large-scale mobilizations, covering about 20 states into a network of decentralized local institutions and people's organizations, related to the thematic areas mentioned earlier. A National Coordination Centre (NCC) of the BGVS was established to work out the planning and monitoring of the activities of the state units. A major component of the SDTT funding was for the capacity-building of the state, district and sub-district level cadres of BGVS for its various projects. The proposal to the SDTT had emerged from a visioning exercise initiated from 2002 at the district level, consolidated into state and national plans in 2003. Regional coordinators had been appointed to monitor the execution of these plans from 2004 onwards supported by a three-member Finance Committee. Academic Resource Centres for basic education located in Bhopal and for Samata Self-Help Groups based in New Delhi provided national support for two of the projects mentioned above. In April 2004, a major workshop was held in Aligarh for reviewing the modalities of the state planning process for the formulation of the project on Empowerment, Rights and Security.

It appears that while the SDTT provided adequate financial support for capacity building activities through meetings, training programmes, workshops and seminars, actual programme implementation was left to the state and district level units of BGVS to seek financial support from other sources. The former resulted in a major cascading effect of academic supportive activities as seen in Table 2.7. However, the consolidation of these efforts took concrete shape largely after 2005 when BGVS adopted a strategy of concentrated efforts within clusters of gram panchayats in selected blocks/districts and extended these empowering processes right down to the village level. This strategy came to be called as one of 'convergence'.

The details of this phase from 2002 to the present may be found in chapters 7 and 8. To avoid repetition, the defining characteristics of this phase may be stated here in a summary fashion. A significant aspect of this phase was the utilization by the BGVS of its mass base of support in order to undertake advocacy for policy on several issues related to the rights of the marginalized. These were the campaigns for the Right to Food and Work from 2002 onwards, together with the campaign for the

TABLE 2.7 *Number of Workshops and Trainings, SDTT Programmes, 2004–05*

	Basic Education
District Level Meetings	40 district level meetings including core group meetings
State Level Meetings	17 meetings
Teachers Trainings	12 teachers training workshops in which both private and government school teachers had participated
State Resource Persons Workshops	9 state resource persons workshop were conducted in which they were prepared and trained for further trainings they have to do in basic education
Bal Mela Workshops	20 Bal Mela workshops were organized at village, block, district levels for the children
Bal Mela Trainings	10 Bal Mela trainings were conducted for the children
Bal Vigyan Utsava	5 Bal Vigyan Utsavas were organized at village and district levels
Other Activities	Several other activities relating to basic education
	Continuing Education
District Level Meetings	10 district level meetings including core group meetings
State Level Meetings	8 meetings were held at state level
Trainings	10 training workshops were held for the activists
State Resource Persons Workshops	9 state resource persons workshops were conducted in which they were prepared and trained for further trainings in continuing education programme
Workshops	20 workshops were organized at village, block, district and state levels
Trainings	19 trainings workshops were conducted for the skill development and animal husbandry
Orientations	8 orientations were held at village and district levels
Other Activities	Several other activities relating to continuing education
	Samata
District Level Meetings	48 district level meetings including core group meetings
State Level Meetings	20 meetings were held at state level
Trainings	10 training workshops were held for the activists
State Resource Persons Workshops	9 state resource persons workshops were conducted in which they were prepared in areas like health, SHGs
Workshops	24 workshops were organized at village, block, district and state levels
Trainings	18 trainings workshops were conducted for the skill development, empowering women, SHGs and for different small entrepreneurs
Orientations	8 orientations were held at village and district levels
Seminars	4 seminars were held
SHG Meetings	17 SHG meetings were held for the establishing new SHGs and improving the work of SHGs
Other Activities	Several other activities relating to Samata

Source: BGVS, Annual Report 2004–2005, New Delhi.

provision of mid-day meals for school going children; the Right to Social Security that culminated in a major meeting held on September 2–4, 2004; and the campaign for the Right to Education from 2005 onwards. These campaigns were closely articulated with the involvement of BGVS activists in the India, Asia and World Social Forum processes from 2002 onwards; the kalajathas for Peace, Unity and Sovereignty conducted between September 8 and October 2, 2003; and the nation-wide Janadhikar Kalajathas (People's Rights Cultural Caravans) held from November 2007 to January 2008.

The second defining feature of this phase has been the attempt to concentrate and converge its education development interventions within clusters of gram panchayats accompanied by direct training of about eight resource persons – half of whom would be women – within each gram panchayat. The major Samata network of Self-Help Groups covering 127 districts, 226 blocks and 323 clusters of 1,673 gram panchayats within 16 states facilitated the strategy of convergence. This strategy through the Samata network covered close to 16,000 participants, more than half of whom were women. The double-pronged strategy that was a distinctive feature of this phase promises to be the broad direction that BGVS could possibly take in the future. This will be discussed in greater detail in the concluding chapters 10 and 11.

6. Organizational and Strategic Issues

From a network of PSMs in 1989, the BGVS had by 1992, in a matter of three years, become an all-India organization with state and district level units in 17 states/Union Territories (UTs), Uttar Pradesh being considered as two units. It had a fairly extensive total presence in about 150 districts in these states. It may be pointed out that the creation of this organizational network for mobilization and facilitation of the literacy campaigns was created at the behest of the Department of Adult Education, Government of India and the NLM. By 1993, the BGVS was reported to have played a major role in project initiation and implementation in 55 out of the then 132 literacy campaigns in these states/UTs. By 1995, this figure had risen to 101 districts out of 250 district literacy campaigns in the states of its presence. The figures of rise in BGVS presence, as also in the number of TLC districts, indicate the massive expansion of the literacy campaigns into the Hindi-speaking belt of the country. The impact of this much needed even though reckless expansion, without adequate preparation, would be felt in a stark manner during the 1995 to 1998 period, with several stagnating literacy campaigns.

Assessing its own contribution from 1989 to 1994, the report of the BGVS General Council meeting held in Madras in July 1994 highlights the following (BGVS, July 1994: 3):

1. Strong state level teams in 17 states/UTs and a presence through district level groups in 150 districts.
2. Training and orientation to several literacy activists and administrators at various levels.
3. Several publications on aspects of training, organization, monitoring, problem solving, environment creation and evaluation that have served as guides to not only the 150 districts of its presence, but also to other parts of the country where the literacy campaigns were running.
4. A significant role in initiating 120 campaigns and direct involvement in implementation in about 80 districts.
5. Capacity-building at the state level to handle different aspects of the campaign.
6. Support at the national level to the NLM and associated organizations in all aspects of the campaign.

However, the rapid finance and need driven expansion of the literacy campaigns at the behest of the Department of Adult Education was beginning to tell. The BGVS General Council identified the following problems in their relations with the district campaigns (BGVS, July 1994: 4):

1. The growing tendency to bureaucratize or 'collectorize' the projects and the marginalization of the BGVS in some districts. The literacy campaigns were beginning to be viewed as a 'standard' government programme.
2. The expansion was overstretching the capacities and human resources within the BGVS. State and district administrations were hesitant to release persons on secondment as was suggested by the NLM. "The futility of trying to start TLC projects in districts where no preparations have been made is affecting the morale of several activists."
3. False reporting and false declarations of literacy achievement were on the rise, despite clear instructions on evaluation suggested by the

Dave Committee Report and accepted by the NLM. A people's movement was thus being reduced to a target-oriented programme with achievements being declared at any cost.

The tensions between the administration of the literacy campaigns at the state and district levels and the BGVS were beginning. The 1995 report of the BGVS states that in 45 districts, the BGVS was eased out or was constrained to withdraw from the literacy campaigns (BGVS, December 1995: 15). The report attributes this growing phenomenon "to the tendency to totally bureaucratize the TLCs. In some instances, we could resist such moves with the support of the NLM. However, there are also cases where even the NLM had to sit tight and watch. In the extreme case of Bhiwani district, Haryana, the district administration even resorted to police force to oust the BGVS and other people's groups. The result, as could be imagined, was the total collapse of the programme" (BGVS, December 1995: 16).

Several BGVS state units, in collaboration with the state administration or independently, had begun to review the problem of a growing number of sterile literacy campaigns in Madhya Pradesh, Orissa, Assam, Himachal Pradesh, Bihar and Uttar Pradesh. According to the preliminary assessments, more than 40 per cent of the total number of sanctioned literacy campaigns had lost their dynamism. The Department of Adult Education and the BGVS still viewed each other as partners in the NLM working towards the success of the campaigns, as may be seen from the following statement: "We should seek the support of the NLM which has been championing the spirit of people's movement for literacy. The conflict between NLM's compulsions to offload money on the one side and stagnation of projects and spread of campaigns without adequate preparations on the other, has to be urgently resolved" (BGVS, December 1995: 17). A concern to review the strategy of the literacy campaigns and to seek alternatives through decentralization and local specificity was beginning to be felt. "Our experience shows that a time has come to systematically decentralize the campaign and also to evolve new models of TL campaigning. The present-day Collector-centric district model has more or less outlived its purpose" (BGVS, December 1995: 17).

Further substantiation of the foregoing analysis may be seen in the data in the Table 2.8, for the period till December 1995:

TABLE 2.8 *BGVS Involvement in TL-PL Campaign Districts, 1995*

	States	*Total districts*	*No. of TLCs*	*Districts where BGVS, played a major role in running the campaign*	*BGVS role in environment creation*	*BGVS role in training*	*Districts with no BGVS role in running the campaign*	*Districts where BGVS was pushed out or withdrew*
1.	Assam	23	18	3	3	2	3	2
2.	Orissa	30	17	7	15	6	4	2
3.	Bihar	55	16	9	15	1	1	2
4.	Haryana	17	11	7	7	8	4	2
5.	Himachal	12	12	5	12	12	1	3
6.	Punjab and Chandigarh	15	6	4	4	4	2	–
7.	UP (West)	20	14	8	9	5	1	3
8.	UP (East)	44	20	3	15	3	14	–
9.	Rajasthan	31	17	2	5	4	1	–
10.	Tripura	4	3	1	2	2	1	–
11.	Tamil Nadu	22	–	–	–	–	–	–
12.	A.P.	23	23	11	16	11	1	1
13.	Karnataka	20	20	13	15	8	4	8
14.	Kerala*	14	14	14	14	14	–	14
15.	Pondicherry**	–	Total					All
16.	Maharashtra	31	–	4	8	5	–	–
17.	Madhya Pradesh	49	49	10	20	16	10	8
	Total	410	250	101	160	101	47	45

* KSSP participated fully during the first phase only.

** Pondicherry Science Forum (PSF) was 'pushed out' of the campaign after the first phase.

BGVS/PSM groups played an important role in the initial environment creation in almost all districts through BGVJ 1990 and 1992, Samata Jatha 1993, Hamara Desh project 1993–94, BGVS Jatha 1995 (UP), and various other projects.

Source: BGVS, Report to the General Council Meeting, December 11–12, 1995, Hyderabad, New Delhi, 1995: 15.

The report to the BGVS General Council (December 1995: 12) analysed the organizational strengths and capacities of the different states where the BGVS had a presence. It categorized the states, from this perspective, in the following manner:

1. States that emerged from a strong PSM base and evolved further through involvement in the literacy campaigns and related activities: Kerala, Tamil Nadu, Andhra Pradesh and Pondicherry.
2. States which started from very little and developed strong organizational networks through literacy campaigns in several districts: Himachal Pradesh and Bihar.
3. States, which had some initial base or no base at all, but which can develop a fairly good network during the literacy campaigns with additional inputs on planning and capacity building: Haryana, Punjab, Karnataka, Assam, Orissa and Tripura.
4. States which needed a lot of support to improve capacities and develop their network. BGVS presence had been recent in these complex social contexts: Rajasthan and Uttar Pradesh. Incidentally, these were the states where special jathas were held in 1995 and 1996, respectively.
5. States were the BGVS had not been able to develop due to various limitations: Gujarat, Maharashtra and Delhi.

The following Table 2.9 presents an analysis of the status of the BGVS at the district level in 1998 (BGVS, February 1998: 15). In 17 states/UTs (Uttar Pradesh being taken as two units), the BGVS was present in 138 (38%) out of the then total 359 districts of these states/UTs. In these districts, it had adequate organizational capacities to plan and execute the literacy campaigns and related development projects. In 79 (22%) districts in these states, it had adequate number of activists who, however, were dependent on the state core group for guidance. In 84 (23%) districts in these states, the organization was in the formative stage. In 58 (16%) districts in these states, BGVS had no organizational basis. The foregoing data suggest that in about 60 per cent of the districts in these states, the BGVS had an adequate presence to make a significant difference to the literacy campaigns, if permitted and if the strategy was appropriate to the given contexts. A major problem that it was facing was in resolving its conflict between participation, despite the reservations of the administration in some districts, and a critical withdrawal to chalk out its independent path in view of the negative and bureaucratized direction which the campaigns had taken.

TABLE 2.9 *BGVS – Organizational Profiles in States and Districts, February 1998*

	States	*Name of State Organization*	*Total No. of Districts*	*BGVS Presence in Districts*			
				A	*B*	*C*	*D*
1.	Andhra	BGVS, A.P. + JVV	23	10	5	7	1
2.	Assam	Gyan Vigyan Samiti, Assam	23	10	5	8	–
3.	Bihar	Bihar Gyan Vigyan Samiti	30	30	–	–	–
4.	Gujarat	BGVS Gujarat (NR)	–	–	–	–	–
5.	Haryana	Haryana Gyan Vigyan Samiti	17	4	5	8	–
6.	Himachal	Himachal Gyan Vigyan Samiti	12	4	4	4	–
7.	Karnataka	BGVS, Karnataka	20	9	9	1	1
8.	Kerala	BGVS, Kerala + KSSP	14	14	–	–	–
9.	Maharashtra	BGVS, Maharashtra (NR)	30	–	7	12	11
10.	Madhya Pradesh	Madhya Pradesh, BGVS	45	10	12	15	8
11.	Orissa	BGVS, Orissa	29	10	5	7	7
12.	Punjab	BGVS, Punjab and Chandigarh	14	9	5	–	–
13.	Pondicherry	BGVS, Pondicherry (NR)	1	1	–	–	–
14.	Rajasthan	Rajasthan, BGVS	32	3	3	3	23
15.	Tamil Nadu	BGVS, Tamil Nadu + TNSF	29	13	7	3	6
16.	Tripura	BGVS, Tripura	4	4	–	–	–
17.	UP (West)	BGVS, UP (West)	21	6	6	8	1
18.	UP (E and C)	BGVS, UP (East and Central)	15	1	6	8	–
		Total	359	138	79	84	58

Source: BGVS, General Council Meeting, February 7–8, 1998, Bangalore: 15.

Notes: A. Districts which have enough capabilities to independently plan and execute projects.
B. Districts with a good number of activists, who need support from the state group.
C. Organization in formative stage.
D. Districts with no organizational contact.
NR Not registered.

By October 1999, the marginalization of the BGVS by the Department of Adult Education and its growing alienation from the effective policies and practices of the literacy campaigns had reached its peak. The report to the General Council suggests that in states like Bihar, Assam, Tripura, Himachal Pradesh, Punjab, Haryana, Madhya Pradesh, Rajasthan and Orissa there were districts and blocks where several BGVS activists were struggling to assist in the literacy campaigns despite the negative attitude of the officials at various levels. In states like Uttar Pradesh, Tamil Nadu and Maharashtra, the officials had not been inviting the BGVS representatives to the monthly monitoring meetings, as was prescribed by the NLM. Even, the NLM was beginning to accept that most of the literacy campaigns, especially in their PL and CE phases, were facing stagnation. The predicament as regards the direction the BGVS should take in the context of the above-mentioned factors influencing its trajectory is brought out in the following statement: "While the NLM has not been able to come up with any substantial policy change to revitalise the programmes, we have to recognize the fact that we also have not been able to create any feasible alternative models. Our efforts to develop grass root level gram panchayat models of TL-PL did not take off. Our efforts to intervene in CE and develop workable pilot CE models are yet to take a clear shape" (BGVS, October 1999: 13).

The document draws attention to two approaches of the state units with respect to the literacy campaigns. While some of the state units had practically withdrawn in the context of a shrinking space for meaningful intervention, other units still considered the literacy campaigns as their central thrust for various development interventions despite various externally imposed limitations. While suggesting a state-specific approach, the report fears that, "It may not be possible to go along with the NLM approach in most of the places. We may have to carve out our own alternative within or outside the routine TL-PL-CE programmes" (BGVS, October 1999: 13).

BGVS was also experiencing the problems of having to run a mass organization with only a few full-time activists, who were paid a nominal honorarium. The report to the General Council of February 1998 suggests that the "availability of manpower is a problem that is faced by most of the state units. Unfortunately, in most of the units, the concept of a BGVS 'activist' is synonymous with a paid full-time worker. Somehow, the concept of an activist, who is not dependent on an organization for her/his living, has not worked out well in most of the states ... Despite earnest effort, most of the state units are not in a position to support the activist with self-generated funds ... . In this context, it is essential to

TABLE 2.10 *BGVS State Organizations, February, 2002*

	State and Organization	*Dist. Units*	*Dist. Centre*	*Presence in Blocks*	*GVK/ Units*	*Member-ship*	*Full-Timers*	*Sub-Com-mittee*	*Remarks*
1.	Andhra Pradesh BGVS/JVV	20	3	100 block 300 mdl	NA	30,000	30	9	Spl. committee for BGVS
2.	Assam GVSA	12	9	NA	NA	NA	10	4	SRC
3.	Bihar/ Jharkhand GVS	26	8		2,600	33,000	7	6	–
4.	Chhatisgarh BGVS	–		–	–	–	–	–	Presently part of MP, BGVS
5.	Haryana HGVS	10	9	10	10	3,000	3	NA	Spl. BGVS co SRC
6.	Himachal/ HGVS	10	2	50	3,000	22,737	NA	11	SRC
7.	Karnataka KBGVS	15	8	50	4	1,200	5	NA	–
8.	Kerala, KSSP	14	NA	152 block 950 GPs	1,477	45,051	70	10	Spl.com. for BGVS IRTC
9.	Madhya Pradesh GVS	28	10	48	350	1,829	11	7	SRC
10	Maharashtra MGVS	9	4	25	25	265 activist	6	5	–
11.	Orissa BGVS	12	11	143	NA	8,000	NA	NA	–
12.	Pondicherry PSF/BGVS	1	NA	3		550	NA	3	CERD
13.	Punjab BGVS	10	5	71	NA	NA	3	6	–
14.	Rajasthan BGVS	8	5	13	NA	NA	8	5	Own building
15.	Tamil Nadu TNSF/BGVS	23	7	115	NA	18,000	50	4	–
16.	Tripura BGVS	4	NA	NA	NA	NA	NA	NA	SRC
17.	UP BGVS	23	10	56	305	6,500	6	6	–
18.	Uttaranchal BGVS	–	–	–	–	–	–	–	Presently part of UP
	Total	225	81	836	7,771	1,70,132	209	76	

Source: BGVS, General Council Meeting, Dhanbad, February 2002: 8–9.

Note: All the state organizations are part of the AIPSN and have been participating actively in the AIPSN activities.

NA–Information not available.

evolve a long-term approach to both human resource management and finance resource management" (BGVS, February 1998: 16–17).

By October 1999, at the time of General Council meeting, the relationship between the National Centre of BGVS and the state units was under serious consideration. BGVS was moving in the direction of far greater autonomy to the state units which were already registered separately. It was visualized that the central office would increasingly act only as a resource and liaison centre, devolving all organizational, leadership and financial functions to the states. Seed money support was already being limited to only the states of Rajasthan, Bihar and Uttar Pradesh. It was hoped that decentralization would move further to the district level.

By 2001, BGVS was present through units in 20 states and union territories. It had played an active role in supporting around 200 district literacy campaigns in different aspects of literacy intervention (BGVS, 2001: 9). It had been able to reach out to around 2,000 blocks in the country. About 2,500 literacy activists of the BGVS were devoting more than half their time to the activities of the organization, besides thousands of volunteers who participated actively in programmes as and when needed. The organization estimated that about 20,000 village/panchayat level, local units or Gyan Vigyan Kendras could be formed (BGVS, May 25–27, 2001: 3). Table 2.10 provides an indication of the organizational spread of the BGVS by February, 2002. While evolving into a major organization of literacy and social development activists, supported by a network of PSMs, it had been unable to involve other NGOs in any substantial numbers. This was largely due to the self-limiting priorities of existing NGOs and the voluntary character of the literacy movement where only a few full-time activists received a nominal honorarium.

In a number of states, for example, Bihar, Assam and Himachal Pradesh, the organization was making its presence felt in the local self-governing bodies through the participation of literacy activists and neo-literates, many of whom were women. Individuals had been elected to a number of these bodies (BGVS, February 2002: 11). As the report to the General Council meeting of February, 2002 states, "The emergence of a more self-confident and more informed local level leadership consisting of women and people belonging to oppressed sections has been one of the major achievements of the literacy movements" (BGVS, February 2002: 12).

The above-mentioned report draws attention to the need to promote women and persons belonging to oppressed sections to leadership positions to a great extent, as also the need for second and third level leadership. By February, 2002, the representation of women in state executive committee was as follows:

TABLE 2.11 *BGVS, Women Representation in State Executive Committees, February, 2002*

	State	*Total No. of E.C. Members*	*Total No. of E.C. Members (Female)*
1.	Assam	18	6
2.	Andhra Pradesh	14	2
3.	Bihar/Jharkhand	17	3
4.	Haryana	42	10
5.	Himachal Pradesh	31	8*
6.	Karnataka	25	4
7.	Kerala	45	12
8.	MP/Chhattisgarh	32	11*
9.	Maharashtra	18	7
10.	Orissa	15	00
11.	Punjab	27	2
12.	Pondicherry	29	7
13.	Rajasthan	18	3*
14.	Tamil Nadu	47	11
15.	Tripura	10	–
16.	Uttar Pradesh	23	5
	Total	411	90

* Including State Secretary.

Source: BGVS, General Council Meeting, Dhanbad, February, 2002.

The table would suggest that less than 25 per cent of the membership of the state executive committees was constituted by women, with states like Andhra Pradesh, Bihar/Jharkhand, Karnataka, Orissa, Punjab, Rajasthan and Uttar Pradesh in particular, need greater involvement of women.

By February, 2002, at the time of the General Council meeting of the BGVS at Dhanbad, the organization was active in 16 states plus two that had been carved out of Bihar (Jharkhand) and Uttar Pradesh

TABLE 2.12 *BGVS-State Level Activities: An Overview, February, 2002*

	State and Organization	*Literacy and Related Activities*	*Other Activities*	*State Projects*
1.	Andhra JVV/BGVS	Partial presence in some of the ZSS like Nellore, Nalgonda, Vijayanagaram	Jeevanshala programme in Wyra block of Khamman district PHA activities	Mobile library programmes in four mandals with support from DPEP, orientation to thrift groups, teachers' training
2.	Assam, GVSA	Continuing education programme in seven blocks, constant support to ZSSs through SRC	Panchayat resource mapping in 30 GPs, Prochesta, self-help groups of women, block selling campaign	Disaster management programme, teachers' training and in-depth studies for DPEP, sanitary mart, environment awareness programme
3.	Bihar and Jharkhand, Bihar Gyan Vigyan Samiti	Active participation in ZSS in 12 districts of Bihar-Jharkhand, implementing pilot CE programme in five districts	Active SHGs in seven districts, active involvement in PHA, implementing Jeevanshala, initiated GVV process in select districts	Literacy to health programme with support from UNICEF, follow-up of PHA
4.	Chhattisgarh Bharat Gyan Vigyan Samiti	UNESCO study of PL	Active participation in struggle against privatization of BALCO	NA
5.	Haryana, Haryana Gyan Vigyan Samiti	Running the State Resource Centre	Participation in PHA, seminar on female feoticide, Kalajathas in five districts in November-December, 1999, Jeevanshala in Samalkha block	NA
6.	Himachal Himachal Gyan Vigyan Samiti	Running State Resource Centre, active participation in Mandi, Kullu ZSSs	Active participation in PHA	NA

Cont'd…

Cont'd…

7.	Karnataka BGVS Karnataka	Pilot CEs in four districts initiated in previous project, partial presence in some ZSSs	Active participation in PHA organized science-related seminars, publication, primary education	People's science programmes, primary education programmes
8.	Kerala KSSP/BGVS	Nominal presence in the State CE Programme	Active participation in People's Plan Programme, Education Reform Programme, People's Soap, SHGs	NA
9.	Maharashtra, Bharat Gyan Vigyan Samiti	Active participation in the Nasik Literacy Programme, Organizing Pilot CE Programme in two districts in self-supported manner	Active participation in PHA organized Gyan Vigyan Jatha 2001 in 11 districts, Samata self-help group formation progressing well, science communication, balmelas, publication, *Jan Vachan*	NA
10.	Madhya Pradesh Gyan Vigyan Samiti	Active participation in the SRC Bhopal functioning, Pilot CE programmes in two districts	Active participation in PHA, Nine GVVs-initiated, Samata self-help groups in 13 districts active participation in Fujrath Earth Quake relief work and Orissa cyclone relief	Training programmes for Panchayats, Swasakti Programme
11.	Orissa Bharat Gyan Vigyan Samiti, Orissa	Pilot CE programme in three districts, partial involvement in three ZSSs	Active participation in Cyclone Relief Work, SHG formation in Jagatsinghpur, participation in PHA	Punar Nirman Abhiyan in Jagatsinghpur with AA and unnayan, projects with OSDMA, UN House
12.	Punjab, BGVS Punjab and Chandigarh	Implementing pilot programme in Kotkapura block, partial presence in five ZSS	SHG programme in Kotkapura block publications, rural libraries, vocational centres	NA

13.	Rajasthan, BGVS, Rajasthan	Implementing Pilot CE Programme in two districts, undertook impact of PL study (UNESCO) in Pali district	Running 12 Jeevanshalas in slum areas and one *gramin* vidyalay, SHG active in two districts, PHA activities	Child rights project in a district with support of UNICEF Jeevanshala project with state government. Girl child project with UNICEF
14.	Tamil Nadu, TNSF/BGVS	Pilot CE programme in five blocks, undertook impact of PL study in Virudunagar, publishing quarterly neo-literate newspaper, developed two folk primers, village arithmetic	Malar as a model SHG, literacy to primary education programme, literacy to women empowerment through SHGs, literacy to health programme. Very active participation in PHA	NA
15.	Tripura, BGVS, Tripura	Active participation in PL-CE programme in the state, running SRC, publication of neo-literate material, pilot CE Programme in three GPs.	Participatory Resource Mapping in six GPs, active PHA. PHA Kalajatha to Dakha.	Environment awareness, PRM and watershed.
16.	Uttaranchal/UP, Gyan Vigyan Samiti UP and UA	Active participation in nine ZSSs, Pilot CE programme in seven districts	Active participation in PHA and various health-related programmes, SHGs in four districts	Multi-sector approach to health with UNDP support, Bal Swasthya Abhiyan supported by WHO and UNICEF.

Source: BGVS, General Council Meeting, Dhanbad, February 2002.

Note: NA–Data not available.

(Uttaranchal). Table 2.12 indicates that a number of the activities in these states were closely linked to the post-literacy and continuing education phases of the literacy campaigns, given that the districts in the majority of the states had reached a continuing education phase, which provided a certain 'formal legitimacy' to other developmental activities. The BGVS had launched several of these. Some of the state BGVS units had also taken the initiative to organize state level projects with funding from sources other than that from the NLM through the initiatives of BGVS central office.

In 2002, BGVS had a 93-member General Body with eminent educationists, social workers, literacy activists and the representative of NLM, as members. The General Body had elected a 13-member Executive Committee, which included the NLM nominee. Four sub-committees assisted the Executive Committee in specific areas: the literacy campaigns (TL, PL, CE), primary education, literacy to health, women and literacy (Samata).

Despite the lack of financial support from the central office of the BGVS, due to the cessation of Central Government funds under the National Democratic Alliance regime at the centre from 1998 to 2004, the state units persisted with several activities as discussed in the text and were able to expand their organizational base. By 2005 the organizational status was as shown in Table 2.13. The BGVS had a presence in 19 states and 258 districts within these states as compared to 225 districts in 2002. Its membership had grown to 2,22,566 by 2005, from 1,70,132 in 2002. There were 258 full-time activists (209 in 2002) working within several projects undertaken by the BGVS, together with several thousands of grassroots volunteers.

The report to the General Council, held in Bhopal during December 28–29, 2005, drew attention to many important organizational issues that needed to be debated in order to strengthen the organization. A need was felt that the state units become more self-sufficient in terms of their ongoing projects while supporting a few full-timers at the state and district levels. Other avenues for funding needed to be explored such as a possible membership fee policy. There was need for infusing the organization with younger persons who could take up leadership roles while the more experienced leaders could continue to remain useful to the organization. While creating a network of grassroots institutions and people's organizations was recognized as

TABLE 2.13 *Organizational Status of BGVS in States, 2005*

	State and Organization	*District Units*	*District Centres*	*Presence in Blocks*	*GVK/ Units*	*Member-ship*	*Full-Timers*	*Sub-Com-mittees*	*Remarks*
1.	Andhra BGVS/JVV	20	3	100 blocks 300 mandals	–	30,000	30	9	Special Committee for BGVS
2.	Assam GVSA	14	9	8 blocks 300 GPs	100 GVV	2,500	10	4	SRC
3.	Bihar GVS	22	8	199 blocks 800 GPs	2,652	33,000	7	6	–
4.	Chattisgarh BGVS	10		–	–	–	–	–	
5.	Haryana HGVS	6	9	20 blocks	12 BM	5,000	5	6	Special BGVS co SRC
6.	Himachal HGVS	12	2	43 blocks 438 GPs	3,000	40,000	–	11	SRC
7.	Jharkhand BGVS	16	–	60 blocks 320 GPs	1,400	2,800	10	3	
8.	Karnataka KBGVS	14	8	45 blocks 8 GPs	8	1,850	6	4	–
9.	Kerala KSSP	14	NA	152 blocks 950 GPs	1,477	45,051	70	10	Special Committee for BGVS IRTC
10.	Madhya Pradesh MPBGVS	24	10	68 blocks	350	16,000	10	6	SRC
11.	Maharashtra MGVS	13	4	25 blocks	25	265	6	5	–

Cont'd…

Contd.

12.	Orissa BGVS	12	11	143 blocks	–	8,000	–	–	–
13.	Pondicherry PSF/BGVS	2	–	7 blocks commune	12 BE	600	25	4	CERD
14.	Punjab BGVS	10	5	71 blocks	–	–	3	6	–
15.	Rajasthan BGVS	8	5	18 blocks 56 GPs	–	3,000	8	5	Own building
16.	Tamil Nadu TNSF/BGVS	23	7	115 blocks	–	18,000	50	4	–
17.	Tripura BGVS	4	–	40 blocks	5	5,000	8	5	SRC
18.	UP BGVS	27	10	56 blocks 700 GPs	305	10,000	6	6	–
19.	Uttaranchal BGVS	7	–	17 blocks 99 GPs	40	1,500	4	2	
	Total	258	91	1,187 blocks , 3,971 GPs		2,22,566	258	96	

Source: BGVS General Council Meeting, Bhopal, December 28–29, 2005: 16–17.

the need of the hour, it was recognized that such processes would require ongoing professional support of persons who would necessarily remain in close contact with villages. A greater number of persons from amongst dalits, minorities and women could be playing a leadership role towards widening the base of the organization while not promoting sectarian views (BGVS, 2005: 18).

The BGVS National Executive Committee decided that it would be useful if there were an exchange of activists across states in order to have a mutual sharing of experiences. This exchange was conducted during the period from September 1 to October 8, 2007. The BGVS teams in the following states played host in the initial round: Himachal Pradesh, Kerala, Tamil Nadu, Jharkhand, Bihar and Assam. These were the states where the organizational base and project activities were comparatively stronger. The host states also sent their activists to other states. The duration of the visit was about a week. The BGVS national centre undertook the coordination of the exchange programme. The exchange of activists enabled almost the entire second level leadership to participate, 40 per cent of whom were women. The participants found this a useful sharing experience and suggested that this process should continue. A total of 550 persons were reported to have participated in this exchange programme (BGVS, 2004–2008, 2008: 45).

Table 2.14 indicates that by 2008 the BGVS had a base in 22 states, 316 districts covering 2,009 blocks, 21,064 gram panchayats and 51,469 villages throughout the country. An additional 414 urban and semi-urban areas had some presence of BGVS activities. The organizational strength had risen from a membership of 1,70,132 persons in 2002 to 2,22,566 in 2005, and finally to 2,70,535 by 2008. A presence was newly established in Arunachal Pradesh, Manipur and Meghalaya during the previous three years, together with a revival of its base in Gujarat. Most of the states were independently registered but federated under the banner of the BGVS. The General Body consisted of 100 members, which included a 13-member Executive Committee and two permanent invites from the All India People's Science Network (AIPSN). Providing a participatory and federative character to the General Body was the fact that it was comprised of three members from each state, the outgoing Executive Committee and 15 members nominated by the current Executive Committee. In contrast with the sizable strength of the Samata Women's Network, the Executive

Committee at the national level had still a 23 per cent women's participation and a variation from 5 per cent to 40 per cent in the states.

TABLE 2.14 *BGVS Organizational Status of States, 2008*

	Name of State	*Districts*	*Blocks*	*Panchayats*	*Town Areas*	*Villages*	*Membership*
1.	Andhra Pradesh	23	572	264	64	518	(JVV) 34,502
2.	Arunachal Pradesh	3	3	6			
3.	Assam	17	50	300	8	3,500	5,000
4.	Bihar	23	162	1,944	12	2,417	38,215
5.	Gujarat	7	2	22	–	54	1,610
6.	Haryana	9	26	130	33	130	3,000
7.	Himachal Pradesh	12	45	1,000	20	–	45,000
8.	Jharkhand	14	51	1,000	12	3,000	24,020
9.	Karnataka	16	45	75	40	100	2,800
10.	Kerala	14	141	699	57	1,196	(KSSP) 32,666
11.	Madhya Pradesh	26	54	855	60	2,565	10,393
12.	Maharashtra	14	10	30	7	45	450
13.	Manipur	5	5	10			
14.	Meghalaya	2	2				
15.	Orissa	28	91	451	35	2,158	9,200
16.	Puducherry	2	4	50	2	71	951
17.	Punjab	20	135	3,500	10	3,500	35,000
18.	Rajasthan	10	13	80	3	415	3,300
19.	Tamil Nadu	29	500	10,000	20	30,000	(TNSF) 12,000
20.	Tripura	3	21	–	3	–	53
21.	Uttar Pradesh	28	60	578	18	1,500	10,375
22.	Uttarakhand	11	17	70	10	300	2,000
	Total	316	2,009	21,064	414	51,469	2,70,535

Source: BGVS General Council Meeting, Tirupati, July 21–22, 2008: 33.

Part II

Major Projects

3

Natural Resource Management (NRM) with Community Participation

1. Participatory Resource Mapping (PRM), 1993–97

Participatory Resource Mapping (PRM), initiated in 1993, was a major programme of the BGVS. Through this project, the BGVS with the help of the All India People's Science Network (AIPSN) intended to make "… major interventions in the field of land and water by extending the participatory approach (validated during the literacy campaign) to bring about a grass roots level economic regeneration through local level planning and sustainable development" (BGVS, 1996–97: 10). The major objective underlying the conception of the programme was thus the empowerment of the community around basic needs. The PRM programme "includes land literacy by mapping the status of terrain, land use, water resources and local assets wholly by the villagers; followed by the stages of resource literacy, organization building and development action planning" (BGVS, 1996–97: 10).

It appears that while the initiation of PRM was being contemplated, the Rajiv Gandhi National Drinking Water Mission (RGNDWM) had approached the BGVS for its involvement in a water and sanitation programme on a pilot basis. The aim was to strengthen the programme by using PRM to maximize community participation which had been lacking in the implementation of water and sanitation programmes in the country (BGVS, July 1994: 18–19). The BGVS then took up the programme for implementation as a technical consultancy to RGNDWM to begin with. The annual report submitted to the BGVS

General Council in 1994 suggests that the following two factors influenced the initiation of the PRM programme by the BGVS:

1. The RGNDWM thought that the involvement of local people in drinking water and sanitation programme had been lacking despite it being one of its major objectives. It was felt that the programme could be linked to the literacy campaigns and could benefit from the existing network of BGVS/PSM linked to literacy (BGVS, July 1994: 18).
2. BGVS viewed this as an opportunity to link land and water to literacy, to empower communities with knowledge concerning their livelihood and sustainable economic activities for community benefits (BGVS, July 1994: 19)

The programme was by and large drawn from the experience of the Kerala PRM with successful literacy campaigns and Panchayat Resource Mapping, only this time the programme strategy was different. This has been attributed to the fact that "a totally different environment with regard to infrastructure and organizational set-up necessitated substantial alteration in the programme strategy" (BGVS, July 1994: 20). Hence, a new approach which was largely dependent on the fund of villagers' knowledge about the terrain and their experience and perceptions was more acceptable. "The programme envisaged preparation of three thematic maps on terrain features, land use status and water utilization structures and other community facilities after intensive environment-building and mobilization of volunteers. Collection of data related to land, water and socio-economic status in structured data format also formed part of the exercise. Subsequent to mapping, the key volunteers and scientific assistants undertook a combined evaluation of thematic maps and prepared a derivative map for action planning. To internalize local level action planning and implementation, formation of user committees at hamlet, village and gram panchayat (GP) level were also envisaged" (BGVS, July 1994: 20).

Using the PRM, the BGVS thus implemented the following two programmes:

1. WATSAN, from July, 1993 to August, 1995.
2. Watershed Development Project from August, 1995 to October, 1999.

2. The Integrated Drinking Water and Sanitation with People's Participation (WATSAN) Project, 1993–95

The main objective of the project was to evolve and implement participatory planning for drinking water and sanitation. The funds for implementing this project were provided by UNICEF amounting to Rs 28 lakh. The WATSAN project was launched on July 1, 1993, on an experimental basis, incorporating the application of PRM. Though the project was sanctioned initially for one year, it was later extended by one more year, i.e., upto June 30, 1995. Four blocks were selected from different districts across four different states. These were: Muthukuluthur (Ramanad–Tamil Nadu), Bhanjanagar (Ganjam–Orissa), Kashipur (Purulia–West Bengal) and Chainpur (Palamau–Bihar). One had the opportunity of visiting the last site. The blocks were selected in consultation with the BGVS/AIPSN activists. The criteria for selection of the blocks were water scarcity, backwardness and organizational strength (BGVS, 1994: 19).

A Technical Core Group was formed in July, 1993 having two members initially and to which one more member was added later on in January, 1994. The Core Group provided technical know-how, support materials and necessary organizational assistance. It was reported that, "though the project commenced its activities in July, 1993, it took almost 3 to 4 months to actually start the work in all the four areas"; the justification being that, "the implementation process was not hurried deliberately to give time for the activists to get clarified the philosophy of the programme" (BGVS, July 1994: 19–20).

The project was kicked off with a National Orientation Workshop organized at IRTC, Mundur, Kerala. The project coordinators, organizers, scientific assistants and a few government officials linked to rural development from the four states were oriented (BGVS, July 1994: 20). The following were core activities undertaken under the project (BGVS, December 1995: 31):

- Block level training for resource persons
- Gram panchayat and revenue village level training for volunteers
- Participatory resource mapping and data collection by the volunteers
- Compilation of thematic resource maps on terrain features, land use, water resource status and community facilities by the volunteers

- Compilation of panchayat and revenue village level database by the volunteers
- Mapping of communication and resource literacy to the community at the hamlet level by the volunteers
- Formation of community organizations at hamlet, village, gram panchayat and block level
- Participatory action planning by the community
- Finalization of action plans by the local organizations
- Formation of implementation committees at appropriate levels to implement development programmes.

The annual report to the BGVS Governing Council, 1994, discusses the initial implementation process in greater detail. It highlights the efforts taken, problems encountered and remedial actions and the nature of response from the villagers, activists and concerned organizations. It also brings out the location-specific differences in the strategy adopted for the initiation of resource mapping in the blocks selected for the implementation of WATSAN. By the end of 1994, modalities for evolving an action plan through local committees and relevant social structures were the main efforts that were made to internalize planning at the grassroots level. It was observed that it was a time-consuming process and beset with unanticipated hurdles in various localities (BGVS, July 1994: 22).

The following specific activities were undertaken through the four blocks selected for the implementation of WATSAN by the end of 1994 (BGVS, July 1994: 20–22):

Muthukulathur, Tamil Nadu: Kalajathas were organized in 91 hamlets out of a total of 157. Dialogue was initiated with the villagers in 12 revenue villages out of a total 37. Two block level training camps were organized to train the key resource persons. Revenue village level training of volunteers and subsequent mapping were undertaken in 12 revenue villages. On completion of mapping, the hamlet level user committees were formed in four revenue villages, through which discussions were initiated on local action with regard to planning, implementation and monitoring of development activities and proper usage of land and water (BGVS, July 1994: 20).

Bhanjanagar, Orissa: The campaigning was launched among the elected gram panchayat members and key government functionaries. Key resource persons were identified by the project organizing group and a block level orientation workshop was conducted. An environment-building campaign, mainly through personal interactions with the village elders and youth and other publicity means, was held in four gram panchayats out of 20 and user committees were formed to take up the local level planning and related activities.

Kashipur, West Bengal: The PBVM sought the help of the Block Panchayat Samiti to organize the mobilization. Key resource persons were identified initially for six gram panchayats and they were oriented in a block level workshop. Subsequently, gram panchayat level training was undertaken in three gram panchayats and the mapping was completed.

Chainpur, Bihar: Due to the absence of PSM and a literacy campaign in the past, work was started from the grassroots level organization building by forming project implementation committees in all the 24 gram panchayats. The initial interaction at the 24 gram panchayats helped to identify key volunteers and a block level training was organized subsequently. As part of the environment-building for implementation of the programme, kalajathas were conducted in panchayats. Training and mapping was then organized in six panchayats. In one of the panchayats, user committees were formed at hamlet, village and gram panchayat levels, through which activities related to planning were undertaken. By the end of 1994, efforts were on for organizing a local group at the block level. A review workshop on the PRM project was organized at Coimbatore to share the experiences of the PRM programme implemented in the districts of Ramanathpuram (Tamil Nadu), Ganjam (Orissa), Palamau (Bihar) and Bankura (W. Bengal). The workshop, attended by about 40 activists and experts, resulted in a project for extending the PRM to more districts where TLC was successfully implemented.

It can be seen that great efforts were taken to implement the project. All the above activities were implemented meticulously with the participation of the village communities in the project. However, the successes achieved were not without problems. According to the BGVS Report to the General Council, the following problems were encountered (BGVS, July 1994: 20–22):

It was observed that in Muthukuluthur, while the strong base of TLC helped generate volunteers for mapping, the mapping process itself did not evoke much response from the villagers. A need for intensive environment-building was felt and subsequently undertaken.

In Bhanjanagar, due to non-consolidation of literacy efforts the campaigning that was launched among the elected gram panchayat members and key government functionaries was rendered ineffective.

The project also suffered a serious organizational setback "due to the lack of attention by the selected project organizer". Another problem faced was "discontinuities in technical activities due to intermittent resignation and recruitment of scientific assistants".

In Kashipur, the lapse of not providing a local organizer by the PBVM had affected the smooth functioning of the project. Another problem was "the reluctance on the part of scientific assistants to stay in the field and lack of coordination of their activities".

A major problem common to all the four blocks was the lack of communication between the volunteers and the entire village community based on the maps prepared by the volunteers. The problems were later "sorted out through motivating the village community to have a number of deliberations based on the maps prepared by the volunteers".

Another constraint in the programme was that "the process of making user committees functional by themselves was found to be a time-consuming process". In addition, BGVS also met with a broader problem of social dynamics, particularly in Muthukuluthur where "the deep-rooted caste rivalries and confinement of societal activities to the respective hamlets pose considerable problems in the smooth sailing of the programme" (BGVS, July 1994: 20).

The following were discernible factors which played a positive role (BGVS, July 1994: 20–22):

In Muthukulathur, a local voluntary organization of women (Maharam) played a significant role in the entire process, as the project generated enthusiasm among the activists who were involved through the TLC. It was observed that the organization had the potential to turn into a 'functional catalyst for participatory actions in the area'.

Wherever the mapping was undertaken a qualitative change was observed among the villagers. It was observed that "the effectiveness and accuracy of mapping of local resources by volunteers from the community had been established beyond any doubt, irrespective of the character and composition of the community". It was found to be "an excellent tool for consolidating literacy and empowerment of the community". It was observed that they were able to come out with constructive criticism on various developmental activities and were able to suggest viable alternatives.

According to the report to the BGVS General Council Meeting, December 11–15, 1995 (BGVS, December 1995: 31), the following were the outcomes of the WATSAN project by the end of that year:

1. Micro-level database in the form of thematic maps and tables, prepared by the local people were available at each village where the work was completed.
2. A total scientific appraisal on the land, water and social problems and prospects of each village by the villagers themselves was available. This had led to an urge for a better living environment.
3. The literacy on land and water had generated a powerful and highly informed demand for development. This included specific projects of their choice which they knew would be effective and relevant to their needs.

3. Watershed Development Project, 1995–99

The Watershed Development Project was another programme which was implemented using PRM. The aim was, "to achieve conservation and development of watershed, to improve its ecological well-being and thereby enhance its productivity and life-supporting system for the betterment of the people and their environment through the people's participatory method" (BGVS, 1997: 11). The project included the protection, rational management, sustainable development and utilization of natural resources (BGVS, 1997: 11; BGVS, 2001: 7).

The project was sanctioned to the BGVS by the ministry in August, 1995 for setting up of four regional centres for helping the states/project implementing agencies (PIAs) in implementing watershed development projects according to the guidelines of Government of India. The project was sanctioned for a period of three years. A project grant of Rs 50 lakh was sanctioned for the implementation of the project (BGVS, 1998: Annexure 1).

The operational objectives, in accordance with the ministry's sanction, as mentioned in the report to the BGVS General Council, 1998, were:

1. The BGVS , New Delhi, would set up four regional centres:
2. The BGVS, through these regional centres, would work as support groups for helping the state/project implementing agencies.
    (a) to delineate the watersheds,
    (b) to recruit and train the watershed development teams (WDTs), and
    (c) offer continuous technical support through the programme period.

3. 20 clusters would be identified during 1995 and 1996, and this would be followed by the identification of 20 to 25 new clusters every year in the subsequent years (BGVS, 1998: Annexure 1).

Thus BGVS was given a clear mandate to identify, orient and train PIAs from among the PSM/BGVS groups and other NGOs to take up watershed development projects.

An implementation committee was constituted at the national level which had eminent administrators and technical experts in the field of rural development. The function of the implementation committee was to formulate policies and regulations and monitor the progress of the project. For the purpose of project execution, a multi-disciplinary national core team was constituted comprising of persons with experience in watershed development. The national core team operated from four regional centres. The locations of the regional centres were Delhi, Pune, Calcutta and Palakkad.

A workshop on sharing the experiences on watershed development project was held in 1995 at Hyderabad. Ten key papers were presented highlighting the field level experience in implementing the watershed management programme. The workshop helped in the preparation of a methodology for the implementation of the project.

The methodology involved mainly two steps: pre-project assistance and the assistance during the project implementation (BGVS, 1998: Annexure 1). During the pre-project assistance stage, the village community was provided training to enable them to develop an understanding of their resources through PRM. The pre-project stage involved mainly three steps which helped in the identification of suitable village clusters for taking up watershed development projects and awareness creation. The BGVS has detailed these activities in its publication, "A Guide for Conducting PRM and Resource Literacy as a Preparatory Activity for Watershed Development Project".

The pre-project activities which are briefly outlined in the report presented before the BGVS General Council, 1998, were as follows (BGVS, 1998: Annexure 1):

1. *Organizing sensitization camps:* These helped in the sensitization of BGVS activists in areas such as: the necessity of decentralized development, importance of watershed mode of development and the relevance of PRM and the features of the government-sponsored watershed projects.

2. *Conduction of PRM:* PRM was conducted in selected villages, during which the activists along with the local population were trained for four days in resource mapping. Subsequent to this training, the local people, assisted by the activists, completed the mapping of the complete area of the proposed watershed. A BGVS publication, "Handbook for Land Literacy" was used as a guide for conducting PRM.
3. *Post-PRM workshop and resource literacy:* These were the sessions conducted after the preparation of the maps from which a plan of action emerged. Upon completion of this activity, a decision was taken on the plan of action for submitting a proposal for watershed development.

The pre-project assistance stage of the implementation process was followed by the second step, viz., assistance during the project implementation. This stage involves the following activities (BGVS, 1998: Annexure 1): Training in technical and managerial aspects appropriate to the location, exposure to other watershed projects, sharing experience among BGVS/AIPSN-PIAs and with other PIAs, and support through consultants, wherever necessary.

Additionally, the BGVS Watershed Development Project provided technical and organizational support to the PIA for the following activities (BGVS, 1998: Annexure 1):

1. Preparation of literature:
   - (a) Technical manual, covering all technical and social aspects, to be used as reference material by the PIA, watershed conservation team (WCT) members and consultants
   - (b) Training modules, to cover appropriate and sustainable technologies, social organization and project management
   - (c) Publicity material for environment-building
   - (d) Handbook for Watershed Development on the lines of Handbook of Land Literacy
   - (e) Guide for conducting PRM
   - (f) Draft of a source book for watershed based development
2. Setting up a reference library with books and occasional papers:

   A reference library, consisting of about 1,800 titles (including booklets) had been set up at Delhi. These were borrowed/consulted by activists, resource persons, experts, etc.
3. Translation of appropriate literature in regional languages.

Translation of training material prepared by BGVS was carried out by the respective state units.

By the end of 1998, the following 11 sensitization camps were conducted in various states as follows under the project:

TABLE 3.1 *Sensitization Camps under Watershed Development Project, 1998*

	States	*No. of Participants*
1.	Paramakkudi, Andipatti and Pondicherry, Tamil Nadu;	186
2.	Tumkur and Bangalore, Karnataka	20
3.	Bhopal, Madhya Pradesh	10
4.	Pune, Maharashtra	32
5.	Jaipur, Bindranhera and Sawai Madhopur, Rajasthan	111
6.	Chandigarh, Punjab and Haryana	32
7.	Solan and Shimla, Himachal Pradesh	72
8.	Agartala, Tripura	33
9.	Patna and Dhanbad, Bihar	75
10.	Palakkad, Kerala	72
11.	Bankura and Calcutta, West Bengal	10
	Total	652

Source: BGVS, General Council Meeting: February 7–8, 1998, Bangalore, New Delhi 1998, Annexure 1(a).

PRM was conducted in 28 village clusters, covering about 63,000 hectares. Post-PRM workshops and resource literacy sessions were conducted in the following places: Muthukulathur, Ramanathpuram district, Tamil Nadu; Andipatti, Vaigai district, Tamil Nadu; Girgaon, Kolhapur district, Maharashtra; Bhanjanagar, Ganjam district, Orissa; Kyamanahalli, Tumkur district, Karnataka; Chippabarod, Baran district, Rajasthan. New projects sanctioned by the Council for Advancement of People's Action and Rural Technology (CAPART) were initiated in the Muthukuluthur block, Ramanathpuram district, Tamil Nadu and Bhanjanagar block, Ganjam district, Orissa. A pre-planning workshop was conducted at Ramanathpuram. A training workshop for WCT was conducted at Bhubaneshwar. Exposure visits were conducted to Ralegan Siddhi and Social Centre, Piplagaon, both in Maharashtra, for 30 activists/WCT members. A national workshop was conducted on sharing experiences for AIPSN/BGVS state units at Pune during October 27–30, 1996. Expert advice was obtained for the implementation of Muthukulathur project from scientists of Tamil Nadu Agricultural University and from scientists of Orissa Agricultural University for the Bhanjanagar project.

The following were the achievements (BGVS, 1998: Annexure 1; BGVS, 1999: Annexure A.4):

1. Regional Centres: Four regional centres were set up at New Delhi, Pune, Calcutta, Palakkad and they were fully functioning by the end of 1998.
2. Delineating Watersheds: The BGVS helped in delineating 33 watersheds by the end of 1999.
3. Help to states and the PIAs.
    (a) The BGVS, through the regional centres, helped the various PIAs, states and other collaborating agencies in various ways such as recruitment of WDTs, proposal preparations and their forwarding, providing technical support, assistance in conduction of PRMs, participation in meetings, studies, and developing research proposals.
    (b) The BGVS assisted the Tamil Nadu Science Forum, the PIA of watershed development project at Muthukulathur, in the recruitment of eight members of WDT and in training them in 1996–97. It similarly helped in the recruitment and training of five members of WDTs in Bhanjanagar block in Orissa; 18 members of WDT of five Kerala panchayats (Meyil, Madakathara, Mezhuveli, Vallamkannur, Kodumaon) during 1997–98 and 156 members of WDT in Purulia district.
    (c) BGVS provided continuous technical support to the identified PIAs.

The foregoing sections show the immense amount of efforts that were put in towards the promotion of watershed development and for taking people from literacy to land and water management. The following Table 3.2 shows the participatory resource mapping exercises carried out over nine states by March, 1997. These covered a total of 63,339 hectares. As a result, a very large number of proposals for watershed projects were submitted by the PIAs. While the project achieved successes on many counts, it also faced some problems. The BGVS report to the General Council 1998 points out problems encountered in dealing with the government agencies, viz., CAPART and the Department of Wasteland Development, Ministry of Rural Areas and Employment, such as inordinate delays in sanctioning of projects submitted by PIAs, misinterpretation of project objectives, adamant stands and holding up payment of sanctioned grant instalments, etc. (BGVS, 1998: Annexure 1; BGVS, 1999: 6). As a result the Executive Committee of BGVS unanimously decided to wind up the project with effect from October 31, 1999 (BGVS, 1999: 6).

TABLE 3.2 *Participatory Resource Mapping (PRM) Conducted till March 31, 1997*

District	*Place*	*Area*
Kerala		
Kasargod District	Uduma	2,017 ha
	Peelicode	1,487 ha
Kannur District	Kaliasseri	1,700 ha
	Mayyil	1,444 ha
	Muzhakunnu	838 ha
Kozhikkode District	Oonchiyam	900 ha
Malappuruam District	Vallikunnu	1,513 ha
Palakkad District	Pallassana	2,937 ha
Trissur District	Madakathara	3,200 ha
Ernakulam District	Pallipuram	1,600 ha
Kottayam District	Kumaraka	5,166 ha
Pathanamthitta District	Mezhuvalli	1,444 ha
Kollam District	Clappana	1,745 ha
Alappuzha District	Aryad	6,800 ha
Tamil Nadu		
Ramnathpuram District	Muthukulathur*	11,500 ha
Vaigai District	Andipatti*	3,996 ha
Tripura		
West Tripura,	Jampuri Jala	NA
North Tripura	Pani Sagar	NA
Bihar		
Palamau District	Chainpur*	–
	Neura	2,000 ha
Dhanbad District	Dhanbad	750 ha
	Topchanchi	2,220 ha

Cont'd...

Cont'd...

Dharbhanga District	Mathurahi	3,220 ha
Saharsa District	Purushottampur	315 ha
Madhepura District	Shankarpur	3,000 ha
	Mahadevpatti	4,500 ha
Madhya Pradesh		
Dewas District	Chandpura	1,900 ha
Orissa		
Ganjam District	Bhanjanagar*	–
Karnataka		
Tumkur District	Kymanahalli	2,080 ha
Maharashtra		
Kolhapur District	Girgaon	800 ha
Yavatmal District	Poplani**	450 ha
Nanded District	Nandgaon**	1,350 ha
Rajasthan		
Baran District	Chippabarod	3,000 ha
West Bengal		
Purulia District	Kashipur*	–
Total Area of Participatory Resource Mapping done 63,339 ha		

Notes: * Participatory Resource Mapping completed in 1994, under a project by Rajiv Gandhi Mission for Drinking Water and Sanitation.

** Participatory Resource Mapping done after April 1, 1997.

Source: Bharat Gyan Vigyan Samiti, General Council Meeting: February 7–8, Bangalore, New Delhi, 1998.

There were two other major programmes that were closely related to the entire concept of NRM at decentralized levels with people's participation. One was the programme *Desh Ko Janein Desh Ko Badlein* (Let's Know and Change the Country), which attempted to create decentralized organizational forms for analysis and action on a range of official development programmes as they reach out to villages. The second focused, as the name suggests, on the local self-governing bodies which were expected to play an active part in development administration according to the 73rd and 74th amendments to the Indian Constitution. While the Integrated Drinking Water and Sanitation Project and the Watershed Development Project were discontinued after 1995 and 1999, respectively, due to discontinuation of funds, the processes such as PRM were learnt by a cross-section of BGVS cadres and were continued through other programmes related to decentralized governance and the convergence of activities. However, a Watershed Development Project was initiated in Bhanjanagar district, Orissa with the support of CAPART.

4. Desh Ko Janein Desh Ko Badlein, 1995–98

Desh Ko Janein Desh Ko Badlein (DJDB) was one of the later programmes implemented jointly by the BGVS and the AIPSN. The aim of the programme was "to help ordinary people as well as the activists to examine analytically and critically the processes and products of 'Development' during the five decades of India's freedom" (BGVS, 1996–97: 12–13 and BGVS, 2001: 7).

The programme was designed for the empowerment of the poor through the formation of SHGs and strengthening of Panchayati Raj as a tool against vested interests. All this was to be carried out through a guided process as the objective was "to help the villagers to 'see' what they 'feel' and to involve the weaker sections in the development of self-help groups" (BGVS, 2001: 8). The programme had two major components – educational activities and developmental activities. The educational activities were focused around discussions on subjects such as development of local economy, access to natural resource, public finance, power, telecommunications and transport, employment opportunities, the promises and realities of education, health, the plight of the weaker section's women, SC-ST and minorities, people's right to information, and Panchayati Raj (BGVS, 2001: 7). The implementation of the educational activities involved the formation of a local study group of 10 to 15 activists in each gram panchayat of the selected field area, about four village level discussion groups of about 50 to 60 persons and with at least half of them being women. It was proposed that the study groups through the discussions would prepare study reports on the above-mentioned educational activities in about 10,000 gram panchayats (BGVS, 1996–97: 12–13 and BGVS, 2001: 8).

The developmental activities were geared towards undertaking development actions such as: field investigations, preparation of area development plans and establishing the area-based groups. Field investigations were to be carried out around a number of themes like the status of people's livelihood, economy and technology, laws, status of the local self-government, and people's science knowledge, culture and social life as a major part of developmental activities. Action plans were to be formulated in sessions with technologists and scientists (BGVS, 2001: 8). It was reported that under this programme, a series of Jan Sansads (People's Parliaments) at the block, district and state levels were

Meera, a young, vibrant and energetic sitting member of Shimla Municipal Corporation, is the daughter of a farmer's family of Balson Theog village of Himachal Pradesh. After completing her studies upto the 10th class in her village, she came to Shimla to pursue her higher studies. Today, Meera has two master's degrees in sociology and history from Himachal Pradesh University.

Since her student days she started questioning various social and political issues concerning the common masses which later on developed as a spirit to fight against all odds in life and society. This brought her in contact with Himachal Gyan Vigyan Samiti (HGVS), the state unit of the Bharat Gyan Vigyan Samiti, where she got a forum to raise her voice and focus on various issues like women's literacy, campaign against female feticide and organizing women to form self-help groups.

Meera also obtained a diploma in women empowerment from Indira Gandhi National Open University and got a government job in the Kandi Project, integrated watershed management and mid-Himalayan project. But she soon realized that she was not someone to go on working as a government employee throughout her life. She left the job to become a full-time activist of HGVS. In the People's Science Movement (PSM), she got married to Giyanand , a PSM activist and ex-state secretary of HGVS. She got more opportunities to intensify her struggle on different fronts. She taught voluntarily in various schools. She has also participated in the campaign on human-wildlife conflicts and the monkey menace in the state. The support she has extended to the local orphanages and the strong stand she has taken against the local liquor mafia are well-known in the local communities.

These are the reasons why Meera, even after fighting an election against powerful and rich candidates supported by other powerful leaders and lobbies, won with a comfortable majority. In the past two and half years she has continuously spoken on behalf of common people in the municipal corporation. She has a son of six years and she is successfully managing to look after him and other family matters.

(Interviewed by Asha, BGVS, December, 2009)

organized and a final convention was held at Nalanda in October 1998, coinciding with the eighth AIPSC (BGVS, 2001: 7–8).

5. Linkages with Panchayati Raj, 1995 ...

The aim of the programme was to strengthen the Panchayati Raj system and to build the literacy network along with it in the gram panchayats. It was reported that almost all the state BGVS units were interested in developing linkages with panchayati raj institutions. A number of states organized different kinds of training programmes for elected panchayat representatives independently and in collaboration with agencies like UNICEF. Madhya Pradesh BGVS undertook a massive programme in August–November, 1995 to train panchs, sarpanchs and gram sabha sachivs of 27 blocks in 25 districts. Training was imparted to 9,200 panchs and sarpanchs of 2,300 gram panchayats. The experience of the Kerala People's Plan Campaign served as a big boost to the state units. During the months of September–October, 1996, the BGVS National Centre coordinated a programme with the help of BGVS Kerala, KSSP and Kerala State Planning Board to give field exposure to representatives from different state units to the Kerala Peoples' Planning Campaign. These representatives also participated in a seminar organized at Trivandrum and undertook extensive field study trips to selected panchayats of Kerala where the planning campaign was being operationalized (BGVS, February 1998: 11).

A material preparation workshop on PL-CE-Panchayati Raj Linkage, was held at Trivandrum from May 4 to 10, 1997, to prepare material on the basis of the Kerala People's Planning Campaign and to workout possible linkages between PL-CE programmes and gram panchayats. Ten resource persons from different states participated in this workshop (BGVS, February 1998: 8). Another workshop on PL-CE-Panchayati Raj linkage was held at the IRTC, Mundur, Palghat from June 14 to 22, 1997, to share the experiences of the Kerala Planning Campaign and to develop linkages between PL-CE and Panchayati Raj institutions in other states. In all, 62 activists from 17 states participated in this workshop (BGVS, February 1998: 8).

In the year 1998, a four-day national workshop on TL-PL-CE and linkages with gram panchayats was held during May 7–10 at Dehradun to discuss the overall strategy of developing linkages between PL-CE programmes and gram panchayat development plans. Presentations were made by the Assam and Kerala units on the results of the panchayat development reports that they had prepared during

Usha was born in a lower middle class family in Beguserai, Bihar. Her father was a government servant at Baroun thermal station. They were five sisters and one brother in the family. Though her parents were interested to educate their children, financial constraints and social prejudices were creating obstacles.

At the age of 12, Usha got married to a boy 11 years older than herself. By the age 16 she had become a mother of a child. But Usha was not one who would give up. She was constantly looking for betterment and one day in 1993 her efforts succeeded as she came in contact with BGVS through a health workshop. The next year she was given the responsibility of Samata activities in Barbati panchayat. Her hard work and commitment soon caught the eyes of the leaders of the literacy movement in the state and the same year she became the district convener of Samata; a responsibility she undertook for a further 10 years.

Her husband, other members of the family and the community were totally against her work with the People's Science Movement which meant going from village to village, from door to door for the cause of the literacy. But Usha was determined. She had to take both her sons with her while going for work related to the literacy campaign. Usha kept on working hard to build a women's organization in that area. In the year 2001, Panchayati Raj system was implemented in the state with the 73rd and 74th Amendments of the Constitution. Usha was backed by the local people and activists to fight the election. She not only fought the district council election, but won it with a very good margin. She was elected as the vice-president of the district council and for the next six years remained at that post and worked enthusiastically.

Usha kept on working with the BGVS even after becoming a member of the legislative council in the year 2003. She was given the responsibility of the state president of BGVS, Bihar which she successfully carried on for two consecutive terms till 2009. She used to raise various issues of the common people in the legislative assembly and tried to convert each 10th class school upto 12th class. People's representatives started getting travelling allowance. She fought continuously for proper implementation of different government policies. Today, at the age of 41, she is an arts graduate. Usha is still busy struggling for people's rights, for the cause of female literacy, empowerment of women representatives and education.

(Interviewed by Asha, BGVS, December, 2009)

April–June 1998. "The Assam experience clearly showed the possibility of developing strong linkages between the PL-CE action programme with the development needs of the community" (BGVS, October 1999: 8). One visited the Assam programme and would share this view. The workshop was attended by delegates from Himachal Pradesh, Haryana, Punjab, Uttar Pradesh, Assam, Bihar, Karnataka, Kerala, Tamil Nadu, Andhra and Orissa. All the state units were expected to prepare a minimum of five Gram Panchayat Development Reports with strong linkages to PL-CE programmes (BGVS, October 1999: 8).

The interface with Panchayati Raj was also brought about through various programmes such as Literacy and Resource Literacy, Literacy to Land and Water Management, Hamara Desh, Desh Ko Janein Desh Ko Badlein (DJDB), Samata Vigyan Utsav (SVU). In fact, Panchayati Raj featured in almost every mass programme or mela at the state, district, block and village levels as one of the issues for discussion. For instance, in melas organized from village to state levels under the SVU, one of the corners for discussing specific issues was kept for Panchayati Raj (BGVS, 2001: 6). A six-day Samata workshop was held on 'Literacy, Women's Empowerment and Panchayati Raj' at Bhopal during May 7–12, 1995. 140 women from 18 states and two union territories participated in this workshop in which the role of elected representatives of the panchayat, especially women, was one of the key issues for discussion.

Under the DJDB programme, Panchayati Raj was a prominent theme among the many subjects which formed the educational activities. Workshops were also organized in May and June, 1997, respectively, by the BGVS National Centre in collaboration with the AIPSN, at Trivandrum and Palghat to discuss the details of panchayat development report preparation as part of the DJDB programme. As a follow-up of these workshops, most of the state units had started work on the preparation of panchayat development reports (BGVS, February 1998: 11).

4

The Mobilization of Women and Samata

1. The Samata Jatha, 1993

The BGVS jatha of 1990 was a large-scale programme for creating a demand for literacy through people's mobilization. It also aimed at initiating an organizational framework to facilitate literacy. The activities of the jatha according to BGVS reports covered over 1,00,000 villages in the country and set in motion a chain reaction of minor literacy processes. However, there had not been a concerted and focused mobilization of women. The literacy campaigns that followed covered a large number of non-literates, the majority of whom were women. In addition, there was a major contribution of women and girl children as volunteer instructors and jatha performers. It was estimated that out of the total number of volunteers and learners, two-thirds were women. However, women were absent from positions of leadership. Apart from this structural shortcoming, there was a need to place women's issues on the agenda of the literacy campaigns and to establish linkages with the women's movements. Experience suggested that linkages to ongoing movements, whenever carried out, had led to a heightened impact of the jathas. This was so in the case of Chamoli in Uttar Pradesh and in the districts of Raipur, Durg and Bilaspur in the Chhattisgarh region of Madhya Pradesh (Dighe et al., 1991: 84). The jatha of 1992 which concentrated on the six northern states, while having one of its six themes literacy for women's emancipation, did not address women in any specific manner. However, during January 11–13, 1992, an attempt was made to relate the concerns of BGVS with the Mahila Samakhya Programme in a national workshop.

In view of the growing demand for a special emphasis on women, it was decided to undertake a national women's jatha called Samata – a jatha of women for education, equality and peace. This was discussed at the Executive Committee of the NLMA and communicated to the Ministry of HRD by a letter dated March 10, 1993. As a preparatory background to this decision, a national level organizing committee was formed with various national level women's organizations being represented. A convention was held at Delhi in December, 1992 where about 150 women delegates from all over the country participated. This was preceded by a brainstorming session in Madras in October of the same year. A national level Samata kalajatha production camp was held at Rohtak from January 16 to 31, 1993. Four major themes for the Samata jatha were identified: women and literacy, the girl child, women and work and women and communalism. The last assumed significance in the context of increasing communalism in the country after the demolition of the Babri Masjid. The outcome of the workshop was 11 plays and action songs as well as a documentary on the situation of girls – *Hindustan ki Betiyan* (Daughters of Hindustan). This was followed by five regional training workshops to translate/transcreate the scripts into regional languages with local relevance. While the jathas that followed suggested a homogenization and centralization of themes, this was offset to some extent by the introduction of local songs (Sharma, 1993: 23). District level Samata conventions followed. The Samata activities received wide publicity in the media.

Eight jathas set out from March 8, 1993, from Trivandrum, Kanyakumari, Aurangabad, Madhubani, Gauhati, Shimla, Dhankanal and Jaipur. More than 250 women artists participated in these jatha programmes covering a total of 611 points. The jathas converged at Jhansi with an additional 500 women delegates on April 8, 1993. They had performed plays and songs over a period of a month reaching out to a reported number of over two lakh women, men and children. Performances took place in a variety of settings such as market places, outside schools, in an auditorium, on railway platforms, or even at *mazars* and temples. Performances were often preceded by speeches of local representatives and followed by an exhibition on the theme of the jatha. For example, in Madhya Pradesh, posters that were created as part of a pre-jatha activity called Abhivyakti (expression) were exhibited. These posters were done during an open day of creative expression in Bilaspur district. In Arian, Rajasthan, the exhibition depicted the methodology of two innovative programmes for education – the Shiksha Karmi and the

Lok Jumbish (Sharma, 1993: 7). A significant aspect of the popular response to the jathas was that resources for the reception and arrangements for the performance were raised locally. This was in keeping with the spirit of volunteerism of the literacy movement.

The plays in the jatha were reported to have often met with dramatic responses from the audience. In Madras, the women gave a very enthusiastic response to the performance of Agnikund, a play depicting the multiple burdens borne by women. The principal of a local school came on stage to state that this was essential viewing at boys' colleges. In Bihar, after watching a performance of an anti-arrack song, a drunken old man came on stage with a bottle in hand. He went on to describe his life and stated his decision to give up drinking. There was a strong and positive response in places that had suffered from communal violence to the play 'Aaj Ki Raat Hum Jagate Rahenge'. The audience could immediately identify with the play. In Punjab, the performance of Kamahi Devi had to be interrupted twice due to rain and hail. The audience was game to shift the stage thrice (Sharma, 1993: 9, 11, 13).

The jatha strategy was to first reach out to those who could initiate literacy interventions in urban areas, to be followed by local intensive jathas that would reach out to the rural population. A comment on the messages in the performances was that they focused largely on the injustices suffered by women to the relative neglect of women's experiences that reflected a sense of confidence, strength and the possibility of change (Sharma, 1993: 7). This appears to be as result of the inexperience and the relatively early involvement of the participants in the cause for women's rights. Women's organizations participated in the conventions and as members of the local organizing committees. Inadequacy of time and the novelty of the effort explain the inadequacy of the involvement of women's organizations. The jatha succeeded to a great extent in focussing attention on the issue of female illiteracy and its relation to gender equity. Several states formed Samata groups at the state and district levels as a follow-up.

2. The Samata Network, 1995 ...

It was unclear at the end of the jatha whether the mobilizations around Samata would crystallize into an organizational formation or would serve as a broad forum of various activities relating to women's education and empowerment. It was felt that the various states would determine the process based on their ongoing experience (Sharma, 1993: 27). During the years immediately following the Samata jatha of

1993, the activities could not be coordinated at the national level due to the lack of suitable full-time activists. However, different states formed state and district level Samata groups, e.g., Bihar, Madhya Pradesh, Himachal Pradesh, Orissa, Assam and Tamil Nadu. Other states formed women sub-committees of BGVS. The Bihar Samata group organized kalajathas in 19 districts. Tamil Nadu and Pondicherry initiated two comprehensive programmes for imparting legal literacy to women. Andhra Pradesh developed several women's groups in Nellore followed by a women's savings movement in other parts of the state (BGVS, July 1999: 18). Several activities and mobilizations of women were carried out in the following years such as the quarry workers' struggle, the anti-arrack movement, the struggles of unorganized workers, thrift and credit societies, and the movement to engage women in greater social and geographical mobility through learning cycling (Balagopal, 1992; Ilaiah, 1992; Shatrugna, 1992 and 1998; Akash, 1993; Anveshi, 1993; Reddy and Patnaik, 1993; Athreya and Chunkath, 1996; Dighe, 1998).

In May 1995, a national core group for Samata was constituted with 10 members. Several national, regional and state level meetings followed. A major six-day workshop on literacy, women's empowerment and Panchayati Raj was organized in Bhopal in May 7–12, 1995. The objective was to review the Samata experience and the participation of the women in the literacy campaign. Around 140 women from 18 states and 2 union territories participated. An action programme and several state initiatives resulted as a follow-up of this meeting, e.g., activities relating to the involvement of women in Panchayati Raj, legal literacy and thrift groups. Legal literacy training in 18 districts of Karnataka and jathas to sensitize women on Panchayati Raj issues in Andhra Pradesh were some of the highlights of this process. A periodical entitled Samata was brought out by the national centre.

While retaining a primary involvement in the literacy campaigns, most of the BGVS state units also felt the need for developing their capacities to relate to other developmental activities, by 1995 (BGVS, 1995: 12). Based on the assessment provided by the state BGVS units, 12 states were involved in Samata activities with relevant sub-committees. Of these, the states of Assam, Himachal Pradesh, Eastern Uttar Pradesh, Bihar, Madhya Pradesh and Tamil Nadu were assessed as performing at a level that was above the average expectation. The jatha in Uttar Pradesh during February, 1995, while generating a high degree of participation, did not have a special focus on the issue of gender equity. The rapid expansion of the literacy campaigns over new districts and their growing stagnation or routinization began to have an impact on the BGVS involvement in the campaigns. A concern to revise the strategy and to save the spirit of a people's movement within the campaigns was articulated in the documents of the time (e.g., BGVS, 1995: 17–18).

Two regional workshops were organized during 1996 to train state level women activists for conducting Samata Melas/Vigyan Utsavas (Samata Science Festivals): at Shimla for the northern region during June 11–14, 1996 and Nellore for the southern region during August 1–4, 1996. About 160 women activists were trained in each of these workshops. The training covered issues such as women's education, health, domestic work, violence, personality development, Panchayati Raj, cycling and cycle repair, and anti-alcohol campaigns. A national review was conducted in New Delhi with the participation of 35 women from 17 states in August, 1996. The formation of women's savings groups received extended support at this workshop. The BGVS project proposal for January 1997 to December 1998, approved by the NLM in November, 1996, but with a much delayed sanction, planned to develop strong linkages between literacy and women's empowerment based on the above-mentioned experiences and using village Samata Vigyan Utsavas as a mobilization strategy (BGVS, 1996–97: 17). The objective was to mobilize women and to create organizational forms right down to the village level. Apart from providing a platform for the articulation of women's issues and the dissemination of information, it was hoped that a leadership would emerge among the women at decentralized levels (BGVS, February 1998).

A national level meeting of Samata state coordinators and resource persons was organized at Delhi during January 15–16, 1997, to work out the details of Samata Utsava. This was followed up by several meetings during 1997 of the National Core Group and of the state coordinators at the regional level. Eighteen states undertook activities ranging from state to village levels. Among these Andhra Pradesh, Bihar, Himachal Pradesh, Kerala, Madhya Pradesh and Punjab stand out as states with over a 100 village level Samata Melas/Utsavas (BGVS, 1996–97: 25).

A national convention of Samata activists was held at Topchachi, Dhanbad, from October 22 to 26, 1997, to review the progress, Samata Vigyan Utsav. Ninety activists from 12 state units participated in this review. Some of the important experiences under small savings and economic activities that were discussed are described briefly:

The Didi Bank in Dumka district, Bihar, arose as a result of the Jago Behna mobilization of women during the literacy campaign. By

TABLE 4.1 *Workshops, Melas and Programmes Organized under Samata, 1997–2000*

States	State Level Workshop					District Level Workshop					Block Level Workshop					Village Level Workshop				
	Jan.-Dec. 1997	Jan.-Dec. 1998	Jan.-Dec. 1999	Jan.-Sept. 2000	Total	Jan.-Dec. 1997	Jan.-Dec. 1998	Jan.-Dec. 1999	Jan.-Sept. 2000	Total	Jan.-Dec. 1997	Jan.-Dec. 1998	Jan.-Dec. 1999	Jan.-Sept. 2000	Total	Jan.-Dec. 1997	Jan.-Dec. 1998	Jan.-Dec. 1999	Jan.-Sept. 2000	Total
1. Assam	3	6	7	4	20	10	24	3	9	46	0	147	12	15	174	64	39	71	56	230
2. Andhra	2	4	0	2	8	17	17	0	0	34	7	26	0	0	33	134	165	0	0	299
3. Bihar	5	4	2	2	13	53	51	27	17	148	0	924	6	31	961	161	1,067	0	0	1,228
4. Haryana	1	17	0	0	18	3	21	0	0	24	10	6	0	0	16	86	915	0	0	1,001
5. Himạchal	2	2	7	3	14	9	3	4	3	19	30	0	59	60	149	280	0	0	0	280
6. Karnataka	3	0	0	0	3	6	4	0	0	10	2	21	8	0	31	1	37	9	0	47
7. Kerala	2	2	0	0	4	14	22	0	0	36	90	39	0	0	129	1,250	101	0	0	1,351
8. Maharashtra	1	6	4	1	12	0	1	2	2	5	0	1	3	0	4	0	6	3	0	9
9. Madhya Pradesh	1	1	10	0	12	27	2	6	0	35	0	12	0	0	12	0	0	0	0	0
10. Orissa	4	2	3	2	11	6	16	5	0	27	0	0	0	0	0	20	0	0	0	20
11. Punjab	1	3	0	0	4	12	8	4	0	24	30	2	4	0	36	878	35	6	20	939
12. Pondicherry	1	0	0	0	1	1	0	0	0	1	0	0	0	0	0	0	0	0	0	0
13. Rajasthan	3	4	2	2	11	4	5	8	1	18	1	4	0	2	7	70	2	10	10	92
14. Tamil Nadu	2	0	0	0	2	11	2	0	0	13	7	0	0	0	7	38	0	0	0	38

15. Tripura	3	2	0	0	5	4	4	0	0	8	2	14	0	0	16	19	14	4	0	37
16. UP (East)	2	4	5	1	12	4	0	7	1	12	0	6	18	0	24	0	17	3	0	20
17. UP (West)	3	7	0	0	10	0	7	0	0	7	0	2	0	0	2	0	15	0	0	15
18. West Bengal	2	0	0	0	2	12	0	0	0	12	8	0	0	0	8	48	0	0	0	48
Total:	41	64	40	17	162	193	187	66	33	479	187	1,204	110	108	1,609	3,049	2,413	106	86	5,654
Grand Total:	162					479					1,609					5,654				

Source: BGVS, Project Completion Report: January 1997–September 2000, New Delhi, 2001, Annexure 2.

February, 1998, 500 savings groups had been formed. Each member had saved an average of Rs 100, while the total collection had been about rupees nine lakh.

The Poduppulakshmi programme in Nellore district, Andhra Pradesh, began in 1992 after the anti-arrack agitation of the literacy campaign. Women of one small village were inspired to launch a blockade against arrack in their village. The struggle soon spread to the district and the state leading to the declaration of prohibition. The SHGs that followed were run with the help of teachers and Anganwadi workers under the auspices of the District Rural Development Agency (DRDA). Two lakh women were enrolled in 6,980 savings groups. Each woman saved a rupee a day and made weekly deposits. Rupees 13 crore had been saved. About 400 groups had sought loans from financial institutions for economic activities.

During the post-literacy phase of the literacy campaign in Madurai district, Tamil Nadu, 836 groups with 13,000 members were formed by 1998. Rupees 26,000 were collected at the district level every year. Each member saved Rs 10 or Rs 20 depending on capacity. Some of the groups had moved into production of items such as cleaning powder, spices, pickles, jam and ink. In some villages, the groups had undertaken to run ration shops at fair prices and canteens.

The Mazdoor Kisan Shakti Sangathan (MKSS) of Rajasthan is an organization working with poor farmers. Some of the activities emerging from the savings movement were the running of fair price shops and small production units. These cooperative societies provided a forum for discussion and intervention on issues concerning education, health and gender justice.

A number of Tamil Nadu districts consolidated the formation and networking of women's savings groups during this period. An important feature of these groups was that they considered themselves as a women's movement, undertaking savings as one of their activities. The MALAR group of Kanyakumari district is an important example and will be discussed separately (Chapter 9, Section 3). Samata in Andhra Pradesh undertook a valiant, though unsuccessful, mobilization against the efforts of the state government to lift prohibition which was promulgated as a result of the efforts of the women of Andhra Pradesh, especially of Nellore district. Saharsa district in Bihar experienced a major mobilization of women from backward communities.

In the year 1998 Samata regional workshops were held in May and July. A total number of 7,500 Samata Vigyan Utsavas were conducted by October, 1999, reaching out to around two lakh women (BGVS, October 1999). Eighteen states in all were involved in the various programmes organized under the banner of Samata between January 1997 to September 2000. The BGVS data in the Table 4.1 would suggest that 1998 was the high point in terms of number of Samata related activities at the state (162), district (479), block (1,609) and village (5,654) levels, gradually fading out over the years 1999 and 2000. Of the 18 states that participated, the ones in which more than 200 activities were held at the village level during the period January 1997 to September 2000, were the following in order of significance: Kerala, Bihar, Haryana, Punjab, Andhra Pradesh, Himachal Pradesh and Assam.

Some of the weaknesses identified during the conduct of the Utsavas were the lack of adequate numbers of resource persons with organizational skills, inadequate coordination between BGVS organization and the Samata groups, and the lack of proper follow-up plans. A major Samata national workshop on the linkages between PL, CE and the women's small savings movement was held at Nagercoil from January 10–14, 1999, to learn from the experience of the MALAR savings movement in Kanyakumari district. Close to a 100 women activists participated in this seven-day workshop.

By February, 2002, Samata had spread to about 6,000 villages as a result of sustained efforts over the years since 1993. Samata jathas in around 1,500 points, Samata Vigyan Utsavs in over 8,000 villages and more than 8,000 SHGs in 500 blocks of 14 states contributed to this spread. Efforts were being made to establish linkages between Samata and other women's groups/organizations beyond the network of the PSMs within particular states. Issues such as violence against women, women's rights, right to information served as a binding thread with other organizations in joint mobilizations. The challenges, as seen in the report to the General Council of February, 2002, were to consolidate the network, develop the capacities of the members of the different groups and to reach out further to weaker sections (BGVS, February 2002: 1). Table 4.2, based on available data, suggests that there were in all 9,794 Samata SHGs in at least 72 districts, 259 blocks and 4,298 villages, of 14 states. Tamil Nadu/Pondicherry, Bihar/Jharkhand, Assam and Madhya Pradesh/Chhattisgarh head the list having the largest number of such groups.

TABLE 4.2 *Samata SHGs in States, 2002*

	State	*District*	*Blocks Covered*	*Village Covered*	*No. of Groups*
1.	Assam	NA	NA	NA	2,000
2.	Andhra Pradesh	1	2	NA	150
3.	Bihar/Jharkhand	13	87	1,186	2,035
4.	Haryana	3	3	4	4
5.	Himachal Pradesh	2	15	432	600
6.	Karnataka	NA	NA	NA	100
7.	Kerala	NA	NA	NA	200
8.	Maharashtra	7	7	13	39
9.	Madhya Pradesh/ Chhattisgarh	17	24	386	1,082
10.	Orissa	7	10	219	804
11.	Punjab	1	1	2	2
12.	Rajasthan	3	3	26	48
13.	Tamil Nadu/Pondicherry	13	100	2,000	2,700
14.	Uttar Pradesh/Uttaranchal	5	7	30	30
	Total	72	259	4,298	9,794

Source: BGVS General Council Meeting, Dhanbad, February, 2002.

Note: NA = Data not available.

Neelam Devi is a 48-year-old widow, landless resident of village Hawidih, Baheri block, Darbhanga district, Bihar. She was earlier illiterate but started studying during the literacy campaign. Later, she herself became a convener of the village committee, the panchayat and the regional committee. She gradually acquired a command over reading and writing.

After undergoing training for Self-Help Groups (SHG), she formed one and became its Secretary. Savings were regular. She also undertook training for sewing and embroidery. She got a loan from the bank and started a small enterprise. She has also trained a number of women and the process is still going on. She purchases cloth from the wholesale market and sells readymade clothing. Presently, there are three persons who sell her clothing from door to door. She earns about rupees four to five thousand per month and looks after four children. One daughter has been married. With this saving from her income she has formed 42 SHGs within five panchayats till the present, and is a leader of the federation of SHGs.

(Edited from BGVS, SDTT Project 2004–08, 2008: 24)

By 2005, the Samata SHGs had risen in number to more than 25,000 units with several independent district level federations, their own offices, training centres and monthly newsletters. Reporting in 2005, the report of the Secretary to the BGVS General Council states:

> "The Samata Self-Help Groups are unique since they are not linked to governmental schemes, bank loans or other forms of stereotyped notions of micro-credit schemes, and have a self-reliant structure with full-timers. They are consciously involved in women's empowerment and are not mere saving and lending groups. While that makes them unique, it also renders them somewhat fragile to a host of external competitions and threats" (BGVS, 2005: 14).

Our observations in the field would suggest that this was true to a great extent. Undoubtedly, the Samata SHGs were facing competition from project funded micro-credit groups sponsored by governments, banks and international agencies. Attempts were made to develop a community solidarity, autonomy and a critical perspective through training programmes, regular meetings and a wider solidarity in the form of district level federations among the SHGs sponsored by BGVS in order to counter the wider threat:

> "The other important difference is that official SHGs remain merely micro-credit initiatives. The Samata SHGs by design are larger women's collectives where social, cultural and political perspectives are imbued both at the perspective and action levels through trainings, jathas, etc., Samata SHG women are involved in issues of education of children, health and panchayat issues as well" (BGVS, August 2006: 9).

By 2008, the Samata groups had moved beyond economic savings for domestic purposes into social, cultural and even political processes. Initial loans that were taken were generally for the following purposes: to repay debts from the money lenders, medical purposes, children's education, birth of a child, marriages and festival occasions. The loans were gradually moving into the area of economic enterprise in order to enhance the value of production in existing occupations, group enterprises and opening small shops. Some of these activities were agriculture, food production, crafts, medicines, garments, pickles, umbrella making, bakery and cloth weaving. It was reported, and our observations suggested, that in most cases the status of women within the domestic sphere and the local communities had changed for the better. The limited economic independence had generated a sense of self-confidence, reinforced by the regular meetings among women and

TABLE 4.3 *Samata Activities, 2008*

State	*Total RP Training*	*Total Vocational/ Entrepreneur Training*	*Total Parti-cipants*	*Samata Vachan-anlya*	*Total Samata Shops*	*Total SHGs*	*District-wise Federation*	*Production Activities*
1. Assam	8	9	1,050	–	26	3,124	Prochesta State Federation	–Weaving, designing, development and production centre at Chadarpur of Kamrup –Bamboo work –Tailoring -Craft making
2. Bihar	22	15	1,225	56	5	3,305	AWARD Nawada MASKAS Kairmur SAMBAL Begusarai Sakhi Madhepura SAMMA Saharsa	–Sattu –Bakery –Cloth whitener ink (neel) –Juices
3. Chhattisgarh	2	–	86	16	20	620		–Rice collection and selling –Bamboo work –Fisheries
4. Haryana	5	4	348	14		14		–Running small grocery shops –Tailoring
5. Himachal Pradesh	5	6	580	2,663	2	3,000	MASHAL Mandi	–Sale of inner wear –Preservation of fruits and vegetables and sale -Ladies purses, sweaters, school bags -Vermi composting–preparation and sale

6. Jharkhand	16	8	1,048	–	–	–		–Papad making –Canteen –Small grocery shops
7. Karnataka	2	10	656	12		307	Belur-Hasan	–Readymade garments –Papad making and selling –Tea powder –Herbal medicines, oil, pain killers –Candle making –Turmeric –Shaking powder, Vermi compost
8. Madhya Pradesh	14	12	1,907	22	12	1,118	AWAZ Jhabua Riyadarshani Chindwara Samridhi Bhind	–Pickles, spices –Purses, bags –Tribal art and craft –Soap making –Flour mill –Vermi compost –Midday meal
9. Maharashtra	2	6	306	10	–	65	SAMATA Beed	–Soap making –Running small shops
10. Orissa	4	17	768	–	2	1,498	SAPNA Jagatsinghpura, Jharsuguda, SAMATA Bargarh	–Dairy development –Fishery –Goat –Grocery –Fodder and cultivating –Food processing –Rice and vegetable market –Weaving

Cont'd...

Cont'd…

11.	Pondicherry	20	45	2,745	–	30	–	SAMAM	–Agriculture –Fishery
12.	Punjab	1	1	72	–	–	–		–Fodder and cultivating –Rice and vegetable market
13.	Rajasthan	12	16	888	39	2	162	Baran in Process	–Agriculture –Dari and galicha –Garment exporting and designing –Accessories making
14.	Tamil Nadu	45	75	5,184	4	–	5,500	MALAR THILUR	–Soap making –Food processing –Pickles –Tailoring
15.	Tripura	5	29	2,329	50	22	2,700		–Tailoring; Readymade garments –Fishery, Pulses –Running canteen, Barber work
16.	Uttarakhand	9	1	611	–	–	116	Pithoraghar, Chamoli	–Tailoring centre in Haridwar and Chamoli
17.	Uttar Pradesh	14	30	1,840	70	13	221	ASTHA Sultanpur MUMTAZ Alighar SAKAR Ghazipur Sarigarh Raibarlly	
	Total	186	284	21,643	2,956	134	21,750		

Source: BGVS, General Council Meeting, Tirupati, July 21–22, 2008: 51–53.

the discussions of social issues. The groups generally had a multi-caste character within which they mixed freely and occasionally ate together. In many states such as Madhya Pradesh, Bihar, Jharkhand, Rajasthan and Himachal Pradesh group members had stood for panchayat elections and won (BGVS, August 2006: 10–11).

Table 4.3 suggests that there were 21,750 SHGs covering 17 states by 2008. A total of 186 training programmes for resource persons had been held and 284 such programmes to promote entrepreneurship development in defined vocational spheres. A range of production activities that were locally relevant had been initiated. Apart from sponsoring women for workshops related to vocational skills conducted by other organizations, Samata had opened training centres at Chandrapur, Kamrup district, Assam in weaving and designing and a women's enterprise at Jaipur, Rajasthan for garment manufacturing and export. About 134 Samata shops were providing outlets for the different products produced in Samata groups, apart from taking advantage of fairs organized by state governments and the local markets. About 2,956 libraries had been established. Most of the SHGs had been federated at the district level, thus providing a wider solidarity and organizational base for influencing local self-governing systems.

An attempt was made to converge the health-related interventions of BGVS with the SHGs. Towards this, a national workshop was held in Hyderabad followed by state and district workshops. The SHGs and their federations have been involved in the campaign for a relevant Micro Finance Bill together with other organizations like Nirantar, AIDWA and NFIW. Around 1,700 members of different SHGs participated in a national convention held in Delhi followed by a rally culminating at Jantar Mantar, Delhi (BGVS, 2008: 24). Major activities that have converged around the SHGs, other than those directly related to savings and the utilization of these funds, have been NREGA, the mid-day meal scheme under ICDS, the initiation of libraries and wall papers. Women health activists have taken an active part in the local committees in the states of Uttarakhand, Tamil Nadu, Uttar Pradesh and Bihar. Some of the challenges faced by the Samata network, as mentioned in the document above, were fostering micro enterprises as a means to women's empowerment in all spheres of life and providing technology and marketing support.

5

The Literacy to Health Project

1. An Overview

The Literacy to Health Project (LHP) was initially funded by the Ministry of Health and Family Welfare. It was one of the activities initiated by the BGVS in 1993 where literacy was attempted to be broadened out into a wider developmental agenda. The LHP, in fact, was a continuation of the health programme of AIPSN. Prior to the formation of the BGVS, health had been one of the critical areas of intervention undertaken by individual state contingents of the PSM (BGVS, 'Note on Perspective Programme of BGVS/AIPSN', 1994). The more specific objectives of LHP of the BGVS were "to use health education inputs as a part of TL-PL-CE programmes, to improve child health status in a measurable manner and to intervene in women's health issues" (BGVS, 2001: 21). With these objectives in view, the health sub-committee, in consultation with the BGVS state units, identified a number of districts where the LHP could be launched with the help of literacy activists and the local community.

A LHP national workshop was organized during January 23–25, 1992, at New Delhi. Around 30 health professionals, most of whom were actively involved in the literacy campaigns and other PSM activities, participated. The meeting discussed approaches to integrating health with the PL-CE programme for measurable improvement in health parametres such as total immunization, safe drinking water and sanitation. Later on, planning workshops were held in Lucknow and Delhi during September 16–18, 1993. These workshops helped in finalizing a set of guidelines for implementation at the state level. The following steps were planned in each district (BGVS, 2001: 21):

- Formation of a district level Literacy to Health core group.
- Training of the Literacy to Health core group.
- Identification and training of the village health activists.
- Environment creation for ensuring community participation in the programme.
- Health survey in selected villages.
- Preparation of the Village Health Register.
- Awareness-building and health education campaigns through health booklets prepared for neo-literates.
- Preparation and implementation of People's Health Plan for the village/gram panchayat.

The LHP was implemented in two phases: Phase I from March 1994 to December 1995 and Phase II from January 1996 onwards.

Phase 1: March 1994 to December 1995

The Ministry of Health and Family Welfare sanctioned the LHP in December, 1993, for implementation in 20 districts. The actual implementation of the first phase of LHP was initiated in March, 1994. The emphasis during this phase was on health communication, participation, health survey and local level planning. An extensive health education campaign was implemented in 15 districts all over the country with a focus on Sampark Andolans (contact movement) which was implemented through village level group discussions and kalajathas centred around core messages expressed in 15 booklets. The districts undertaking this campaign were Madhepura, Jehanabad, Nawadah, Begusarai and Bhabua in Bihar; Chamoli in Uttar Pradesh; Mandi in Himachal; Rohtak in Haryana; Bilaspur in Madhya Pradesh; Kurnool and Nellore in Andhra; Ganjam in Orissa; Ramnathpuram and North Arcot in Tamil Nadu; Bankura in West Bengal (BGVS, February 1998: Annexure 4). A Literacy to Health workshop was held during February 9–11, 1995 at Nellore. In this workshop, the experiences of the LHP were reviewed and discussions were held to explore the possibility of extending the LHP to other parts of the country. Around 60 activists and doctors from different states participated in the workshop. They were trained in undertaking health education programmes and formulating local level health intervention programmes in TL-PL districts (BGVS, 1996: 3). The first phase of the LHP was to have concluded in December, 1995. In most districts, however, this work was continued for at least one more year.

Phase 2: January 1996 onwards

The second phase proposed 'intensive work going beyond health education to health interventions' in eight districts (BGVS, February 1998: Annexure 4). Projects were submitted to the Ministry of Health from these districts. It was proposed to be a phase 'for deeper interventions' including: (i) training of health activists, (ii) operationalization of panchayat level action plans, (iii) local level monitoring, (iv) surveillance of health status and maternal and child health, (v) bringing about measurable improvements in child health through health education and better utilization of existing primary health centre services. In each of the districts selected for the phase two programme, field level work was planned to be taken up in 10 to 20 gram panchayats. Nellore district was, however, already in the midst of a 400 village Arogya Deepam Programme. Work was newly initiated in Baran district in Rajasthan. During the year 1996, a number of national sub-committee meetings, workshops and seminars were held including a meet arranged by the National Institute of Health and Family Welfare (NIHFW), New Delhi. In November, 1996, Project BGVS 1997–98 (Mass Literacy Campaigns, Post-Literacy and Continuing Education, Health and Development) was submitted to the Project Advisory Committee (PAC) of the NLMA. The project proposed LHP in 20 selected districts (BGVS, February 1998: 28).

A 'Literacy to Health: Review-cum-Planning' workshop was held at Rohtak during January 14–15, 1997. The workshop reviewed the experience of ongoing LHPs in Ramnathpuram (Tamil Nadu); Jehanabad, Madhepura (Bihar) and worked out plans for extending the programme to other states. Around 40 participants from 10 states participated.

Until January, 1997, full-fledged activities under the phase two LHP were implemented only in four districts of Tamil Nadu and two districts of Bihar. Not much was achieved in terms of health programmes and activities in the remaining LHP districts. Other than that, the health resource persons who were developed by that time were utilized in Samata and other BGVS programmes.

The limited coverage has been attributed to the failure in sanction of the second phase programme by the Ministry of Health and Family Welfare. There had been changes in officers at the ministry and the original commitment to follow the first phase of health education by a second phase of health intervention could no longer be tenable. The ministry, however, sanctioned this second phase for the district of

Ramanthapuram in Tamil Nadu. A year later, a similar project was sanctioned for Vellore district by the Department of Science and Technology (DST) under its Science and Technology for Women scheme. And another year later, three districts in Bihar got funding support from UNICEF for this programme.

The possibility of conducting this phase with funds available under the budgetary head of Literacy to Health of the BGVS project sponsored by the Ministry of Human Resource Development (MHRD) was explored. There were three problems with this. Firstly, the funds required for the eight districts were considerably more than what BGVS had. Secondly, the funds were for a health education programme and its use for a health intervention programme could not be clinched satisfactorily within the BGVS. And thirdly, this initiative had to be launched at a time when funding from MHRD itself was uncertain and the release of the grant had been considerably delayed. A decision was taken to use a smaller level of funds to continue the first phase activities in these 10 districts hoping for eventual sanction of the second phase from one or other source. This strategy worked for Bihar and Tamil Nadu where UNICEF funding took over, but it had to be allowed to peter out in the remaining districts as no funds could be secured. The lack of a full-time team or coordinator in Delhi following up funding or giving the extra push needed for a programme to continue, voluntarily contributed to the eventual dying out of this initiative in many districts (BGVS, February 1998: Annexure 4).

A national workshop on 'Literacy to Health' was held at Pune during July 2–5, 1998. In this four-day workshop, 22 activists from Haryana, Karnataka, Maharashtra, Rajasthan, Tamil Nadu and Tripura participated and discussed the overall strategy for the second phase of Literacy to Health. The major outcome of the workshop was "... a commitment to initiate block level programmes, one each in Haryana, Karnataka, Maharashtra, Rajasthan and Tripura in the next six months" (BGVS, October 1999: 9).

A provision was made for the LHP in the BGVS project 1997–98 for some work that was to be done in 1998. However, due to various reasons such as raising objections and seeking of clarifications by MHRD on certain items in the proposal, the sanction and payment of grants was delayed. Eventually, the second phase did not take off fully by the end of 1998 (BGVS, February 1998: Annexure 4 and BGVS, 2001: 22). The exceptions to this, however, were the states of Tamil Nadu, Bihar and, much later, Uttar Pradesh. The Tamil Nadu BGVS/Tamil Nadu Science Forum (TNSF) extended its LHP to one more district in 1996 with the help of the Department of Health and Family Welfare and Tamil Nadu State Government, another district with the help of DST in 1997, and in 1999 it extended the programme to seven districts with the help of UNICEF. Bihar Gyan Vigyan Samiti was able to implement the second phase of its LHP with the help of the UNICEF. The UNICEF also supported BGVS, Uttar Pradesh to undertake a major People's Health Awareness Campaign (BGVS, February 1998: Annexure 4). In 2001, a massive programme of the second phase type was launched in two districts, Rae Bareilly and Pithoragarh.

The People's Health Assembly (PHA), 2000

In October 1999, the BGVS was approached for its active involvement in the PHA that was planned to be organized in Dhaka in December, 2000. The assembly was being organized by several people's health groups and coordinated by Gana Swasthya Kendra, Bangladesh. The main objective of the assembly was "to critically assess, from the point of the people, the achievements and shortfalls of the Health for All by 2000 target" set at the Alma Ata Declaration. This was discussed in the BGVS General Council meeting held at Bhubaneshwar on October 28 and 29, 1999. The General Council resolved that the BGVS should fully participate in the PHA programme. It was also proposed in the meeting that "a number of programmes like a series of block, district and state seminars on chosen people's health topics, kalajathas to focus on the present state of health, a national health assembly at Calcutta preceding the Dhaka International Assembly, an Indo-Bangladesh joint kalajatha may be organized by the BGVS-PSM groups" (BGVS, February 2000: 12).

The BGVS played a major contributory role in setting up a national coordination committee of 18 national networks – all those who had been active in the area of health policy or community health action. In the course of the year 2000, with no central funding whatsoever, the programme was able to reach out to over a 1,000 blocks, spread over 300 districts of the country. In each of these blocks, the basic issues that the campaign addressed could be explained and by the process of surveys and conventions the concerns were contextualized.

The process of selecting delegates to attend the state, national and international conferences of the PHA served to consolidate the process of identifying a leadership for advocacy and community level action in health. State teams emerged for health action, which so far had not happened in those states, where funding was not available. The BGVS which had hitherto mostly worked in isolation from other NGOs and

TABLE 5.1 *People's Health Assembly (PHA) Activities and BGVS, 2000*

	BGVS	*State Convention*	*No. of Delegates*		*No. of Districts Covered*	*PHA–Books/ Posters/ Booklets*	*Other Major Activities*	*No. of Collaborating Organizations*
			Calcutta	*Dhaka*				
1.	Andhra Pradesh	12th November 2000	160	6	17	*PHA books in Telugu *Thirty Posters *PHS booklet on drugs *Developed three formats for: 1. Mandal level enquiry 2. Group discussion 3. Village level door to door survey	*Two-day district level workshop in seventeen districts *Local enquiry in 410 villages (100 mandals) *30,000 women were interviewed (including children under five years) *10,000 deliveries were studied *Three State level workshops *National level workshop (Hyderabad)	7
2.	Assam	19th November 2000	76	5	12	*PHA pamphlets	*Three State level workshops *Four Health awareness melas *Health survey form (distributed) *Training: at district, block and Panchayat level *10 District health charters *Letters to doctors	24
3.	Bihar	19th November 2000	190	8	22	*PHA Hindi brochure *Training handbook *Four set posters *Developed four formats for: 1. District level interviews 2. Mandal level interviews 3. PHC level interviews 4. Village level enquiries	*State level policy dialogue *Health Jatha (Nine district level) *Cycle march (Nine district level) *Protest rally (Ten district level) *Seminar (Seven district level) *Seminar (One state level) *District conventions *Block conventions *100 Block level workshops	24

Cont'd…

Cont'd…

4.	Haryana	1st November 2000	70	6	8	*Book on female feticide	*National workshop on female feticide *Five district level seminar on health for all *Eight district level workshop *Block audit in each district	20
5.	Himachal Pradesh	16th November 2000	82	6	–	*Four PHA books in Hindi *Five Health books	*District level seminar and workshops (July) *Block level health seminars (September) *District level health assembly (October) *State level health assembly (November) *PHA Kala Jatha	–
6.	Karnataka	26–27 November 2000	180	–	20	–	*Five Kalajatha teams	–
7.	Kerala	15th November 2000	98	7	–	*PHA books in Malayalam	–	–
8.	Madhya Pradesh	26–27th November 2000	70	7	17	*PHA Hindi brochure *Training handbook *Four set posters *News bulletin *Jan Swasthya Samvad	*Two Regional workshops *17 district level workshops *20 two block level workshops *Village level enquiries	–

9.	Maharashtra	18–19th November 2000	75	8	15	*PHA books in Marathi *Posters, etc.	*Three state level workshops *15 district level workshops *42 village level health dialogue *Health march from Pimpri-Nigdi (Pune) *Health slide shows *Four health dialogue	44
10.	Orissa	11th November 2000	160	10	25	*PHA books in Oriya *Five PHA posters *Newsletters "Dear Dr–Dear Patient" *Audio cassettes on health *State health status report	*Six zonal level meetings *25 district level workshops *Three district level training camps for trainers *One block level training camp *Six "block health enquiry"	18
11.	Pondicherry	12th November 2000	60	3	5	–	*Five Kalajatha teams were trained *Kalajatha teams covered 25 districts of Tamil Nadu	16
12.	Punjab	–	20	–	–	–	–	–
13.	Rajasthan	27–28th November 2000	72	3	11	*PHA booklets *Posters *Phad (banner) writing by neo-literates	*11 district level workshops *Three state level workshops *Village level enquiries	10
14.	Tamil Nadu	26th November 2000	150	20	25	*PHA books in Tamil *Posters *Booklets	*Kalajatha *Poster campaigns *Despatch of Dear Dr Letters *25 district conventions *Hundreds of block conventions, meetings, etc.	30

Cont'd...

Cont'd…

15.	Tripura	–	70	7	–	–	–	–
16.	Uttar Pradesh	26–27th November 2000	82	6	28	*PHA Hindi books *Posters *Booklets etc.…	*Nine district level workshops *Panchayat level Jan Adalats *Block level PHAs *Regional workshop (entire state was divided into eight regions)	137

PHA Activities in Delhi:

* Health Mela
* Signature campaign
* PHA rally from Feroz Shah Kotla to Lal Quila via Daryaganj
* Jhanki
* Eighteen organizations joined in the rally
* Press conference and press release

PHA activities in Gujarat:

*75 delegates participated in the National PHA, Calcutta

Source: BGVS General Council Meeting, Dhanbad, February, 2002.

other peoples movements, learnt to work as part of a coordinated strategy with a number of NGOs and social movements.

Table 5.1 presents a picture of the process as it got consolidated by the time of the General Council Meeting of the BGVS in February, 2002. In all 16 states were covered through a process that included state conventions, district level mobilization and meetings, awareness generation through various publications, surveys at the village level, training programmes and charters of demands. The PHA also served to network with several other organizations working in the sphere of health. Mobilizations at the village, district and state levels were followed up by a national level convention in Kolkata and the PHA at Dhaka.

2. LHP: Organization and Intervention

Organizational Structure for LHP

A national level BGVS/AIPSN health sub-committee had been formed which provided overall supervision to the LHP programme. This committee coordinated the national level health activities and was also involved in developing active state level committees. At the district level, there were district committees constituted of volunteers. The functions of most state offices were to help develop the district organizations, promote sharing of experience among them and coordinate with the centre. They also played a major role in explaining the programme to officials and political figures at the state and district level. The state coordinators also helped state and NLMA officials as well as the collectors as literacy consultants. Most of the workshops, meetings, conventions, etc., held at the state level and in districts were directly organized by the state level functionaries, i.e., by the state coordinators in their role as consultants, with the national centre playing only a coordinating role. Even in planning future programmes, the state committees decided the actual programmes within the agreed framework, with the national centre playing only an advisory role (BGVS, 1989–93: 8).

Project Inputs

Workshops, orientations and trainings were organized at the national, state and district level from time to time. Activities such as key resource persons' camps, lectures, training camps, women's workshops, post-literacy workshops and MIS workshops were organized from time to time within states, at the regional levels and at district levels. The following activities were organized, particularly at the state level:

(a) *Regular training and review workshops held along with field visits:* This was the most important activity through which capability-building in the BGVS took place.

(b) *Special orientation programmes were conducted for the doctors:* These were conducted on topics such as: Health policy and economic policies, resurgence of infectious diseases, privatization of health care, drug policy and rational drug use, understanding the medical profession (professional problems), and community and panchayat initiative to improve health care. The doctors who were oriented in these camps were able to help as resource persons/or in work amongst doctors.

(c) *Publications and production of reading/training material:* A set of 15 books was published for the neo-literates. These books contained simple messages on common health problems of individuals, families as well as communities. Due consideration was given to the specific health needs of women. The books covered the following topics:

1. "Why Do We Become Sick?" – a basic introduction to understanding what health and disease are.
2. "Water Borne Disease" – explains how the commonest diseases, i.e., water-borne diseases spread.
3. "How to Make Drinking Water Safe" – a-do-it-yourself approach to family level and community level intervention for safe drinking water.
4. "Sanitation Waste to Wealth" – a community level approach to sanitation.
5. "Of Darkness and Light" – a poetic appeal against child marriage and marriage of girls before they are 18.
6. "Preparing for the New Arrival" – on antenatal care.
7. "Women's Health and Women's Rights" – a primer on how patriarchy is the major cause of women's ill-health.
8. "We Can Choose" – a book on family planning that does not recommend family size, but which rearticulates contraception knowledge as empowerment and provides basic information.
9. "Our Body, Ourselves" – an introduction to the human body.
10. "One Magical Morning" – a popular skit on male and community responsibility in pregnancy and child care.

11. "Mysteries of Adolescence" – this book alone in this series is taken from the VHAI publication.
12. "The Child Must Survive: Nutrition" – key messages to prevent child malnutrition and child deaths.
13. "The Child Must Survive: Immunization"
14. "The Child Must Survive: Diarrhoea" – both prevention and management at family and community level are discussed.
15. "The Child Must Survive Coughs and Colds" – an introduction to preventing mortality from acute respiratory infections (BGVS, 1994).

These books were meant for mass circulation, for reading to groups, for reading by neo-literate and, last but not the least, for adaptation to street plays and songs – a large number of which were scripted and performed

Punam Devi is from Baank village, Begusarai district, Bihar. She is thirty-two years old. She is married and has five children. Punam Devi belongs to the Dalit community and works as an agricultural labourer. She participated as a learner in the village total literacy campaign and post-literacy programme.

When Punam initially joined the literacy centre, regular attendance was difficult due to her workload at home and in the fields. But with consistent motivation from the literacy volunteer, she became a regular participant at the post-literacy centre. During the post-literacy programme, she became aware about the Government Act concerning equal wages for men and women. She completed four primers as a part of the total literacy and post-literacy programmes. Today, she writes letters to her husband, Braham Deo, who has migrated to Lakhimpur (Assam) for work. She also signs her name for the money orders.

Punam said that she came to know, through the post-literacy programme, that there is an Auxiliary Nurse Midwife (ANM) in the village who is supposed to come to the village on a daily basis, but does not. Through the post-literacy programme she has joined a saving and credits group named Sambal. Punam is now the president of one Sambal group.

Today, she is actively involved in encouraging parents to enroll their children in schools, in providing assistance during immunization camps and in mobilizing other women in her community to learn to read and write and join self-help groups.

(Edited from BGVS, January 2002: 131)

in all these districts. These 15 books were designed as a minimum essential health knowledge package that every adult in society must know. The topics also reflected government priority areas where there were existing projects that people could better utilize. The central Ministry of Health also stepped in to print thousands of these booklets for circulation in the states in five different languages.

For the second phase, in addition to the above, a series of training manuals of five parts called the "Peoples Initiatives for Primary Health Care" were planned of which four parts were published (as three books) in English. They were Health Campaign Guide Book (2,000 copies) book 1: Addressing Women and Child Health Needs (2,000 copies); book 2: Village Medical Kit and First Aid (2,000 copies); Books 4 and 5 as Book 3: on the control of communicable disease ran out of funds, though its text was ready and was in use in all training camps. Placing health on the Panchayat Agenda was the trainers guide published for the first phase.

3. The Case of Tamil Nadu and Bihar States

A brief account of the LHP implemented during the second phase in the two states which had remained active during this phase beyond 1998 is given below. This section is drawn largely from the BGVS Annual Report, February 7–8, 1998: Annexure 4.

1. The objectives of the programme were:
   - Improving the health of people by better utilization of government services and by the community's self-help efforts. This involved both health education and also a special focus on child health,
   - Expanding Samata women's empowerment activities and organization in a sustainable manner,
   - Meaningful intervention in panchayats,
   - Promoting policy level health changes by improving understanding of health policy and sensitizing all concerned sections in this effort.
2. The organizational aspects of the programme were:
   - Training and developing support for a cadre of totally voluntary health activists – one for each village necessarily women.
   - One full-time trainer or high quality part-time person to provide support/training to every 10 health activists (to cover a cluster of 10 villages).

- Regular maintenance of a Village Health Register, that identified children at risk and kept track of vital health data and which could be used for assessing what impact the health programme had made.
- Periodic environment-building activities built around health programme events.
- Active planned sensitization and involvement of elected panchayat leaders.
- A proper mix of community level intervention organized by the health team with regular family level visits and interventions done by the health activist herself.
- Fresh approaches were sought in specific areas of health care such as: child health, women's health, TB and leprosy control, immunization, provision of emergency/basic first-aid and curative services.

The coverage in Tamil Nadu was 60 villages in Ramnad district (4 blocks), 60 villages in Vellore district (2 blocks), 20 villages in Virudhunagar district (1 block) and 10 villages in Pudukottai district (in 1 block).

The proposed plan of expansion in Tamil Nadu was to cover 60 villages each in nine blocks of five districts – Buvanagiri in Cuddalore district; Anaicut in Vellore district; Andipatti in Theni district; Kariapatti, Watrap and Tiruchuli in Virudunagar district; Sakkotai in Sivaganagai district. Based on voluntarism and internally generated resources, the programme was to be sustained in the earlier blocks as well as expanded to 60 villages in Kanyakumari district linked to women credit groups. In addition to the health programme, regular seminar/hall meetings were organized at the state and district levels, as also publication and sales of materials on health policy. The proposed coverage in Bihar was 40 villages of Jehanabad district, about 5 villages of Madhepura district and 5 villages in Dhanbad.

It is very clearly set out in the programme objectives that the programme did not aim at duplicating the existing government health programmes, but it would complement them through a sustainable organization of people for participation and self-help. Programme objectives also reflect a commitment to strengthen the involvement of the local self-governing bodies, i.e., the gram panchayats in their role in people's health. The programme activities, therefore, revolved around capacity-building of volunteers – 'necessarily women', trainers and panchayat leaders. The programme also included improved community level health interventions by the health teams including those by the health activists.

4. Some General Issues and Reflections

From the various annual reports submitted by the BGVS to its General Council, a broad assessment can be made of the direction within which LHP has progressed and the outcome of the process of implementation in terms of the organization of the programme.

The LHP seems to have made rapid progress during the first phase. The first phase was taken up and implemented with much enthusiasm in most of the targeted districts. The momentum it generated and successes it achieved in the initial few districts (10) led to some more districts (10) being taken up. The depth of coverage in this phase was variable. All districts had one or more rounds of volunteer training, kalajathas and health education campaigns. However, only eight districts completed the process of conducting surveys and evolving participatory action plans in the village. According to the BGVS Annual Report, December 11–12, 1995, encouraged by the outcome of the first phase in the first round of districts, there were nearly 16 new districts which had come forward and shown willingness to take up the first phase programmes. These districts were to be considered in the second round of first phase projects. These were: Morigaon and Dhemaji (Assam); Solan, Kulu, Sirmour and Chamba (Himachal Pradesh); three districts from Bihar; one district of Orissa; rural Bangalore and Tumkur (Karnataka); two districts of Punjab; Datia (Madhya Pradesh); and Pauri (West Uttar Pradesh) (BGVS, 1995: 25). Though the trainings for many of these districts for a first phase programme were completed, due to lack of sanction of these districts by the Ministry of Health programme the planned expansion did not occur.

While the second phase programme made a staggered progress due to the stalling of funds from the Ministry of Human Resource Development during the initial stages, it seems to have picked up momentum in the year 1999. It is reported in the Project Completion Report 1997–2000 brought out by the BGVS in 2001 that the LHP started doing well in Jehanabad, Madhepura and Dhanbad districts of Bihar and North Arcot and Ramnathpuram districts of Tamil Nadu. It is further reported that the Village Health Registers had become operational in these districts and that the health sub-committee of the BGVS extended the programme to Maharashtra, Assam, Rajasthan, Tripura and Uttar Pradesh (West). These states had been carrying out the preliminary work in line with the planning. The LHP was visualized as linked to the pilot CE programmes. By the end of the year 2000, work was at different stages in 11 districts of nine states. Pilot programmes which were initiated at Ramanathpuram district of Tamil Nadu and Jehanabad district of Bihar made considerable progress. The LHP in these districts demonstrated that "the health awareness built upon the enthusiasm generated through literacy can lead to perceptible changes in the health indices of the concerned villages/GPs" (BGVS, 2001: 21–22). The exact level of improvement in child health and the other outcomes of this approach are part of a voluminous project outcome report submitted to the UNICEF for the seven blocks in Tamil Nadu where the programme was conducted from 1999 to 2001. The programme on the whole generated a great deal of interest and enthusiasm among the activists operating at the state level and below. The first phase programme objectives were achieved to a great extent and the second phase was beginning to show promising results.

The overall impact of the LHP can be assessed in terms of the following:

1. *Networking:* The LHP, being linked to the TL-PL-CE programme of the BGVS had a readily available network of activists, volunteers, and resource persons. It is for this reason that the state sub-committees were able to provide a sound institutional structure that was already in place for implementation of the LHP. In the absence of which the BGVS, or any organization for that matter, would not have even thought of undertaking such a mass level programme. The LHP had contributed to the strengthening of the existing volunteer network of the BGVS.
2. *Organizational capacity-building:* The numerous trainings and workshops held for activists and volunteers helped them in the acquisition of skills for implementing the programme activities such as health communication, participatory health survey and local level planning. At times the expression of needs and demands for training in technical skills related to health programmes came from the activists themselves. Towards the end of the first phase, the local activists were able to take up the programmes on their own initiative. The widely circulated 15 booklet series and the training manuals on 'Placing Health on Panchayat Agenda' were found extremely useful.
3. *Resource material:* The aforementioned set of 15 books was also produced for the neo-literates which possibly helped generate

interest among the neo-literates and sustained their motivation. A look at the titles of these books points suggests their appropriateness to the lives and needs of the neo-literates, especially the women.

4. *Arousal of interest among the state groups:* The successful implementation of the first phase programme definitely aroused the interest of other state groups. They showed their willingness to initiate the programme in their respective states while the proposal for the second phase was being planned. This demonstrates the relevance and the usefulness of the programme when implemented alongside the literacy campaigns.
5. *Increase in the level of motivation of the state groups:* It was also observed that the grassroots activists and volunteers participated in the trainings and workshops in large numbers and with great enthusiasm. In addition, they demanded more training programmes particularly in the technical aspects of the health area. On the whole, the implementation of the first phase of literacy to health activities improved the confidence and motivation of the volunteers.
6. *State initiatives in health education and community level action:* In almost all states, despite lack of funding for a second round of first phase programmes or for any second phase programmes, many initiatives in health education became possible and took place because of the capacities that were enhanced. A few major examples of these are:
   (a) In all Samata programmes, the health component was included as a central component. This was especially so in the Samata Vigyan Utsavas and later in the micro-credit networks. The health team trained for the LHP were almost invariably the resource persons for these initiatives.
   (b) In the cyclone relief programme in Orissa, the major interventions in the initial phase were in diarrhoea control. In the next year, a number of health-related interventions were launched with support from state level funding agencies, including a major campaign against heat stroke and a general health awareness campaign.
   (c) In Assam, a number of campaigns against water-borne diseases were launched both as part of their post-literacy effort and also supported by UNICEF.
   (d) In Andhra Pradesh, a round of health awareness and health education programmes, including kalajathas were conducted with state government support.

(e) In Uttar Pradesh, with WHO and UNICEF support, a number of child health awareness and health education programmes were undertaken.

(f) In Pondicherry, health and sanitation kalajathas were organized twice, in 1998 and in 2000, and in Tamil Nadu kalajathas covered over 15 districts in the year 2000.

The report of the BGVS General Council, December, 1995, also suggests that the activities in some districts were highly successful as they benefited from the infrastructural support of a large number of medical professionals associated with the programme and their organizational networks; for example, Nellore district of Tamil Nadu. While others such as North Arcot and Ranathpuraum (Tamil Nadu), Mandi (Himachal Pradesh), Chamoli (West Uttar Pradesh) achieved the programme objectives to a great extent (BGVS, December 1995: 23). As regards the core group and sub-committee functioning in the implementation of the LHP, it fared from good to very good in the states depending on TL-PL campaign capabilities of different BGVS state groups (BGVS, December 1995: 13). The project not only worked towards increasing awareness but also towards helping the neo-literate to internalize health behaviour. The project had the potential of growing into a people's organization to demand improved public health services and infrastructure.

A number of reasons contributed to the successful outcome of the first phase as compared to the slow progress of the second phase. Firstly, funding was available. Secondly, the BGVS was at that time just emerging from literacy programmes and could more readily accept a health education programme as compared to a health intervention programme. Thirdly, the resources and skills needed for the second phase programme were of a much higher order than the first phase programmes. Finally, whereas during the first phase, it was possible to learn and implement with little guidance; the second phase needed a higher quality of support and the central organizational mechanism for providing this was weak. Over a five-year period, however, many of these difficulties had become less of an obstacle.

The JSA continued over the years 2000 to 2007 with selected districts within particular states of BGVS presence taking part in various health-related advocacy activities and project implementation. The BGVS attempted to align its health-related activities with that of the National Rural Health Mission (NRHM), 2005 to 2010, one of the largest government-sponsored health programmes undertaken in independent

India. The programme covered 18 states and attempted to improve not only health services and institutions, but also to create a decentralized base of demand for health rights and entitlements. Community monitoring of health services constituted an important part of the implementation. The BGVS, with the assistance of the AIPSN was involved in Orissa, Rajasthan, Jharkhand, Madhya Pradesh, Tamil Nadu and Karnataka. An important activity was the formation of health and sanitation committees at various decentralized levels and the orientation of these committees (Gyan Vigyan Varta, March 2009: 12). In Uttarakhand, Madhya Pradesh and Jharkhand, ASHA health workers have been closely aligned with the BGVS health activities. The BGVS continued to play a major role in the People's Health Movement consisting of close to a thousand organizations in the country.

Towards the latter part of the decade, an attempt was also made to converge health-related activities with the relatively widespread network of Samata. The Second National People's Health Assembly of Jan Swasthya Abhiyan (JSA) was held in Bhopal from March 23–25, 2007. The theme was Defending People's Health in the era of globalization. More than 500 BGVS activists from 15 states participated (BGVS, 2004–08, 2008: 79). In addition, 42 organizations, movements and networks took part and the total participation was more than 2,000; half of whom were from the AIPSN-BGVS network. Several journalists, social scientists, medical personnel, politicians, government officials and policy makers were reported to have taken part in this assembly. As a prelude to the assembly, BGVS Madhya Pradesh had organized health assemblies in 10 districts and also at the state level in Bhopal during February 27–28, 2007.

A stark and disturbing conclusion that emerges from the review of the LHP is the uncertain fate of people's programmes that are largely dependent on finances from central and state governments and other external agencies. The vicissitudes of the programme are closely related to the vagaries of funding from changing governments, administrations and their ideological perspectives. The same was largely true for the programme on Natural Resource Management. This conclusion is, in some ways, quite different from the fate of programmes such as Samata and the SHGs, the Basic Education of Children, Reading and the Library movements and Publications. The latter set of programmes was in educational terms, substantively more closely related to the literacy campaigns and its participatory philosophy, was articulated with the felt needs of the major participants – women and their need for solidarity, self-confidence and relative economic independence; their children with their demand for basic education; and the adult neo-literates, educated literacy activists and literates through the formal system who responded to libraries and reading material. These factors contributed to the autonomy and the self-sustainability of the latter processes. This is not to suggest that the mere finance, management and technology dependent aspects of development interventions need not be undertaken by people's organizations, but only to draw attention to the conflicts and predicaments that are implicit in these processes. These mobilizations are perhaps more amenable to and interface better with government and people's 'institutions' in the formal sense of the term, rather than taking the expression of people's 'organization' formations.

6

Literacy and the Basic Education of Children, Reading and Social Awareness

In this chapter, we would be covering several activities of the BGVS related to the basic education of children: The Joy of Learning (JoL) Campaign, the Cosmic Voyage Programme and the Jeevanshala (the NFE/UEE projects). We would also be covering the mobilizations towards social awareness and the spread of learning such as the Jan Vachan Andolan (JVA, the People's Reading Movement) towards setting up libraries and the several publications brought out at the national and state levels of the BGVS in relation to the literacy campaign and other related programmes. The rationale for this approach is that it covers the basic educational needs of children and the general concerns for critical social awareness of adults, within the broader meaning of adult education.

1. Joy of Learning (JoL) Campaign, 1994, Cosmic Voyage, 1995 and Other Astronomical Events

Two important events that formed the context for BGVS involvement in the Universalization of Elementary Education (UEE) were the Nine Country Summit for Education for All (EFA) held at New Delhi in December, 1994 and the initiation of the District Primary Education Programme (DPEP) in several states. Earlier in 1992, BGVS had organized a ten-day national workshop at the National Council for Education Research and Training (NCERT), New Delhi, on the Universalization of Elementary Education (UEE) in collaboration with the Ministry of Human Resource Development (MHRD). Several strategies for the basic education of children were outlined during this workshop. It was clear that while the literacy campaigns created a demand for basic education for children, the very objectives of the former could not be met without attention to the latter. The 42nd round of the National Sample Survey (NSS) had shown that a major factor for school drop-outs was the quality of education and the pedagogical processes in the classroom which led to disinterest among the learners. It was felt that a participatory, campaign mode would stimulate the interest of children and would motivate parents towards sending children to school. Organizations like the KSSP, Eklavya, other members of the AIPSN and of the BGVS had been involved in elementary education and non-formal education (NFE) earlier. The need to involve the gram panchayats in the schooling systems was also felt.

The JoL project planned to launch the campaign in 250 districts of the country (BGVS, February 1998: Annexure 8). The proposal was submitted to the Executive Committee of the NLM at its meeting during August 3–4, 1994. The MHRD sanctioned the proposal on September 7, 1994. Children were categorized in two age groups, 6–7 years and 12–14 years. Programmes were formulated for each of these groups. Major components of the programmes were: children's science festivals, creative competitions, science picnics, exhibitions and village learning festivals. The objective was to make the teaching-learning process enjoyable and to relate learning to real life situations with the involvement of local communities.

An outline of the major steps in the JoL process is presented below. A national core group was constituted in March, 1994, to coordinate the programme. Several meetings of the core group were held, together with state visits. State level core groups were also constituted together with committees at the district, block and panchayat levels. The gram panchayat, the VEC (village education committee) and teachers were actively involved with strong linkages with the education department and district literacy committees.

Training workshops were held to identify subject areas, activities and materials for the festivals. Ten activity corners were identified: mathematics, science experiments, science through the kitchen, imagination and creativity, story-telling, songs and games, the environment, a science walk/picnic, technology and history. States were free to adapt these corners according to their needs. All the states started organizing training programmes from August, 1994. Children's science festivals were held at the village, block and district levels. An average of 200 children participated in a given gram panchayat. The festival lasted for four days and was conducted in a guest-host mode where half the children were from nearby villages. On the last day of the festival, the children and resource persons organized an exhibition.

A national JoL festival was organized in New Delhi from November 7–14, 1994. This event brought together around 500 children from different states, 500 children from Delhi and 300 resource persons. The festival received wide acclaim from the media, educationists and the general public. Most of the district level JoL programmes were organized soon after the national festival. These were held in 258 districts.

A second round of JoL programmes, under the head of Cosmic Voyage, was undertaken between August and October, 1995, using the special event of the total solar eclipse on October 24, 1995. New themes such as sky-watching and eclipse watch were added to the regular programmes. Efforts were made to consolidate the human resources generated through the first round. A total of 136 programmes in combination with cultural items on the significance of total solar eclipse were organized. Kalajathas were held covering the states of West Bengal, Bihar and Eastern Uttar Pradesh with performances at 67 points; and over the states of Rajasthan, Madhya Pradesh and central Uttar Pradesh with performances at 69 points. These two jathas converged on Allahabad on October 10–11, 1995. Brahamanand Melas were held on October 27–28 at 30 points on the line of totality. More than 50,000 sun-watching filters were distributed during the campaign. Apart from the foregoing activities planned at the national level, a number of states conducted their own programmes in connection with JoL-Cosmic Voyage.

Several materials by way of books and posters were produced in connection with JoL. These materials are being used by different UEE, NFE programmes. At the conclusion of JoL, it was reported that around 258 melas were held at the district level, 1,000 at the block and 12,000 at the village level during the project period. A total of 203 workshops were held in 16 states and 3,842 resource persons were trained in state level programmes/workshops. In all 7,240 persons were trained in 258 district level training camps held in 19 states. Around 1,046 melas were held at the block level and 12,491 at the village level. The total participation at the block level with a rate of 150 persons per mela would suggest a coverage of 1,56,900 persons; and at the village level with a participation rate of 350 would total to over 4 million persons, according to BGVS reports. About 19 books were published through the central office in connection with JoL and 60 in all by 12 states.

2. The Jeevanshala Programme, 1995

The concern for working for the universalization of elementary education in a manner linked to literacy for adults arose from the very start of the literacy campaigns in 1990. The demand emerged from the non-literate adults themselves who sought improvement in the schooling system and access to it for their children. The BGVS held several workshops and a project "Non-Formal Education (NFE) of a Different Kind" was conceived. This project was sanctioned by the NFE division of the Ministry in March, 1996 (BGVS, February 1998: Annexure 3).

Preliminary work for Jeevanshala, first called "Non-formal Education of a Different Kind", was initiated in 1995. It had the objectives of providing life-based education to out-of-school children in a block, while ensuring that they move back into formal schools. The approach was that of a mass campaign for UEE with a focus on a block, unlike the literacy campaign model that concentrated on a district. Each NFE centre would be working in two shifts covering 30 to 40 children each. Thus, all the out-of-school children in a given area would be covered. The objectives outlined in the proposal were:

1. To develop a life-based and improved curriculum for non-formal education which can influence the formal curriculum as well,
2. To impart training in such an approach and through a participatory methodology to NFE volunteers who too can later contribute to the training of formal school teachers,
3. To select such a block for running Jeevanshala centres, such that the centres cover all the out-of-school children of the block; to run in parallel, a back-to-school programme so that the children shift from Jeevanshala centres to regular schools.

A national meeting was held in July, 1996 at New Delhi towards operationalizing the Jeevanshala programme. State units which expressed interest in taking up this project were requested to prepare the ground work like the formation of core groups of interested academicians and a primary survey of a selected block of the 6–14 age group who were not enrolled or had dropped out from the schooling system. A two-day national workshop was held in Chandigarh during October 20–21, 1996 as a follow-up to this initial work. About 23 representatives from Haryana, Punjab, Himachal Pradesh, Andhra Pradesh, Bihar, Orissa, Assam, Tamil Nadu and Western Uttar Pradesh took part. Two pilot blocks were selected for initial implementation: Wyra, Khammam district of Andhra Pradesh; and Samalkha, Panipat district of Haryana. Another project covering three gram panchayats of Navada district, Bihar was added later on. The Jeevanshala projects were sanctioned for a period of five years. The other states were requested to continue with the preparatory work. A follow-up workshop was organized in New Delhi from December 18–19, 1997 where participants from 10 states took part (BGVS, February 1998: Annexure 3).

The following description of the process in Wyra block, Andhra Pradesh, provides an illustration of the functioning of Jeevanshala. A total of 2,738 children were identified in 29 villages during the survey of the block. Gramsabhas were held in all the villages and VECs and Mother Committees were setup. A door to door campaign was organized and the project was formally started in August, 1997. By early 1998, 12 centres were running through volunteers who met once a week to share their experiences. Several workshops and training programmes were held during 1997. A bridge course book, a draft of an instruction manual for the first phase of NFE and a training manual were prepared by the academic core group. By October, 1999, NFE centres, locally called Manabadi, were started in all the 29 villages. Around 75 volunteers were working in the project of whom four served as cluster coordinators. Enrolment festivals were organized during April 6–12, 1999 in 30 villages. More than 8,550 adults and 3,150 children took part. More than 10,000 persons came to visit the exhibition that was held on the occasion. This was followed up by a festival at the block level and an educational seminar in August, 1999, at the district headquarters. Several teachers, education officers and personnel from BGVS and other related educational programmes participated.

The NFE project in Samalkha block, Panipat district in Haryana started in April, 1997. A survey conducted in 33 villages identified about 200 children of whom 90 per cent belonged to scheduled and backward castes. Teachers were trained in batches till May, 1998. The Jeevanshala project was started in Navada district, Bihar, in November 1998. By October, 1999, 58 Jeevanshalas were running with the help of 62 trained teachers. Around 1,658 children were enrolled and five books were published. The Maharashtra unit initiated the Jeevanshala programme in Akkalkuva block of Nandurbar district entirely on the basis of local support. By 2000, it was seeking to sustain this initiative with the help of support from aid agencies.

The enrolment status of the three block projects upto March 31, 2000 was as in the following table:

TABLE 6.1 *Enrolment Status of Jeevanshalas (upto March 31, 2000)*

Project	*Target*	*Enrolment (% of Target)*	*Average Attendance (% of Enrolment)*	*Back to School (% of Enrolment)*
Nawada	2,050	1,633 (79.7)	911 (55.8)	220 (13.5)
Wyra	2,287	2,287 (100)	720 (31.5)	561 (24.5)
Samalkha	1,808	1,496 (82.7)	751 (50.2)	503 (33.6)

Source: BGVS, Jeevanshala: Ek Zalak, presented at the National Workshop on Sharing Experiences of on NGOs on Experimental and Innovative Projects under the MHRD Schemes, March 23–24, 2000 at NCERT, New Delhi: 6.

The data suggest that while enrolment rates of identified out-of-school children were relatively high, the average attendance tended to be low. This could be partly explained by the difficult social and economic conditions of the children and the turnover of instructors. The latter was due to the delayed sanctions and consequent delay in payment of the meagre honoraria. One of the objectives was to phase out the centres by facilitating the entry of children to the formal school. The data indicate that by March, 2000, this percentage was relatively low. Given that the programme was at a mid-way stage, the initial gains of children returning to formal education are to be appreciated.

The report to the General Council Meeting of the BGVS in February, 2002, provides an overview assessment of the interventions in children's education. It was felt that the objectives of covering nearly all the out-of-school children in a block was largely achieved in Wyra and Samalkha. Nawada was not planned having this objective in mind. The back-to-school component was fairly well-established in Wyra and Samalkha.

The pedagogical process of a schooling system that links life to education was found to be complex at the primary level. Linking to productive activities cannot be established in a mechanical manner for primary children. A child orientation in the teaching-learning process and the contextualization of learning within culture and community had been achieved in a fairly creative manner. Across caste, communication was facilitated to a great extent, as seen from the integration of the Musahar children with other castes in Nawada and the community participation in Wyra. District resource teams had emerged which could serve the organization both at the state and national levels.

A review of the work with children over a decade suggested that different interventions would require different capacities based on the process. For example, campaigns like the JoL emphasized mobilization but were difficult to sustain on their own; teacher networks facilitated the involvement of teachers in more child-sensitive approaches; balmelas were largely event-based, but did not necessarily have an impact on the classroom; Jeevanshalas required substantial training and pedagogical inputs, but their sustainability depended on financial support; professional academic inputs were needed to impact on the government schooling system, as seen from the efforts of Eklavya and KSSP; the proposed Gyan Vigyan Vidyalayas would require a high level of community participation, managerial skills, academic and financial support. These efforts were not mutually exclusive but complementary to each other in their impact (BGVS, February 2002).

At the General Council meeting of the BGVS in October, 1999, a resolution was passed to further institutionalize the Jeevanshala process through the initiation of Gyan Vigyan Vidyalayas (GVV). This would be an initiative for an alternative and innovative schooling system to be coordinated by the BGVS. A detailed plan for initiating pilot GVVs in 13 districts was formulated. A four-day national workshop was held at Aligarh University in February, 2001, to discuss various aspects of this programme. The Madhya Pradesh BGVS had already initiated nine GVVs in different districts. However, at the time of reporting to the General Council Meeting in February, 2002, the GVV movement could not materialize for want of resources. It was felt that while state units might be in a position to start GVVs with the support of local communities, minimal resources would be required for training of the volunteer teachers. Discussions had been held with organizations such as Alternatives, AID and Asha, in this connection. The possibilities for aid were further limited by the decision of the BGVS not to accept financial support from an agency that would require the invoking of the Foreign Contribution Regulation Act (FCRA) (BGVS, February 2002: 5–6).

3. Gyan Vigyan Vidyalayas (GVV), 2004 ...

In a sense, the GVV programme was a continuation and a consolidation at another level of the earlier Joy of Learning (JoL) festivals held throughout the country and the Jeevanshala programme conducted in three blocks. In the context of the growing religious fundamentalism in the country, which was penetrating the educational system and its curricula, and the rising religious intolerance that was manifesting itself in communal conflicts especially under the National Democratic Alliance (NDA) government in the centre led by the Bharatiya Janata Party (BJP) during the period 1998–2004, the BGVS was increasingly seeing the GVVs as an educational strategy to counter these processes. The practical merits of this justifiable approach will be discussed later. However, the following quotation from a review report to the Sir Dorabji Tata Trust which was financing the BGVS during the period 2004–08, emphasizes this point:

> "These GVVs would strive to provide a secular space for imparting education of equitable quality and promote scientific temper, democratic and secular values. We assumed that by using our organizational capabilities, a large number of community schools could be opened to redress the many shortcomings of the existing school education, while also fighting the communalization of education"(BGVS, August 2006: 1).

In a document brought out in 2008, entitled the Sir Dorabji Tata Project, 2004–08, a vision for BGVS's involvement in basic education is stated:

> "The Basic Education Program of BGVS is based on the vision and understanding that large-scale efforts are needed, within the Governmental system and outside it, to help increase access of children to schools, to create teaching-learning materials that are of interest and relevance to children so that they are retained in schools, and to provide institutional platforms where children have learning opportunities that are transacted in a joyful manner, which implies reducing and eliminating fear, trauma and boredom from the processes of learning. In this manner it is hoped that the essential triangle of education – inclusion, equality and quality shall be strengthened.
>
> BGVS also considers it important that basic education should stress as much on the affective domain as it usually does on the cognitive. Therefore addressing questions of values, feelings and emotions are as important as teaching various subjects. In particular, the Basic Education Programme lays stress on values such as cooperation, peace, democracy and secularism, within an over all critical pedagogy" (BGVS, 2004–08, 2008: 12)

Explaining the teaching-learning methodology undertaken by the GVVs, and hence implicit in the training of teachers, the BGVS states in one of its reports that:

"the methodology shall be based on creating a fear-free learning environment, centred around activity, exploration and discovery, critical analysis and creativity, keeping the child's social and cultural location in mind. In the process values pertaining to democracy, secularism, cooperation, respect for pluralism and peace will be transacted. No particular religion shall be promoted in the GVV. Respect for each religion will be fostered. Accordingly, songs, stories and activities promoting equality and respect for different identities shall replace religious prayers and rituals" (BGVS, March 2007: 6–7).

Based on its experience of constraints while collaborating with government, such as changes in government and their ideological perspectives and the fact that such work could be undertaken within the preset designs of government schemes, the BGVS decided to take the local community as its partner. The GVVs that emerged were owned and supported by the community. It was felt that this would ensure greater freedom in designing teaching-learning processes and management practices and local community support would be more sustainable in the long term. By promoting democratic and secular values and a critical pedagogy, these schools could also act as a counter to schools of organizations that promoted religious intolerance.

An important component of the GVV process was the formation of the School Management Committee (SMC). The GVV was to be registered in the name of the SMC and not the BGVS. The former had democratic powers and responsibilities over all aspects of the GVV. Its functions were to conduct a survey for identifying children for enrolment in the GVV, identifying a male and female potential teacher from the local community for training, the location for the GVV, mobilizing resources, where necessary, for constructing/repairing a community structure, collecting textbooks from children who had cleared a particular standard and initiating and establishing linkages with other BGVS programmes and with the gram panchayat. The visualized tasks were many and for this purpose trainings and orientation programmes were held for the members of the SMC (BGVS, August 2006: 2–3).

A major training programme for resource persons was held for the states undertaking the GVV programme, Orissa, Jharkhand, Bihar, Madhya Pradesh and Uttar Pradesh during May 3–10, 2005 at the BGVS conducted national Basic Education Resource Centre (BERC), Bhopal. A total of 61 participants from these states attended the programme. Some of these participants were later involved in national level workshops on various aspects of basic education and about 60 per cent of them contributed as state level resource persons. It was decided that training programmes would be held for potential teachers of GVVs in at least two phases of 15 days each (BGVS, April–November 2005). Another major national level, resource persons' training was held for 10 days in June, 2007, at Pachmari, Madhya Pradesh. About 37 participants took part and the training focused on grade IV and V CBSE textbooks. By 2008, 20 similar state level training programmes for resource persons were held covering seven states (BGVS, January 2007–August 2008, 2008).

Chandeswari Prasad is a resident of Dinapatti village, Madhepura block, Madhepura district, Bihar. He was participating actively in social activities and the villagers had high expectations from him. He has been an old activist of the BGVS, concerned about the development of his village which was a subject of discussion with friends. There was no school in the village and most of the children remained out of school. The Gyan Vigyan Vidyalaya (GVV) was initiated in the village with the help of villagers. A piece of land was got. A managing committee was formed and Chandeswariji was given the responsibility of Secretary. This was a very good start. Villagers started collecting funds, bamboos, iron sheets, etc. Labourers from the village worked hard in constructing a small building with two rooms. Parents were happy observing the teaching of the teachers. Teacher Namita took a lot of interest.

The children gradually lost their hesitation of seeing her as a daughter-in-law which she was seen in the beginning. Parents, the managing committee and the children participated actively in the process of taking collective decisions like organizing daily meetings, asking children to sit around to understand their problems and to sort them out, providing equal opportunities to everybody. These issues became important discussion points in the village. The meetings of the Managing Committee facilitated the disbursement of fees collected from the students. Many of the quarrels that were continuously going on the village decreased as the result of the people being compelled to come together in good and bad times. It became a routine for the villagers come to the school in the evenings and have meetings.

The district administration soon converted the GVV into a recognized school as part of a special drive under Sarva Shiksha Abhiyan. Chandeswariji has now become a teacher in the gram panchayat school.

(Edited from BGVS, SDTT Project 2004–08, 2008: 15)

The following Table 6.2 provides some indication of the spread of the GVV process over different states. A total of 576 GVVs had been established over 62 districts of eight states by 2008. This coverage included the venture schools that pre-existed in Assam and where BGVS was providing teacher training and some material support. The GVVs in Bihar and Jharkhand were assimilated under the Sarva Shiksha Abhiyan scheme. In response to a community demand for some certification and to provide greater flexibility in the curriculum, discussions had been held with the National Institute of Open Schooling (NIOS) so that certification could be provided by NIOS rather than state departments. Community support, apart from identifying a local potential teacher for training, had been through land for the school building, building materials and labour for construction, community contributions for teachers' salaries and for sponsoring some children, and grains for the meals at the schools.

TABLE 6.2 *BGVS Gyan Vigyan Vidyalayas, 2008*

	State	*District*	*No. of Schools*
1.	Assam	16	242
2.	Bihar	9	14
3.	Gujarat	1	6
4.	Jharkhand	5	16
5.	Madhya Pradesh	11	60
6.	Orissa	8	179
7.	Uttarakhand	1	7
8.	Uttar Pradesh	11	52
	Total	62	576

Source: BGVS, SDTT Project, 2004–08: 22.

Note: Including the GVVs in Bihar and Jharkhand which were recognized by government under SSA and other existing government schools where special GVV inputs were provided, the number of GVVs works out to about 1,200.

BGVS had continued with its range of out-of-school programmes such as Balmelas (Children's Fairs), Bal Sansad (Children's Parliament), Gyan Vigyan Kendras (Centres for Scientific Knowledge) and libraries. In fact, some of these school-related programmes were additionally seen as entry points to the initiation of GVVs with community support. A total of 430 Gyan Vigyan Kendras had been set up during the period 2005–08 covering eight states and about 2,459 Bal Manches had been organized

(BGVS, 2004–08, 2008: 22). Apart from various child-centred activities, these fora were reported to have produced children's literature such as magazines, broad sheets and wall newspapers. BERC at Bhopal, Madhya Pradesh, supported by senior educational activist of BGVS, had been providing academic support for material production, teacher training and curriculum development to the GVVs, especially to those in the northern Hindi-speaking states. A resource team of about 30 persons had been formed at the national level. A fruitful academic collaboration had been established with agencies such as Pravah, Avehi-Abacus, Eklavya and Khoj. A national level workshop was held covering resource persons from the states of Madhya Pradesh, Bihar, Jharkhand, Uttar Pradesh, Orissa, Assam and Gujarat. Teacher trainings for 15 days were conducted annually for each state during the period 2005–08. A guide book for teachers and resource persons for implementation in the GVV schools had been produced at a workshop conducted by BERC.

The BGVS was aware of the inadequacy of the number and duration of these teacher training sessions in order to achieve sustainability of innovative classroom practices (BGVS, 2004–08, 2008:16). Some of the challenges faced by the GVV basic education programme were reported to be a lack of BGVS organizational support for the GVVs, some non-functional school management committees, inadequate resource persons to provide academic support, lack of external monitoring of the schools resulting in the isolation of the school teacher and problems in sustaining the enthusiasm of teachers without adequate honoraria (BGVS, 2004–08, 2008: 21).

During the period 2004–08, BGVS had also worked with the government system on various programmes on basic education within states such as Maharashtra, Andhra Pradesh, Bihar, Jharkhand, Orissa, Jammu & Kashmir, Kerala, Karnataka, Tamil Nadu and Uttarakhand; and with national institutions and processes such as the NCERT, NUEPA, the National Knowledge Commission and MHRD. These partnerships had generally been in the areas of teacher training, curriculum development and policy formulation. For example, by 2006, the organization had trained 1,524 government teachers from 10 states and had established 424 libraries attached to government schools in five of these states (BGVS, 2005–06, 2006: 8). The policy of collaboration with government had been part of a belief that the state had the primary responsibility of providing access and quality education to children under the Right to Education, 86th amendment to the Constitution.

4. Jan Vachan Andolan (JVA), and Publications, 1994 ...

The JVA was first initiated by BGVS in the Virudhunagar district, Tamil Nadu. It was later systematically adopted as a national programme (BGVS, January 2002: 170). Prior to the public reading sessions during jathas, workshops were held to write books, plays and songs, and volunteers were trained in the methodology of public reading during the jathas. The volunteers would read out to an audience of a couple of hundred people gathered in the village square. Reading aloud would stimulate popular interest in books and motivate villagers to purchase and read them. These reading sessions also provided feedback to writers for neo-literates.

A need was felt for a major initiative to develop good, low-cost reading material and spread the culture of reading at the mass level. The JVA was a country-wide campaign in response to this assessed need. It was initiated during the course of the 1994–96 project of the BGVS. A programme of this nature could also be interfaced with the PL and CE phases of the literacy campaigns. A two-day workshop to review JVA in different states was conducted at New Delhi on August 12–13, 1996. Around 37 persons from different states participated.

Writers' workshops were held at the national and state levels. By February, 1998, 17 writers' workshops were held at the state level together with 27 training programmes; 104 training programmes at the district level and 141 at the block level. A total number of 3,838 village level melas were organized for the purpose of book distribution. By February, 1998, 259 books were published under the auspices of JVA. Apart from new books, there were several adaptations of renowned classics, books of science and a variety of topics of popular interest. The foregoing data from 18 states (BGVS, February 1998: 26) is an underestimate because some of the states had not reported.

The Jan Vachan Utsavas, the festivals undertaken under the auspices of JVA, varied from 3–5 days in various places. The festivals included book exhibitions, reading programmes, door to door campaigns to introduce books. The books were priced between rupees two and three to make them affordable to the neo-literates. JVA also introduced a series of children's science books meant for village level children and priced at rupees eight.

The JVA provoked an excellent response, but of a short duration. A concern is expressed in the documents of the BGVS as related to the inability of short-term mobilizations to consolidate into a movement and/or a process of institutionalization. "Why are we not able to develop

Anju Kumari Paswan lives in Baank village, Begusarai district, Bihar. She is 25 years old and belongs to the Dalit community. She has completed her school education upto 10th standard. She is married and has one daughter. She participated in the total literacy and post-literacy programmes as a volunteer instructor and secretary of the Samabal (self-help) group for women.

According to Anju, the real charm of the literacy process during the post-literacy phase was the diversity of initiatives and interventions. She was involved in teaching at the literacy centre, taking part in Sambal Self-Help Group meetings, as well as mass mobilization activities for collective reading, immunization, and school enrolment. She was also active in organizing and conducting Samata Vigyan Utsava meetings and teaching children at the non-formal education centre Vikalp Shiksha Kendra. She explained that conducting these activities was not very easy, but the training and support which she got from the district team helped her in taking these responsibilities.

Anju believes that all these initiatives raised the expectations of neo-literates but they were unable to help them further. For instance, she said 'We did not do any income generation and skill development programme, but from the start we had been talking about doing this. Nearly one and half years ago we organized a cloth cutting-cum-library workshop. Women energetically participated in this workshop and really liked this type of learning. But we have made no efforts in this direction'.

(Edited from BGVS, January 2002: 137)

the JVA programme into a nation-wide rural library movement? Almost everywhere, even in remote villages people were willing to buy books. Why couldn't we pursue this further and create a culture of reading among the people and a culture of book selling among our activists?" (BGVS, February 1998: 13).

The BGVS initiatives had given rise to a vast number of publications. A listing of some of these may be seen in Appendix 2. It is near impossible to present an accurate record of the number of these publications of various types that were brought out in relation to various programmes, in different states, and at various levels (national, state, district, block, village). During January 1994 to December 1996, in connection with the JoL programme alone, 19 publications were brought out by the Central Office and several in regional languages by the states: Assam 12, Bihar 4, Gujarat 7, Himachal Pradesh1, Karnataka 3, Madhya Pradesh 4,

Maharashtra 3, Orissa 4, Punjab and Chandigarh 5, Rajasthan 4, Tamil Nadu 7 and Uttar Pradesh 6; i.e., 79 publications in all. Between January 1997 and September 2000, the BGVS had published 475 good quality, low-priced, neo-literate literature as part of its Jan Vachan Andolan, towards creating a movement for village level libraries (Appendix 2). Of these, 148 books were brought out in Hindi, 12 in Urdu, 22 in Telugu, 32 in Assamese, 6 in Malayalam, 5 in Kannada, 49 in Marathi, 65 in Oriya, 76 in Punjabi, 54 in Tamil and 6 in Bengali.

The foregoing data provide a clear indication of the diversity and the significance of the publications towards promoting learning and regional culture. Apart from the vast material relating to the strategy of the literacy campaigns and its different phases, publications by way of training manuals and information materials were brought out in relation to programmes such as Gender Empowerment, the Samata Jatha and the Samata Vigyan Utsava; the Joy of Learning, Cosmic Voyage and Jeevanshala; Health; and Natural Resource Management. In addition, there were periodicals like the *Gyan Vigyan Sandesh/Vartha* in Hindi and in English; *Samata*, on gender empowerment; *Prawah*, a newspaper for Hindi-speaking neo-literates; *Akhsar Sainik*, a Hindi periodical for literacy volunteers; and *Jeevanshala Update* on elementary education and NFE. Several of the state and district units were also bringing out periodicals, e.g., Uttar Pradesh, Assam, Himachal Pradesh, Haryana and Maharashtra. The periodicals served to share field experiences and acted as rallying points for organization to a lesser degree.

A brief analysis of the contents of some of the JVA publications is in order. The literature under JVA was effective in conveying its messages in a clear manner that was entertaining at the same time. It was done in a manner that would normally hold the attention of a neo-literate. The content related closely to the lives of its potential audience and the struggles that they underwent. A few feasible solutions were gently suggested when a problem was highlighted. Health, hygiene and cleanliness occupied an important space in the literature. The natural and human environment was discussed in a simple manner with adequate illustrations.

Basic science and rational solutions for situations were depicted in an accessible manner. The idea was to present science as present in everyday life. The evolution of science and reasons for various natural phenomena were described in an engrossing manner in the booklet "Vigyan Ke Prayog", so that scientific experimentation becomes an interesting sport for the learners. In a similar manner, "Bachhe Aur

Taraju" discussed the laws underlying the act of balancing. The illustrations in this book were in a style similar to that of traditional story-telling. A fascinating book was "Bachhe Kise Banten Hai" which discusses the biology related to child birth. The book was in fact a story addressed to children telling them about their arrival in this world. "Visva Ki Kahani" illustrated several aspects about the secrets of the universe, the solar system, the natural environment and the laws of nature. The environment was another major subject area. Facts about the environment were discussed through stories with explanations and messages that were communicated in an indirect manner. In fact, there was little need to explain because the stories themselves were very powerful. "Daani Ped", the charitable tree, told a story about the relationship between human beings and their environment. The simple story was convincingly written to suggest that every element of nature was of some use to human beings.

Awareness of one's rights constituted another important area of writings. The BGVS literature conveyed awareness about living with dignity and self-respect. "Na Bara Na Chota" was a small booklet in the form of a poem with strong visuals. The poem provided several reasons to convince people not to accept a person as bigger or stronger, just because a person was rich. It also condemned discrimination based on religion, culture and gender. Gender sensitization was an important message in some of the writings. They discussed the difficult and deprived circumstances that face a large number of women. The lives and achievements of eminent people was another body of writings. The book "Aaise The Gandhi" related a number of incidents from the life of the father of the nation. The message conveyed was that Gandhi was not a distant figure, but a person closely related and relevant to the lives of ordinary people.

The promotion of literacy was the primary thrust of the entire effort. The effort was towards learning through experiencing, even in the process of learning to read and write. The focus was on using the familiar for the recognition of alphabets. For example, "Khel Khel Mein Shiksha" was a 16-page booklet that insisted on the importance of the recognition of alphabets without pairing them with just one word each. The message was conveyed that a single alphabet could be taught by a number of methods if one was observant. Leaves, dry branches, flowers, fruits and even shadows could well be used for this purpose. The shapes of objects could be associated with the entire range of alphabets. The actions of everyday life were closely related to the shapes of alphabets.

The learner was encouraged to use imagination to discover the shapes of alphabets in different objects encountered in everyday life. The entire range of BGVS literature for learning seemed to take the position that there was no end to progressive and imaginative ideas to make learning more interesting and relevant. The exercises were highly participatory and encouraged both learners and educators to get involved in the process of learning. The BGVS literature may be seen as an important contribution to the relation between literacy and learning and to a range of human rights.

Much care was taken to see that the publications responded to the field experience in implementing the range of BGVS programmes. For example, the Annual Report, 2005–06 provides a summary view of what the field level cadre considered as relevant for creating awareness in relation to particular programmes:

> "Samata
> Self-Help Groups (SHGs): Basics of savings and borrowings, book-keeping, transparency and reconciliation, annual report making, etc.
>
> Samata Groups: Preventive health, sanitation, anatomy and physiology, reproductive health, food and nutrition, vaccination, women's rights, women's skills, gender aspects of economics and politics, arts and crafts.
>
> Basic Education
> Basic Education Teachers: Fundamentals, handbooks, syllabus, subject books, testing and examination techniques, teaching methodologies, games and tasks, etc.
>
> Basic Education Coordinators: Fundamentals, handbooks, pedagogic theory and practices, comparative studies on children's education, etc.
>
> Continuing Education (CE)
> CE Sanyojaks/Sanyojikas: Fundamentals, CE handbooks, wall newspaper publishing, setting up library, organization building, survey methods, Soochna kendra working, resource raising and book keeping, record keeping and reporting, etc.
>
> CE Coordinators: Fundamentals, follow-up tasks, coordination tasks, record keeping, etc." (BGVS, 2005–06, 2006: 4).

By 2006, 270 village level libraries had been established within continuing education centres where the first phase of training of the coordinators had been carried out (BGVS, 2005–06, 2006: 17). During the period 2005–08, there was a second round of new publications and reprints of earlier editions. This was largely sponsored by the grant from the Sir Dorabji Tata Trust (SDTT). The following Table 6.3 gives a summary account of these publications.

TABLE 6.3 *BGVS Publications, 2005–08*

	Name of the BGVS Centres	*Titles*	*Copies*
1.	BGVS National Centre Delhi	205	3,89,000
2.	BGVS Orissa	13	26,000
3.	BGVS Karnataka	10	20,000
4.	BGVS Assam	10	16,000
5.	BGVS Puducherry	4	8,000
6.	BGVS Andhra Pradesh	7	7,000
7.	BGVS Tamil Nadu	20	40,000
8.	BGVS Maharashtra	27	53,000
	Total	296	5,59,000

Source: BGVS General Council Meeting, Tirupati, July 21–22, 2008: 69.

The table suggests that 296 titles with 5.59 lakh copies were published during the period 2005–08. Most of these titles were published by the national centre in Hindi. State units from Orissa, Karnataka, Puducherry, Andhra Pradesh, Tamil Nadu and Maharashtra were actively involved in publications in the regional languages and their distribution through the Jan Vanchan Andolan (People's Reading Movement) and libraries. A number of district literacy committees had been purchasing these books for their CECs, as also several voluntary agencies.

7

National Campaigns for Rights

The strength of an organizational network across the country that is closely connected with a mass base at the district, block and even village levels is demonstrated by the engagement of BGVS in advocacy on various rights issues at the national and state levels, especially after 2002. The BGVS was involved in mobilizations, kalajathas, training programmes and other capacity-building activities of its members towards conventions and other forms of mass demonstration. Some of these mobilizations and advocacy activities are discussed below.

1. The Campaign for the Rights to Food and Work, 2002 ...
This campaign was initiated by a writ petition submitted to the Supreme Court in April, 2001, by the People's Union for Civil Liberties, Rajasthan (PUCL vs Union of India and Others, writ petition, civil, 196 of 2001). The petition sought that the country's food stock be used to protect people from hunger and starvation. The public interest litigation that followed led to Supreme Court hearings at regular intervals and interim orders. On November 28, 2001, the Supreme Court directed state governments to introduce cooked midday meals in all government and government assisted schools within six months. This was one of the first successes of the Right to Food campaign at the legal level. Cooked midday meals were introduced in all primary schools as a result of another Supreme Court order of April, 2004. With about a hundred million children covered under the country's midday meal programme, this constitutes the largest nutrition programme in the world. The larger public campaign was intended to compliment the legal process and to make up for inadequacies of a purely legal approach.

The Right to Food campaign was an informal network of individuals and organizations, with BGVS and its state units being an important component. The campaign recognized the fundamental right to freedom from hunger and under-nutrition for which equitable and sustainable food systems was a necessary condition. This was closely connected to entitlements related to livelihood security such as the right to work, land reforms and social security. The demands included the following: a National Employment Guarantee Act, universal midday meals in primary schools, universalization of the Integrated Child Development Services (ICDS) for children under the age of six, effective implementation of all nutrition-related schemes, revival and universalization of the public distribution system (PDS), a social security arrangement for those who are not able to work, equitable land rights and forest rights. The mobilization and advocacy led to the enactment by the Indian parliament of the National Rural Employment Guarantee Act (NREGA) in August 2005. The Act has been in effect in rural districts across the country since April, 2008. The Act guarantees every rural household 100 days a year of manual work at minimum wages within a five kilometre radius. A failure to provide work gives the applicant and the potential worker the right to draw an unemployment allowance. A failure to receive wages within 15 days entitles the worker to receive compensation for late payment of wages. Social audits are a statutory requirement under the NREGA, and the NREGA guidelines define social audit "as a continuous process of public vigilance". Public audits and Jan Sunwais (public hearings) have been other methods of ensuring accountability and transparency to local communities.

The foregoing and the following information is based on BGVS 2004–08, 2008: 69 and the following pages. Several mobilization activities had been undertaken as part of the campaign which included public hearings, rallies, dharnas (sit-ins), padyatras (marches), conventions, action research, media advocacy and lobbying with members of Parliament. On April 9, 2002 such activities were held throughout the country as part of a 'National Day of Action on Midday Meals'. BGVS units in Jharkhand, Madhya Pradesh, Bihar, Chattisgarh, Uttar Pradesh, Maharashtra and Rajasthan undertook demonstrations before the chief ministers' residences and before the offices of district collectors. About two lakh children were given food as part of this demonstration. Several state governments initiated cooked midday meals in primary schools following from these actions. On September 19, 2004, a national convention on Employment Guarantee and the Right to Work was held in New Delhi. During hot summer months of May–June, 2005, BGVS played a leading role in the Rozgar Adhikar Yatra (Right to Work Journey) as part of a 50-day tour of the country's poorest districts to demand immediate enactment of a National Employment Guarantee Act. The Right to Work was seen as the primary aspect of the fundamental right to live with dignity. Five-member kalajatha teams travelled for 10 days, the trips and the songs being earlier developed in a BGVS conducted workshop. The yatras covered the states of Haryana, Rajasthan, Gujarat, Maharashtra, Madhya Pradesh, Chattisgarh, Jharkhand, Bihar, West Bengal and Uttar Pradesh. About 93 district conventions and 6 state conventions were held during this programme, together with several public meetings and press conferences. An important slogan conveyed through posters and pamphlets was 'Give Work to Every Hand, Give Full Value to Every Work'. The BGVS followed up the passing of the NREGA in August, 2005, with surveys of the under and unemployed in districts, social audits, public hearings and trainings programmes regarding the rules and regulations of the Act. In addition, two-day training programmes were held for eight persons, four males and four females, from each of 1,673 panchayats in the country where BGVS was engaged in a strategy of concentration and convergence of programmes.

National conventions were held in Bhopal in June 11–13, 2004; Delhi, September 19, 2004; in Kolkata, 2005 and in Bodhgaya in April, 2007. The BGVS was the primary organizer of the Bhopal and the Bodhgaya Conventions. The Bhopal Convention was held to share experiences of field actions and to plan for the future; around parallel thematic workshops, a plenary session and cultural activities. The convention ended with a large rally and a public programme. The Convention on Employment Guarantee and the Right to Work held in Delhi included 300 participants from 80 organizations. The morning sessions had brief presentations from the participating organizations and invitees from the Planning Commission and the government. Parallel workshops were held in the afternoon on mobilization activities and the draft Employment Guarantee Act.

The Convention on the Right to Food and Work, November 18–20, 2005, held in Badu, near Kolkata, drew about 400 participants representing a range of organizations working on these issues, together with few international participants. The Convention at Bodhgaya, Bihar was held during April 6–8, 2007. The speakers recalled the long history of land struggles which had resulted in some land distribution in this region. However, issues like poverty and hunger, cards for persons below the poverty line and education were still a matter of concern. An important feature of this convention was the participation of several trade unions, agricultural labour organizations and a delegation from Bangladesh. The nature of the organizational structure was explained: A steering group comprised of representatives of 10 national networks and two support groups, a secretariat with an advisory group comprised of the steering group members and invited members from local campaigns. Discussions were held on the Integrated Child Development Services (ICDS) programme which was supposed to cover the health and nutrition needs of children below the age of six, mothers, adolescent girls and pregnant women. Attention was drawn to the landmark judgement of the Supreme Court of December 13, 2006, which directed government to universalize ICDS by December, 2008.

From February 18–22, 2005, the BGVS in collaboration with the Ministry of Environment and Forest and several persons and organizations from the cultural field organized a festival in celebration of 'Nature and the Environment' at Mavlankar Auditorium and its lawns in New Delhi. The festival served to highlight issues such as the right and the need for the sustainable uses of natural resources, climate change, the displacements resulting from large dams and the extraction of resources and the unsustainable use of energy, water and forest resources. The festival had an important component of tribal art and culture (BGVS, 2005).

2. Social Forums, 2002 ...

As part of its strategic critique of globalization processes and communalism during the phase 2002–04, the BGVS decided to participate in the processes of the World Social Forum (BGVS, 2005: 7–8). Regional workshops were held at Hyderabad, New Delhi, Guwahati and Trivandrum as part of a process of generating awareness about the issues underlying the World Social Forum (WSF) and the mobilizations necessary to spread this awareness. A cadre camp was held from July 18–20, 2002 at Pachmarhi, Madhya Pradesh with 109 participants from 20 states of the presence of BGVS and the AIPSN. This camp served the purpose of awareness generation about the Asia and the World Social Forum (ASF, WSF) processes. The sessions that were held over these three days covered the following topics: Introduction to the WSF process; globalization and self-reliance; the impact of globalization on education, health, gender relations and food security; and the communalization of society. The camp was followed by mobilization activities at the district and sub-district levels. A special women's consultation and core group meeting related to the WSF process was held in Delhi on November 20, 2002. BGVS took an active part in the ASF held in Hyderabad in January 2–7, 2003. About 1,500 activists travelled to Hyderabad at their own cost. This was preceded by a major camp for its activists and some grassroots mobilization.

The WSF was held in Mumbai during January 16–21, 2004. BGVS was an active member of the India Organizing Committee and influenced the approach to this large-scale meeting. State units used this as an opportunity to hold meetings and contact programmes even at the sub-district level. BGVS kalajatha groups performed in various localities of Mumbai during the course of the WSF. About 1,500 activists of BGVS travelled at their own expense to participate in the forum.

The Indian Social Forum was held in Delhi from November 9–13, 2006. There were 796 participants belonging to AIPSN and BGVS. BGVS organized three conferences related to their work on rights issues: education, development and continuing education. The Madhya Pradesh, Bihar and Uttar Pradesh units conducted workshops, while cultural teams from Madhya Pradesh and Haryana engaged in performances. An exhibition of BGVS publications was organized on the occasion (BGVS, 2004–08, 2008: 80). BGVS members participated in the ninth World Social Forum held in Belem, Brazil from January 27 to February 1, 2009.

3. The Jathas for Peace, Unity and Sovereignty, September 8–October 2, 2003

These jathas need to be seen in the historical context of the times; the strengthening of processes of globalization, on the one hand and of fundamentalism, internationally and in the country, on the other. The events in Gujarat in 2002 were a stark symptom of a national process of the communalization of society that was taking place during the rule of the NDA headed by the BJP from 1998–2004. The war on Iraq by the government of the United States was also ongoing. The jathas were thus seen as a counter to the processes taking place in the country as well as a mobilization effort towards the WSF process whose concerns had national relevance. As stated in the report to the General Council Meeting, Bhopal, December 28–29, 2005, "Our activities in literacy and education, in health, in promotion of science and self-reliant development, have all been premised in the belief in the three pillars of peace, unity and sovereignty" (BGVS, 2005).

Elaborating on the spirit underlying the national level jathas for peace, unity and sovereignty and taking off from the refrain of Arundhati Roy, 'they be few and we be many', at the World Social Forum held in Porto Alegre, Brazil in 2003, a BGVS leaflet on this jatha states:

> "If it is so, if we the forces of light and reason, are so overwhelmingly larger in numbers, why do they succeed today in their evil designs? It is because they are one and we are still divided. Can we come together? Come together with all our differences, in fact make our differences our strength? The People's Science Movement believes that we can. We can come together, with the common purpose of beating back the forces of darkness. Many amongst us will have thought of different paths to reach the same goal – let us come together while retaining our beliefs in these paths" (BGVS, 2003: 1).

Organizing committees towards preparation for the kalajatha were held in Bhopal, Wardha, Ahmedabad, New Delhi and Jaipur. A seven-day national kalajatha script production workshop was held at Bhopal from July 22–28, 2003. About 25 well-known theatre personalities and writers from all over the country and two master trainers from each of the BGVS state units participated in this workshop which resulted in about 20 core scripts, skits and songs. These were to be adapted at state level workshops, together with the production of local specific programmes. Parallel to this workshop, a material production workshop was held to generate booklets, leaflets, neo-literate materials and posters on various themes that would be the focus during the jathas. About 120 people participated in the workshops and the resources were contributed by participants, other organizations and the community amounting to a value of over Rs 10 lakhs.

The kalajathas were eventually conducted all over the country from September 8 to October 2, 2003, details of which are to be found in the Table 7.1. There were 41 jathas in all, of which nine were regional jathas. These covered 1,120 places in 258 districts concluding at five nodal points: Wardha, Delhi, Khatkhat Kalan (the birth place of Bhagat Singh), Champaran and near Sabarmati Ashram in Gujarat. The jathas had also covered nine districts of the communally-charged situation in Gujarat. It was reported that close to rupees five crore towards the costs of the jathas were raised locally from various BGVS state and district units, community contributions, donations, food grains; sale of books, cards,

TABLE 7.1 *Kalajathas for Peace, Unity and Sovereignty, September 2003*

	State	*Jathas*	*Districts Covered*	*Progra-mme Spots*	*States Crossed*	*Culminated at*	Other Features
1.	Assam	Due to rains and floods, jatha activities to be taken up in various districts after October 2, 2003					An 18-member jatha team participated in Champaran
*2.	Andhra Pradesh	1	8	29		Wardha	Pondicherry–Tamil Nadu–Andhra Pradesh–Maharashtra
3.	Bihar	2	26	105	1	Champaran	Posters: 1,000, Booklets: 1,000, Banners: 100, Two Jathas
*4.	Chattisgarh	2	17	40	2	Wardha	Two Jathas Madhya Pradesh–Chattisgarh Jatha
5.	Gujarat	1	9	23	1	Sabarmati	Even at affected areas Jathas performed well. Good response. Folders: 15,000
6.	Haryana	1	8	8	2	Jalianwalabagh and Khatkat Kalan	Resource collection: District donation, Food grains
7.	Himachal Pradesh	1	10	44	2	Jalianwalabagh and Khatkat Kalan	Resource collection: Donation, Books sale
8.	Jharkhand	2	14	85	2	Champaran	Two jathas
*9.	Karnataka	1	13	25	2	Wardha	Kerala–Karnataka–Maharashtra–Wardha
*10.	Kerala	1	13	54	3	Wardha	Kerala–Karnataka–Maharashtra–Wardha

*11.	Madhya Pradesh	4	27	149	6	Wardha Champaran Delhi and Sabarmati	Four Jathas culminated at different points. Jathas entered into seven states Folders: 5,000, Posters: 10,000, Banners: 1,000, Audio Cassettes: 1,000
*12.	Maharashtra	4	27	35	18	Champaran	Three regional jathas culminated at Wardha Kerala–Karnataka–Maharashtra Jatha Madhya Pradesh–Chattisgarh–Maharashtra Jatha Pondicherry–Tamil Nadu–Andhra Pradesh–Maharashtra
13.	Orissa	Jathas postponed due to floods.					
14.	Punjab	1	7	72	1	Jallianwalabagh and Khatkat Kalan	Jatha inaugurated. Culminated at two places. MP, Rajasthan, Himachal and Haryana jathas culminated here.
15.	Rajasthan	1	14	50	3	Jallianwalabagh and Khatkat Kalan	District seminars on social issues
*16.	Tamil Nadu	1	4	48	4	Wardha	Pondicherry–Tamil Nadu–Andhra Pradesh–Maharashtra
17.	Tripura						
18.	Uttar Pradesh	3	35	46	2	Delhi	Three jathas

Cont'd...

Cont'd...

19.	Uttaranchal	1	14	62	3	Delhi	Resource collection: District donation, Food grains. 15 Jathas. Covered maximum number of villages.
*20.	West Bengal	14	12	245	2	Champaran	
	Total	41	258	1,120	54		

Note: * Indicates states from within which state and regional jathas emerged.
Total no. of state jathas: 41
Total no. of regional jathas: 9

1. Pondicherry–Tamil Nadu–Andhra Pradesh–Maharashtra
2. Kerala–Karnataka–Maharashtra
3. Chattisgarh–Maharashtra I
4. Chattisgarh–Maharashtra II
5. Madhya Pradesh–Rajasthan–Uttar Pradesh-Delhi
6. Madhya Pradesh–Maharashtra
7. Madhya Pradesh–Uttar Pradesh-Bihar
8. Madhya Pradesh–Gujarat
9. West Bengal–Bihar

Culmination points for the jathas were: Champaran, Delhi, Jalianwalabagh, Khatkat Kalan, Sabarmati and Wardha.

Source: BGVS 2005.

posters and Samata soaps (BGVS, 2005: 8–9). Funding support from the central office was not available at the time due to lack of financial resources. This as well as other activities of the period 2002–04, are clearly indicative of the rootedness of the organization and the decentralized, local support that it earned from village communities.

4. The Education Activists' Assembly on the Right to Social Security, September 2–4, 2004

This assembly was held from September 2 to 4, 2004 at Bhartiyam Grounds, New Delhi. It was held in the context of the United Progressive Alliance (UPA) coming to power and the need felt by BGVS to impress on the new government the importance of renewing the participatory processes related to education and literacy. The Minister for Sports and Youth Affairs and the Minister for Human Resource Development, Government of India, were chief guests at this coming together of the BGVS network on the issue of the literacy campaigns. It was felt that rights relating to the social sector could be closely articulated with the literacy campaigns. There were about 6,000 delegates from all over the country. Serving and retired government officials who were associated with the literacy campaigns spoke on the occasion appreciating the role of BGVS activists and reiterating the need for a government collaboration with civil society organizations and people's movements. Several neo-literate women, some of whom had become members of the gram panchayats, spoke on the occasion as also academicians and activists working in the education and cultural sectors. Cultural teams of the BGVS from different parts of the country performed and several trade unions, people's organizations and movements extended their support through their active participation (BGVS, 2005: 11–12).

The topics discussed at the assembly included literacy and health; right to food, work and information; science and culture; religious toleration and plurality. A demand note was read out and presented to the Minister, MHRD. It was reported that close to 6,000 activists who participated had travelled at their own expense, once again symbolizing the fact that voluntarism in the BGVS was quite active (BGVS, 2005: 11).

The assembly was followed up with a note dated November 12, 2005, to the MHRD with suggestions for the restructuring of the literacy efforts in the country. Attention was drawn to the sharp contrast between the early years of the literacy campaigns when the mobilizations led to almost 12 million volunteers and an enrolment of close to a 100 million persons, leading to an unprecedented rise of 13 per cent in the literacy rate during the decadal period of 1991 to 2001. It was pointed out that several activists on the ground were still willing to serve the national cause of literacy for development; as seen from 6,000 representatives travelling to Delhi for the assembly at their own expense. Education for development could be an important way of converging recent positive legislations. Towards this it was suggested that there was a need to closely relate the district literacy committees with the gram panchayats, following from the 73rd and 74th Amendments to the Constitution. Additionally, a single Continuing and Lifelong Education Programme (CLEP) was suggested to bring together important keywords with their programmatic implications: Information/Education, Livelihoods and Governance. A massive mobilization was still needed in order to give the campaigns a major rejuvenation (BGVS, 2005).

The BGVS followed up the above-mentioned note with a project proposal to the NLM entitled 'Education for a New India'. This was approved by the meeting of the Project Approval Committee (PAC) held in October 2006. However, the proposal was not sanctioned till date (BGVS, 2008: 19).

5. The Campaign for the Right to Education, 2005 ...

The Central Advisory Board on Education (CABE) had prepared a draft for a bill in August, 2005, on the Right to Education with necessary budgetary provisions. Members of BGVS had taken an active part in this process. A campaign was launched by the BGVS in association with the AIPSN. A national assembly was held at Kozhikode in Kerala from July 8 to 10, 2005, in collaboration with the AIPSN and NCERT. The main themes of the assembly were the National Curriculum Framework, 2005 proposed by the NCERT and the draft bill on the Right to Education prepared by the CABE. Ten other conventions were held in different states to mobilize support for the bill. The draft bill was published in several languages for wider dissemination.

The central government diminished the value of the draft bill to a model bill which state governments were supposed to introduce. Knowing that this was tantamount to shelving the bill, a strategy of advocacy was sustained by the BGVS to reverse the process. During October 2–3, 2005, a national Right to Education workshop was held with the participation of representatives of several states, about 42 mass organizations and some educational institutions. Discussions focused on the National Curriculum Framework and the Right to Education Bill. A campaign committee was formed. In January 12–13, 2003, a national convention was held in New Delhi followed by a conference on Education for All held on June 7, 2007 which was coordinated by BGVS. Resolutions were passed by gram panchayats where BGVS was present and sent to the Prime Minister to implement the bill. This was accompanied by a large-scale signature campaign and a CD of songs highlighting issues concerning education. BGVS also joined hands with NAFRE and the public campaign for a common school system in opposing the move to shift responsibility to the states. It was also involved with the Knowledge Commission to prepare a draft bill that would remove the shortcomings of the CABE draft (BGVS, August 2006: 13). In February, 2008, the Prime Minister called for a central legislation and BGVS members were involved in the process of redrafting the bill and campaigning for its introduction in parliament. Individuals from BGVS also lobbied with Members of Parliament from different parties and addressed a meeting of the Parliamentary Standing Committee of MHRD.

The Right to Education Bill was finally passed by the Rajya Sabha on July 20, 2009, and by the Lok Sabha on August 4, 2009. It was notified as an act on September 3, 2009, entitled as the Children's Right to Free and Compulsory Education Act. The act operationalizes the fundamental right of every child between the ages of 6 to 14 to education. Some of the major objectives of the act are an obligation on the part of the state to provide education, the formulation of a curriculum that is consistent with the Constitution and that provides quality education with quality teachers, the participation of civil society, especially women, in school management committees and a proportionate reservation of seats for children of low income groups from the vicinity of a school. Some of the debates relating to the limitations of the act still continue. However, the act might be seen as a step forward, subject to due corrections based on experience.

The BGVS in association with the AIPSN has had a tradition of utilizing astronomical events to generate awareness among children and other community members. Similar to the Cosmic Voyage held in 1995, were attempts to create a sense of critical, scientific awareness such as the programmes related to the 'Transit of Venus' held at Banaras, Barabanki, Meerut, Rae Bareilly, Muradabad, Rampur, Kanpur and Aligarh in Uttar Pradesh, on sequential dates from May 24 to June 3,

2004. A major event was watching the total solar eclipse under the banner of Surya Grahan Utsava (Festival of watching the solar eclipse) held at Patna, Bihar during July 20–22, 2009. These events might appear as relatively insignificant, but have had a major mass level impact in counteracting superstitions which are reinforced within a context of semi-feudalism and patriarchy.

6. The Nationwide Janadhikar Kalajatha, November 2007–January 2008

BGVS had been involved in several networked campaigns for human rights, as discussed above. It was found necessary to carry the message through a nation-wide Janadhikar Kalajathas (Cultural Caravan on People's Rights) during November–January 2007–2008. Unlike earlier kalajathas, the focus of this one was to a greater extent on the district and sub-district levels. The kalajathas were organized by state teams in 20 states. About 6 plays and 15 songs were prepared in script writing and production workshops held at the state level. A significant feature of this jatha was that it had moved into clusters of panchayats within blocks where convergence trainings had earlier been conducted. An additional feature was that an attempt was made to sell the large number of publications brought out by BGVS during the course of the kalajatha.

Table 7.2, based on available incomplete data, provides a picture of the decentralized scale of operation of this kalajatha. In all 1,235 gram panchayats within 714 blocks of 305 districts were covered by sub-groups of 46 jathas. This involved 781 artists, about one-third of whom were female, based on the available genderwise break up. It was estimated that the jathas were able to reach out a population of over 13 lakh persons.

> Khublal Mahato, aged 46, is a resident of Topchanchi, Dhanbad district, Jharkhand. He works in the education department. He saw the performance of the kalajatha in the village. He got so motivated that he insisted that the performance be held in his nearby native village as well. Even though this could not be done, he arranged for food for the kalajatha team members. He still campaigns for the organization and has become a member of the local BGVS unit.
>
> (Edited from BGVS, SDTT Project 2004–08, 2008: 42)

TABLE 7.2 *BGVS Janadhikar Kalajatha, 2007–08*

	Name of State	*No. of Dis-tricts*	*No. of Blocks*	*No. of GPs*	*No. of Jathas*	*No. of Artists*			*Starting Date*	*Culmination Date*	*Total Points*	*Approx. no. of Audience*	*Fund Collection (Rs)*	*Books Sold*
						M	*F*	*T*						
1.	Andhra Pradesh	12	–	240	4	50	10	60	15/12	7.01.08	240	–	–	–
2.	Arunachal Pradesh	5	13	40	1	6	4	10	19/11	5.12.07	40	80,000		
3.	Assam	8	18	102	1	8	8	16	7/11	6.12.07	98	1,00,000	–	20,997
4.	Bihar	28	73	98	2	23	16	39	22/11	10.12.07	117	1,00,000	26,000	17,000
5.	Gujarat	7	–	40	1					18.03.08	40			
6.	Haryana	18	–	–	2	35	35	70	14/11	2.12.07	105	80,000	2,50,000	50,000
7.	Jharkhand	18	101	126	3	41	21	62	27/12	11.12.07	126	80,000	3,00,000	11,000
8.	Karnataka	21	–	–	6	78	12	90	14–22/12	6.01.08	200	1,00,000	–	–
9.	Kerala	14	–	–	6	–	–	125	–	–	360	–	–	3,50,000
10.	Manipur	9	–	–	1	20	–	20	14/11	8.12.07	40	1,50,000		
11.	Madhya Pradesh	27	70	–	2	18	4	22	20/11	20.12.07	130	1,00,000	29,000	6,000
12.	Maharashtra	14	–	38	1	18	6	24	24/11	8.12.07	38	24,000	25,000	1,800
13.	Orissa	29	120	120	2	24	09	33	18/12	10.12.07	122	73,000	50,000	55,000
14.	Pondicherry	2	5	38	1	11	4	15	23/11	6.12.07	50	12,500	–	–
15.	Punjab	20	–	–	3	35	10	45	22/12	26.01.08	200	80,000		
16.	Rajasthan	10	17	100	2	23	7	30	14/11	10.12.07	130	50,000	70,000	3,500
17.	Tamil Nadu	29	90	103	3	31	14	45	24/11	5.12.07	103	1,00,000	–	50,000
18.	Tripura	4	207	110	3	27	5	32	14/11	11.12.07	51	63,000	–	10,000
19.	Uttar Pradesh	26	–	120	2	23	5	28	24/11	16.12.07	120	60,000	16,000	7,500
20.	Uttarakhand	11	–	–	1	11	4	15	11/11	10.12.07	82	85,000	10,000	16,000
	Total	305	714	1,235	46	482	174	781			2,352	13,37,500	7,76,000	6,01,473

Source: BGVS General Council Meeting, Tirupati, July 21–22, 2008: 66.

8

The Convergence of Literacy/Education with Development through Concentrated Decentralization

The period from 2002 to 2008 was marked by addressing policy issues at national and even global levels, as well as integrated practice at the local, micro level of clusters of gram panchayats, with resource persons for the same. The previous chapter largely covered the ground of the predominantly former process as part of which there were major campaigns and conventions for Rights, participation in the World Social Forum (WSF) processes and major kalajathas on relevant national issues. These macro, organizational, networking and communicational processes, and expressions of solidarity served to create a mass demonstrational basis and support system for advocacy with government at the policy level. This chapter focuses on the latter process of attempting to reach out to decentralized levels through capacity-building for convergence and concentration of sustained, day-to-day efforts for nurturing programmes towards institutionalizing people's organizational forms. The report to the General Council of the BGVS in Tirupati, Andhra Pradesh during July 21–22, 2008, hints at this two-pronged approach:

> "Attempts were made to develop capacities of the activists upto the panchayat level by providing National and State level resource persons through various programmes, training, workshops and campaigns. Efforts were made to influence the policies through mass mobilization. Members of BGVS who were on various bodies/committees tried to influence the decision-making processes as in the case of Right to

Education Legislation or formulation of Eleventh Five Year Plan, so far as allocations on Literacy and Continuing Education were concerned" (BGVS, 2008: 19).

1. The Proposal for Decentralized Institutionalization, 2002 ...

The BGVS had been aware of the need for sustaining its mass mobilizations and institutionalizing them at decentralized levels through various forms of people's organizations and institutions, right from 1998. Reports to the General Councils of BGVS had been sensitive to this need. However, the process picked up from 2002 and gained momentum from 2005 when a strategy and practice for convergence was beginning to take shape. A programme of decentralized planning was initiated from October, 2002, wherein each state unit was given some initial guidelines to prepare a five-year plan and a long-term vision. This was meant to be a planning process from the lowest organizational units of BGVS over a period of a year. Work plans were thus prepared with central capacity-building support for visioning exercises, analysis of organizational strengths and weaknesses, need assessment, human resource planning and data handling (BGVS, 2005: 10).

The state plans were consolidated into a national plan and, after a budgeting exercise, evolved into a three-year consolidated project proposal. The local organizational forms, as visualized in the proposal were to be GVVs, Bal Manch (children's forum) for basic education, CECs and libraries for adult education and SHGs under the banner of Samata. Mobilization activities through campaigns and publications resulting from the Jan Vachan Andolan were to be supportive activities. This proposal was then presented to and accepted by the Sir Dorabji Tata Trust (SDTT) for sponsorship.

During the first two and half years of the project funded by the SDTT, i.e., from 2004 to 2006, the BGVS had undertaken training programmes for 88 resource persons and a further training within 375 panchayats of 96 districts covering 16 states. In all 268 libraries were started within these panchayats. A total number of 18,871 persons had participated in these trainings which were geared towards enabling them to take up the multi-dimensional responsibilities at the sub-district level. This was part of a larger strategy of linking CECs with activities such as health, women's groups, libraries, wall newspapers and the formation of Charcha Mandals (discussion groups) (BGVS, 2004–08, 2008: 35).

2. The Concept and Strategy of 'Convergence', 2005 ...

The concept and strategy of convergence generally followed two basic principles: concentration of efforts within defined geographical areas at decentralized levels, generally a panchayat, moving on to a cluster of panchayats; and the convergence of related social development programmes within these defined geographical regions. The formation of a trained resource group of eight persons within each gram panchayat, half of whom would be women, was part of this initiative. The large network of Samata Women's SHGs constituted a potential organizational base for the convergence of different programmes: literacy, the Integrated Child Development Scheme (ICDS), Bal Manch, libraries, the GVVs of basic education; skill development and vocational training, Right to Work and the NREGA, Right to Food, the PDS and the Midday Meal Programme, watershed development, health and NRHM, at the level of socio-economic survival; and the Right to Information and the strengthening of the gram sabhas of the local gram panchayats within the context of local self-governance. Several documents and manuals were prepared for the guidance of trainers who would be training the panchayat level resource persons engaged in the strategy of convergence. It was visualized that the efforts at integration would evolve into organizational forms such as Bal Manch, Kisan Manch, Yuva Manch and the Samata Women's SHGs for different categories of persons which could serve as pressure groups for accountability and delivery from the gram panchayats. The effort was entitled as a Citizen Education Programme for Democracy where aspects of democratic, political participation through gram sabhas would be closely linked to socio-economic development. Training manuals were brought out in Hindi, Assamese, Oriya, Bengali and Telugu. Training programmes were held in two spells of six days each for the village level resource persons.

A manual prepared for the training of panchayat level resource persons states some of the key objectives of the initial, two-phase training programme, of six days each. The trainings were being conducted not in a cascading manner, as was the general style of BGVS, but directly by a district level resource team supported by national level resource persons. The objectives of the training were:

- "To equip and install a group of social activists in a contiguous area with certain level of awareness and understanding.

- To develop a group of activists who have faith and concern about their surroundings especially in the community.
- To develop a group of activists who have faith in collectivism.
- To develop confidence in the activists for understanding the surroundings and to realize the social issues and its causes and to prioritize the area of interventions by understanding the scope and limitations and develop strategies by taking into consideration the objective realities.
- To motivate the participants to take the challenge of continuous learning through self-learning, collective learning and experiential learning.
- To develop the skill of transaction or communication by understanding the context, need and the level of the participants (BGVS, August 2007: 4).

The topics covered were 'Our Surroundings, the World Around Us', which covered the ecological, socio-economic, cultural and political context of the participants and government interventions through various programmes; understanding BGVS; Samata, SHGs, Panchayati Raj, Continuing and Lifelong Education (CLEP) and linkages with the different BGVS initiatives. The sessions also covered practical aspects of how to prepare a local level plan of action with the involvement of the gram sabha and the gram panchayat.

The 11th Congress of AIPSN was held in Guwahati on February 2–5, 2006 with a focus on convergence of the programmes of BGVS and of government within the decentralized, concentrated context of contiguous gram panchayats. The attempt was to provide a strategic vision for the organization around the concept of 'convergence'. About 430 participants from 20 states of the country took part and almost all the executive committee members of BGVS were present. Discussions were held on various aspects of basic education, continuing education and Samata. A detailed report was prepared as an advocacy document for submission to the NLM for inclusion as part of its national plans (BGVS, 2004–08, 2008: 79).

During August 6–7, 2006, a major convention of BGVS activists was held at the convention centre, Indira Gandhi National Open University, New Delhi. This was under the banner of 'Education for Decentralized Democracy and Development' with the participation of about 350 activists from 18 state units. The focus of this convention was on self-reliance of state units in the context of depleting BGVS central resources from government and other agencies and on the above-mentioned strategy of convergence. By this time, about 1,500 panchayats were covered by convergence training programmes. The convention was addressed by the Union Minister of Panchayati Raj, Youth Affairs and Sports and the Union Minister of State for Human Resource Development, apart from BGVS activists and other concerned intellectuals.

On August 21, 2006 a meeting was held to work out the strategy for convergence. This involved BGVS state coordinators and executive committee members. Several visioning exercises were held during the period 2005–07 for the new and existing BGVS leadership in order to work out a strategy for the next 10 years. As part of this exercise, an organizational camp was held at Jaipur during May 4–6, 2007 in which 125 key activists of BGVS participated. The issues discussed were the strengths and limitations of the present state level organizations, the changing role of the BGVS within newly emerging contexts and papers entitled 'Vision on Futuristic Plan' and 'A Great Leap Forward' by M.P. Parameswaran, ex-President of BGVS. The former paper suggested a coverage of about 300 blocks (out of the 6,000 odd blocks in the country) each having approximately three contiguous clusters of five gram panchayats each. This would result in a sizable effort of concentrated convergence covering close to 5,000 gram panchayats out of the more than 2,00,000 gram panchayats in the country during the three-year period of 2008–11 (BGVS, 2008: 93–94). The second paper drew attention to the fact that the Government of India, through its various departments, had more than 2,700 schemes aimed at poverty alleviation. Estimates suggested that an average district got finances in the range of Rs 250 crore to Rs 500 crore per annum on these schemes; which would imply that each gram panchayat would be receiving funds in the range of Rs 50 lakh to Rs 100 lakh per year. There was a need for an integrated and convergent approach to the utilization of these funds, for which a group of about 10 trained resource persons within each selected gram panchayat could serve as an important pressure group and a channel for efficient and accountable utilization (BGVS, 2008: 119–120).

During the period October to December 2007, several regional level planning and review meetings were held to consolidate the convergence strategy. This process was brought to a head through a National Experience Sharing workshop held during January 1–3, 2008, on the

Ranjit Kumar is 28 years old. His father Shri Ram Sevak is a former Sarpanch (head of the gram panchayat). His wife is presently Sarpanch of Nararpuri panchayat. He is the Secretary of the Gyan Vigyan Samiti (Literacy Committee), Khajouli block and is also Joint Secretary of the Block Literacy Committee. He had participated in the national workshop of the convergence strategy organized by Saharsa, Bihar. He had also organized the training programme for convergence for a cluster of villages in his block and has now become the state level resource person for training in other districts.

Ranjit Kumar says, 'On two occasions I have led the dharna (sit-in) and demonstration programmes in front of the block headquarters which were organized against the corruption in government development programmes. The Block Development Officers and the block head along with their goondas (goons) attacked our peaceful dharna and lodged cases against us. I managed to get out on bail and continued the struggle under Right to Information (RTI). Meanwhile, myself and my friend were trapped in many cases. When information was sought from Block Development Officer under RTI Act, we didn't get it. When the same was sought from the Deputy Development Commissioner of the District Rural Developmental Agency, instead of information we got threats. Then we appealed to the District Authority, Madhubani. Neither information nor justice was provided by them. They only asked for clarifications from the Deputy Development Commissioner and during this period the whole family was threatened by the authorities.

After this, I approached the State Information Commissioner. I visited them frequently and faced a lot of problems during the hearing at the State Commission. After that the Block Development Officer came to my house to provide the information. They did not even charge for the photocopies. All the authorities from top to bottom were together. Still without giving justice to me, my case has been closed by the Information Commission. Till today I am a victim of their anger.

(Edited from BGVS, SDTT Project 2004–08, 2008: 37)

linkage between Continuing Education and Samata as part of the convergence strategy. This workshop was held in Bhopal and involved 70 participants. A similar workshop was held during December 29–30 of the same year.

Table 8.1 presents a picture of the attempt to bring about an integration between social development programmes and the Samata network through the trainings for convergence by 2008. A total of 1,673 gram panchayats were covered which were located in 323 clusters. This concentration of efforts was carried out in 226 blocks within 127 districts of 16 states. There were in all 15,852 participants, more than 50 per cent of whom were women.

TABLE 8.1 *Continuing Education – Samata, Convergence Training till 2008*

State	*No. of Districts*	*No. of Blocks*	*No. of Clusters*	*No. of GPs*	*No. of Participants*		
					M	*F*	*Total*
1. Andhra Pradesh	6	8	19	101	475	420	895
2. Assam	17	23	35	175	522	850	1,372
3. Bihar	18	31	35	177	1,371	1,374	2,745
4. Haryana	1	1	1	4	16	16	32
5. Himachal Pradesh	8	17	17	84	311	291	602
6. Jharkhand	9	24	35	178	700	900	1,600
7. Karnataka	9	10	10	46	187	262	512
8. Madhya Pradesh	8	20	37	185	892	737	1,629
9. Maharashtra	5	6	7	30	154	140	294
10. Orissa	13	22	31	172	498	662	1,160
11. Puducherry	1	2	5	25	83	127	210
12. Punjab	5	5	10	50	–	–	500
13. Rajasthan	7	7	11	54	319	210	529
14. Tripura	4	20	26	169	628	900	1,528
15. Uttarakhand	7	10	11	55	197	322	519
16. Uttar Pradesh	9	20	33	168	789	823	1,725
Total	127	226	323	1,673	7,142	8,034	15,852

Source: BGVS General Council Meeting, Tirupati, July 21–22, 2008: 58.

An analysis of the limited available data on the social background of the participants in the trainings (BGVS, 2004–08, 2008: 39), suggests that 21 per cent belonged to the OBCs and 22 per cent were from the SC, ST communities. A small minority of 2 per cent were from the Muslim community. Almost 54 per cent of the participants in the training programmes were newer, post–2000 entrants to the BGVS organization.

Sunita Devi of Sadamau gram panchayat, Masoli block, Barabanki district has only passed high school. She became a BGVS member in 2006. She has attended all the gram panchayat level training programmes and meetings for the convergence of projects. After getting fully trained, she formed the panchayat level committee and became the coordinator. She also established the Kishori Manch for young women.

A library was opened with the support of BGVS. She herself runs the library which is located in her house. It has 300 books and she has asked for more. She has helped the local team to bring out a wall paper. She and other village level resource persons/facilitators have conducted a village survey. A women's SHG has been formed and another is in the process of formation. She and her colleagues have generated awareness among the villagers about the Midday Meal Scheme and NREGA. A Bal Manch for children, a Mahila Manch for women and a Kisan Manch for farmers have been formed. She has facilitated the participation of children in the GVV which has recently been setup.

(Edited from BGVS, SDTT Project 2004–08, 2008: 36)

9

Some Illustrative Cases

1. The Case of Mandi District, Himachal Pradesh

BGVS has a strong organizational base in the state with the involvement of educationists and prominent persons who were closely connected with activists at the field level and the village level participants in its diverse programmes. It had played an important part in providing leadership to the Mandi district literacy campaign. The campaign was launched in the district in June, 1992. A massive motivational and environment-building campaign was followed by the creation of committees from the district to the village level. The coverage of the district was done in a block-wise manner over the following year. The post-literacy programme was sanctioned in July, 1993, for six blocks and in March, 1995, for the remaining four blocks. The district reported that 1,17,742 persons were enrolled out of the 1,51,753 non-literates who were identified. A total number of 79,762 (53% of the identified non-literates) persons were reported to have completed the three primers during the literacy campaign. The vast majority of these persons aged 9 to 45 were female. The post-literacy programme was conducted through Jan Chetna Kendras (People's Awakening Centres), libraries that were located at the ward level.

Continuing Education in Mandi District: One visited Mandi District in June, 2000. The literacy campaigns in the state and in the district had, by and large, entered the Continuing Education (CE) phase. Mandi district had reconceptualized the structure of the Nodal Continuing Education Centres (NCECs) and Continuing Education Centres (CECs) to suit the dispersed geographical character of the gram panchayats. It had set up 382 NCECs, one for each gram panchayat, and 2,582 CECs within each of the wards of the gram panchayats in the district. The district had 10 blocks. The CE programme had begun in 1998 in three phases, and had at the time of the visit covered all the blocks. Eight gram panchayats were being coordinated by a zonal coordinator and the block by a block coordinator for the CE programme.

The District Literacy Committee, within which the BGVS was providing leadership, had visualized that a gram panchayat with an approximate total population of 3,000 would be having a population of 1,500 (50%) in the 15–35 age group. A nodal CEC could be set up at this gram panchayat level to serve the needs of approximately 1,000 (66%) literates from the formal education system, 300 (20%) neo-literates from the literacy campaign and about 200 (13%) non-literates that still needed to be covered. A gram panchayat would generally have seven wards, each with a population of 215 persons in the age group of 15–35. Given the scattered nature of hamlets/wards and the hilly geographical terrain, one CEC within each ward would have to be set up. A library would cover the ward as a unit, whereas other programmes could take the gram panchayat as a unit. The unit costs of the Mandi district continuing education programme per enrolled neo-literate/non-literate per annum was working out to approximately Rs 75.

The programmes that were being conducted through the CE centres were in the areas of health, primary education, credit and self-help groups, and the diffusion of information to generate awareness. Apart from the CE centres, other major activities related to education were the promotion of 100 per cent enrolment within elementary education and the setting up of Mother-Teacher Associations attached to schools. It was reported that while all these structures for community participation in elementary education had been formed, about 20 per cent were active. Activities in the area of health covered aspects of safe delivery and mother and child health, pulse polio and AIDS campaigns, and awareness on the harmful effects of addiction to tobacco and alcohol. About two lakh persons had participated in health jathas that had 347 performances throughout the district. These were conducted almost entirely with people's financial contributions. Activities related to conserving the environment were awareness campaigns relating to polythene bags, the celebration of environment days, forestry programmes in three blocks and steps to eliminate forest fires. Women's empowerment and the creation of SHGs was a follow-up to the Samata Vigyan Utsavas held during 1997–98. Apart from savings, the women's groups were important fora for the diffusion of health information and linkages with Panchayati Raj institutions.

ILLUSTRATION 9.1 *Aspects of Continuing Education*

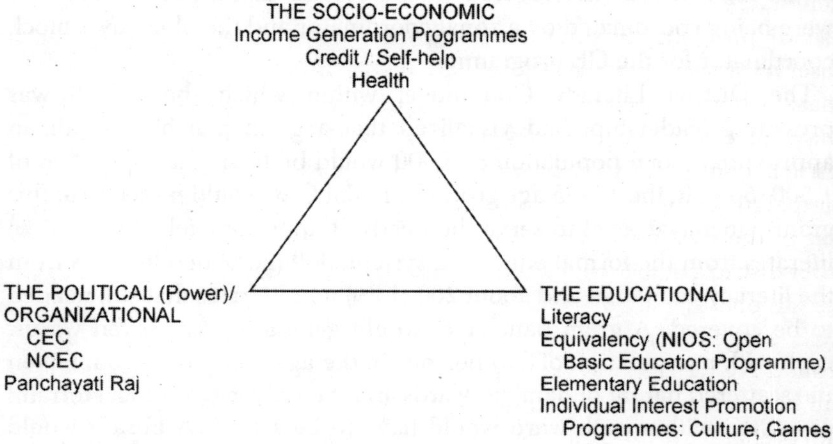

Some General Issues and Reflections

The central scheme of CE visualized activities initiated by the NCECs and CECs along the following dimensions, drawn largely from UNESCO's Appeal Programme. One would like to represent them as follows:

The foregoing visualization of programmes in three broad areas covering: Credit/self-help and income generation programmes of a socio-economic nature and health; people's organization-building and human resource development around NCEC and CEC structures together with strengthening the system of local self-governance through Panchayati Raj; and more specifically, educational programmes of a literacy, equivalency, elementary education and individual interest promotional character. These need to be seen as overlapping dimensions of a CE thrust at decentralized levels.

The Mandi district CE efforts and organizational structures may be seen as highly exemplary, setting a standard for the CE programmes in the country which were largely floundering. However, an overview of the CE initiatives in general, and in Mandi district in particular, would suggest several issues relating to CE. The gaps in centralized financial support between the literacy, post-literacy and continuing education phases of the literacy campaign cause severe setbacks to the flow of initiatives and mobilization at decentralized levels. These phases need to be seen in an integrated manner, both in substantive and financial terms.

The literacy phase throws up a diversity of learning needs within a decentralized population, ranging from non-literacy to neo-literacy and persons who have dropped out of formal education systems at the elementary level. Addressing these needs in a convergent manner poses several problems to educational activists. At the national level, one observes a tendency to declare a particular district formally in the CE phase; whereas the majority of learners might still be in the preparatory phase of the literacy campaign. While this was not true for Mandi district, considering its relatively high levels of literacy prior to the campaign and the positive results in terms of literacy outcomes at the end of the campaign, this concern is valid for a significant number of other districts in the country which might be formally designated to be in the CE phase.

CE suggests, in organizational terms, an institution-building phase around NCEC and CECs. In effect, if the foregoing is true, there might still be the need for social mobilization for learning which characterizes the preparatory phase of the literacy campaigns. The formation of community based, people's organizational forms might, however, be initiated right from the start of a literacy campaign. These provide a developmental organizational basis and a wider relevance to literacy efforts. CE programmes that count on government extension departments of a developmental nature are faced with a predicament. Development needs, especially in the CE phase, are of a convergent nature; whereas the departments are structured in divergence. Considering this departmental segregation, it becomes difficult to draw on government as a major resource for developmental inputs.

Repeat Visit to Mandi District, Himachal Pradesh, June, 2005

Another visit was made to this district, this time at the instance of the Sir Dorabji Tata Trust which was funding the national project of BGVS from January, 2004. This visit, approximately five years after the first, served the additional purpose of assessing the status and transformation of the adult education efforts of BGVS in the district and the state.

Nagwain Technology Research Centre, Mandi: The visit to Mandi district began with a late evening meeting with several BGVS activists in Nagwain. Some 30 people from different districts and towns throughout the state had come to participate in this meeting. This show of strength served to indicate the extensiveness of BGVS's efforts in the state and the uniqueness of its interventions in Mandi district, in particular. Most of the persons present were government servants who had given their time voluntarily to the organization and had come all the way from Shimla, a five-hour drive away. This organizational strategy meeting was on the following day. Some of them had stayed back for the meeting with us and drove overnight to Shimla.

Some of the issues that emerged from the overview that was presented to us by persons from different districts were as follows. There is considerable awareness of the need to institutionalize the different activities of BGVS and to relate literacy to various developmental concerns. There was a concern about the shortage of financial resources at the state level, since the state government was reluctant to give its 25 per cent share of funding for the CE programme. The funds from the centre had been exhausted. As a result, there was some problem in sustaining the involvement of the BGVS activists.

Changes in the political character of state level governments had not impacted the programme in the past and it was felt unlikely to do so in the future. This was except for the matter of financial resources. The activist and participant base was sufficiently large and diverse to accommodate different political perspectives.

The training programmes conducted by the central team of BGVS were found to be useful. The state level activists felt the need for ongoing academic research support from the central office, given that literacy was not seen as a short-term process. The state BGVS team was somehow able to sustain the continuing education activities from the people's own financial resources and by generating resources from government and other agencies at the state level. It was reported that Mandi district had some 3,000 volunteers and another 30,000 persons had expressed their interest in getting involved with the BGVS programmes in various ways.

The origin of the Technology Research Centre at Nagwain was a result of the initiative of the Delhi Science Forum which began its activities in the area with a major workshop on science and local knowledge in 1983. With financial assistance from the Department of Science and Technology they began work in two sectors: Leather under which some 250 persons were trained in the use of appropriate technologies for the local market and pottery. The latter attempted to use new technologies and to expand the product range. In 1989, the centre had become independent with its own management. A building was constructed in 2001 with assistance of CAPART. The centre also engages in training programmes and demonstration in the areas of horticulture, nursery plants, organic farming and vermi compost. A cold storage unit using appropriate technology had been constructed in collaboration with the Indian Institute of Science. The centre that we visited was primarily engaged in leather work and making squashes of fruits and served as a sub-centre of the main unit which was in Manori. A network of other sub-centres covering aspects of blacksmithy, pottery and construction technologies served to provide technical skills for income generation within the literacy campaigns and the continuing education activities of BGVS in the state.

The literacy and post-literacy phases of the literacy campaign had been completed in all the districts of Himachal Pradesh at the time of our field visit. There had been a break in central financial support for the CE programme. Funding had been provided only to Mandi district and here too the central sponsorship for three years was over. There were 3,037 gram panchayats in Himachal Pradesh, but due to constraints of funds, the BGVS wished to focus on 10 per cent of these panchayats. The continuing education efforts in Mandi district had covered all 10 blocks and the felt priority was to consolidate these activities. This district, as well, was facing severe budgetary constraints and lack of flexibility over budgetary heads and geographical coverage as regards the limited funds that were available.

Raha Village, Nagwain Gram Panchayat: Our visit was to a CEC in this village. There was a small group of articulate and outspoken women. They reported that about 25 women from the village were active in the literacy campaign and had become literate. They now meet on the 12th day of every month in the home of the village headman where a small library is also housed. They borrow books, read and discuss them together in the meetings. The collection of books in the library was small, though apparently much used, and the women felt the need for more books for them to be able to expand their reading.

A SHG was formed by 12 women in the village and it was reported to be very successful. The SHG had savings of about Rs 20,000 and the money was earning a small interest. Loans were generally spent on the education of children, for marriages and other domestic expenses. Some had also taken up income generating activities. The women had undergone training in bag making and had begun to make cloth bags, crocheted covers for television sets, teddy bears and other small things which they sold in the local market. The profit was quite substantial, for example, a cloth bag produced for around Rs 30 could be sold at about Rs 70.

Pondoh Gram Panchayat: There were eight SHGs in Pondoh; seven of them were linked to the bank. They reported that the bank was happy to lend them money, considering their track record of transactions and repayment. We were meeting a small group of relatively older women in this village since several of the younger ones were busy because of the school holiday. While the women were quite involved in the activities of the saving groups, they did not seem to have much interest in the CEC and its library.

Nodal Continuing Education Centre (NCEC), Jugan Village, Badsu Gram Panchayat: We met an initial group of 15 women and as we spent time the group swelled as others joined it. Several women were literacy activists who had been involved in the earlier literacy campaign and the post-literacy phase. They were now engaged in income generating work. They spoke nostalgically about the literacy campaign and how it had provided them a public platform and a sense of deep involvement. They had also helped to set up Jan Chetna Kendras (People's Awareness Centres) within different gram panchayats.

One of the activists reported that she had been involved since 1998 with the BGVS and had been to Dharamshala for training. On her return she had helped to form nine SHGs. Very soon, several income generating activities had started. Many of the women were keen that their daughters be educated and wished to put aside money for this. The first loans that were taken were the most difficult, since the women wondered about their capacity to repay. The fact that the women had been able to independently earn an income had improved their standing within the home and the local community. In the case of the person being discussed, she was a panchayat coordinator for BGVS and her only income was Rs 200 a month at the outset. With the help of the National Bank for Agriculture and Rural Development (NABARD) she had been able to set up a small tea stall and gradually her income rose to around Rs 3,000 a month. She said that she was now confident while speaking at public fora. The group under her leadership was trained in bag making and tailoring. The group was engaged in bag making, tailoring and the making of vermi compost which they sold to the villagers. The group has about Rs 75,000 in savings.

This NCEC covers 10 gram panchayats. The panchayat coordinators meet regularly and each ward of the panchayats has a SHG. The CEC in this panchayat together with its library was well used. They were keen to add to their collection. The women reported that seeing the success of their small enterprises even young boys and men wanted to be trained and set up SHGs.

Some General Issues and Reflections

Mobilization and Institutionalization: One of the overall issues faced by the BGVS in its work across the country and in diverse contexts is: How can an organization as diverse and as differently constructed out of mainly volunteer work move out of a mobilization mode into an institutional one? This question can perhaps be largely answered by taking a closer look at the functioning of the SHGs.

Mobilization and Institutionalization, SHGs: These are institutions which meet the felt needs of women and emerge almost naturally from mobilization processes of this section. They are also institutions that do not need much infrastructure and salaries. They are not only able to pay for themselves in a self-sustaining manner, but can also be profitable to some degree. While addressing the issues of relative economic independence for women and providing them a forum for meeting, reading and discussions, they make a considerable difference to the self-esteem of their members. At the heart of the SHG activity is not only the economic improvement in women's lives, but the overall improvement that this leads to the lives of their families. Women are able to interact and sell in the market place, they are able to have some degree of control within the family and are able to interact with other SHGs, do accounts, deal with banks and assume financial responsibility. The base provided by this activity gradually develops, under appropriate leadership, as a base for raising awareness on other issues such as female feticide. A structure of federation is gradually emerging within Mandi district, closely linked with the Samata network and federations in other districts/states.

Consolidation of BGVS Development Initiatives: In the case of Himachal Pradesh, and Mandi district in particular, these have generally been as regards Samata SHGs, CECs and mobilization for the Jan Vachan Andolan (People's Reading Movement). Even though the CECs are not functioning upto expectation due to the financial crunch, the formation of SHGs and their involvement in CECs and the libraries have gathered pace. The women were in general very aware of the importance of literacy and the education of their children. Even though some of them may have lapsed into illiteracy because of breaks in the funding of the CEC programme, they were determined that their children should be educated. This also had the effect that women would pay greater attention to health, sanitation and their own economic activities. Given the fact that elementary education in Himachal Pradesh is comparatively well-established, the local BGVS had taken the decision not to initiate GVVs. As regards the libraries, our observations in some other states may be seen with respect to Mandi district as well. The books if well-used tend to be utilized primarily by children, adults and BGVS activists who have had the opportunity of formal education through the schooling system. This is not necessarily a negative practice, since literate members of local communities are expected to gain benefits from the CECs and their libraries. In some instances, the books tend to be relatively new or locked away and out of reach in a cupboard. In both cases, the neo-literates and persons with a fragile literacy who have emerged from the literacy campaigns tend to be left out. What proportion of the readership are neo-literates is an open question, as also the types of books that they do read with facility and appreciation. A survey conducted by BGVS of the users of the libraries would help to answer this question.

Convergence of Institutionalised Efforts: Mandi district serves as an important illustration of the consolidation and convergence of different educational and livelihood-related activities, sponsored by different sources and consolidated around varying institutional formations. Some of the broader institutional initiatives have been the Technology Research Centre with its sub-centres, AIPSN, Samata and several developmental programmes sponsored by governments thanks to the good relations that the local BGVS has with government. It has generally been upto the initiative of the state and district units of BGVS to seek other sources for programme implementation, considering that external sources of funding have been largely to the central office for capacity-building.

2. The Case of BGVS, Dhanbad District, Bihar–Jharkhand

BGVS in Dhanbad district needs to be analysed in the context of the specific features of its functioning in the undivided Bihar state. Field level activists reported the significant impact on primary education as a result of the demand for schooling in some districts of the state, the impact on caste relations, on health and to a limited extent on gender relations. By the end of 2000, state level BGVS personnel reported a strong presence in 21 out of the then 55 districts. A BGVS report for the year 1997 states that there were 5,404 full time members and 45,329 affiliated members in 28 districts of the state. Sub-committees had been set up for training, post-literacy, the JoL Project, health, natural resource literacy, on women issues, for cultural mobilization and academic matters, and for the Desh Ko Jano Project. While BGVS was involved in the literacy campaigns in a selective manner in 21 districts, in nine it had played a key role. Significant work had been carried out in Begusarai, Madhepura, Saharsa, Khagaria, Kaimur (Bhabhu). A distinctive characteristic of BGVS in Bihar had been that it was largely constituted by persons drawn from the weaker sections. The literacy activists were predominantly from the district and sub-district level and a majority of them had some experience of earlier participation in democratic movements such as the Jai Prakash Narayan movement for 'total revolution', the student's movement and the anti-emergency struggles during 1975 to 1977. The leadership reported that while literacy activists were highly enthusiastic and efficient in action, their capacities in financial management, academic and documentation work needed to be enhanced.

The Jharkhand state unit of BGVS was established in 2003, three years after Jharkhand became a separate state on November 15, 2000. The Jharkhand unit had reached out, in particular, to tribals by taking up issues of food security, right to work and the monitoring of NREGA.

The Literacy Campaign in Dhanbad District, Jharkhand State

The following is based on a report of March, 2002, from one of the members of the district leadership and one's field visits to the district on two occasions. Although the literacy campaign programme was launched in Dhanbad district on September 8, 1994, its origin can be traced to the initiation of the BGVS jatha in July, 1990. The jathas were held at 110 different places in which altogether 50,000 people took part. Under the influence of the jatha, about a dozen youths took the initiative to set up the local BGVS. Some of these youths had been influenced by the earlier Jai Prakash Narayan movement and Left ideology. They formed a core committee. This was followed by organizing kalajathas. The jathas drew youth in large numbers and as a result of this mobilization process the organization developed its network. Four kalajathas were organized to cover the whole district from October 2 to November 14, 1992. Saksharta Vahini (groups of literacy activists) were formed in coordination with the district administration in July, 1992. It was during that period that some members decided to concentrate on a village and make at least one village fully literate. A village named Kachchra of Baghmara block was selected and it achieved a high degree of literacy.

The literacy campaign was started in five panchayats on October 2, 1993. Teaching-learning activities were initiated among 4.87 lakh non-literates throughout the district from September 8, 1994. In the first stage, only 3.67 lakh non-literates were supplied first standard books. In the second stage, all 4.87 lakh non-literates were supplied books. Along with kalajathas, padyatras, wall writing, organizational training and survey (one-day) were conducted before starting the teaching-learning sessions. Nearly 5,000 people participated in the one-day survey. About 50,000 volunteers, 2,500 head teachers and 250 resource persons were trained.

Some of the achievements of the literacy campaign conducted by the BGVS, Dhanbad district may be summarized as follows. Literacy committees had been formed in 180 out of the 185 panchayats and in 1,085 out of the 1,275 villages. It was reported that messages could be sent to people in the villages within two days. There was a strong organizational network from the district to the villages.

Literacy campaigns were linked with the problem of minimum wages. A separate primer was prepared called Kala Sona (Black Gold). The unorganized labourers working in the coal dumps were being given a very low wage. The literacy campaigns helped the labourers to get united and to use their union, under which they had been fighting for their rights. Major campaigns were launched against alcoholism. One of the literacy volunteers called Buddhu Mahto was killed by a liquor baron. Poor people without any provision of relief were enabled to become red card holders in the public distribution system of food grains.

About 54,000 children were enrolled in schools within a day on the 'school chalo' slogan pursued by the BGVS and Saksharta Vahini (the literacy committees). Enrolment in the schools increased due to such environment-building. About 200 schools were opened for giving education to approximately 40,000 children. There was an increase in women's participation as literacy volunteers and key trainers. Due to this, a large number of women's groups were formed at different levels. Surveys of pregnant women and children were conducted in about 150 villages and health committees were formed. Over 200 village libraries were opened. Neo-literates visited, read and borrowed books from these libraries. Approximately 600 SHGs were formed by the women. These SHGs had over Rs 12 lakh deposits in their accounts. There was a significant participation in the pulse polio campaign. The literacy groups of Dhanbad district took an active part in providing immediate relief and help to the victims of cyclone in Orissa during October, 1999. According to the 2001 Census, Dhanbad district stood first in rural literacy, both in Jharkhand and Bihar.

Seven out of the eight blocks in Dhanbad district were among the top 25 most literate blocks in the state. Following a Supreme Court judgement for providing midday meals to children in all the schools, the state government issued orders for the same in February, 2002. On April 7, 2002 (World Health Day), 50,000 children were given midday meals under public pressure with the involvement of the BGVS. The children participated in a demonstration in front of the chief Minister's residence in support of the demand for the midday meal.

Jitpur Village NCEC, Topchachi Block, Dhanbad District: One visited this NCEC in January, 2001. This NCEC catered to the needs of a total population of 22,000 in two gram panchayats. The NCEC had a 15-member executive committee and a seven-member core group responsible for different programmes. The CEC at the village level also had an executive committee and a core group. Several mobilizational activities had been undertaken, such as panchayat resource mapping exercises followed by a Panchayat Development Report, Jan Vachan Utsavas and Samata Vigyan Utsavas. SHGs had been established as well as cultural groups of local artistes and a football team. Education through the CECs had taken a wider development character through health awareness campaigns and the creation of a Village Health Register, the formation of 22 SHGs, resource mapping exercises with linkages to the gram panchayat, the sale of low-cost books and the starting of village libraries, and a skill development programme based on a need assessment survey.

Some problems were reported at our meeting and in the documentation such as getting adequate technical resource support, the local committees not being regular in their meetings, sustaining various activities due to inadequacies in financial and academic support, establishing links with the government development departments, the interference of local vested interests and gram panchayats that were, for practical purposes, non-functioning (BGVS, February 2002).

Continuing education activities had also been initiated on a substantive scale in the villages of the nearby Tundi block as seen during our visits to Bangaro, Sitalpur, Odratand and Laharbadi villages. The important feature of this block was that while formal development institutions like health and education had come to a standstill as a result of the tension and violence between the state machinery and militant people's organizations, continuing education appeared to be the major substantive developmental input that had popular support. Public institutions such as schools, panchayat offices and health centres had come to a standstill with all their furniture and equipment ravaged by people who were caught in a cycle of violence between the state machinery and militant people's organizations. One visited the following gram panchayats in Tundi block, Dhanbad district: Nawada gram panchayat, Mariadeh gram panchayat with its revenue villages of Sitalpur and Mariadeh, Majhiladoh with its revenue village of Odratand, Tundi gram panchayat itself with its revenue village Laharbadi and Lodheria panchayat within which the revenue village of Gopinathpur falls.

3. The Case of Mahalir Association For Literacy, Awareness and Rights (MALAR), Kanyakumari District, Tamil Nadu

MALAR offers a useful illustration of how mobilization around literacy, towards a women's movement, can be consolidated through village level organization, networking and sustainable institutionalization. The following information about the organization is drawn largely from the Annual Report of the Fifth District Conference held in July, 2000. Other documents supplied by the organization and our field visit in February, 2001 helped to complete the picture.

As the name suggests, MALAR is an organization of women for their social, economic and educational emancipation. The organization, administered by women, was formed in 1995 under the guidance of the Tamil Nadu Science Forum (TNSF). The forum had taken an active part in the literacy campaign in Kanyakumari district which ran from 1991 to 1995. This successful campaign mobilized more than one lakh learners, but was suddenly withdrawn in 1995 by the administration. A mass base that had been mobilized felt frustrated and convinced the TNSF to evolve an alternative. What followed was an ambitious experiment in organizing poor women through a network of credit cooperatives that was relatively independent of government administration.

By July, 2000, it had a total membership of 17,700, comprised of 885 SHGs spread over the entire district. By February, 2001, when we visited the district, the number of groups had increased to 1,090 with a membership of approximately 22,000. And by 2006, it was reported that MALAR had formed 1,600 groups with more than 30,000 members and transactions of more than Rs 22 crore, with Rs 7 lakh as savings. About 60 micro enterprises, most of which were individual-based, were already initiated (BGVS, 2005–06, 2006: 14). While the organization was administered by women and was independent of government, it had close networks with government agencies, banks, non-government organizations and resource persons drawn from various sectors of society.

The organizational structure with frequency of meetings was as follows:

- Revenue Village Level SHGs (approximately 20 members with a President, Secretary and Treasurer); weekly meetings held,
- Gram Panchayat Committee (comprised of village coordinators each of them looks after approximately five SHGs); meetings held according to need,

- Block Committee (of all village coordinators); monthly meetings held on the first Saturday,
- District Committee (of all block coordinators, each of them look after approximately 50 SHGs and the office bearers and advisors); monthly meetings held on the third Saturday,
- A district conference held annually, preceded by block and panchayat/group level conferences.

By July, 2000, the savings of the different groups amounted to Rs 77 lakhs and the amount of loan taken by them was Rs 2,59,33,905. The following Table 9.1 suggests that the trend has been a movement from obtaining loans for redemption of debts and for consumption purposes, to economic activities such as agriculture, animal husbandry and micro enterprises. The table also suggests that the relative significance of purpose, ranked according to the number of persons taking a loan, was as follows:

TABLE 9.1 *Purposes for Which Loans Were Utilized, MALAR, July, 2000*

Number of Persons	*Purpose*	*Amount*
1,989	Liquidation of loans	32,60,600
1,580	Redeeming ornaments	30,64,900
1,463	Education	24,37,000
1,379	Medical expenses	16,33,250
1,126	Trading	17,52,200
1,106	Micro-enterprises	9,93,450
923	Other purposes	15,17,245
814	Animal husbandry	3,06,763
757	Agriculture	11,92,850
755	House construction	29,42,100
703	Marriage	27,55,800
610	Making ornaments	1,06,82,210
145	Ration card	1,40,000
45	Electric connection	10,000

Source: MALAR, Annual Report Presented in the Fifth Annual District Conference, July 28–29, 2000, Kanyakumari, 2000: 4.

The following micro-enterprises had been initiated: readymade garment centres, training and poultry development at two centres, training in hand embroidery at two centres, training in milkgova making, training in coir making for two groups, and coconut oil extraction. Apart from the foregoing, several members were engaged in individual economic activities such as running shops, selling vegetables, grocery trade, pottery, basket making, coconut leaf thatching, animal husbandry, farming on leased lands, weaving, curd making, and tailoring. Some of the MALAR groups had established contacts with programmes such as Development of Women and Children in Rural Areas (DWACRA) and Swarna Jayanti Gram Swarozgar Yojana (SGSY).

One of the major reasons for the economic and organizational sustainability of MALAR has been the operationalization of the principle of sharing of interest on group/district loans given at the rate of 24 per cent and bank loans at the rate of 12.5 per cent per annum, in the following manner:

The SHG transactions were designed to ensure not only the self-reliance but also the self-sustainability of the groups. Each of the group members contributed an annual membership fee of Rs 10 and a minimum saving of Rs 20 per month (i.e., a minimum amount of Rs 5 every week) to their respective groups. Each group contributed an amount of Rs 50 per month to the District Level Federation, which went towards the reserve fund at the district level. The individual personal loans were available to members from the SHGs and group loans were available to the SHGs from the Federation at a rate of 24 per cent per annum on a reducing balance of the principal amount. Private money-lenders in the region generally charged between 60 per cent and 120 per cent rates of interest.

The income distribution was as follows:

Interest on loan to members from the SHG at the rate of 24 per cent: 50 per cent to Group, 30 per cent to Village Coordinator, 20 per cent to District Committee.

Interest on loan to the SHG from district at the rate of 24 per cent: 50 per cent to Interest Reserve Fund (for paying back to the group), 20 per cent to Village Coordinator, 30 per cent to District Committee.

The District loan was given from the Rs 50 per group, which was contributed per month, repayable with 12 per cent per annum interest to the group after five years. Other income to the District Committee consisted of the Rs 10 annual membership fee from each member.

Interest on Revolving Fund (a grant under Swarna Jayanti Gram Swayamrojgar Yojna): 50 per cent to Group, 10 per cent to Village Coordinator, 20 per cent to Social Security Fund, 20 per cent to District Committee.

The District Committee incurred major expenses on the following items on each of the SHGs every year: individual passbooks, rubber stamps, membership forms, loan forms, loan cards (repayment), register in duplicate for monthly accounts, bank loan forms, resource paper every month, registration certificate copy for bank account opening, introduction letter to the bank, sponsorship letter for bank loan.

The organization had conducted several training programmes for enhancing the administrative and financial capacities of its members and office bearers. Visits to other districts and states had also facilitated this process. MALAR had actively participated in the health movement coordinated by BGVS at the national level and had interfaced with programmes such as Convergent Community Action (CCA) of the UNICEF and government welfare schemes such as the provision of latrines and housing.

The group's meeting that takes place every week for savings transactions, also served as a forum for discussions. The solidarity emerging from these group-building activities had resulted in several collective actions as reported in the MALAR documents. Members of MALAR had contested the elections to the local self-governing bodies. Micro-credit and micro-enterprise was seen as a tool for mobilizing the unorganized sector. External resource support was provided through full-timers, an advisory committee and resource persons for training, accounting skills, marketing and networking. While voluntarism was emphasized, in the interest of sustainability, a self-generated fund from the group was created which supported a full-time as well as a part-time structure. Working with the government and banking system was encouraged, but it was on the basis of self-reliance and the creation of an organizational structure which advocated changes in policy. Social pressures ensured prompt repayment even without collateral. Since MALAR emerged from the literacy movement, continuing education activities were an important part of its agenda. Arivu Thendral, a neo-literate broadsheet, was discussed at the organizers' meeting every month and later introduced to the savings groups. Neo-literate booklets were purchased and read out at group meetings. Numeracy skills were enhanced through familiarity with accounting procedures. MALAR planned to start libraries around the groups.

The saving groups were classified at regular intervals into three categories on the basis of their performance according to ten basic principles that were considered important for the successful running of the groups:

1. Weekly meetings
2. 75 per cent attendance
3. Minutes of meetings to be recorded and approved
4. Neo-literate material to be bought and read
5. The resource paper to be discussed and debated
6. Reports to be duly submitted along with the reserve fund, interest, etc.
7. A children's science club to be started
8. No defaulters in the group
9. A collective responsibility for lending and repaying
10. Periodical training for production on a regular basis.

The annual report of the organization at the end of five years of its existence assessed the changes that had been brought about by MALAR:

Self-confidence and independence in several who were earlier steeped in indebtedness with private moneylenders,

Sensitivity to social issues and willingness to collectively change them,

Participation by several in the local bodies as representatives,

Major advances in the area of health awareness and in addressing chronic illnesses,

A spirit of entrepreneurship among the women as seen in a movement from savings and self-help, to seeking credit for individual and collective enterprises,

Several banks that had been persuaded to come forward with loan assistance,

Inspired by MALAR, SHGs had been established in 14 out of the 30 districts of Tamil Nadu and in 13 other states of the country under the Samata Micro-Credit Network. There were about 7,000 groups in the network by December, 2000.

The following villages were visited during the field trip:

Muhilankudiyrupu Village, Agasteeswaram Block: There were reported to be 95 learners during the course of the literacy campaign. All of them had become literate. There was one MALAR group functioning in this village with 20 members. It was started in 1999. The women were enthusiastic participants at the SHG meeting. They reported that apart from the economic benefits for domestic purposes through savings, they had deepened their awareness about health and nutritious food. The group had contributed towards solidarity among the members and towards harmonious caste and religious relations within the village. We also visited Kattuvilai village in the same Agasteeswaram block.

Paramankonamtheru Village, Killiyur Block: In contrast with the groups in the earlier mentioned villages, this group was comprised of extremely poor households who were largely engaged in weaving. The group provided loans to tide over the lean seasons and to escape the clutches of the moneylenders. Some attempts had been made to upgrade the technology of weaving.

Some General Issues and Reflections

The MALAR movement of SHGs that accompanied and built upon the mobilization and learning of the literacy phase, demonstrates how mobilizations can lead to processes of institutionalization. Mobilizations towards learning that are divorced from programmes related to livelihood, tend to get dissipated and generally remain ephemeral. On the other hand, a socio-economic programme directed at individualized beneficiaries, divorced from a movement, provides a limited scope and direction without the synergies of collective motivation and mobilization. MALAR is a good illustration of the combination of efforts around mobilization towards learning, followed by organization-building and institutionalization processes towards resolving issues of livelihood. Kanyakumari district had the advantage of a high literacy rate (82%) already at the time of the launching of the literacy campaign in October, 1991. The targeted non-literate population in the 15–45 age group was 1,01,538 persons. Of these, 90,164 learners were reported to have reached the NLM norms of literacy. However, in low literacy districts of the country where an earlier basis of social development and literacy might not have created an already existing aspirational basis for learning; organization around issues of livelihood would need to accompany the processes of mobilization for literacy from the very start of the literacy campaigns. These districts also tend to be the ones where caste, class and gender inequities act as severe obstacles to mobilization and motivation for learning in isolation. The MALAR experience provides important lessons to the NLM on the need for an integrated strategy towards addressing learning that is contextualized within larger mobilization for social development.

As the foregoing data suggest, the inspiration from MALAR and similar efforts linked to livelihood have created a major network of empowered women's groups in the state of Tamil Nadu and within other districts of the country under the banner of Samata. This network has the potential of giving the literacy campaigns a much needed character of a women's movement. One observed the tremendous enthusiasm among the women and an urge to learn to enhance their economic independence during our field visits. The linkage to basic livelihood needs, the motivation of the participants channelized and organized into SHGs, the provision of an independent space for women to interact and articulate their needs, the capacity-building efforts of the organization and its inbuilt financial mechanisms for ensuring autonomy, lead one to the conclusion that the MALAR process is highly sustainable.

The academic inputs towards capacity-building are worthy of note. The first and fourth Saturday meetings at the block level provide an opportunity for the block and village coordinators to interact and review their work. In addition, the neo-literate broadsheet and monthly resource paper are introduced and discussed. There is generally a talk on a subject of current interest accompanied by songs and sharing of experiences. A training programme for village coordinators and office bearers of the groups is organized once in six months to go into issues relating to accounting, report writing and general awareness. Personality development trainings have been conducted twice so far for the block coordinators. Annual days and festivals provided for other opportunities for meeting and cultural expression. The foregoing ensured that the technology of finance and accounting systems are closely articulated with an ideological perspective in terms of solidarity and social awareness.

An important lesson to learn from the Kanyakumari experience is the constraints and limits to government–voluntary sector collaboration and the reasons behind these limits. The collaboration between the BGVS and district administration came to a dead end towards the conclusion of the literacy campaign. Changes in government personnel, differences in ideological perspectives between a bureaucratic extension and finance driven approach and a mobilizational, people-centred one, and differences in styles of functioning were some of these reasons. The future of social developmental mobilizations like MALAR in their impact on the political economy is unclear. What is evident is that they do not necessarily translate into electoral gains of a party political nature. The dynamics and logic of the latter in their relation to popular aspirations are quite different from and parallel to many micro, decentralized processes of people's mobilization. The latter have their own independent and relevant space and need to be recognized as such. What appears likely in the visualisable future is some impact on the local self-governing bodies in the rural areas through acting as pressure groups and alternate forms of people's representation from below. This process has already begun in the Kanyakumari district. It is a process of power/politics to the people from below; a democratization of civil society in a manner that it can increasingly challenge the state for equitable distribution and human rights. An important feature of the accounting systems and regular review meetings of MALAR was the transparency of the entire process. Creating the possibilities for the right to information ensures the accountability of the office bearers at various levels.

Was MALAR experiencing the ironical logic that those who need savings the most have little to save and thus tend to be left out of the savings movement? One raises this question because the impression one gets from observations of some of the groups is that they tended to be of the already literate prior to the campaign and generally more secure in economic terms. In any case, MALAR would need to be sensitive to this possibility. However, internal evaluations of MALAR have shown that very few people are left out for want of money to save. The district has only 4 per cent Dalits. Yet there are several SHGs of dalits and some mixed groups in MALAR. The movement has served to reduce the caste barriers in the groups. An important issue is whether the transition to individual and collective micro-enterprise and participation can be sustained in the face of the onslaught of an inequitably liberalized economy that is market and finance driven in a top-down manner.

In addition to its ongoing activities, MALAR continues today to organize state conferences at regular intervals; the last being held in February, 2009. It has expanded its activities by taking financial support from the Rashtriya Mahila Kosh and has taken an active part in health interventions and the library movement.

4. The Case of BGVS, Assam

The Assam Literacy Campaign was conducted through the BGVS in seven blocks: Sipajhar in Darrang district, Dhemaji in Dhemaji district, Lahol in Dibrugarh, Chandrapur in Kamrup, Mairabavi and Lahorighat in Morigaon, and Raha in Nagaon district, covering 115 gram panchayats, within six districts. The CE programme was financed directly by the NLM. The selection of the blocks was on the basis of the participation that had been generated during the literacy campaigns and also keeping in mind the ethnic diversity of Assam. In all 115 NCECs had been established and 960 CECs. In the remaining 17 districts of the state, the programme was largely government-initiated.

The BGVS in this state had played a leading role in mapping the resources within panchayats. As regards the SHGs, the following Table 9.2 provides an analysis of the coverage of Prochesta, i.e., women's self-help groups, in seven blocks. By October, 2001, there were 902 such groups with a total membership of over 14,000. A sum of approximately Rs 24 lakhs had been deposited and Rs 3 lakhs had been loaned. The largest number of groups was in Sipajhar block in Darrang district, Dhemaji block in the district of the same name, and Lahorighat in Morigaon district. In Dhemaji block, the BGVS was active in 11 of the 15 gram panchayats. Nine NCECs and 85 CECs had been established. The BGVS had a limited presence in 17 out of the 23 districts in the state. The women's groups were acting as focal points not only for savings, but also as groups for discussion and pressure on the gram panchayats.

TABLE 9.2 *BGVS, Prochesta in Seven Blocks of Assam, October, 2001*

Name of District	*Name of Block*	*Total No. of Groups*	*Total Members*	*Total Deposit (Rs)*	*Loan Amount (Rs)*	*Total Annual Subscription (Rs)*
Darrang	Sipajhar	331	5,559	8,38,792	1,26,520	13,010
Dhemaji	Dhemaji	160	2,132	3,67,281	94,700	11,350
Dibrugarh	Lahowal	32	382	1,23,547	10,100	1,950
Kamrup	Chandrapur	23	364	87,223	13,500	1,310
Morigaon	Moirabari	67	1,089	1,65,226	38,836	4,690
Morigaon	Lahorighat	155	2,664	4,09,631	36,080	7,470
Nagaon	Raha	134	2,083	4,11,295	3,500	3,510
Total 6	7	902	14,273	24,02,995	3,23,236	43,290

One visited Assam in February, 2001. District and state level data helped to complete the picture emerging from one's observations. *Sipajhar block in Darrang district* has 25 gram panchayats and approximately 10 wards in each panchayat. The literacy campaign had begun in 1992, the PL phase in 1995 and the CE phase was initiated from January, 2000. The block had participated in several of the BGVS national level mobilizations over the years, for example, the Samata Jathas, the JoL Campaign, and what was distinctive of this block and the state was the creation of panchayat development reports in a participatory manner. Seven such reports had been completed at the time of the visit and eleven were being prepared. The reports were a starting point for several activities such as SHGs, named 'Prochesta', among women, bridge building efforts, sanitation initiatives, the construction of ponds and other water harvesting measures, the selection of beneficiaries for housing and pension schemes. These activities emerging from CECs had enhanced the self-confidence of participants, especially women, and had served to establish contact with government development departments. Monthly wall magazines and fortnightly newspapers served to diffuse information. The activities were run, to an extent of 90 per cent, on people's contributions. The panchayat development reports were entirely financed by the people.

In *Hazarikapada village* which was visited, there were 22 SHGs. The village was relatively large with a population of 15,000 in 10 wards. Half the number of approximately 500 non-literates in the 9–45 age group had been made literate in the village. Continuing education activities were in the area of agriculture, drinking water, health and sanitation.

In *Dhemaji block, Dhemaji district* there were 15 gram panchayats. Almost 85 out of the 150 wards had been covered by CECs. The activities included SHGs, health camps, awareness campaigns relating to floods, panchayat development reports, libraries and wall magazines.

Repeat Visit to Assam, September 30–October 5, 2005

The revisit to Assam, about five years after the first visit, served as an insight into the progress of the BGVS activities in Assam, and in *Kamrup and Naogaon districts* in particular. The earlier districts that were visited were Darrang and Dhemaji.

The Venture Schools: A specific feature of Assam was the large number of so-called Venture Schools started at the initiative of local communities and supported by them. A community school was formed when there was a perceived need for a school, in addition to the government school which was at some distance from the village or the hamlet. The community provided the land and the finances for the school building. Volunteer teachers who had generally completed their higher secondary education or graduation were appointed by the community. They received a normal honorarium from the fees charged from the students which was generally Rs 10 to Rs 20 per month; if at all there was any financial remuneration. The government provided only the text books and the curriculum that was followed was that of the regular government schools. A Venture School generally passed through three stages before it was taken over by government, a process that could last about 15 years: (a) Permission to start, (b) Recognition of its academic programme, and (c) Financial provision by the government. It was reported that about 80 per cent of the pre-1990 Venture Schools had been absorbed by government and were currently being run under the jurisdiction of the education department.

BGVS was attempting to provide training to teachers and some teaching-learning materials to those Venture Schools that had generally not been absorbed by government. There was an estimated number of 15,000 Venture Schools in Assam and an additional 39,150 provision schools run by local self-governing bodies. The latter were recognized by government and enjoyed the benefits of financial support. This did not cover all the Venture Schools. BGVS had concentrated its efforts with respect to Venture Schools in seven blocks of Assam: Sipajhar, Chandrapur, Raha, Moirabari, Lahorighat, Dhemaji and Lahowal. Data about the number of such schools, the students and teachers are provided in the following Table 9.3.

TABLE 9.3 *Venture Schools within Seven Blocks of BGVS Intervention in Assam, 2005*

Blocks	*No. of Schools*	*Boys*	*Girls*	*Students*	*Teachers*	*Ratio Student:Teacher*
Lower Primary	259	10,871	9,743	20,614	671	31:1
Middle Elementary	243	10,730	12,616	23,436	1,536	18:1
Total	502	21,601	22,359	43,960	2,207	20:1

Efforts had been made in the Venture Schools that had not been covered for training under the District Primary Education Programme (DPEP) or related programmes. For example, from January 22–31, 2005, a training was held covering 24 schools, nine of which lower primary and 15 middle elementary. A total of 80 teachers drawn from 16 gram panchayats in four districts – Kamrup, Naogaon, Morigaon, Darrang – undertook this training. Some of the themes covered were education through games, developing a questioning mind, teaching-learning materials, education through work, English, mathematics, science, social science and environmental education, drawing and evaluation systems. The trainers were drawn from local institutional resources and the BGVS National Resource Group. Another training programme was held from July 21–31, 2005, covering 21 schools, 9 lower primary and 12 middle elementary. The training covered 61 teachers, 42 males and 19 females, drawn from 16 gram panchayats within 10 blocks from four districts – Kamrup, Barpeta, Jorhat and Gowalpara. Apart from the training programmes, the salaries of two coordinators for basic education, one for Samata and one accountant were covered from the funds received from the Sir Dorabji Tata Trust (SDTT) since 2004.

The Prochesta Self-Help Groups (SHG) under Samata: This work had been going on from January, 1998 till the present. The SDTT funds had been utilized for the capacity-building of these SHGs, especially in the areas of maintenance of accounts and expansion to new centres. The following Table 9.4 provides information on the district-wise coverage of these SHGs for 2005.

TABLE 9.4 *BGVS Prochesta SHGs under Samata, 2005*

District	*Total Number of Groups*	*Total Member*	*Total Deposit*	*Group Loan (in Rs)*
Barpeta	74	1,328	1,90,082	25,600
Bongaigaon	807	13,971	29,20,358	11,04,630
Darrang	390	6,136	10,33,298	1,90,584
Dhemaji	194	2,482	4,59,143	1,32,000
Dhubri	33	439	1,09,970	11,100
Dibrugarh	42	412	1,38,227	10,100
Jorhat	44	703	2,73,453	47,600
Kamrup	77	874	1,95,218	13,500
Morigaon	266	4,326	7,51,302	1,74,521
Nagaon	143	2,177	4,29,200	12,450
Nalbari	21	314	37,437	4,320
Sibsagar	25	411	1,02,034	54,850
Sonitpur	89	1,415	2,94,550	96,535
Tinsukia	73	1,059	1,88,225	15,500
Goalpara	331	2,779	4,93,863	27,465s
Total 15	2,609	38,826	76,16,360	19,20,755

It is quite evident from the table, considering the number of groups, their membership and their financial transactions, that the SHGs had been receiving a significant response from the women. This could well be the most important impact of BGVS's efforts towards linking the literacy campaigns to other development activities, in Assam as well as in other states. As one will see below, the SHGs have not only been a form of savings and loans for largely domestic purposes, but they have had an important impact on the status and relative economic independence of women. It was reported that 40 per cent of the Samata members were neo-literates who had come through the literacy campaigns. The following Table 9.5 provides data on the varied activities of Samata during a single year September 2004–September 2005.

TABLE 9.5 *Prochesta – Samata Activities in Assam, September 2004–September 2005*

	Name of the Activity	*No. of Participants*	*Area of Coverage*
1.	Two state level workshops on Women and Development	100 (panchayat coordinators and Samata group members)	9 districts
2.	Panchayat level workshop on Women and Development	2,250 (45 × 50 panchayats)	9 districts
3.	Four capacity-building/trainings for panchayat and block coordinators	156 panchayats and block coordinators	12 districts
4.	Production centres	2 trained Samata members	Chandrapur
5.	Panchayat level workshop on SHG Management and Social Development	4,300 women (50 × 86 panchayats)	Tinsukia district
6.	Samata groups	2,609 SHGs	15 districts

Continuing Education Centres (CEC): The SDTT funds had also been utilized for strengthening 10 CECs, one in each of 10 districts of Assam. The activities consisted of formation of a library generally at a location provided by the local community, conducting an information diffusion centre, a discussion forum, cultural activities, sports and a wall magazine. Networking with the GVVs, which had taken the form of inputs in Venture Schools in the case of Assam and the Prochesta SHGs, was another important activity The state BGVS was conducting 210 CECs in the seven blocks within the six districts of its concentration in Assam. It was also running three institutions for academic resource support for the literacy campaigns, Jan Shikshan Sansthans, one in each of the districts of Silchar, Kamrup and Jorhat.

The Jan Vachan Andolan (Peoples's Reading Movement): It had helped to bring about 150 publications related to literacy, basic education, environment, health, panchayat planning, science and income generation. These publications served to provide much needed reading materials for the libraries within the CECs.

Barsajai Middle Education School, Belpola Village, Kamrup District: This Venture School was started in 1996. It ran classes from grades five to seven with six teachers. In the absence of any training organized by government for the teachers, even under the DPEP, the primary role of BGVS in this and other selected Venture Schools was to provide trainings for the teachers as well as some teaching-learning materials. The teachers in the Venture Schools were found to be highly motivated, despite receiving only a nominal financial compensation from the community, if any. Service to the community, the social status that arose from the appreciation and the possibility of being absorbed some time in future as regular teachers with a government salary was the motivation for their enthusiasm. This was in a context where opportunities for middle class, salaried employment were anyhow scarce for the educated unemployed. The teachers generally made up by way of motivation and commitment for what they lacked as regards capacity enhancement from any formal training prior to the intervention of the BGVS. As regards the students, it was reported that the achievement levels of these Venture Schools were of an equivalent standard, if not higher than that in the normal government schools in the region. This was confirmed by our observations through random visits to the class rooms, observations of the teachers conducting the classes and pointed questions to the students.

Guwahati Bodo Middle Education School, Kamrup District: This Venture School was started in 1985 and had three rooms, one for each of its grades five to seven. There were five teachers. The majority of the students as well as the teachers belonged to the Bodo tribal community.

Nisbogorigueri Lower Primary School, Sahari Panchayat, Raha Block, Naogaon District: There were four teachers in the school which conducted classes for grades one to four. The school was started in 1988. The teachers had a lower level of qualification (higher secondary) than the teachers in the earlier mentioned schools who were atleast graduates. About a 100 students were packed into a single large room which had classes with respective black boards, spaced out from each other.

Dighaliati Middle Education School, Dighaliati Panchayat, Raha Block, Naogaon District: Started in 1995, this school was conducting classes for grades five to seven. Of the five teachers, three were graduates and two had a higher secondary degree. There were 84 students in all. Our discussions in this and the earlier mentioned Venture Schools suggested that there was a demand for these schools, despite the fact that there might be a government school within the jurisdiction of the gram panchayat. The explanation given was that the existing government schools could not cater to the needs of all the children within the scattered habitational pattern of the gram panchayat, with schools situated across rivulates and highways that made it difficult and hazardous for the students to access them. Besides, the commitment of the teachers and the sense of ownership of the local community made a big difference in the exercise of educational choices. We paid a brief visit to the relatively small school, *Mulankhatha Adarsha Lower Primary School, Manipujai Panchayat, Barpujai block* in the same district.

Thakuchi Middle Education School, Chandrapur Panchayat, Chandrapur Block, Kamrup District: This Venture School had a beautiful location provided by the community on a hill top, overlooking a rivulet and the green fields of the village. It conducted classes for grades five to seven, with 140 students and six teachers. It was started in 1993. This particular school charged a nominal fee of Rs 10 per month from the students and Rs 70 per annum for various equipments of sports. The tribal groups in the region – Kargis, Bodos and Rabas who formed about half the population of the gram panchayat – were represented among the students and the teachers.

Prochesta Samata Self-Help Groups, Dighaliatai Panchayat, Raha Block, Naogaon District: This was a meeting of women members of seven SHGs from three gram panchayats. The SHGs were being conducted by Samata, better known as Prochesta in Assam. The meeting was held in the spacious, covered entrance of the sanctuary of the Shankar Deo Temple. Monthly meetings were reported to be held regularly and this was one such meeting. Some of the women had brought along their children for a meeting that was to last for the larger part of the day. The women reported that the regular coming together served to maintain the ongoing records of loans taken, interest accrued and recoveries; besides ensuring transparency and accountability. Apart from the economic benefits of the SHGs, these fora served to discuss issues related to health, family planning and other social development concerns. These groups had started in 2004 with contributions of Rs 20 per month per member. The annual interest rate that was charged on loans worked out to a relatively high percentage of 24 per cent; but the women reported that this was affordable considering the cooperative nature of beneficiaries. The loans were utilized for preparing traditional weaving materials, embroidery and articles such as dolls and bags for domestic purposes and for sale in the local markets.

Prochesta Samata Group, Baladmari Panchayat, Balijana Block, Goalpara District: Several of the engagements for this day of heavy downpour had to be reorganized. We met 12 members of a SHG who belonged to the

Muslim community. They were engaged in preparing bags and embroidery work in a small room. It was a matter of consternation that they could engage in their intricate and skillful designs considering the limited space. In the neighbouring *Agiya Panchayat* we met another dozen members of a women's SHG who belonged to the Garo community. They were engaged in handloom weaving. The raw materials were purchased in common through a collective loan and the finished products were sold in the markets of the region; the income being distributed among the members according to their productive capacities. The products were of a high quality and represented the best of traditional designs. It was reported that there were 47 groups in the Balijana Block. They were being supervised by an enthusiastic coordinator who received five per cent of the membership fees as a honorarium and Rs 300 per month for travel expenses. These groups were spread over seven gram panchayats. One per cent of the income of the groups went towards central office expenses and to provide a nominal honorarium to the coordinators at various levels – panchayat, block, district and state.

Nodal Continuing Education Centre (NCEC), Dighaliati Panchayat, Raha Block, Naogaon District: This centre was an extension unit of the agricultural university that was presently being used for the purposes of continuing education. It was in a dilapidated condition because of a recent flooding in the region. It was reported that 10 NCECs in Assam had been taken up for special attention and were being supported by the SDTT funding. The one visited was not one of the 10, though Naogaon district had one such NCEC. This NCEC had prepared its panchayat development report; mapping the natural, human and institutional resources within the panchayat towards planning and demanding accountability from government development schemes. The Jan Shikshan Sansthan (JSS, People's Education Institution) Training Sub-Centre, Chandrapur Panchayat, Kamrup district which was visited in an urbanized setting conducted training programmes that largely met the needs of the lower middle classes – screen printing, the use of computers, repairing power tillers, metal cutting, candle making and driving vehicles. The Production Centre, started in April, 2005, in the same panchayat and district also formed part of the continuing education activities of the state. It was being run in a well-constructed facility provided by the Block Development Office, with training facilities such as handlooms and residential accommodation. Two women served as handloom weavers and were being trained to become trainers. The women had already started production activities which found a sales outlet in the surrounding regions and in Guwahati city.

We concluded this field revisit to Assam with a meeting of the BGVS General Council. While providing us an opportunity to follow progress reports from different regions, the meeting also served the purpose of feedback and seeking clarifications based on the field visits. A summary content of our interactions may be found in the following sub-section.

Some General Issues and Reflections

Geographical Concentration, Convergence of Programmes and Institutionalization: BGVS in Assam is one of the better performing states. This may be largely seen as a result of the concentration in seven blocks within six districts of the state. Concentration in geographical space had resulted in some degree of convergence of development interventions related to adult education. This had also facilitated the consolidation of human resources within BGVS and associated community-based volunteers towards involvement in the various activities. The organization has a team of committed and competent field coordinators. Another important factor contributing to the comparative success of BGVS's efforts in Assam has been the greater level of institutionalization of mobilization and capacity-building processes through people's organizational forms and formal institutions. This has taken the shape of three JSSs, 10 NCECs and 210 CECs; other training centres in livelihood skills; interventions through training programmes for teachers covering 502 already existing Venture Schools in seven blocks of six districts; and the network of 2,609 SHGs of Samata-Prochesta covering 15 districts.

Pedagogy in the Venture Schools: Observations of the Venture Schools in Assam, within which the BGVS has provided training programmes, suggest that learning outcomes are adequate, especially when compared to government schools. The teachers were enthusiastic about their work and had whole-heartedly welcomed the BGVS training given that they were generally neglected by government, not only in terms of financial assistance but also as regards academic inputs. However, the pedagogical processes that were observed suggested that there was a continuation of rote learning, reading in a monotonous or rhythmic manner with lowered levels of comprehension. Our observations indicated that greater emphasis might be placed on 'How learners learn, and hence, are taught?' and 'Why they learn?'; rather than on 'Whether they learn?' and 'What they learn?', to the relative exclusion of the former. This may be done by underlining the principles implicit in meaningful teaching-learning rather than concentrating on the 'technology' of pedagogy. The former processes are more amenable to transfer of skills and motivation for learning over subject areas. The foregoing is an inference drawn from observations of classroom teaching-learning, given that we had not witnessed a training programme in Assam.

The Continuing Education Centres (CECs), their sustainability and relevance is a wider issue covering such activities in Assam and throughout the country. The challenge to innovation in terms of literacy, understood in a limited sense, is of reaching out through relevant modes of communication and interaction with the scripted word. It was reported that in Assam only about an estimated 20 per cent of the non-literates enrolled in the literacy campaigns would have sustained their literacy because of various gaps in earlier programme funding and lack of adequate continuing education facilities. An additional problem appears to be the fact of coming to a fixed place – a centre/library – for 'knowledge' acquisition, rather than the 'mobility' of knowledge moving out to life situations; especially in a context where habitations are dispersed like in Assam. In such situations perhaps mobile libraries that move on bicycles for selling books at weekly marketplaces could perhaps be tried out. Even though the JVA had helped to publish about 150 booklets related to literacy, basic education, the environment, health, panchayat planning, science and income generation, it is not clear who actually reads these books. Is it the BGVS activists, village-based volunteers, the literates through the formal education system or the neo-literates and in what proportion? Do the materials correspond to their areas of interest and do the books reach out to the formal schools? A small-scale readership survey should serve to unravel this issue.

Organizations that are confronted with such difficult geographical contexts of learning and socially limited learning environments tend to neglect the basic education of the neo-literates and the non-literates, in its restricted sense, to shift attention to other related social development interventions such as training centres for livelihood skills which are relevant and respond to an immediately felt need. As has been discussed earlier, the Samata Prochesta Network has gained widespread legitimacy and has been a major source of economic and social empowerment of women. This network has tremendous potential of serving as decentralized pressure groups on local self-governance for accountability and equity in administering development schemes.

5. The Case of BGVS, Rajasthan

The Rajasthan unit of BGVS was established in 1992, as a branch of the national BGVS at the initiative of the People's Science Network (PSN). The following is based on an undated document (probably in 2001) of the local BGVS and one's field observations, especially in Jaipur and Baran districts.

BGVS has a network of district committees in eight districts. In others it operates through the Zilla Saksharata Samiti (ZSS). The organization consists of writers, journalists, college and school teachers, students, unemployed youth, women, and elected representatives. At the state level, BGVS has a state committee of 45 persons and an executive committee of 16 persons. The state committee is the body deciding all matters of the state unit. The executive committee meets every two months. At the state level, district level committees and an executive committee have been formed. The selection of functionaries for these units is carried out through elections. The organization was, by the end of 2000, still in the process of forming block level and village level units. The entire structure is voluntary. Full-time paid employees are a minimum and are kept on a project basis. As a mass-based organization, the main strength of the BGVS is its large volunteer cadre. There were more than 3,000 volunteers all over the state. BGVS has mainly worked in the fields of literacy, science popularization, women's and children's education, and child rights in Rajasthan. Some of the programmes of BGVS, Rajasthan, were as follows:

Literacy: Environment-building programmes consisted of organizing kalajathas, padyataras (marches), volunteer melas and orientation camps. Training was conducted for developing training modules and organizing training at the state and district levels for resource persons, master trainers, and volunteers. In terms of material development, the BGVS helped the ZSSs to prepare primers, other reading materials and training modules. Concurrent evaluation of the literacy programme was carried out in two districts, Banswara and Bhilwara. BGVS was involved in running classes in Alwar, Baran and Pali districts. In Dholpur district, 10 panchayats in Rajakhera block were taken up to develop a model. In these villages, women's groups as well as youth groups have been created. JVA, to create a people's culture for reading specially for those learners whose literacy skills were fragile, was undertaken. Close to 100 books had been published by March, 2002, of which 25 were for children. Jan Vachan Shivirs (camps) were organized, books were read out and thereafter discussions were organized. JVA jathas were also organized in four districts to create awareness and for the sale of books. 10 ZSSs had bought these books as part of the PL and CE programmes. About 11 community level libraries were being run by Bal Manch (children's groups) in Baran, Kota, Jaipur and Dholpur districts.

As part of CE, BGVS Rajasthan had been running continuing education pilot projects sanctioned by the NLM. Two nodal and 18 CECs had been running in Dholpur and Baran districts. The main activities were running libraries, equivalency programmes, women empowerment programmes, literacy groups and the Bal Manch.

Child Rights and JoL Campaigns for Children: This was carried out in 100 villages between 1994 to 1996. Child rights programmes were taken up to consolidate the efforts of the JoL campaign and to increase the participation of children in the panchayats and schools. This was carried out with the support of UNICEF and the Education Department in 100 villages of eight districts. About 30,000 children were covered in this programme. Bal Manch were constituted by open elections of children in the villages and by the end of 2000, 60 such fora had been formed. Each Manch has 11 to 16 members and care has been taken to ensure girls' participation. There has been about 40 per cent representation of girls in these Manch. The Manch exist in Baran, Kota, Dholpur, Alwar, Pali, Jaipur, Sikar and Karauli districts. Through these organizational forms the children had started intervening in the development process. They had started libraries, taken an active part in pulse polio campaigns, had organized cleanliness drives in the village and had even taken up issues of child marriage.

Science Popularization: Jathas had been regularly organized for exposing superstitions and spreading science in the villages. A large number of low-cost scientific aids which are used in schools had been acquired. The Cosmic Voyage Programme was organized during the total solar eclipse in 1995. BGVS took up a massive awareness programme and a kalajatha was launched along the line of totality of the solar eclipse. At 11 points, stations were set up for safe watching and approximately 10,000 people watched the solar eclipse.

Primary Education: BGVS had made two kinds of efforts in primary education, the Janshala programme and the GVVs. The Janshala programme was being run in collaboration with the Government of Rajasthan in the slums of Jaipur. BGVS had taken the responsibility of the Vidhyadhar zone. About 13 Janshalas were running in these slums. BGVS had started the GVV in Kota district. By 2002, 200 children had been enrolled in this school.

Women's Development: BGVS had aimed to work closely with women who had participated in literacy activities. Samata Vigyan Utsava (SVU) was one such initiative. The programme was organized in a mela style in which various issues relating to women were discussed; for example, health, education, women, science and technology, kitchen science, home-based production, women and violence and small savings. These issues were reported to be transacted in a participatory manner, the idiom of the woman being used like role plays, stories, games, posters and demonstrations. This was a part of the national coordinated programme and was taken up in five districts.

Self-Help Groups (SHGs): Around 38 groups had been formed in three districts, Baran, Dholpur and Karuli. There were 550 members and more than Rs 75,000 had been deposited by these groups. Internal loans had started and one group had taken a loan from the bank. One Credit Cooperative Society had been registered in Natai village, Baran district, with 125 members.

Pathak Manch: As part of CE, women Pathak Manch (reading clubs) were formed. Issues discussed in these Pathak Manch were health, the girl child, primary education and violence against women. There were 500 members in these groups.

In addition to the above programmes, BGVS had also undertaken Participatory Resource Mapping to create awareness and optimize the use of natural resources. This was carried out in Baran and Sawai Madhopur districts. BGVS was, however, not able to actually implement this watershed development programme because funding from the government was delayed. The organization had also worked closely with panchayats and had undertaken training of women representatives in Baran and Alwar. Among BGVS's main strengths was its cultural wing consisting mainly of village youth volunteers. The youth were reported to be good at developing plays and cultural programmes aimed to educate. BGVS had taken out several kalajathas at the state and district levels since its inception. It had also been continuously involved in networking with various other groups in the state. Apart from the literacy network, the organization was part of the Right to Information movement, the campaign against atrocities on women and human rights networks.

The Nodal Continuing Education Centre (NCEC) in Natai Village, Shahbad Block, Baran District: Baran district, located in the south-east of Rajasthan, is dominated by tribals, largely from the Sahariya community. It is one of the most underdeveloped districts with a literacy rate of 28 per cent, a female literacy rate of 13 per cent, and that among tribals 4 per cent. One visited the district in March, 2002. There is only one Primary Health Centre (PHC) and a TB centre in Shahbad block which is quite inadequate given that 40 per cent of the Sahariya tribals are reported to suffer from TB according to a health survey of 10 gram panchayats conducted by the BGVS.

The campaign in the district started in 1994 and in the initial stages the BGVS played a major role in all aspects of the campaign. However, the district team was later marginalized by the administrative bureaucracy. Utilizing its network of activists, the team moved into linking literacy with other development issues like natural resource management, health, women's empowerment and child rights. There had been a major gap between the literacy and PL phases of the campaign leading to a serious problem of relapse.

The NCEC in Natai was largely amongst Bangladesh refugees who were rehabilitated in this village in 1971. There had been a good response from them during the literacy campaign. There was a strong women's group that had participated in programmes against alcoholism and atrocities on women. The NCEC was started in October, 2000, in a place provided by the gram panchayat. It was being relocated at the time of our visit to a site provided by the villagers and constructed through community participation. The NCEC covers a total population of 16,000, largely from the OBCs and the Sahariya tribals. About 14 reading clubs had been formed and 11 were in the process of formation. The members in each group were about 20. Libraries had been established in most of the villages covered by the NCEC in spaces provided by the gram panchayats. Three SHGs had been formed and five were in the process of formation. The Bal Manch, a formation of children, was playing an important role in running the libraries and in motivating the learners to come to the CECs. A girl child week was celebrated in September, 2000, with posters and essay writing competitions on issues relating to girl children. Health melas had been organized to diffuse information on health issues.

The following Table 9.6 provides some details of the coverage of programmes and villages under the NCEC:

TABLE 9.6 *NCEC, Natai Village, Shahbad Block, Baran District, 2002*

	Name of NCE/CE Villages	*Library*	*Reading Circles*	*Self-Help Groups*	*Bal Manch*
1.	Natai	1	3	2	1
2.	Samraniya	1	2	1	1
3.	Agronda	1	1	In process	1
4.	Faridua	1	1	In process	1
5.	Gajrata	1	1	In process	1
6.	Dhansuri	In process	In process	In process	1
7.	Khushyara	In process	In process	In process	1

Source: BGVS, Continuing Education Programme in Rajasthan, Jaipur, 2002.

There have been several problems in running these NCECs. Some of these had been political interference, unsatisfactory experience with past saving groups and the banking system in programmes organized by the government, the large gap between the literacy and the CE phases resulting in dropout and lack of motivation, volunteer dropout as a result of the marriage of women volunteers. Financial constraints had led to severe problems in running these centres. The local BGVS hoped to confront these issues through volunteer training and concentration on SHGs, skill development programmes, health initiatives and equivalency programmes for the neo-literates linked to the National Open School.

Repeat Visit to Baran District, Rajasthan, August, 2004

The objective of this visit was to study the functioning of the NCECs and the CECs in villages. The project visualized forming reading circles and establishing community level groups of women, children and youth. Field visits were planned to Baran and Kota district, but due to unprecedented rains and floods the visits to villages in Kota were cancelled. However, one had the opportunity of interacting with BGVS activists at the district and state levels.

Kelwara Village, NCEC: This NCEC covers 10 village level CECs. Libraries had been established in each of the 10 villages as a result of cultural mobilizational activities and organization-building. Reading circles were running in four of the villages. The involvement of the participants in agricultural operations was reported to have resulted in breaks in the process of the reading circles and literacy classes. SHGs had been formed in these villages, with training in stitching and embroidery in two of them. The organization had been able to establish village level formations for the coming together of children, youth and farmers. About 300 children were members of the Bal Manch. One had an opportunity of interacting with the children and was impressed by the potential of these organizational forms for leadership-building.

Four SHGs had been formed in and around the Kelwara gram panchayat and a Computer Training Centre had been established. The participants generally took loans for agricultural production and a few borrowed for consumptions purposes. Interactions with the women suggested that they were largely from the upper caste and from relatively more economically secure households. It was reported that this was partly due to the agricultural season when persons from lower income and caste groups could not afford to attend meetings and thus lose wages. An attempt was made to shift the sewing classes to the nearby Danita village and in order to reach out to Saharia tribals. The various mobilization activities and social formations had, to some degree, reduced caste distances by bringing together persons on common platforms. We met the literacy instructors from the surrounding villages who appeared adequately motivated and trained considering their relatively moderate levels of education. Most of them had completed high school. The records of the various centres had been adequately maintained.

Balda Village, SHG: We had a meeting with the largely Rajput members of the SHG who had a relatively secure economic background. It appears that the SHGs have an internal mechanism of self-selection, with those who can afford to save or are engaging in savings. This complex issue would need to be addressed in a manner that interventions reach out to those who are in the greatest need of economic and educational interventions. On the other hand, as reported at the state level meeting in Jaipur, these organizational formations had served as an effective counter to fundamentalist forces through the organization of the rural middle classes and castes.

Uni Village: This village in contrast was populated by households from the Saharia tribe which was one of the most disadvantaged in socio-economic terms. We met in the traditional 'Bangla' (community centre) where only males were traditionally allowed. Some concessions were made for girl children below the age of puberty and for women to perform functions of cleaning and decoration. However, we observed a few women and girl children entering the Bangla and speaking up. Only two girl children from the village were reported to be going to school.

The monthly wage to annual labourers during the six months, when some form of agricultural employment was available, was Rs 1,200. The BGVS programme had not really taken off in this village, even though a coordinator had been appointed. The participants were enthusiastic to engage in a cultural performance despite their generally anomic attitude. BGVS, Rajasthan, would need to address the larger issue of how educational interventions can take root within those sections of society that are confronted with dire issues of socio-economic survival.

Kheria Village: This village, though also inhabited primarily by Saharias, offered an interesting socio-economic contrast to the previous one. A meeting was held in a more modern style Bangla that had a brick and cement, concrete structure. However, the traditions of the community in terms of exclusion of women from the Bangla persisted. The meeting began with the males, youth and adults, seated in the Bangla and the women outside without shelter in the rain. After a session of song and instrumental music, the question of gender-based segregation was posed to the assembled males. There was much resistance, especially among the older generation, to breaking away from tribal traditions despite their accepting the rationality of the principle of inclusion. However, the traditional leadership of the *mukhya* (headman) took a stand as a consequence of the discussions and suggestions. He persuaded the women to enter despite some hesitation of a section among them. The meeting ended with joint and separate singing by men and women sitting together within the Bangla; with the mukhya, a senior woman from the tribal community, the resisting male elder and the visitors sitting in front of this now inclusive group. The event, as reported to us, was seen as a historic occasion for the community and a journalist-cum-BGVS activist recorded it in the press. This occasion indicates, to some degree, the wider social relevance of BGVS interventions, despite the fact that literacy and basic education might have made little headway within the extremely difficult socio-economic circumstances.

Chandan Khera Village: The Kherwa community, recognized as a scheduled tribe in the neighbouring states but not in Rajasthan, largely populated this village. The various activities and organizational formations of the BGVS had taken root among this community which, despite its poor economic background, revealed a high degree of aspiration for mobility.

Meeting in Jaipur with BGVS Coordinators at the State Office: The aborted trip to Kota due to heavy rains and flooding in the rivers of the semi-arid region resulted in a few activists coming down to Jaipur for the meeting.

It was reported that the BGVS programme is run primarily in the Kherawad block of Kota district. The main tribal groups are the Bhils and the Meghvals. Mining is predominant in the hilly region and agriculture in the plains. SHGs had been started in two villages and village development reports had been conducted in six of the ten villages under the coverage of this specially financed project. Some of the problems that were reported at the meeting were the high transportation costs to reach out to scattered villages. The activists drew attention to the need for the continuing the establishment of village formations and the resource assessment through the village development reports. This could serve as the basis for skill training and the following were tentatively identified: welding; soap, chalk and candle making; tailoring, embroidery and the making of school bags; computer training; food processing; and training in skills related to agricultural production such as the use of high yielding varieties in mustard and gram for which some training programmes had already been initiated with the resource support of the Bio-Technology Centre of the Jamia Hamdard University, New Delhi.

Some General Issues and Reflections

The following comments are largely based on the 2004 status of the projects of BGVS, Rajasthan, in the selected blocks. The organizational formations of children, youth and women through social and self-help grouping have been established, as also village libraries. The CECs and the literacy classes were generally weak considering the harsh socio-economic circumstances of the proposed beneficiaries. Despite efforts made by the BGVS and government through earlier literacy campaigns, the number of neo-literates who could take advantage of the CECs was negligible and dispersed over the villages.

It may be noted that the libraries, the Bal and Yuva Manches are primarily directed at school-going children, educated youth and literate/semi-literate adults, most of whom might have been school dropouts at various levels. These sections/age groups would come from generally more secure income groups and middle and upper castes, within what is admittedly a depressed economy, within a fragile ecology. The saving groups among women, as mentioned above, tend to follow a process of self-selection where those who can afford to save a meagre amount tend to become participants and borrowers. CE, as also the CEP of BGVS, is justifiably planned to be for non-literates and neo-literates, as well as for semi-literates and literate persons from generally poor and marginalized households. It is a programme of lifelong learning and meant to be an inclusive programme.

The concern, however, is that the economically and socially marginalized – the scheduled tribes, the dalits, the bonded and child labourers, the migrants – tend to remain relatively excluded from what is primarily an educational intervention backed by other developmental and organizational inputs; despite the conscious efforts of the organization. The BGVS has made efforts in the direction of addressing this predicament, as will be seen from some of the tribal villages selected for our field visits, but with relatively less success on the educational front. Attempts have been made to relate the wider campaigns, for the right to food, the right to information and poverty alleviation programmes, to educational efforts. This is a step in the right direction. Within this scenario, one has found that cultural activities have received a strong response and have taken firm roots. This could well be a form of escape from the harsh realities of everyday life as well as serving the purpose of social mobilization. As has already been mentioned, while narrowly defined basic educational efforts may not have been sufficiently established as yet, the organization has had a wider and significant impact in creating a social and organizational base for countering fundamentalist, cultural-religious influences in the region and for breaking the social exclusions based on caste, religion and gender, largely at a socio-cultural level.

The issues of livelihood would need to be addressed together with interventions for basic education in order to make the latter more meaningful, especially for adults. BGVS could explore the possibility of mobilizing its youthful human resources for soil and water conservation, forest management, utilization of forest produce, food processing and the setting up of agro-industries. This would provide a dimension of functional relevance and a much needed motivation for basic education for adults in an ecologically fragile region. The educational programme could largely focus on youth that has a relatively higher level of aspirations than older adults who are engaged in the struggle for economic survival. Short-term, intensive residential education camps lasting a few weeks have been found to be a useful strategy in Rajasthan as adopted by Doosra Dashak (Saldanha, 2007).

6. The Case of Rae Bareilly District, Uttar Pradesh (UP)

This field visit was part of the second review report, 2005, of the BGVS project that was then sponsored by the SDTT. I am grateful to Urvashi

Butalia for her field notes on which the present writing is based. The field visit for this study was conducted in November, 2005.

The work of BGVS in Uttar Pradesh (UP) concentrated on the following four areas: Samata SHGs conducted in 15 districts; GVVs in nine districts and CE, in 10 districts. The work in the state had been going on since the last 15 years. The visit to Rae Bareilly focused primarily on Samata with some visits to GVVs.

Rae Bareilly, Public Meeting: This meeting was attended by a large number of women and was on the theme of SHGs. They had come from the neighbouring villages by tractor, bus, on foot and bullock carts to attend the meeting. Some of them came later to the BGVS office for an informal meeting. Some executive members of BGVS, Uttar Pradesh, were present. The village level activists whom we met were largely involved in issues concerning health, water, sanitation, the setting up of SHGs and occasionally running a GVV.

A series of Samata Saving Groups were visited in the surrounding villages. Vishnupur had four SHGs that had been running for a year and a half. Each of the women paid Rs 20 a month and met twice a month. Apart from the savings they valued their mobility beyond the home. Maharajganj village had three SHGs with the women paying a similar monthly amount. One meeting in a month was held to deposit money and the other to discuss issues facing them, such as health, the weight of children and the importance of mother's milk. Some expressed a desire to move into small enterprises to prepare incense sticks, envelopes and candles. One woman had taken an emergency loan to treat her husband who, however, had expired. The women were very understanding of difficulties in repaying. Purerani village had a SHG that was a month old. They learnt from the example of another SHG and had saved only a small amount of Rs 480. Cair village also had one SHG which began with monthly deposits of Rs 10, but had increased the amount to Rs 20. The women had been meeting for over a year and exuded a sense of self-confidence. They had also begun to take up local issues such as the placement of the village water tap and expressed their happiness that now they 'did not need to stretch out their hands for seeking assistance from anybody'.

A total of six SHGs were running in Dotra, Pure Hirara, Harpal and Lonara covering some 150 women. They had been giving out loans, but had experienced some difficulty in recovery. In some places, the women were fined if they did not pay back without adequate reasons. Some of the women were willing to take up an agitation for acquiring ration cards. In Avadigaon and Bariarpur there were four SHGs. Women were taking loans for farm work, for deliveries and medical treatment. They suffered some opposition initially from money lenders. In one of the SHGs, none of the women were educated and the husband of the secretary kept accounts. In another SHG the women had got together and confiscated a goat for two days from a recalcitrant member who was not paying back for some time. There were four SHGs in Aimapur village. Loans here were generally repaid as a lump sum and not in installments. Chitvania had three SHGs with relatively educated women and some young girls.

Visit to Gyan Vigyan Vidyalaya (GVV): This GVV was running in the panchayat building next to a government school. It had been set up less than a year ago and some 25 children were attending. The children were smartly dressed and the teacher, a young boy interested in education, was taking his work seriously. The Pradhan (head person) of the village, a woman had been invited to a small assembly of children and their parents. She was requested for a permanent structure for the school in the village. About a dozen children were in a position to pay the monthly fee of Rs 15 and the rest were unable to do so. A committee had been established which met once a month to discuss matters such as punctuality, education content and the capacity to pay fees. The school appeared to enjoy much goodwill in the village.

Rae Bareilly, Meeting with BGVS Executive, Uttar Pradesh: Some of the salient features of the meeting were as follows. The BGVS activists were convinced of the need to institutionalize and consolidate the relatively fragile organizational forms that had emerged from the mobilizations and the literacy campaigns. They were resistant to a notion of institutionalization that would mean setting up offices and creating hierarchies and procedures. They felt that this would be a loss to the open and flexible character of the organization. They were concerned about the lack of funds to provide for even transport and communication facilities which made the organization vulnerable to losing some personnel to other NGOs and institutions entering the field with high salaries. They recognized that Uttar Pradesh was beset by a range of political problems with several interior villages almost cut-off due to poor roads, lawlessness and corruption. The caste factor was predominant in most of the everyday life activities. While the SHGs had rapidly grown in number and were responding to women's needs and the GVVs were beginning to receive community support, the CECs suffered from a dwindling supply of books for the libraries due to the curtailment of national funds. The BGVS field processes were reported to have a good network of support from local institutions. The Aligarh Muslim University, for example, provided training, technical skills for production centres and assisted in conducting public gatherings.

The Samata work in Rae Bareilly through the medium of the SHGs had been widespread and a positive development for the women in terms of their relative economic independence and their growing self-confidence. However, given the political situation, the caste and patriarchal structures within society and the low levels of literacy in the area, the work had been painstaking. The amount of the savings was small and many of the women in positions of leadership needed to have some basic literacy. Much support would be needed to evolve into micro enterprises that are self-sustainable. Other NGOs in the region, the World Bank and other banking projects that tend to be highly commercialized leading to indebtedness in a situation of lack of autonomy and organized strength, had been posing a competition to the BGVS-run SHGs. The caste issue would need to be confronted in a far more central manner given that it permeated almost every aspect of everyday life.

7. The Case of Bhind District, Madhya Pradesh

The BGVS organization in the state covered a diversity of contexts from the Chambal valley to the tribal regions of Jabhua. It had taken a lead role, together with other like-minded organizations, on social developmental issues such as health and midday meals for children. It had assisted the central office in establishing the Basic Education Research Centre (BERC) in the state and providing academic support for various national level programmes.

One visited the district in May, 2007. Gwalior was the closest railway station from Delhi. The primary objective of this visit was to understand the progress of the strategy of consolidation and convergence adopted by BGVS, based on their own experience and in response to suggestions made during various interactions: Mumbai, March 14, 2006; Delhi, May 17–18, 2006 with the participation of several state coordinators; and the review meeting at the BGVS office,

New Delhi, January 4, 2007. Three major programme activities were attempted to be consolidated under the strategy for convergence: Samata Women's Organization and SHGs, the imparting of basic education through GVVs, and CECs that were a result of mobilizations during the literacy campaigns and the libraries/reading movement. Discussions were held with state and district programme organizers, programme activists at the field level and participating women, children, teachers and other community members. This served to complement our field level observations at various sites.

BGVS was active during the early phase of the literacy campaigns in Madhya Pradesh during the 1990s especially during the mobilization for literacy. It was later marginalized as the campaigns were taken over by the state-run ZSSs. In May, 2007, at the time of our visit, it was working in 25 of the 45 districts of the state. A listing of these districts and of the 13 underlined districts, where the convergent approach was being adopted, is given in the following Table 9.7.

TABLE 9.7 *Districts of BGVS Presence in Madhya Pradesh, May, 2007*

Gwalior, Chambal Region	*Elsewhere*	
Bhind*	Tikamgarh*	Bhopal
Morena	Channarpur	Devas*
Datia	Katni*	Indore
Shivpuri*	Jabalpur*	Ujjain
Sheopur (subdivision of Morena)	Shivni	Ratlam
Bhuna*	Chindwara*	Jhabua*
Gwalior	Betul	Mansar*
	Hoshangabad	Neemanch*
	Sihor*	Harda*

Note: Districts with an asterisk sign represent those in which a convergent approach is being attempted.

It may be noted that Bhind is one of the better-off districts with respect to the implementation of the strategy of convergence. It thus offered an opportunity for critically appreciating the potential of the strategy in this and other states with BGVS presence. The following Table 9.8 presents a picture of the active presence of BGVS in gram panchayats, the BGVS membership and the coverage of programmes in all the six blocks of Bhind district which were taken up for coverage.

TABLE 9.8 *BGVS Coverage of Gram Panchayats and Activities in Bhind District*

	Blocks in Bhind District						*Total*
	Bhind	*Raun*	*Lahar*	*Ater*	*Mehgaon*	*Gohad*	
Presence in Gram Panchayats	20/62	10/40	15/65	15/85	15/105	15/90	90/447
Continuing Education Centres (CEC)	7	–	–	–	–	–	7
Gyan Vigyan Vidyalayas (GVV)	5	8	4	4	2	4	27
Women's Self-Help Groups (SHG)	24	16	26	17	21	18	122
Membership of BGVS*	120	80	120	170	210	180	880

Note: *The membership fee is Rs 10 per annum.

An attempt was made to cover approximately 15 per cent of the gram panchayats within each block in the district. It was reported that key gram panchayats were selected on the basis of BGVS's active presence, the response of the people to a felt need and the potential for creating a cluster of approximately five contiguous villages for geographical and programmatic convergence. The foregoing data suggest that apart from the seven CECs scattered over the Bhind block, there are none as yet in the remaining blocks. The CECs were visualized to be a space donated by the local community that could be utilized as a base for meetings in the village, a library, for group readings and for undertaking short-term training programmes. Some reasons that were suggested for the relatively slow progress of the CECs were difficulties in getting a community space, a low level of felt need for a library, restrictions on the mobility of women and lower caste groups and the relative absence of a local full-time person.

GVVs and SHGs, especially the latter, appear to respond to a strongly felt need in the community as their numbers could suggest. The SHGs that had been established on a substantial scale, not only in Bhind district but also in other states, respond to immediate economic needs of a consumption and domestic character. They have also served as a major forum for women to come together and discuss their concerns. This has facilitated, to some degree, the breaking of the constraints of a highly patriarchal, caste-ridden and feudal society in this region. These groups had not yet evolved into micro enterprises based on the acquisition of skills and availability of finances.

An important feature of the approach to convergence has been the strengthening and widening the village level membership of BGVS, as the data suggest. The village level facilitators together with other full-time BGVS activists form the 880 membership base of BGVS in Bhind district.

Sherpur Village, Gohad Taluka: Sherpur lies about 25 km from Malanpur, a major town. It is a large village comprised mostly of farming communities, Thakurs, Brahmins and Jaths. There were a few dalit community members in the village and a substantial number of OBCs, persons from the Khushwa community, whose children were in the GVV. BGVS had been active for two years in this village. The earlier literacy campaign had BGVS participation during the mobilization phase before being marginalized at a later stage. The campaign in literacy terms was, to a large extent, nominal in character with the literacy figures being highly exaggerated in order to fulfil targets.

The GVV situated close to the government school had some 50 children comprised largely of the OBCs, with a few upper caste children. The Kushwas are OBCs and were the largest in number, to be distinguished from the upper caste Kushwaha who added the term Rajat to distinguish themselves from the others. The children were generally in the age group 7–10 years and were being instructed by a local volunteer. Teaching materials were supplied by BGVS. The education was being conducted upto grade five and the classes were held from mid-morning till the afternoon. No midday meal was provided, however, the children used to carry their own food and eat together across communities. The government school in this village was a little away and had a teacher student ratio of 1:150, while the GVV had a ratio of 1:25. The general impression was that the teachers did not teach in the government schools, but were keen on making money through tuitions. Even though the government schools offered a midday meal, the children preferred to come to the GVV or be enrolled in the former, have their midday meal, and yet attend the GVV. The GVV charged a normal fee of Rs 20 a month, whereas the government school charged an admission fee of Rs 150 which was difficult for some to pay, especially given the failure of the rains the previous year.

Our discussions suggested that the villagers felt a sense of collective ownership of the GVV. The school was run by a managing committee with a woman member and was headed by the local doctor. The villagers were keen to bring the curriculum in line with the government school and to get recognition from the National Institute of Open

Schooling (NIOS). They were keen to get proper premises for the school, since it was currently being run in a narrow front room of the village temple and, when possible, classes were being held in the courtyard. The villagers were ready to donate two bighas of land for the school. The rationale for the GVVs, which were apparently evolving as a parallel system to the inadequately run government schools, is discussed separately.

The next halt was at another part of the village to meet women organized as a SHG. The meeting was being held in a room of a local, well-off Thakur household. Some of the women had attended the BGVS training that was held recently. One woman and her husband were teachers in the local government school. Convergence of programmes and cross-sectoral interactions were thus taking place through personnel within the structured boundaries of the village! The women discussed the setting up of the SHG, following the example of another recently constituted 10-member group in the village that was collecting a monthly contribution of Rs 50. Lack of clear understanding of the immediate gains to be attained through monthly contributions in a situation of economic constraints seemed to be the central issue.

We invited the women to join us at the CEC that was being inaugurated in another part of the village in the lower caste area. They were initially reluctant to do so being mostly Thakur women whose caste taboos prevented them, unlike the menfolk, to go to the lower caste areas in the village. The teacher in the family took a fairly progressive stand. We were pleasantly surprised when later at the fairly large gathering for the inauguration of the CEC, these women came as a small group and sat in the front, even though with their heads and faces partially covered. This was seen as a historical step within the social dynamics of the village and might be partly attributed to the six-day training that the women had undergone with a mixed group comprising of several castes. The CEC was being inaugurated in a room donated by villagers in front of a large well and an open space that served as a meeting place. The CEC had a large number of BGVS and other publications, newspapers and was meant to be a place for reading, being read to, and to have discussions on social issues and government schemes.

Towards evolving Sherpur gram panchayat as a locus for the convergence of the key BGVS programmes, a six-day convergence training had been held which included four men and four women from each of five panchayats. According to the reports of the participants, some of the major subjects covered were village life, population, agriculture and the creation of various people's organizational forms covering youth, women and farmers. There appeared to be a strong desire for collective involvement in the economic and social development of the village, mediated through these three platforms. They mentioned the adverse sex ratio in the village (781 females to 1,000 males), erratic electric supply, corruption of government officials and natural disasters like the failure of the rains as a motivation to engage in organized self-help. The BGVS activists were well-accepted in the village for their sincerity and commitment. The activists were concerned about the need to broaden the base of the CEC so that access could be provided to even the non-literate, the lowest and the poorest classes.

Sarva Gaon Village, Gohad Taluka: The population of Sarva Gaon Panchayat was approximately 3,000 persons. The caste composition, as gathered from the villagers at our meeting, was roughly as follows: About 25 per cent belonged to the upper caste Bhumihar and the Thakurs. A substantial proportion of the population of the village was from the Kushwa OBC caste and 17 per cent belonged to the dalits. There was a small number of persons belonging to the Muslim community. Persons in this village had participated in the six-day training. We focused on the nature of the training and on the follow-up activities in the villages. The people who participated in the training were drawn from a cluster of villages: Sarva, Raipura, Ikara, Charenta and Chimka. The last three were villages where BGVS had been working for some time and where contacts and networks had been established.

The follow-up activities in Sarva Gaon included the setting up of a CEC at the home of a person engaged in the dairy business. He had participated in the training and was very keen to do something for his village. Another activity was the setting up of several fora for meetings, information and discussion towards concerted action. Information that was shared was on government programmes and their implementation, occupational opportunities for unemployed youth and possibilities of serving as a pressure group for accountability from the gram panchayat. Funds had been collected from the villages for this purpose varying from Rs 550 from Raipura to Rs 7,800 in Sarva Gaon. The villagers planned to utilize these funds for setting up libraries, buying a cupboard, maintaining records, setting up SHGs and initiating a non-formal school.

The Sarpanch of this village was a dalit, elected on a reserved seat, and a Bharatiya Janata Party (BJP) sympathizer. Most of the persons who participated in our meeting were from the upper caste Thakurs and

Jaths. However, the tension between the BGVS supporters and the gram panchayat appeared to have more to do with political allegiances than caste. When we visited the Sarpanch in the panchayat office, he expressed his willingness to support the BGVS activities and regretted his inability to participate in the meeting due to other constraints.

Kanhari Village, Gohad Taluka: A training of potential village level, facilitators for the convergence strategy was under way. There were about 50 persons from five panchayats on the second day of the training: Lahar, Mehgaon, Atair, Bhind and Gohad. More than half the persons present were from the scheduled caste. Different groups were presenting studies of their respective villages covering aspects of population, area, infrastructural facilities and natural resources. There was a brief discussion on the status of women and the preference for girl children.

Chitawali Village, Gohad Taluka: This village is situated at a considerable distance from the main highway, deep inside the large fields. BGVS had been working here for a considerable period of time, with its volunteer teachers and lawyers receiving a lot of popular support.

The children from the local GVV had progressed to a considerable extent in their learning, reciting verses, playing games, reading from their books with comprehension of what they had read, doing complicated multiplication tables and some writing in English. There was a government school at some distance, but despite the midday meal the children preferred to be in the GVV. The government school teacher was reported to be happy with this arrangement. His only request was that during a school inspection, the GVV should lend its students to the government school for a day! There was a SHG in this village, but the monthly collections were not adequate to start a bank account. The members had a vague sense of what they would like to do with the money that was collected.

Kachonghra Village, Gohad Taluka: A large meeting had been called in this gram panchayat and a number of BGVS coordinators had assembled from the nearby villages. Majority of the persons present were women and girl children in a context where gender segregation is predominant. Some of the women belonged to the local SHG. The occasion was the inauguration of the CEC in the gram panchayat.

That afternoon we had a feedback meeting with the BGVS district team, coordinators of districts from the Gwalior region, some teachers, Anganwadi workers and community members. The meeting was held in a school in Bhind town. Muslims, dalits and persons from the scheduled tribe were few in number.

Some General Issues and Reflections

The following analysis of issues that emerged from our field visit is based on one's observations, informal discussions with the BGVS activists and the formal feedback meeting.

The Strategy for Geographical Concentration and Programmatic Convergence: The strategy for convergence generally centred around a gram panchayat where BGVS had established a base of support and had been able to achieve some degree of sustained activity. The criterion for selection of blocks within districts was there where was a greater need. Villages surrounding a nodal point, a gram panchayat, were gradually brought into the process through repeated contact and building a network of support that was crystallized into a training programme on how to go about pulling together various BGVS interventions in a concentrated and consolidated manner. In Bhind district, all the six blocks were selected because there was a reasonably strong network of work and support. The block coordinators were generally those who had been with the BGVS right from the time of the mobilization for the literacy campaign. About 15 per cent of the gram panchayats were selected within each block. This approach had served to reactivate persons who had been active in the initial phase of the campaign. As mentioned earlier, about four men and four women were selected from each village within a cluster of five villages for a training programme. However, as in the case of Palera block, the participants would sometimes select themselves. It was reported that a number of women from a local SHG had turned up seeking information about the running of the SHGs and they were integrated into the training programme.

The BGVS strategy for convergence implied the consolidation of key programmes towards sustainability over time, at the grassroots village level, covering a set of five relatively contiguous villages, creating a village level cadre of four men and four women who would be facilitators of the programme within each village and supporting these efforts by pooling together the available full-time activists of BGVS. This strategy required a six-day training programme with follow-ups that were still to take place. Four such training programmes had taken place in which 160 persons had been trained. An additional programme was held during our field visit and has been described above. The topics covered in these trainings have been: Our world and the socio-economic environment, the BGVS organization, the Samata organization, SHGs, Panchayati Raj (local self-governance), CE, organization-building, NREG, health, midday meals, the Integrated Child Development

Scheme (ICDS) and the follow-up activities to be undertaken through village level people's organizational forms.

The general view among the local BGVS activists was that the approach of convergence was serving to consolidate their efforts and to provide a strong, village level base of support. The local communities had contributed space, the time of some of the members and even financially towards the activities of BGVS. This was the general view despite stated inadequacies such as the number of training programmes (only two in a given cluster of villages), insufficient time to concentrate on specific issues, lack of clarity about payment to volunteers especially to cover costs of travel for monitoring, inadequate systems for accounting and utilizing the community contributions of finances and the need for greater academic resource support.

Voluntarism and Valuation of Labour: At the time of our visit, the predominant work of the BGVS activists at the block and village levels was carried out on the basis of voluntarism. Some of the full-time activists were paid a token and variable amount based on their maintenance needs and the cost of travel. The teachers of the GVVs received a small amount that varied according to the nominal contributions of the number of children enrolled in their classes. The sum paid per child was generally Rs 10 per month. The BGVS in Madhya Pradesh appeared to be faced with the predicament of not making the programme and its activists finance/salary dependent, maintaining the driving force of voluntarism that was explicit in its movement and the inadequacy of finances to pay all activists given the scale of its activities, and on the other hand, the fact that other NGOs in the region had been paying salaries for similar work and had been drawing away some of the BGVS cadre. Besides, it was apparent that travel and other communication costs, such as mobile phones, were not covered in all cases and meant a considerable strain on the financial capacities of the activists.

The possibility of paying a nominal honorarium without loss to the spirit of its programmes, based on the requirements of time to be invested in sustaining some of its field activities was suggested by us. The CECs and the SHGs, for example, would require at least two full-time persons – one male and one female – per cluster of five villages. Unlike mobilization and environment-building through cultural communication, the sustainability of grassroots organizations and people's institutions such as GVVs, SHGs and CECs would require training and an investment of time and personnel for nurturing.

Elementary Education: The Jeevan Shala programme and the early GVVs were originally conceived by BGVS as a bridge to the formal system of education. However, these schools were now emerging as a parallel system in response to the popular demand, especially in the less developed regions of Bhind district. Existing government schools were generally non-functional, with high rates of 'formal' enrolment, drop-outs and some degree of discrimination based on caste, gender and religion. Teacher absenteeism was reported to be high and given that the time-on-task was consequently minimal, learning outcomes were reported to be far below expectations. On the other hand, private schools were too expensive for the vast majority. The Shishu Mandirs run by the Sang Parivar lacked a secular and democratic perspective and promoted an ideology based on religious nationalism.

It is in this context that the GVVs attempted to do something different in pedagogical terms, in value orientation and to ensure that children were enrolled and felt a sense of belonging to the school. Our observations suggested that though the facilities provided in the GVV schools were minimal (space, black board, text books, uniforms, meals), the enthusiasm and commitment of the teachers spilled over to the children who were acquiring learning outcomes at a faster pace than what might be found in the government schools. There had been a demand from the villagers for independent certification through NIOS. The BGVS had also attempted to intervene in the government schools through activity centres, training programmes for formal government school teachers together with Education Guarantee Scheme para-teachers. However, the presence of a government school in the vicinity of the GVVs with infrastructure and adequate number of salaried teachers, as was found in the case of a couple of villages visited, would suggest the need for a higher degree of advocacy with government for the effective running of the government schools in the first place.

The Question of Marginalization: Some issues arose from our interactions in Sarva Gaon village in particular. How inclusive were the meetings and the work of the BGVS in general? The caste profile of the work suggests that there was a tendency to concentrate more on the upper and better-off castes. The involvement of dalits and persons from the Muslim community was generally lower than their proportion to the population in the respective villages. Our discussions with the activists suggested that while dalits and Muslims participated in the trainings and the SHGs included these categories of persons, it was found tactically better to initially work with the upper castes, create an awareness among them and then move towards a greater inclusiveness so that the former do not create obstacles to working with the lower castes. Direct work with dalits at initial stages had resulted in a strong resistance from other castes. However, as regards the participation of women, it was noted that significant advances had been made in a highly patriarchal society and a few barriers of seclusion had been broken.

Local Self-Governance: Another issue is a relationship of BGVS activities and village level organizational structures – group of village level facilitators/resource persons, women's/SHG groups, children's groups and village level committees – with the gram panchayat and the gram sabhas. While attempts had been made to involve the gram panchayat members, formal relations had not yet been established. The BGVS members saw the various organized fora that were created as serving as pressure groups on the gram panchayat towards seeking greater accountability and ensuring wider participation through gram sabhas.

Part III

Some Conclusions

10

Generalizations for Theory and Practice

1. Towards a Conceptual Framework for Theory and Practice

The objective of this chapter is to draw out some theoretical generalizations from the preceding chapters that describe the changing contexts and multiple processes of BGVS interventions. Suitable cross-references will be made to earlier chapters and sections to avoid repetition. This and the following chapter is also aimed at suggesting implications for practice for BGVS and for similar social formations which emerge from civil society and have a social developmental thrust in their interactions with the state. The BGVS practice and practitioners have been a source of much inspiration over the last two decades. However, its multifarious interventions; at the same time, at different times, at various levels-village, block, district, state, national – and in different regions, have been a mind-boggling exercise to document and categorize; a veritable challenge to one's critical examination to make sense of the field processes and to one's theoretical imagination to systematize and generalize within some theoretical framework. The outline of conceptual visualization as presented in Chapter 1, section 3, which gradually evolved in interaction with the BGVS and other interventions will be further elaborated in the sections that follow. This concluding chapter also provides an opportunity to sift out and carry forward my earlier writings on the literacy campaigns, with specific references made to them and to other related literature. An underlying concern is a response to the stark question which holds both state and civil society accountable: What are the conditions for the possibility of the radical social transformation as enjoined by the Constitution – its fundamental rights and directive principles, in particular – and the UN charter on human rights to which India is a signatory, becoming a reality? What has been done and should be done about it?

Opinions, over time and in the contemporary context, sharply differ about the concept of civil society, its definition (if at all such a definition were possible), its constituents and the relation of civil society to the other parametres that constitute social systems. This is not a study on the nature and concept of civil society in itself at a theoretical level and as it evolved historically, but is an attempt to tease out in a relatively inductive manner the meaning of really existing civil society processes in contemporary India in relation to the state as seen in the context of the literacy campaigns. One will thus adopt a modest position of referring to the reader important historical overviews of the concept, as for example in Chandhoke (1995 and 2003), the collection edited by Elliott (2003), especially its introductory chapter, and Kaviraj and Khilnani (eds., 2006).

Most theoretical and empirical discussions of civil society justifiably tend to see it in a contentious relation with the state and in the public sphere. However, to varying degrees, they fail to locate this dynamics of conflict and collaboration well within the broad political spectrum of power understood as a struggle for control over a wide range of resources; from the ecological and economic to the social, educational, cultural, religious and relating to ethnicity, and on to the ideological, and the more strictly speaking, political. Most analyses also tend to work within what one considers to be a reductionist triad of the state, the market and the community/civil society. These formulations neglect the interrelation between the dimensions of the triad, the tensions within the entire system of relations and the internal contradictions within each dimension. Each is not homogeneous but fraught with conflicts in their heterogeneous disparities and contradictory interests that demand resolution. Most importantly, the formulations almost completely skirt the issue of ideology as an important determinant of the social transformatory potential and direction of the different social formations – organizations, institutions and agencies – that constitute each of the above-mentioned poles of the triad and civil society formations and the state, in particular.

Partly as a corrective to received knowledge and more importantly as a result of learning from the extraordinary complexity of field interventions that have a positive, such as the BGVS and others, or even a reactionary social transformatory potential one was forced to evolve over an extended period of time a tentative conceptualization that is presented below. The field practices in a complex yet rapidly changing developing society like India posed a serious challenge to one's received social science wisdom. Surely, they did not seem to fit into the neat categories that were largely drawn from the experiences of advanced capitalist societies.

The discussions and analysis in this chapter might be summarized and structured in terms of the following theoretical framework and visualization, which is a more specific elaboration, in the light of the preceding chapters, of the outline presented in Chapter 1, section 3. The value addition of this formulation, in theoretical terms, is that it uncovers the tensions and contradictions within and between various dimensions of a social transformatory process. Further elaborations within each of the components of this frame of reference will be found in each of the sections that follow. It is one's contention that the strength of this conceptual framework is that it permits an almost infinite variation in articulation in a tessellated manner corresponding to the complexity of changing contexts of reality and representational discourse, yet retaining the essential components of the frame – contexts/structure, intervention/agency and ideology/value – as constant.

The Ecological and Socio-Economic Context, at the national state and sub-district levels, is a given context for the BGVS intervention. It defines the limits to the possibilities of intervention, yet demands such an intervention. It might be analysed in macro and micro terms. An important economic tension within this dimension is that between the market for capital and the market for labour that are related to each other at both micro and macro levels: markets being seen as a symbolic representation of economic exchange relations. The socio-economic context comes as given, structured inequity based on class, caste, gender, religious community, other identities and inequitous access to educational and other institutional opportunities and resources. Equity in access to and quality of basic educational opportunity is one such major distributional factor. This dimension constitutes the Social Spatial aspect of intervention. It may be noted that the very act of intervention by the primary social agents in the literacy campaigns – the BGVS as a social formation within civil society and the state – gives rise to changes in context, since human agency and ensuing processes are located within given contexts. The distinctions between the dimensions that follow is for epistemological analytical purposes of what is in reality a unitary ontology of social being.

The Intervening Agency acting in Time and through a Historical Process might also be analysed in a bi-polar manner, cutting across socio-economic-ecological contexts and structures and attempting to change them. This constitutes the wider Political (power for control over resources and for their redistribution through organization, strategy and action) dimension of intervention. For the subordinate in particular organization becomes an important symbolical representation of the capacity to exercise power. Major intervening agencies might be analysed in terms of the BGVS, a mass organization of networked, social development activists, emerging from the People's Science Movements (PSM) in civil society and in relation to the state and its agencies; another major actor in the literacy campaigns and developmental intervention.

Cutting across the foregoing two dimensions is the relatively subjective aspect of contending Ideological Perspectives loaded with Value. This too may be seen in a bi-polar manner in tension, where the perspective of the BGVS did not always coincide with that of the state and, in fact at times, was in conflict with the latter. Literacy, though not exclusively so, since it is closely articulated with other forms of communicational, cultural and ideological practices, acquires the status of perhaps a hegemonic symbol of knowledge transmission. The foregoing could be represented as follows and the subsequent sections will follow this tri-dimensional, though interrelated and overlapping, conceptual classification.

What then is the definition of civil society that emerges from the BGVS experience in relation to the state in the context of the literacy campaigns? By raising this question, I am aware that I am entering into a territory where angels (meaning, scholars more competent in this specialized area than I am) fear to tread. More than a definition, I will attempt to provide a description of a conceptual, analytical area corresponding to civil society practice at an empirical level. Firstly, civil society might be defined as a non-statal, political process that is yet closely articulated with the state in a contentious relation. Both state and civil society correspond to the public, political sphere of social systems. Civil society, as also the state, is in empirical terms comprised of a vast range of collective associations, organizations, institutions and bodies. The social formations within civil society include both, ascribed/primordial identities and their social formations as well as voluntary, achieved ones. State and civil society as political processes are in a contested relation in the exercise of power understood in a broad sense as control over a range of resources, including educational ones; a

ILLUSTRATION 10.1 *The Structure of the Analysis*

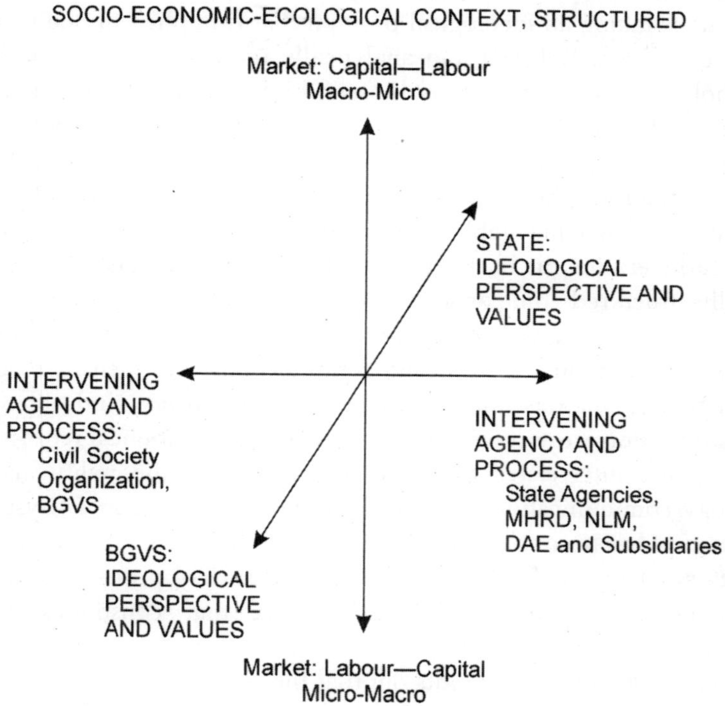

reality that introduces the concept of the market. State and civil society are framed by the relatively 'objective' dimension of ecological and socio-economic contexts with their contradictions as well as the overlapping dimension of relatively 'subjective' processes such as culture, the communication of symbolical meaning systems and, importantly, ideological perspectives which shape individual and collective subjectivity and action. Each of the above-mentioned tri-dimensional, overlapping aspects of social systems, of which civil society is a constitutive part, is fraught with internal contradictions and in its relations to the other parametres; thus constituting social systems in tension towards change.

This conceptual analytical triad can also be utilized for understanding each part. Civil society processes and their constituents, apart from their political relation to the state, cannot be fully understood without reference to structured and conflicting contexts and ideological stand points. Ideology serves to distinguish between the 'progressive', social transformatory potential of the vast array of social formations within civil society. While suggesting the aforementioned, one is aware that one is taking an ideological position that is implicit in one's social science analysis. Referent and analytically relevant aspects of unitary and holistic social systems may be seen both in terms of the relatively distinct and focused part as well as in articulated relation to the whole; to use the much used concept of, in a dialectical manner. One might also consider the metaphor of Gestaltic perception where analytical focus is perhaps humanly inevitable and creates 'figures' of attention without necessarily erasing the back 'ground' of consciousness. The identities of socially structured contexts also involve human agency, because structures are meaningless if they are sanitized against collective human actors, their differing interests and contradictions, and their ideological inclinations. Markets/finance/labour, politics/power and literacy/communication are as it were iconic in character; symbolical representations of the interrelated reality of the economy, the polity and of ideology/communication in intimate articulation within social systems. An attempt has been made, as will be seen in the entire text, to map the trajectory of the BGVS as a complex, civil society process along the above-mentioned three-dimensional matrix that constitutes social systems.

Femia (2006: 140–141) points out that the classical Marxian tradition viewed civil society as part of the infrastructure of social systems, whereas Gramsci saw civil society as a constituent of the superstructure because of the educational, ideological and cultural systems that seek 'consent' in society. I would suggest that this apparent antinomy could be resolved by identifying the essential layered contradictions of social systems as suggested above. It is important not to consider infrastructure, superstructure and the state; the economy, ideological processes and the polity; and for that matter, class structure, consciousness and political interests/actions of social agencies, in a reductionist and hence reified manner. In the final instance, the three dimensions suggested above are essentially parts of unitary, holistic social systems. The epistemological challenge is to arrive at the core of this social ontological unity – the 'being' of a class, as it were – through modes of analytical access that can only be approximations and representations. Pannikar justifiably draws attention to the dangers of reductionism in Indian historiography in the analysis of the Indian nation:

> "As such locating the nation either in the economic or the political alone, as is the case in the bulk of Indian historiography, without tracing its connection with the cultural, has remained an incomplete exercise. The communal historiography has taken advantage of this void in order to attribute an exclusively cultural character to nationalism" (Pannikar, 2009: 35).

A further specification of the foregoing analytical and conceptual formulations would be in order. I undertake this with much reservation, given that it runs the risk of parodying a conceptual framework through the apparent prescription of relatively stable locations within what is essentially a classificatory frame of reference that is in reality in a state of

ILLUSTRATION 10.2 *State and Civil Society: Social Formations*

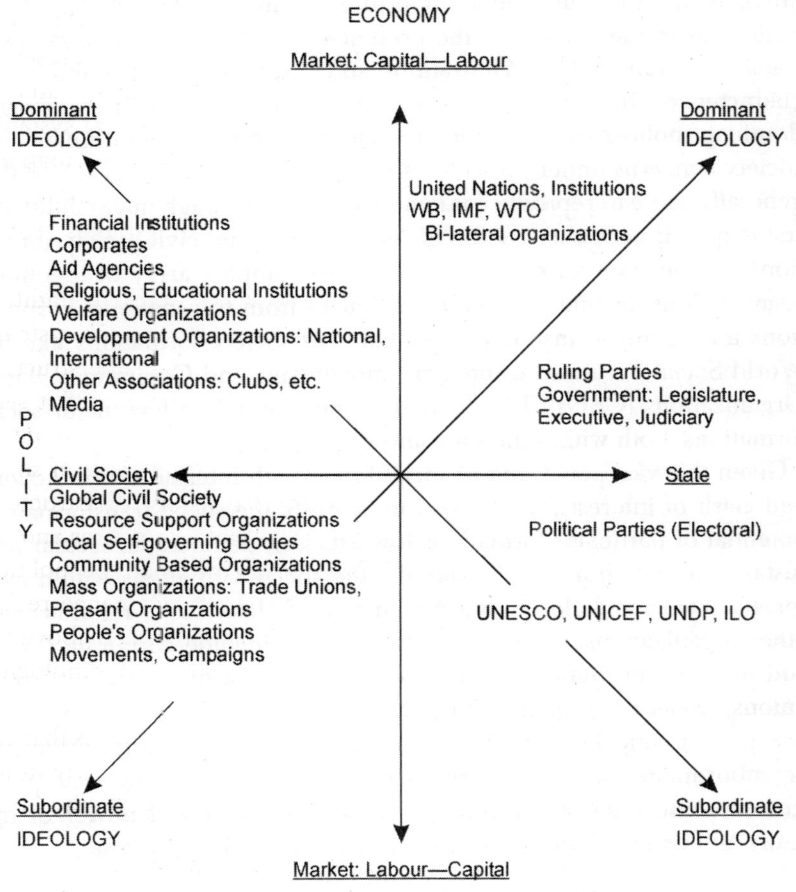

constant flux. Being an attempt at classification, the visualization bears all the limitations of such an effort. I offer the following tentative illustration with the foregoing and other qualifications towards hopefully arriving at more effective communication. It would be a misreading of my intentions to view the aspects visualized in the illustrations within this text as stable, reductionist reifications of what are in effect an attempt to represent a dynamic social reality in the process of transformation.

The tension between civil society and the state within the sphere of the polity is framed by the overlapping structural dimension of the primary contradiction between monopoly capital and relatively assetless labour in the arena of the economy. The iniquitous structural principles of class, caste, tribe, patriarchy, religious marginalization and other subordinating identities have a mutually reinforcing effect on access to literacy enablement, to educational opportunities and on knowledge distribution; as in the context of the present study. There is a vast range of statal and trans-statal organizations and institutions that embody the character of the state as an instrument that primarily represents dominant politico-economic interests and responds to subordinate civil society concerns under pressure of mobilization and advocacy, and that generally serve to reproduce iniquitous systems through maintaining the status quo, if necessary by force. As with the state, civil society formations demonstrate an even more vast and complex array of identities, organizations, institutions, bodies, agencies from transnational corporations and financial institutions, global civil society formations like the World Social Forum to campaigns, movements and Community-Based Organizations (CBOs). I have tried to identify only a few major social formations, both within the state and civil society.

Given this vast panorama of social forces with internal contradictions and clash of interests, how does one identify the social transformatory potential of particular formations towards just, democratic, secular and sustainable directions? For example, the social formations within civil society would include quite a mixed bag of class, caste, religious and other organizations; a multiplicity that would include corporate bodies and financial institutions; communal and terrorist organizations; trade unions, peasant organizations, non-electoral political parties and non-party political groups. It is here that ideology – whether dominant or subordinate, whether close to the monopolizing power of politico-economic interests or contributing to the organized power of the many and its social impact – serves as an important touchstone.

To go back to the illustration and the possible location of particular entities, there is a need for further qualifications. Identifications are necessarily tentative and based on relatively consistent trends in policy and practice within a situation of flux. For example, there is a need to distinguish the role of multilateral bodies such as the World Bank (WB), the International Monetary Fund (IMF) and the World Trade Organization (WTO) from that of UNESCO, UNICEF, UNDP and ILO, even though they all function within the framework of the United Nations. Ruling parties and elected governments with their arms of the legislature, executive, judiciary, the armed forces and the police are the most tangible expressions of the state in the public eye. It is within civil society that one can understand "how ordinary people receive state power. A state without civil society appears both disembodied as well as disembedded" (Chandhoke, 2003: 24). So also are electoral political parties that constitute the state, perhaps a matter of some debate, which are, in most instances, mere governments in waiting and increasingly far removed from the concerns of civil society and their mass organizations. As pointed out by Kumar (2000: 2778), the historical consolidation of the constitutional state from the perspective of a liberal civil society required universal adult franchise. Liberal civil society could not then act against its elected statal institutions, thus consolidating liberal hegemony. On the side of civil society, the multiplicity of forms, the complexity of shifting strategic positions related to contexts and interests and divergent approaches and sub-formations within a single entity (eg., NGOs with a developmental wing as well as an activist one) all serve to defy attempts at any firm classification.

With governments in alliance with corporate bodies behaving in a schizophrenic manner, the uncovering of ideological positions and their translation into trends in social impact based on deep-rooted interests emerging from the way in which social systems are structured introduces some consistency in frameworks of classifications. Consider, for example, the current ruling electoral powers responding to civil society mobilizations and advocacy and introducing positive policies and legislations related to the rights to food, work, micro-credit and the rights to natural and forest resources in the sphere of the economy; the 73rd, 74th and the Panchayat Extension to Scheduled Areas (PESA) amendments to the Constitution that brought about decentralization of governance and powers to gram sabhas and gram panchayats, together with the right to information which is an important step towards accountability and transparency within the polity; and the right to free and compulsory education at the elementary level which is a small step towards equitable knowledge distribution. On the other hand, the same governments in power do not hesitate to undermine the very livelihood and natural resource base of the poor in the name of liberalizing markets through projects relating to Special Economic Zones (SEZs) and contracts for mega projects for mining, dams and industrialization within a peculiar notion of economic growth through primitive accumulation, displacement, forcible eviction and pauperization that create conditions for the very impossibility of mass literacy, education, health and the enhancement of the social development sector. The broad typology suggested is only indicative. One has attempted a similar exercise earlier (Saldanha, April 2008) drawing on a broad classificatory framework of non-party, political formations suggested by Sethi (1984).

As mentioned earlier, the above-mentioned conception of civil society evolved primarily through academic confrontation with a variety of intervention strategies over the last three decades and only to a secondary degree as a process of assimilating academic literature on the subject. However, without intending to misinterpret the writings of others, it would be useful to consider any resonances. Chandhoke comes close to a definition of civil society which one is in agreement with when she writes:

> "The space where these affirmations of, and contestations to dominant historical blocs takes place, is the public sphere of society, in other words civil society. Civil society is simply the sphere where groups organized on class and other social bases – gender, sexuality, race, ethnicity, environment – engage in political and ideological struggles" (Chandhoke, 1995: 168).
>
> And further on:
> "The world of production, the exploitation and the oppressions of the production process, are rendered opaque by the ideology of the market" (Chandhoke, 1995: 193).
>
> And in a later writing:
> "The politics of affirmation and contestation do not occur in a vacuum, but in the overlap of the state, the market, society, and the family" (Chandhoke, 2003: 33)

The introduction of the ascriptive institution of the family within the public forum of civil society would suggest the need to break down sharp distinctions between the ascribed and the so-called achieved. While the foregoing extracts do bring out the contending relations between state and civil society, the internal contradictions of each and their relation to the market and production processes, one would have appreciated a sharper and more definitive status given to ideology, values, culture and other communicative processes of knowledge transaction. This relatively independent, yet intimately articulated, sphere of human existence is hinted at in the following:

> "But this makes civil society valuable only as a site and as a cluster of values intrinsic to democratic life. For civil societies are what their inhabitants make of them, always keeping in mind that their thoughts and their social practices will be permeated by the logic of both the state and the market. Civil society is constituted by the politics of power as much as it is constituted by the politics of protest. And it is this aspect of civil society that transforms it, in Hegelian terms, into the 'theatre of history'" (Chandhoke in Elliott (ed.), 2003: 260).

A clearer position on the role of ideological contestation in relation to civil society, state and markets is taken by Robinson in his analysis of Hindu nationalism within the more strictly ideological discourse, liberalization and economic reforms and the emergence of new forms of civil society activism within the polity. While acknowledging the limitations of western political theory to adequately represent these Indian social phenomena, he writes:

> "Our principle argument is that the civil society domain does not constitute an organizational vacuum divorced from political society, and that ideology provides an important site of contestation in civil society around which groups and organizations mobilize in conscious pursuit of normatively defined interests. Contrary to received wisdom, we would suggest that religion and ethnicity provide critical reference points for mobilization and contestation within civil society, and that organizations founded on these ascriptive categories should not be dismissed as primordial and thus outside the realm of modern civil society ...
>
> This is not simply to acknowledge that civil society is inhabited by organizations with conflicting normative claims, but to recognize that these are engaged in multiple struggles for ideological supremacy in various arenas of civil society" (Robinson in Elliott (ed.), 2003: 374).

With reference to the more specific context of literacy, a formulation by Street (1984 and in Mukherjee and Vasanta eds. 2002: 49ff) that appears to have acquired substantial legitimacy within academic discourse, is the tension between what he calls the 'autonomous' model of literacy and the 'ideological' one. The former discourse is characterized by an implicit claim to the technical neutrality of literacy and suggests that the acquisition of literacy has certain positive cognitive consequences that serve as a break from the generally negative cognitive implications of orality. As opposed to this position, he suggests an ideological model which emphasizes the contexts of 'literacy practices'. Literacy practices are justifiably seen as embedded in cultural contexts and values. The meanings given to literacy and its varying uses in situations are seen as socially constructed by participants. I find that the analysis of Street and his concepts of literacy events and practices are useful for an understanding of literacy interventions within given social contexts and their pedagogical and cognitive implications. However, the designation of an 'autonomous model' given to what is in effect claimed to be a relatively transcendental, reified conception of literacy as a neutral, techno-managerial process is quite unfortunate. For, what could be more ideological in character, not only in the classical Marxian sense of ideology as 'false consciousness' but also in its generalized usage as a system of ideas that guides action, than an academic discourse on literacy that claims for itself a universal representation, when in practice it is a dominant one that represents minority interests. I would rather tend to view the tensions within the academic writings and practices on literacy as both within the ideological sphere (as discussed above) and representing a tension between a dominant cultural hegemony on literacy that seeks 'consent' and a contending, subordinate one in the Gramscian sense of the terms (Saldanha, 2008a and b).

In the light of the foregoing theoretical formulation, we will move on to a further analysis of the three dimensions mentioned above.

2. Contexts: Interventions in Contexts of Uneven Development

An assessment of the history of the BGVS suggests that there were two primary factors that influenced its trajectory; the external environment and the organizational dynamics and strategies internal to BGVS, in response to the former. Factors related to the external environment may be seen as those related to the shifting socio-economic contexts of intervention and those resulting from the interactions with the other major agency in the literacy campaigns – the state/government and the character of its official literacy programmes. The strategies of the BGVS were largely in response to the changing spaces provided to it by the government and the shifting regional focii of the campaigns. This will be discussed below:

One can turn one's attention to the socio-economic context. Literacy was introduced within a context of lack of political priority, especially during the 1994 to 1997 phase, and generally within underdeveloped regions where aspects of caste, patriarchy and economic inequity reinforced each other to act as obstacles to the introduction of a relatively soft input like literacy. This was especially true of the low literacy districts of the northern Hindi-speaking belt. The literacy campaigns adopted a strategy, here as also elsewhere, of first mobilization for literacy and then linkages with development. This strategy could work in the relatively high literacy districts of Kerala and in other parts of India, during 1988 to 1993. A past history of struggle and social reform movements had prepared a socio-economic, political and cultural base for this approach. This strategy proved to be inadequate in contexts where socio-economic survival was the felt priority and 'literacy in isolation' was a relatively weak input. It was only after 1994, learning from the experience of the campaigns especially in the north and when the campaigns at the national level were entering the PL and CE phases, i.e., when there was an official legitimacy for developmental linkages, that the BGVS called for a change in strategy to one that was further decentralized, integrated and interlinked with developmental issues. The report to the BGVS General Council of July 9–10, 1994, held in Madras, states:

> "In no other state there was a people's movement comparable to the KSSP, in its wide reach and in its commitment to literacy. The BGVS was formed, initially to put literacy on national agenda and to evoke a massive demand for literacy. These two objectives were satisfactorily achieved by the BGVS, through the BGVJ 1990. Soon the objective was enlarged: to build up a people's delivery system for literacy, as exemplified in Ernakulam. This demanded, first and foremost, building up of people's movements in various states, comparable to the KSSP. This is not an easy task. KSSP grew to the present level over a period of two to three decades and through a variety of social interventions. To achieve that growth in a couple of years, through a single point agenda of literacy is too much to ask" (BGVS, 1994: 35–36).

Undertaking a review of the strengths and weaknesses of the literacy campaigns, in the context of comparative data from the 1981 and 1991 censuses and the learning achievement levels that were emerging from the early campaigns of 1989 to 1993, one had come to the conclusion that, "It appears impossible to confront mass illiteracy in low literacy states/districts without major interventions on the socio-economic front such as land reforms, income generation measures and mobilizations on issues of caste and the status of women" (Saldanha, 1999: 2025). A major irony in the unplanned expansion of the literacy campaigns during the period 1994 to 1997, the next phase, was that they entered regions where the need was the greatest but where the capacities in terms of human and institutional resources were also the least prepared to implement the campaigns in a participatory manner and to fruitfully utilize the funds. Consequently, these campaigns tended to become finance driven, neglecting the initial mobilizations and the decentralized organizational structures for participation.

Historical experience of twentieth century campaigns had suggested that they were generally undertaken in the context of major politico-economic transformations, thus serving as a break to the linkage between adult illiteracy and underdevelopment (Arnove and Graff, 1987; Bhola, 1984). However, in the Indian context, there were no dramatic changes in the political economy that would create more equitous structures of opportunity. This would have made literacy competencies translatable into fulfilments of democratic and economic entitlements and rights and thus provide a motivation for literacy. In this situation, the campaigns during the early years from 1989 to 1993 had adopted two major strategies, primarily at the initiative of BGVS:

> "1. Create a process that comes close to a cultural movement for literacy in a localized area through environment building programmes that incorporate folk culture, especially in the preparatory phase. While this strategy attempted to offset the lack of reformed structures of opportunity that create the possibility for more equitous entitlements and heightened aspirations, generally in post-revolutionary situations, it was too weak in itself to counter the hard reality of socio-economic underdevelopment in low literacy districts.
>
> 2. Create a democratic decentralized structure for participatory implementation that draws together three major social resources – government/local self-government, the academic community of teachers and students at various levels, and the voluntary organized/unorganized sector. This strategy attempted to counteract the bureaucratic and authoritarian tendencies of an underdeveloped state with the countervailing pressure of the voluntary sector and civil society. However, the latter was generally too weak in regions where the need for literacy was the greatest or was not given the time and the opportunity to grow in the pace for finance driven expansion, or was at times ignored" (Saldanha, 1998: 400–401).

Both these strategies were relatively set aside in the pace for government-sponsored expansion calling into serious question the sustainability of the campaigns and the fragile learning outcomes.

Our data from the early literacy campaigns in Maharashtra suggested that they were able to penetrate the structures of class, caste and patriarchy that tend to reinforce illiteracy and to reach out to the most marginalized. Almost 66 per cent of the learners in the selected districts were female and the SC, ST and nomadic tribals together constituted 38 per cent of the persons participating as learners. About 6 per cent came from the minority community of Muslims. Considering occupational categories, agricultural labourers formed 48 per cent of the learners and small cultivators 27 per cent. Undoubtedly, these early literacy campaigns in themselves generally failed to transform these structures to any significant extent since they were not accompanied by the organization of the oppressed for political and economic rights. Literacy and the process of achieving it through the campaign approach could at best lay the basis for such organizations to emerge (Saldanha, 1995: 1176).

Attention has already been drawn in Chapter 1, section 1, to the extensive and expanding scope of the 'official', government inspired literacy campaigns, irrespective of their quality of delivery of education linked to development over the last decade. One has also pointed out the decline in the quality of the campaigns, ironically coinciding with their sharp spread during the 1994 to 1997 period. By 1998 and the years that followed over the last decade, isolated traces of what was intended to be a people's movement for literacy could be found in what was largely a stagnating, but large-scale government programme. The scale of operation in a country of sharply contrasting socio-economic and political conditions may be seen from the fact that by August, 2008, it was reported that 95 districts were in the first phase of basic literacy programmes; 120 districts were undertaking projects to cover the residual illiteracy of those who were non-enrolled, dropouts or who had relapsed into illiteracy despite earlier programmes; 175 districts were in the PL phase and 328 districts were carrying out CE programmes (NLM, August 10, 2008: 2). Some of the districts were covering overlapping project phases. These data would suggest that most of the districts in the country, if not all, were covered by one form or other of the existing adult education programmes by 2008. The NLM (August 2008: 12) reported that the literacy campaigns had spread to around 597 districts of the country. Around 221 JSSs and 26 SRCs had been established in order to provide academic resource support to the national literacy programmes. The Eleventh Plan (2008–12) had allocated Rs 6,000 crore for the literacy programmes as compared to Rs 1,250 crore in the Tenth Plan (2002–07). The objective was to attain a literacy rate of 80 per cent by 2011–12 from the 65 per cent in 2001 and to reduce the gender gap in literacy to 10 per cent together with other social and regional disparities by the end of the Eleventh Plan.

This is not to deny that sincere attempts were made by the present Ministry of Human Resource Development, Department of School Education and Literacy to revive the literacy 'campaigns' which had effectively become a 'programme', through intensive 'project' modes. A sum of Rs 1,250 crore had been allocated for adult education during the Tenth Plan period of 2002–07. The costs of providing literacy was estimated to be Rs 45 to Rs 50 per learner depending on local conditions, shared on a two-thirds–one-third basis by the centre and the states. By April, 2005, the NLM claimed that about 30 million persons had been made literate under various literacy programmes over the previous five years as part of its strategy of attaining a 75 per cent literacy rate in the country by 2007. A further 150 districts in the country where the literacy rate and especially the female literacy rate were substantially lower than the national average, were identified for an intensive approach during 2005–07. The number of non-literates in the age group 15 to 35 was estimated to be 36 millions in these districts (NLMA, April 11, 2005: 12). An important attempt in the direction of adopting an intensive targeted approach was the Project for Residual Literacy intended to cover stagnating literacy campaigning districts, especially those having a female literacy rate below 30 per cent. By August, 2008, such projects had been sanctioned to 141 districts in various states. Another project was the Accelerated Female Literacy Programme (AFLP). This was initiated in a context where 47 districts were identified that had a female literacy rate below 30 per cent according to the 2001 Census. Most of these districts were concentrated in Bihar, Jharkhand, Uttar Pradesh and Orissa. Attempts were made to involve female Panchayati Raj functionaries in order to facilitate their literacy. Initially in Uttar Pradesh, eight such districts were brought under AFLP which was implemented by a network of about 100 NGOs. It was reported that 17.10 lakh female learners were made literate out of an enrolment of 24.53 lakh. In Bihar in 15 identified districts, Panchayati Raj functionaries, women volunteer teachers and SHGs were involved. In Orissa, AFLP was sanctioned in nine districts with the participation of 117 NGOs. It was reported that 5.80 lakh female learners out of an enrolment of 9.03 lakh had completed the third primer (National Literacy Mission, August 2008: 7–8). These programmes were undertaken by state governments without the involvement of the BGVS which had by this time been marginalized from centrally sponsored literacy activities. It is possible that the involvement of the BGVS, a formation created and sustained by the government itself during the early years of the literacy campaigns, and other similar organizations with experience would have resulted in better performance.

As mentioned earlier, one has attempted to understand the distribution of literacy over the states and districts of the country, based on the Census data of 1991 and the trends in relation to the data in the 1981 Census, as seen in the following Tables 10.1, 10.2 and 10.3 (Saldanha, 1999). The states and union territories of the country were classified into high, medium and low as in the following tables. Such a classification assumed that the issue of confronting 'residual literacy' in high literacy states, districts and in urban areas needed to be seen in relation to the wider context of 'mass literacy' within other regions of the country. The trends in literacy data between 1981 and 1991 within high literacy states suggested a 'saturation effect' where attempts to address literacy met with a different kind of resistance as compared to the medium literacy states of 'transitional literacy'. The relatively low growth rates of literacy among males, urban areas and within the general population in high literacy areas suggested a catching up of literacy among the comparatively contrasting counterparts through higher growth rates. The low literacy states, largely concentrated in a northern belt of the country, suggested a close relation between literacy intervention and addressing the issues of disparity based on class, caste, gender and regional (urban-rural) contexts. Literacy interventions needed to address these issues, considering the low growth rates of literacy.

A further comparative analysis of the trends in literacy rates between 1991 and 2001 (Saldanha, 2005), the decade of the literary campaigns – holding the classification of the states based on the 1991 Census as constant – suggested a sharp increase in the national literacy rate by 12 per cent, from 52.2 per cent in 1991 to 64.6 per cent in 2001 which has been unprecedented in all the earlier censuses. The sharpest increases had been in the low literacy states, from 41.5 per cent to 57.5 per cent, a growth of 16 per cent as compared to the medium and the high literacy states. While rural-urban and gender differences continued, it may be noted that the highest growth in literacy rates during the decade

TABLE 10.1 *India (States and Union Territories): Literacy Rates for 1981, 1991 and 2001 by Sex and Region*

State/ UT(1)	Literacy Rate for 1981 (7 + Age Group)					Literacy Rate for 1991 (7 + Age Group)					Literacy Rate for 2001 (7 + Age Group)				
	Sex		Region		Total (6)	Sex		Region		Total (11)	Sex		Region		Total (16)
	Male (2)	Female (3)	Rural (4)	Urban (5)		Male (7)	Female (8)	Rural (9)	Urban (10)		Male (12)	Female (13)	Rural (14)	Urban (15)	
High Literacy Rate States (70% +)															
Kerala	87.7	75.7	80.3	87.3	81.6	93.6	86.2	88.9	92.3	89.8	94.2	87.9	90.0	93.4	90.9
Mizoram	79.4	68.6	69.5	88.4	74.2	85.6	78.6	72.5	93.5	82.3	90.7	88.1	80.5	96.3	88.5
Lakshadweep	81.2	55.3	65.3	72.0	68.4	90.2	72.9	78.9	84.0	81.8	93.2	81.6	86.4	88.9	87.5
Chandigarh	78.9	69.3	54.7	76.2	74.8	82.0	72.3	59.1	79.9	77.8	85.7	76.7	76.2	82.4	81.8
Goa	76.0	55.2	61.7	74.0	65.7	83.6	67.1	72.3	80.1	75.5	88.9	75.5	79.7	85.0	82.3
Delhi	79.3	62.6	58.0	73.0	71.9	82.0	67.0	66.9	76.2	75.3	87.4	75.0	78.8	82.0	81.8
Pondicherry	77.1	53.0	57.2	72.2	65.1	83.7	65.6	65.4	79.9	74.7	88.9	74.1	74.3	85.1	81.5
A and N Islands	70.3	53.2	58.2	77.1	63.2	79.0	65.5	69.7	81.7	73.0	88.1	75.3	78.6	86.5	81.2
Daman and Diu	74.5	46.5	–	–	–	82.7	59.4	61.6	81.6	71.2	88.4	70.4	78.3	86.0	81.1
Mean	85.1	72.3	78.5	79.4	78.8	89.9	81.0	86.8	83.8	85.5	91.6	83.8	88.8	86.5	87.8
Range	17.4	29.2	25.6	16.4	18.4	14.6	26.8	29.8	17.3	18.6	8.5	17.7	15.7	14.3	9.8
Medium Literacy Rate States (45–69%)															
Maharashtra	69.7	41.0	46.8	72.5	55.8	76.6	52.3	55.5	79.2	64.9	86.3	67.5	70.8	85.8	77.3
Himachal Pradesh	64.3	37.7	49.1	76.1	51.2	75.4	52.1	61.9	84.2	63.9	86.0	68.1	74.4	89.6	77.1

Tamil Nadu	68.1	40.4	46.2	71.1	54.4	73.8	51.3	54.6	78.0	62.7	82.3	64.6	66.7	82.1	73.5
Nagaland	58.6	40.3	46.2	71.8	50.2	67.6	54.8	57.2	83.1	61.7	71.8	61.9	63.0	86.0	67.1
Gujarat	65.1	38.5	44.7	68.8	52.2	73.1	48.6	53.1	76.5	61.3	80.5	58.6	58.5	79.2	70.0
Tripura	61.5	38.0	46.2	81.7	50.1	70.6	49.7	56.1	83.1	60.4	81.5	65.4	70.2	89.5	73.7
Manipur	64.1	34.6	45.6	60.6	49.6	71.6	47.6	55.8	70.5	59.9	77.9	59.7	65.3	80.0	68.9
Punjab	55.6	39.7	42.5	62.9	48.2	65.7	50.4	52.8	72.1	58.5	75.6	63.6	65.2	79.1	70.0
West Bengal	59.9	36.1	40.9	70.5	48.7	67.8	46.6	50.5	75.3	57.7	77.6	60.2	64.1	81.6	69.2
Sikkim	53.0	27.4	37.6	62.4	41.6	65.7	46.7	54.4	80.9	56.9	76.3	61.5	67.7	84.8	69.7
Karnataka	58.7	33.2	38.8	64.4	46.2	67.3	44.3	47.7	74.2	56.0	76.3	57.5	59.7	81.0	67.0
Haryana	58.5	26.9	38.1	64.7	43.9	69.1	40.5	49.9	73.7	55.9	79.3	56.3	63.8	79.9	68.6
Assam	–	–	–	–	–	61.9	43.0	49.3	79.4	52.9	71.9	56.0	60.9	85.8	64.3
Meghalaya	46.6	37.2	35.5	72.1	42.1	53.1	44.9	41.1	81.7	49.1	66.1	60.4	57.0	87.1	63.3
Orissa	56.5	25.1	38.3	61.6	41.0	63.1	34.7	45.5	72.0	49.1	76.0	51.0	60.4	81.0	63.6
Mean	62.7	36.3	42.8	69.1	50.0	70.2	47.3	51.6	76.6	59.1	79.0	57.7	64.2	82.4	68.5
Range	23.1	15.9	13.6	21.1	14.8	23.5	20.1	20.8	13.7	15.8	20.2	17.1	17.4	10.5	14.0
Low Literacy Rate States (0–44%)															
Madhya Pradesh	48.4	19.0	27.5	60.3	34.2	58.4	28.9	35.9	70.8	44.2	76.8	50.3	58.1	79.7	64.1
Andhra Pradesh	46.5	24.2	29.0	57.8	35.7	55.1	32.7	35.7	66.4	44.1	70.9	51.2	55.3	76.4	61.1
Arunachal Pradesh	35.1	14.0	23.2	57.9	25.5	51.5	29.7	37.0	71.6	41.6	64.1	44.2	48.3	78.8	54.7
Uttar Pradesh	47.4	17.2	29.2	52.0	33.3	55.7	25.3	36.7	61.0	41.6	70.2	43.0	53.7	70.6	57.4

Cont'd…

Cont'd…

D and N Haveli	44.7	20.4	30.7	60.2	32.7	53.6	27.0	37.0	78.4	40.7	73.3	43.0	52.2	85.2	60.0
Rajasthan	44.8	14.0	23.7	54.1	30.1	55.0	20.4	30.4	65.3	38.6	76.5	44.3	55.9	76.9	61.0
Bihar	46.6	16.5	28.3	58.0	32.0	52.5	22.9	33.8	67.9	38.5	60.3	33.6	44.4	72.7	47.5
Jammu & Kashmir	44.2	19.6	27.6	51.6	32.7	–	–	–	–	–	65.8	41.8	48.2	72.2	54.5
Mean	47.0	18.2	28.1	55.8	33.2	55.3	26.2	35.1	65.5	41.5	70.0	43.9	54.1	66.0	57.5
Range	13.3	10.2	7.5	8.7	10.2	6.9	12.3	6.6	17.4	5.7	16.5	17.6	13.7	14.6	16.6
India mean	56.4	29.8	37.1	64.8	43.6	64.1	39.3	44.7	73.1	52.2	75.6	53.1	60.0	75.9	64.6
Range	52.6	61.7	57.1	36.8	56.1	42.1	65.8	58.5	32.5	51.3	33.9	54.5	45.6	25.7	43.4
New States in 2001															
Uttaranchal	–	–	–	–	–	–	–	–	–	–	84.0	60.3	68.9	81.5	72.3
Jharkhand	–	–	–	–	–	–	–	–	–	–	68.0	39.3	46.3	79.9	54.1
Chhatisgarh	–	–	–	–	–	–	–	–	–	–	77.9	52.4	60.9	81.1	65.2

Source: 1. Cols. 2–3 and 6, NIAE, Statistical Database for Literacy, 1991, Vol. 1, New Delhi, 1992 based on Census data
2. Cols. 4–5 based on Census data 1981, Primary Census Abstract, India, General Population Part II B(i).
3. Cols 7–11, NIAE Statistical Database for Literacy, 1991, Vol II, New Delhi, 1993 based on Census data
4. Cols. 12–16 based on Census India website www.censusindia.net/results/state.php?stad=A

TABLE 10.2 *India (States and Union Territories): Literacy Rates for 1981, 1991 and 2001 by Sex and Region*

State/UT(1)	*Literacy Rate for 1981 (7 + Age Group)*					*Literacy Rate for 1991 (7 + Age Group)*					*Literacy Rate for 2001 (7 + Age Group)*				
	Sex		*Region*		*Total (6)*	*Sex*		*Region*		*Total (11)*	*Sex*		*Region*		*Total (16)*
	Male (2)	*Female (3)*	*Rural (4)*	*Urban (5)*		*Male (7)*	*Female (8)*	*Rural (9)*	*Urban (10)*		*Male (12)*	*Female (13)*	*Rural (14)*	*Urban (15)*	
High Literacy Rate States (70% +)															
Mean	85.1	72.3	78.5	79.4	78.8	89.9	81.0	86.8	83.8	85.5	91.6	83.8	88.8	86.5	87.8
Medium Literacy Rate States (45–69%)															
Mean	62.7	36.3	42.8	69.1	50.0	70.2	47.3	51.6	76.6	59.1	79.0	57.7	64.2	82.4	68.5
Low Literacy Rate States (0–44%)															
Mean	47.0	18.2	28.1	55.8	33.2	55.3	26.2	35.1	65.5	41.5	70.0	43.9	54.1	66.0	57.5
India mean	56.4	29.8	37.1	64.8	43.6	64.1	39.3	44.7	73.1	52.2	75.6	53.1	60.0	75.9	64.6
New states in 2001															
Uttaranchal	–	–	–	–	–	–	–	–	–	–	84.0	60.3	68.9	81.5	72.3
Jharkhand	–	–	–	–	–	–	–	–	–	–	68.0	39.3	46.3	79.9	54.1
Chhatisgarh	–	–	–	–	–	–	–	–	–	–	77.9	52.4	60.9	81.1	65.2

Source: 1. Cols. 2–3 and 6, NIAE, Statistical Database for Literacy, 1991, Vol. 1, New Delhi, 1992 based on Census data.
2. Cols. 4–5 based on Census data 1981, Primary Census Abstract, India, General Population Part II B(i).
3. Cols 7–11, NIAE Statistical Database for Literacy, 1991, Vol II, New Delhi, 1993 based on Census data.
4. Cols. 12–16 based on Census India website www.censusindia.net/results/state.php?stad=A.

TABLE 10.3 *India (States and Union Territories): Intra Sex and Region Growth in Literacy Rates from 1981 to 1991 and 1991 to 2001*

States/UT(1)	*Growth in Literacy from 1981 to 1991*					*Growth in Literacy from 1991 to 2001*				
	Sex		*Region*		*Total (6)*	*Sex*		*Region*		*Total (11)*
	Male (2)	*Female (3)*	*Rural (4)*	*Urban (5)*		*Male (7)*	*Female (8)*	*Rural (9)*	*Urban (10)*	
High Literacy Rate States (70% +)										
Mean	4.8	8.8	8.3	4.4	6.7	1.7	2.8	2.0	2.7	2.3
Medium Literacy Rate States (45–69%)										
Mean	7.5	11.0	8.8	7.5	9.1	8.8	10.5	12.6	5.8	9.4
Low Literacy Rate States (0–44%)										
Mean	8.3	8.0	7.0	9.7	8.3	14.7	17.7	19.0	0.5	16.0
India mean	7.7	9.5	7.6	8.3	8.6	11.5	13.8	15.3	2.8	12.4

Source: 1. Growth in literacy from 1981 to 1991, same as Table 1.
2. Growth in literacy from 1991 to 2001, Education for All in India, website www.arunmehta.freeyellow.com

1991–2001 had been among the female and in rural areas, 13.8 per cent and 15.3 per cent respectively, the sections and regions of greatest need.

How does one explain the foregoing data? The discussion in this section would have thrown some light on the serious objective constraints emerging from the uneven development within the country. The discussion has also drawn attention to the expansionist tendency in the national literacy strategy, neglecting some basic subjective, organizational factors that were necessary for meaningful outcomes. Assuming that the tendency to inflate official results was constant over the two decades, it appears that primarily the efforts in elementary education over the decade as well as the literacy campaigns had contributed to a significant extent to literacy in rural areas, among women and girl children and to some degree within low literacy regions. This contribution, if not directly the result of adult education efforts, may indirectly be seen to be the product of the demand that had been created for elementary education as a result of the campaigns. The BGVS, as the initiator of the literacy campaigns and the primary strategist during the late 1980s and early 1990s, could claim due credit for this statistical increase in literacy performance. However, such statistical increases constitute only one indicator of social development and some significant questions remained. How 'functional' was the literacy that had been provided and how sustainable was it? The task of addressing illiteracy of about 300 million persons of the national population aged seven years and above and especially among women, girl children, SCs and STs and among Muslim minorities, while engaging them in adequate social developmental interventions still remains.

Based on the 2001 Census, Prem Chand (2008: 41ff) concluded that two-thirds of the total number of non-literates of the country in 2001 continued to be concentrated in 12 states which had literacy rates below the national level – Bihar, Jharkhand, Uttar Pradesh, Jammu & Kashmir, Dadra and Nagar Haveli, Arunachal Pradesh, Andhra Pradesh, Rajasthan, Assam, Madhya Pradesh, Orissa and Meghalaya. The 193 districts that had a female literacy below 50 per cent generally tended to be the ones where literacy rates were low for SCs, STs and Muslim minorities and generally were located among the 12 low literacy states mentioned above. The literacy rate of the age group 15 to 35 years was 71 per cent in 2001, 81 per cent for males and 60 per cent for females. Considering the movement of age cohorts and the increase in population, the literacy rate in this age group was likely to increase to 76 per cent by 2006, with a decline in the number of non-literates from about 100 million in 2001 to 94 million in 2006.

The trajectory of the history of the BGVS suggests a running internal tension in its organizational and strategic orientation that has not been fully resolved. This is related to the scale of operations that was required of it as it breathlessly tried to keep pace with the expanding government programme. The polarities of this tension may be analysed, at the level of structured social space, i.e., the socio-geographical coverage of the various initiatives, as a tension between the macro and micro as regards the scale of the intervention. Several of the centrally sponsored mobilizations (the jathas), the programmes that emerged and the cascading impact of training programmes/workshops at the central, regional, state, block and village levels, bear traces of this tension. The BGVS was constrained to cover several districts in a number of states given national needs and the expansion of the government-sponsored literacy campaigns to new regions. Its mobilizations for literacy, its related developmental programmes and the training programmes bear traces of a resulting cascading effect, from the national to the regional, the states and the districts/blocks. Dispersed activities (as seen in chapters 2 to 6) were the predominant trend; rather than sustained, intensive and concentrated interventions. It was only as a result of a major shift in strategic approach, initiated in 2002 and consolidated after 2005, that the BGVS was able to achieve a concentration of efforts within selected clusters of gram panchayats in a 'convergent' manner. This has been described in chapter 8.

In the context of a discussion of scale or upscaling a model, it may be noted that this may be achieved by one or a combination of several routes. One approach could be that of aggregation/summation of geographical spaces; an additional coverage of more districts in a relatively continuous manner. This was the general trend with respect to the BGVS efforts that for some time till the late 1990s attempted to keep pace with the government sanctions to literacy campaigns in new districts. Another approach to achieving scale could be a concentration of efforts in selected clusters of villages within blocks/districts and a convergence of diverse project activities. Such an intensive qualitative approach could have a positive contagion/ripple effect with snowballing consequences. It also could serve as a critical reference point, even though focused in a limited geographical space. A third approach which will be discussed below is that of utilizing a relatively extensive, though dispersed, base of presence to impact on policy; which then reverts back on national practice, sometimes beyond the scope of the catalytic organization. This strategy was effectively practiced by the BGVS, if not consciously evolved, post-2002 through networking with other organizations and advocacy for policy change related to the rights of the most disadvantaged, as discussed in chapter 7. An important condition for the possibility of influencing policy change was the vast network internal to the BGVS organization that was achieved over a 20-year period covering 22 states and 316 districts by 2008, together with the decentralized, concentrated convergence within clusters of gram panchayats as mentioned above. This formed the basis of support for advocacy. It would be useful to abstract from the BGVS experience and arrive at generalizations on some of the basic factors that lead to impact on education and development policy.

An important condition for policy responding to field situations appears to be the very fact of the existence of a positive, demonstrative practice. This serves as a reference point, indirectly offering a critique of existing extension activities flowing from policy and a pointer to possible alternative approaches. Mobilizations towards practice – in the present case the literacy campaigns as related to social development – facilitate the creation of a critical mass sometimes resulting in a campaign and/or a movement for change; a democratic pressure emerging from civil society for change in policy. Such mobilizations articulate felt needs or serve to create them, thus forming a mass base of social demand for what is seen as a rightful claim on the state and its policies. Without such a basis of demand, rights tend to be largely a formal and legal framework enshrined to varying degrees in policies and legislations. Mobilizations towards a broadly unifying demand, such as for education/literacy, serve to partly redress the heterogeneity of socially structured communities. If and when they eventually result in the formation of people's organizations and institutions – in the case of BGVS and the literacy campaigns: Village Education Committees (VECs), Bal Manch (children's fora) and those for the youth, women's SHGs under the banner of Samata, CECs and libraries and GVVs – contribute to sustainability through the very physicality and visibility of their presence. These social formations are a potential pressure group on local self-governing bodies for accountability and effective delivery.

At a level wider than the local basis of programmes, there are other key factors that contribute to policy. These are, for instance, the contingent event of individuals within the bureaucracy and political parties that are seeking a solution for problems and are inclined towards change in policy and strategies. The BGVS was fortunate to have such a collection of individuals at the national level at the time of its formation and during the early years of the campaigns. At decentralized levels within districts, this was not always the case. The role of supportive alliances and networks of civil society organizations contributed, to a great extent, to the impact that the BGVS had on policy after 2002. One cannot also underestimate the value of academic researchers and publications that are supportive of policy changes based on alternative practices. They serve to frame positive efforts and draw critical attention to them. An important contributory factor is undoubtedly adequate financial support for implementing the change process.

3. Interventions: BGVS Mobilization, Organization and Strategy in Relation to the State

Mobilization, Organization and Sustainability

This section may be read in the context of chapter 2, especially section 6 on organizational and strategic issues. The BGVS-inspired kalajathas were large-scale mobilizations towards literacy, having definite focii on geographical context, social sectors and clear objectives. The 1990 jatha which was carried out on a national scale intended to identify voluntary literacy activists and set in motion state and district level organizations for implementation, apart from mobilizing non-literates on a large scale. The 1992 jatha concentrated on the northern Hindi-speaking belt with broadly the same objectives. The contradiction between the need for the literacy campaigns in regions of low social developmental indicators and the relative lack of a social basis for implementation was perhaps the sharpest in these states. The Samata jatha of 1993 focused on women and their concerns; what was in fact the most significant segment of the earlier literacy mobilizations even though comparatively neglected in terms of leadership formation and a focus on their specific needs. The 1993–94 campaign in relation to Hamara Desh (Our Country) attempted to broaden out the sphere of literacy intervention into various other development sectors. The jathas of 1995 and 1996 concentrated on states that persisted with a relatively weak organizational basis for literacy, Uttar Pradesh and Rajasthan, respectively. One might observe that the other programmes carried out on a limited scale in selected regions that followed during the 1994–97 period (chapters 3 to 6) had a defined developmental thrust in their relation to the campaigns – natural resource management, health, basic education, publications and the reading/library movement, women's empowerment through Vigyan Utsavas and the formation of saving groups. They were initiated after a process of social mobilization that followed the essential principles of development communication of the kalajathas, if not the cultural details.

Mobilizations were generally followed by major capacity-building exercises through training programmes and workshops held in a cascading manner from the national, regional, state to the district and sometimes to the block and village levels. This helped to consolidate the organization of the literacy activists within the BGVS network for implementation. However, there are often repeated concerns expressed in the BGVS documents about the lack of sustainability on the ground in terms of village level institutions and organizations of the people – the non or neo-literate clientele of the campaigns – as part of a bottom-up process of organization-building. One could summarize these concerns and one's own observations, as the relative lack of the translation of mobilization/movement into people's organizational forms, interfaced by the literacy campaigns and other development programmes. This was a general trend, despite some notable exceptions. While there has been an internal, self-critical awareness within BGVS right from 1998 about the need for establishing people's organizational formations within gram panchayats, the concrete correctives were put in place on a substantial scale only after 2005 (chapter 8).

A movement/mobilization that is accompanied by a social developmental programme creates the necessary conditions for the possibility for institutionalization. Mobilizations run the risk of dissipation into passing, individual and collective short-term stimulation when they are divorced from concrete follow-up programmes. At the same time, a programme that is not preceded by collective mobilization runs the risk of being formally target-oriented without effective impact due to lack of popular participation. Mobilizations provide programmes with the synergetic force of collective motivation and when translated into people's organization forms at local levels, the entire process acquires sustainability and institutionalization through the democratization of civil society. In this context, it would be useful to refer the reader to the concluding chapter of my study (Saldanha, 2007) on Doosra Dashak (The Second Decade), an adolescent education programme for the generation of leadership in rural development in selected blocks/districts of Rajasthan. The concepts of education as related to livelihood issues, scale as related to the qualitative significance of programmes and sustainability as articulated with organization are developed, drawing on the experience of Doosra Dashak which, unlike BGVS, paid attention to people's organizations from the earliest stages of its initiatives. Some quotations from that text that are of relevance to the BGVS might be in order:

> "While the availability of finances is an important issue, the reduction of the very relevant question of sustainability to finances (by some funding agencies) tends to ignore more important concerns such as the institutionalization of relatively flexible and evolving processes into stable social formations. Institutionalization as a process itself tends to be reduced to institution building, that is, the creation of physical structures with adequate finances, personnel, functions and hierarchies. A far more relevant question is the need for grass roots, organizational forms that own and continue the process of development intervention. The creation of community based organizations may be seen as the first and most significant step in the process of institutionalization and sustainability …
>
> If learning related to empowerment processes is to be sustainable, it needs to be collective in its dynamics and result in some form of people's organization. Decentralized autonomy, self-help, and community ownership provide sustainability to relatively external interventions that are necessarily short lived. Empowerment and learning processes for adolescents need to crystallize into organizational forms or else they could dissolve into individually 'empowered' persons, with little sense of direction and versatility in the face of systemic odds. They thus loose their potential for social change" (Saldanha, 2007: 182–183).

Programmes require personnel for implementation; in this case, the literacy activists. Mobilizations, in addition to providing popular, receptive synergy to programmes, foster the generation of activists with a multiplier effect. This is its value addition. The BGVS literacy activists were relatively raw as regards both implementation for literacy and other developmental programmes. In fact, most of them, especially at the district level, emerged from the mobilization itself. The cascading effects of training programmes were geared towards building these capacities within a national organization with state and district affiliations, which was itself in the process of formation. So far as the implementation process of particular development programmes, the BGVS was relatively successful in selected regions. However, in providing programmes sustainability in terms of a mass organized base (socially decentralized space and depth in terms of social energy/value) and time (beyond the literacy phase, into PL and CE) the BGVS interventions fell below expectations.

The foregoing conceptualization of the BGVS interventions in terms of mobilization, training, organization-building of the intervening agency, programmes and their potential decentralized institutionalization through the organization of participant beneficiaries, might be briefly illustrated as follows:

The reasons for the relative lack of sustainable people's organization forms are several. BGVS itself was initiated with the objective of mobilization for literacy and later as an organization for providing academic and strategic resource support to the NLM and the literacy campaigns. After 1994, while the BGVS did not take on the exclusive responsibility for implementing any particular literacy campaign in its totality and was not officially visualized as being responsible for doing so, it was actively involved in the implementation of various development programmes linked to the PL and CE phases of the literacy campaigns. All these activities related to a wider conception of

ILLUSTRATION 10.3 *From Mobilization to Institutionalization Through People's Organizations*

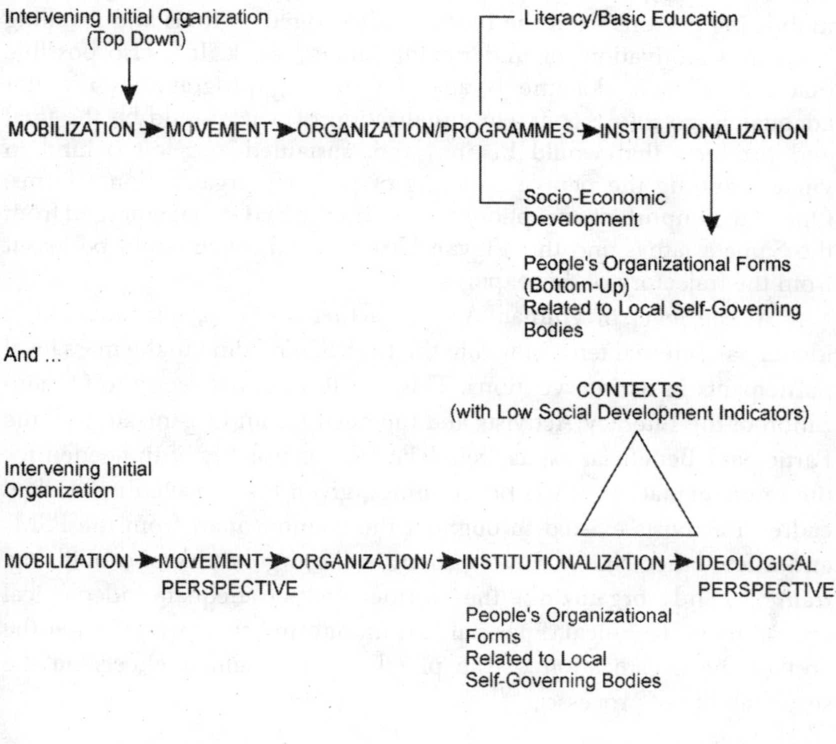

development were expected to be consolidated around selected CECs after 1998. The literacy activists who had emerged through the jathas and most of those involved in conducting them were by and large more familiar with the short-term, relatively spontaneous mobilizations of the jatha mode; and less socialized into the demands of sustained, disciplined implementation on a day-to-day basis that a people's organization or institution-building process would require. The skills with respect to nurturing programmes and creating and sustaining organizations of beneficiaries around them were different from the competencies required for mobilization. The time and energies of the literacy activists were also being claimed by a diverse set of programmes whose strategic thrust was being planned from the central/regional or state levels, thus giving them little time for persisting with ongoing commitments. One must also remember that, apart from a few state and district level full-timers, the vast majority of the BGVS district and sub-district level activists were working on a voluntary basis. Apart from the PSM network of members which was limited in scale considering the extensive national needs for the literacy campaigns, there was no readymade organization for the participatory implementation of the literacy campaigns. This organization had to be created in the very act of mobilizing persons from the most disadvantaged sections and instilling in them a motivation for undertaking literacy work. It is also possible that the strategic documents and the training programmes did not adequately go into a concrete visualization of what would be the final end products that would be nurtured, sustained and left behind in villages among the people in terms of people's organizational forms. One of the important exceptions to this was the SHGs that emerged from the Samata jathas and the Vigyan Utsavas, and much could be learnt from the trajectory of this experience.

At the level of Human Agency acting in Time, one might thus identify an internal tension within the BGVS in relation to the mass level participants in its interventions. This is a tension between the Organization of the Literacy Activists and the need for an Organization of the Participant Beneficiaries, as well. The former was urgently needed for the implementation of the programmes, given that no such networked cadre of activists existed throughout the country apart from the PSMs and a few other NGOs. Involvement in the urgent task of mobilizing, training and organizing the former with adequate ideological commitment, technical, financial and monitoring skills was often at the cost of the organization of the people, with resultant effects on the sustainability of processes.

A major concern about the inadequacy of sustainability of mobilization, for literacy and other programmes through the development of village level people's organization is expressed from 1995. The BGVS Secretary, at the BGVS General Council meeting in Hyderabad in December, 1995, had introduced a perspective note drawing attention to the need for decentralized people's organization. The minutes of that meeting read as follows, "He suggested that it was time to build up the organization at the village level. So far, our attempts had been to spread our network from top to bottom on the basis of a central plan. Now the attempt should be to build up the movement from the bottom to the top" (BGVS, 1995: 4). A further illustration of this growing concern was the question asked in the Secretary's report to the BGVS General Council meeting of 1998:

> "Why are we not succeeding in following up major programmes like Joy of Learning, Cosmic Voyage, Jan Vachan Andolan, Samata Melas, etc., after the initial high pitched rounds? ... We had decided that in order to combat the degenerative trends which have affected the Literacy Campaigns, we must strive hard to develop effective, decentralized, village/GP (gram panchayat) centred models of TL (total literacy)-PL (post-literacy) and CE (continuing education). However, it is a fact that we have not been able to take any effective steps in this direction so far. This has to be considered as a major mistake and every effort should be made by each state to correct this. Unless and until we are able to prove on the ground that alternate sustainable models could be worked out, our criticism will not have much impact. A time-bound plan has to be evolved for this" (BGVS, February 1998: 13, 22).

An honest and extensive review of BGVS organizational functioning is found in this document. It is worthy of credit and emulation by civil society organizations for its critical introspection.

Two major factors leading to the concern for organizational impact might be discerned from the above-mentioned statements. Firstly, is the question relating to the internal strategies and organizational dynamics of the BGVS. The other is the external environment during the years 1995 to 1998 arising from the negative attitudes and bureaucratic tendencies within some of the government-sponsored district literacy committees. The marginalization of the BGVS by the state would be enhanced in the post-1998 period. The Secretary's report to the General Council of the BGVS of February, 1998, suggests that some of the state units seemed to have withdrawn from the field of literacy in response to this situation. It refers to a joint meeting of the BGVS executive committee and the state coordinators which discussed these aspects and "unanimously decided that literacy programmes should continue to be the most important agenda of the BGVS programme. The committee further suggested that we must concentrate fully on village-based integrated models of PL-TL-CE in selected gram panchayats (GPs) of selected districts in the coming year. It was pointed out that all major programmes like Samata Vigyanotsava, Jan Vachan Andolan (JVA), Desh Ko Janein, Desh Ko Badlein (DJDB) may be integrated with this" (BGVS, February 1998: 23).

The question of the relationship between BGVS as an organization of literacy activists and an organization nurturing people's organizational forms may also be seen in the following extract:

> "It seems that there is a broad agreement about the fact that the Jan/Gyan Vigyan Movement that we are trying to build up will be in the form of a massive people's movement. Naturally, the organizations that we build up in the states will have to be in the form of a mass organization. Shall we say that we are in the process of building up a mass organization capable of empowering people with knowledge and science for democracy and self-reliance. In that case, who are the people who should be enrolled in our organizations? What should be the nature and spread of the basic units that we form?" (BGVS, February 1998: 16).

The above-mentioned tension closely parallels the polarities between relatively spontaneous mobilization as part of movements and its sustainability through institutionalization and the creation of people's organizational forms. One of the best examples of the flow of this process and the resolution of this contradiction was the Samata Jatha and the Vigyan Utsavas evolving into sustainable SHGs, for example, in MALAR in Kanyakumari district.

Some of the concerns of the foregoing analysis might be substantiated from the BGVS's own assessment in its report of activities submitted to the General Council Meeting held at Dhanbad in 2002. While recognizing "the emergence of a more self-confident and more informed local level leadership consisting of women and people belonging to oppressed sections", the report states that "the challenge is to help, support and promote them to significantly influence the political and democratic processes" (February 2002: 12). In a moment of critical introspection, the document states that, "there is still lack of clarity about the nature and character of our movement. Are we a mass movement or are we a movement of concerned activists and intellectuals? If we conceive ourselves as a mass movement, we must make use of every opportunity to spread ourselves to more villages of our country systematically". The report suggests that creating community-based Gyan Vigyan Kendras (GVKs) with mass membership and local leadership with adequate academic resource support through institutional structures as a way forward. As regards the character of the organization, one's own view is that the BGVS had evolved into an extensive, nation-wide organization of literacy and development activists in the process of leading a movement within the social developmental sector.

Perhaps the most significant reason for the relative failure to develop people's organizational forms on any significant scale and to thus provide sustainability to the cultural mobilization and developmental interventions was the strategy adopted by the NLM as a result of the Kerala literacy campaign with the involvement of the KSSP and acceded to by the BGVS, especially till 1994. This strategy was in effect one of relatively disarticulated phases: first mobilization for literacy (i.e., the preparatory and literacy phases) and only then organization for other developmental interventions corresponding to the PL and CE phases. This two-phased strategy was neither conducive to the rationale and felt needs of deprived learners, especially in regions of low social developmental indicators, nor was it facilitative of people's organization for development. The literacy in isolation phase could not result in organization of the people, except for non-literates coming together in various types of scattered groupings for learning. By the time of the developmental phase, a significant number had dropped out and/or some of the literacy campaigns had withered away. What was needed, especially in the low literacy districts, was developmental organizations of the people around livelihood issues and for literacy, within an integrated approach to TL, PL and CE, right from the start of the campaigns.

Discussing the possibilities of a 'counterclockwise revolution', a literacy campaign that creates the possibilities for social transformation rather than the other way around, a document of the BGVS raises the question "Can the pointer of social change revolve counterclockwise? Can a massive illiteracy eradication programme lead to conditions which may accelerate social change?" (BGVS, Perspectives, Achievements, Tasks, … and Dreams, 1995: 17). The document goes on to operationalize a strategy that effectively, though implicitly, would visualize literacy intervention before wider social transformation/development:

> "It is generally agreed that a literacy programme should not stop at imparting mere literacy and numeracy. It should make the people aware of the cause of their deprivation and should move forward

towards amelioration of their conditions through organization and participation in the process of development. However, an overemphasis on this aspect, or rather a lack of appreciation of the importance of imparting writing and reading skills had at times resulted in giving 'bhashans' (speeches) to them. Therefore it was decided that the perspective of literacy to be propagated by the BGVJ will be, first and foremost, ability to WRITE and READ" (BGVS, op. cit.: 17).

Implications for Strategy

Literacy interventions, in particular, and social developmental ones in general, such as those in the areas of elementary education, health, access to institutional resources of a welfare state, may be seen as relatively soft interventions. This is not a statement of their relative importance as mediated/indirect interventions, but a statement of their transformative power/potential in sharply polarized politico-economic contexts. Struggles directly related to the latter, i.e., on issues such as land, wages and access to natural resources, are sharper interventions in relation to their social transformatory potential and are generally met with even greater opposition. In a highly differentiated context such as India, a strategy for literacy intervention that emerged from a region of high social developmental indicators and that built upon a past history of social transformation through politico-economic struggles, needed to be operationalized and contextualized in a different manner for regions such as the northern belt of states which might not have experienced such a social history. Purely literacy interventions in these contexts, as during the period 1989 to 1993, were relatively soft interventions and needed to be interwoven with other developmental interventions from the very outset, as seen in the following periods. However, during the period 1994 to 1997, BGVS shifted to the other spectrum of social development to the relative exclusion of adult education for literacy.

Writing in 1998, based on an analysis of the differential performance of the literacy campaigns across the country in contexts of uneven development across states/districts, one had drawn attention to the need for contextualizing the campaign approach so as to be relevant to the ground realities within a vast country (Saldanha, 1998: 401ff). Two broad regions that demanded these adjustments were the regions of low literacy (below 45% literacy rate according to the 1991 Census) as well as the relatively urbanized districts of high literacy (above 70% literacy rate, 1991 Census) with a residual non-literate population. Some of the recommendations based on this study are valid even today. It is ironical that the literacy campaigns faced a contextualized resistance from parts of the country where the objective need for literacy was the most, the former districts, but where the institutional and organized capacities were the least; as well as from the high literacy areas that on the surface required the campaigns the least even though they had the necessary human resource capacities, but perhaps not the time for literacy. These two regions were at contrasting ends of a spectrum of intervention. The distinctive characteristic of the literacy campaigns was organized community participation and its appeal was to the spirit of voluntarism. In the rural areas of medium literacy districts, especially as seen from the data of Mumbai, rural Maharashtra and Goa (Saldanha, 1995), one found that an effective village literacy committee served as a touchstone for the success of the campaigns.

> "These features of the campaign are difficult to attain in high literacy urban areas, as well as in low literacy rural districts of states which may not have had a history of strong local self-governance or of social reform movements. It is difficult to find the equivalent of the village as a micro organizational unit in urban areas. The urban 'mohalla' or 'basti', however socio-economically disadvantaged and excluded, is linked in concentric circles with its larger urban environment and is subjected to a politico-economic and cultural hegemony. Hence, the comparatively lower degree of success. It is like forcing a non-formal element (adult education), weak in motivational value considering other priorities and claims on time for survival, into the informal sector (slum/pavement dwelling workers of the unorganized sector) of formally organized and institutionalised contexts (the urban), where conditions for functional access are clearly defined by commercial value and constrained by time and economic capacity" (Saldanha, 1998: 402).

In high literacy districts, one had suggested a strategy of strengthening the formal, elementary education system and extending beyond that to residual, adult non-literates in the age group 15–45 years with elements of functionality and certification. Campaigns here need to be efficiently managed and targeted to offset the constraints to collective mobilization. In low literacy, rural areas the informal, relatively non-institutionalised contexts favour large-scale mobilization. The convergence of efforts with other developmental programmes becomes an urgent need. In both regions, functionality and organization for participation in development – the two other objectives of the NLM – need to be initiated right from the initial phase (Saldanha, 1999: 2031). It may be noted that contextualization is best attained through participatory organization which provides ownership and rootedness to programmes and the constraints of the lack of a history of organization for socio-economic transformation can be offset to some degree by cultural mobilization and the convergence of development initiatives.

Looking back over the period from the formation of the BGVS in 1989 to the time of the General Council Meeting held at Bhopal, during December 28–29, 2005, the Secretary presented a succinct and insightful historical overview which might be quoted at length:

> "The present Executive Committee took over at a very difficult moment (2002) in the history of our organization. Let me recapitulate briefly. The formation of BGVS was nearly co-terminus with that of the National Literacy Mission, whose objectives and functioning we were able to influence, both in terms of policy and implementation. Consequently, our work-nirmankarya – was in close collaboration with the central government through the NLM … . Though this collaboration persisted from 1990 to 1999, the strains were visible from 1997 onwards since the NLM began to deviate from the essentials of the campaign mode. But still, there was a degree of engagement, which virtually vanished the moment the NDA government took over in 1999. Thereafter the collaboration truly collapsed, as it was bound to. The situation truly worsened by the time the present Executive Committee took over in 2002. The campaign mode was replaced by the bureaucratic and academically unsound Continuing Education program from which we had no choice but to withdraw. The sangh parivar agenda became more and more evident in the choice of collaborating agencies and the use of teaching-learning materials. The disengagement of BGVS also meant the drying out of financial support, the strain of which was very severe by 2002, with even suggestions to close the national office in Delhi.
>
> It is often said that true strength becomes evident during times of adversity, and this is what we could say about our organization for the phase between 1999–2004, and in particular between 2002 and 2004. With literally no financial support at the central level and a hostile religious-fundamentalist government at the centre, our organization not only survived but grew in strength, as was evident from the Peace, Unity and Sovereignty Jatha of September/October 2003" (BGVS, 2005: 4).

Attention has been drawn to the above-mentioned phases of the organization, in the earlier discussions, based on evidence. The differences in strategic orientation for the literacy campaigns of the 1994 to 1997 phase between the BGVS and the Department of Education/NLM were cumulatively felt in 1997. From 1998 to 2004, the distancing between the NLM/Department of Education and the BGVS was reinforced by basic ideological differences with the government in power at the central level. Between 1998 to 2004, government funding was gradually stopped and the organization had to rely heavily on its human resources and the commitment and resourcefulness of the state and district level units. The Jatha for Peace, Unity and Sovereignty, September 8–October 2, 2003, was clearly based on local resources and initiatives. Additionally, its thrust was against the dominant ideology of the time of neo-liberalism, inhuman globalization processes as well as against divisive, religious fundamentalism of all varieties. It was only after 2004 that the dire financial situation of the organization eased with the support from the Sir Dorabji Tata Trust (SDTT). This funding was preceded by a one-off support for the functioning of the national office from October, 2002.

Table 10.4 and illustration present a district-wise coverage of the BGVS over the years for which relatively consistent data are available, 1995, 1998, 2002, 2005 and 2008. Such a comparison of data was possible only for the district level coverage, given that data for other aspects such as number of blocks, panchayats, membership which might have been equally, if not more relevant, were not consistently available over the years. The data for the subdivided states at a later stage have been totalled, respectively. The BGVS presence in districts suggests that with the exception of Kerala where the Kerala Shashtra Sahitya Parishad (KSSP) had a consistent presence in all the 14 districts according to the 2001 Census, all the other states followed the trend of the aggregate. Other higher performing states in terms of extensive coverage were Himachal Pradesh and Tripura. The year 1995 marks a high point of the national district level presence of the BGVS, with a coverage of 87 per cent of the total number of districts according to the 2001 Census. This was followed by a consistent drop between 1998 (77%) and 2002 (48%). The latter decrease corresponds with the decline of the literacy campaigns throughout the country, both in terms of strategic approach and substantive quality of the programme, with a stagnation and even loss of government as well as popular support. The number of districts covered by the BGVS picked up during the period 2005 (55%) to 2008 (60%) indicating a phase of financial support from a non-government agency, SDTT, as different from the withdrawal of financial support from the BJP-led NDA government at the centre during the earlier phase. The 2008 data of coverage of districts still fall short of the pre-1995 expansionist and enthusiastic phase, possibly also indicating a conscious effort on the part of the BGVS to seek a convergence of initiatives in relatively concentrated clusters of villages/blocks within selected districts.

TABLE 10.4 *BGVS, Coverage of States and Districts, 1995, 1998, 2002, 2005 and 2008*

	States	*No. of Districts 1995*	*No. of Districts 1998*	*No. of Districts 2002*	*No. of Districts 2005*	*No. of Districts 2008*
1.	Assam	23	23	12 (23)	14	17
2.	Orissa	30	29	12 (30)	12	28
3.	Bihar–Jharkhand	55	30	26 (55)	38	37
4.	Haryana	17	17	10 (19)	6	9
5.	Himachal Pradesh	12	12	10 (12)	12	12
6.	Punjab and Chandigarh	15	14	10 (17)	10	20
7.	Uttar Pradesh–Uttarakhand	64	36	23 (83)	34	39
8.	Rajasthan	31	32	8 (32)	8	10
9.	Tripura	4	4	4 (4)	4	3
10.	Tamil Nadu	22	29	23 (30)	23	29
11.	Andhra Pradesh	23	23	20 (23)	20	23
12.	Karnataka	20	20	15 (27)	14	16
13.	Kerala	14	14	14 (14)	14	14
14.	Pondicherry		1	1 (4)	2	2
15.	Maharashtra	31	30	9 (35)	13	14
16.	Madhya Pradesh–Chattisgarh	49	45	28 (61)	34	26
	Sub-Total	410	359	225 (469)	258	299 (469)
17.	Gujarat					7 (25)
18.	Arunachal Pradesh					3 (13)
19.	Manipur					5 (9)
20.	Meghalaya					2 (7)
	Total	410 (469)	359 (469)	225 (469)	258 (469)	316 (523)

Notes: 1. The states of Gujarat, Arunachal Pradesh, Manipur and Meghalaya were relatively new states of BGVS presence during the period 2005–08.

2. The districts of the states of Bihar–Jharkhand, Uttar Pradesh–Uttarakhand and Madhya Pradesh–Chattisgarh have been totalled, respectively, for purposes of comparison over time even though these states have been subdivided.

3. The figures in brackets represent the total number of districts for the respective states according to the Census 2001.

Source: BGVS reports of General Council Meetings for the respective years.

An analysis of the comparative performance of different, relevant projects undertaken by BGVS would be in order. Undoubtedly, the

ILLUSTRATION 10.4 *BGVS, Districtwise Coverage, 1995, 1998, 2002, 2005 and 2008*

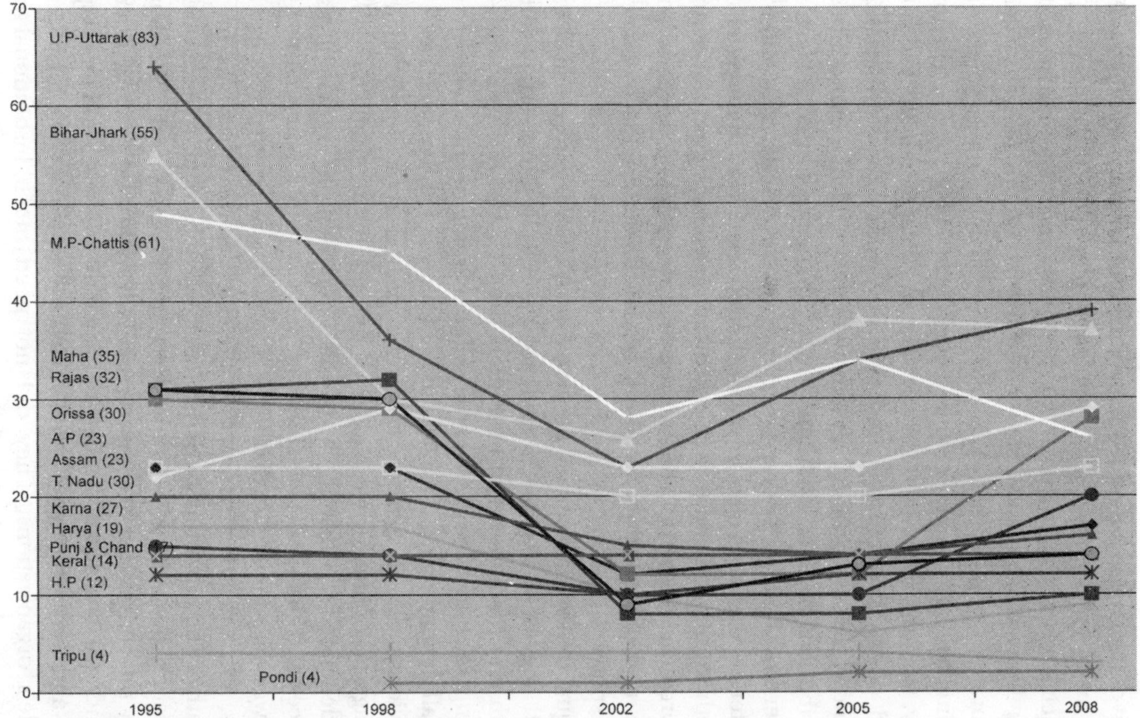

Source: Reports of BGVS General Council Meetings for respective years.

Note: Figures in parentheses indicate the total number of districts in the given states according to the Census 2001.

contexts for the implementation and the objectives of these projects were different making such comparisons not only odious but perhaps not sustainable. However, some insights as regards factors underlying relative impact can be gained from such an exercise, with the qualifications mentioned above. That the implementation of project requires financial support is perhaps a tautological statement. Finances could come from various sources – government, public trusts created by corporations, multilateral UN agencies, bilateral ones, international funding NGOs, national resource support agencies and, most importantly, from the participant beneficiaries. As discussed in the text, BGVS relied on the first three agencies, in that order. Very importantly, it depended for its project implementation on local communities for contributions in cash, kind and labour. These contributions were often greater than that from other agencies as analysed in the text (and in this chapter, section 4). Project implementation, apart from managerial skills, sometimes depends on technological ones depending on the nature of the projects. Above all, the success of interventions depends on felt needs and organizational-building related to these collective interests and aspirations.

A qualitative analysis and observation of BGVS projects in the field would suggest that projects such as Natural Resource Management, Health and the conduct of institutionalized CECs which depended on funding, technical and managerial skill to varying degrees tended to rise and fall depending on the availability of financial and human resources. The vicissitudes of such programmes appeared to be closely related to the vagaries of funding from external sources. In this context, the GVVs also depended too heavily on people's contributions by way of assets, finances and the local availability of persons with a potential to teach. This was despite the fact that these institutions responded to locally felt needs. On the other hand, activities such as mobilizations through kalajathas, the formation of SHGs federated to Samata, other awareness generation programmes, publications and libraries and advocacy for policy reform relating to rights were relatively low on external financial dependence, responded strongly to popularly felt needs and their aspirations, and were conducive to enhancing self-worth and the formation of people's organizations. They did not need much institutional infrastructure or honoraria for full-timers. These activities, as also the concentrated convergence of initiatives within gram panchayats, tended to meet with greater success.

Summary Achievements of BGVS

Assessing the contribution of the BGVS, Mathew (1999: 15ff) identified the following aspects to be of primary significance: placing literacy on the national agenda, being a partner and serving as a strategist of the NLM, extending the contours of literacy through its linkages with various development sectors, establishing the linkage between literacy and women's empowerment, and the emphasis on voluntarism as the driving force.

Writing in 2001, a former Director General, National Literacy Mission (DG, NLM), Government of India, drew attention to the major contributions of the BGVS in terms of generating voluntarism among literacy instructors, producing low-cost teaching-learning materials that had a local specific content, the kalajathas that served as a major communication and mobilizational instrument for creating a demand for literacy by using all forms of media and folk media in particular, and the emphasis placed on the education of women and girl children. The following is a quotation from his presentation which in some senses represents government recognition from some of its sensitive personnel:

> "As their stature grew, they were able to spread their outreach to virtually every state in India. When the National Literacy Mission was formed in India in 1988, nothing of note occurred till after the Ernakulam campaign, which concluded in 1989. Thereafter, structures were set up at the national level for carrying out NFE and literacy activities across the whole country. It was then that a path-breaking decision was taken by the central government. For the first time, perhaps anywhere in the world, at the very apex of the structure, the Bharatiya Gyan Vigyan Samiti was given place. Its members were included in the very highest decision-making body, i.e., the Executive Committee. They were also included in the Projects Appraisal Committee, which assessed projects for their viability and sanctioned funds. Even more importantly, their members occupied positions in the working groups of the National Planning Commission and helped in the formulation of the Ninth and Tenth Five-Year Plans.
>
> Thus the BGVS helped shape policy, being involved in decision-making processes at the very highest levels of government"

The DG NLM goes on to mention some of the implementation responsibilities of the BGVS such as participating in the district literacy committees for the execution of the campaigns and involvement in eight

State Resource Centres responsible for teaching-learning materials and training. He continues:

> "In a word, the Bhartiya Gyan Vigyan Samiti enjoyed perhaps the maximum influence and control at the national/central government level than any NGO in the world. And this influence lasted almost 11 years from 1989 to 2000. The situation has changed marginally over the last year or so, but the BGVS is very much a force to reckon with in the area of NFE and Literacy/Continuing Education even today in India" (Chatterjee in UNESCO China, 2001).

The social reform movement that was initiated by the BGVS through the social development sector, effectively served to generate and enhance human resource capacities through activities within three broad areas of human endeavour:

- Entitlements relating to Livelihood: Programmes such as natural resource management, the creation of self-help and saving groups, encouragement of micro enterprise, programmes relating to health and sanitation, advocacy for policy on the Right to Food and Work and the involvement in the implementation of the National Rural Employment Guarantee Act, the ICDS and the Midday Meal scheme served to promote self-reliance and claims on government development extension.
- Empowerment through Organization: The emphasis on decentralization and voluntarism in the literacy campaign, the creation of people's organizational forms in some cases, for example, among women and children, the involvement in campaigns for the Right to Information, the creation of a network of social development activists in several states and districts throughout the country under the BGVS, the linkages to Panchayati Raj and other local self-governing bodies served to strengthen democracy and demand accountability from the delivery systems of a welfare state.
- Enablement through Learning: The literacy campaigns, the cultural mobilization through the kalajathas, the creation of a demand for and the promotion of elementary education, advocacy for the National Curriculum Framework (2005) and the Right to Education, the setting up of libraries and the promotion of a culture of reading through low-cost publications, all served to establish the link between literacy, language, culture, communication and knowledge generation among the people.

- In the process of engaging in the foregoing, the BGVS was able to effectively focus attention on three crucial social groups:
- Women, who were the major participants in the literacy campaigns, the library movement and in the formation of self-help groups.
- Children, who were the focus in elementary education programmes, the Bal Manch, the GVVs and some of those who served as literacy instructors.
- Youth, who served as the backbone of the BGVS as voluntary educational activists at decentralized levels.

The achievements of the BGVS which have been highlighted at different places during the course of this study may be summarized as follows:

Cultural Mobilization as a Tactical Approach: The mobilization through kalajathas was an innovation as an approach to mobilization for literacy and social development. This may be seen more in tactical terms rather than from a strategic perspective of longer term sustainability of process. It had its limitations as regards the latter, especially in sharply polarized, politico-economic contexts. However, the strength of this approach in terms of generating popular motivation within local communities, among potential learners, instructors and literacy activists towards organization formation, cannot be underestimated. The BGVS has made a significant and widely recognized contribution to creating a cultural climate for literacy. Environment-building and other programmes have not only facilitated adult education, but also created a demand for primary education and for an improvement in the status of women (especially chapter 2, sections 2 and 3).

Placing Literacy and Basic Education on the National Agenda: It may be noted that the 1990s in the country was marked by this important feature. The BGVS and the literacy campaigns may be credited with making this important contribution, especially during the early 1990s, even prior to the national District Primary Education Programme (DPEP) followed by the Sarva Shiksha Abhiyan (SSA) (chapter 6, sections 1 to 3, in particular).

The Literacy Campaign Strategy: The important features of this phased strategy (preparatory, literacy, post-literacy, continuing education) and its major social organizational pillars (the government, the organized and unorganized voluntary sectors and the decentralized teaching-learning community) have been discussed. This national approach suffered from the limitations of a standardized strategy at the cost of contextualization. A major constraint that unconsciously emerged from this strategy, especially during the early years, was an approach of literacy first and then development. The BGVS might be credited with both contributing to the national literacy campaign strategy as well as offering correctives to it, based on experience, especially after 1993 (chapter 2).

The Strength of Voluntarism and a People's Movement Approach: This, as mentioned above, has been a significant contribution of the BGVS. The approach stands in sharp contrast to earlier approaches to adult education in the country (also this chapter, section 4).

Resource Support to Literacy Campaigns through Activists, Workshops, Publications, SRCs and Implementation: The generation of a large number of educational activists and the development of their capacities through workshops and training programmes has been described. The unprecedented number of low-cost publications in terms of the range of thematic issues, languages and functions has been staggering. These have been utilized for the training of activists and as neo-literate reading material. The setting up of State Resource Centres (SRCs) has served to provide institutional academic resource support. The preceding analysis would suggest that the BGVS has also been actively involved in implementing the literacy campaigns in several districts, even though that was not the primary reason for which it was set up at the invitation of the NLM (chapter 2 and chapter 6, section 4).

The Mobilization of Women: An entire section in this study has been devoted to this major contribution and its concrete outcome in terms of an organizational formation, Samata (chapter 4).

Literacy and Development Linkages: Chapters 3, 4, 5 and 6 highlight the special contributions in the areas of establishing linkages between the literacy campaigns and natural resource management, to Panchayati Raj institutions, women's empowerment, health and the basic education of children with social awareness for adults, respectively.

Government-Voluntary Sector Collaboration on a National Issue, on a National Scale: As discussed in the introduction to this study (chapter 1), this interface with all its strengths and limitations has been unique and unprecedented; considering scale, time and impact within the social developmental sector.

A National Mass Organization for Social Development Sector Intervention: Section 6 of chapter 2 on BGVS and the literacy campaigns which discusses the growing organizational network over the years in numerical and geographical terms, and section 3 in this chapter which analyses organization in strategic terms, would suggest that the BGVS stands today as a major social formation that has the potential to make significant contributions within the social developmental sector. The limitations of this formation in terms of its problems to extend itself further into sustainable, community-based, people's organizational forms has also been discussed. This constitutes the thrust of one's major suggestions relating to future directions (chapter 11, drawing on chapters 7 and 8, in particular). The organization has already undertaken self-corrective measures from 2005 (chapter 8).

Mobilization, Networking and Advocacy for Policy and Practice Related to Rights: Utilizing its mass organizational base, the BGVS has played an important role in the formulation of and/or practice relating to the Right to Work and Food, the NREGA, the ICDS and the Midday Meal scheme; the 73rd and 74th Amendments to the Constitution empowering gram sabhas and gram panchayats and the Right to Information; the National Curriculum Framework, 2005, and the Right to Education. It has played an active role in the Tenth and Eleventh Plan Working Groups on elementary, adolescent education and literacy (chapter 7).

Changes in Attitudes and Social Relations with Respect to Caste/Tribe, Gender, Religious Differences and Administrative Personnel: These very significant changes tend to go unnoticed, partly because they do not lend themselves to quantification. Our field observations and discussions in chapter 9 on the case studies, however, drew attention to these very real, personal and social transformations within selected rural communities; all the more important considering the feudal contexts within which they were taking place. They often sprang from the fact of working, dining and sharing together in classroom settings, in training camps and savings groups, while conducting participatory surveys, during conventions; reinforced by the kalajathas, the publications and the social-scientific awareness campaigns. The change in the servile attitude towards political and administrative officialdom in a feudal context of patron-client relations was particularly noteworthy in some instances. It also needs to be pointed out that the very participatory character of the literacy campaigns elicited a heightened spirit of commitment and accountability in several government development officials.

4. Ideological Perspectives in Contention

A Question of Values

At the level of the Quality of BGVS interventions, i.e., the Values implicit in the process, one might interpret an ongoing tension between the participatory, decentralized and a people's movement character which was the organizational perspective of the BGVS, and the general tendency towards bureaucratization, centralization and administrative monopolization of the government. The state, at the national, state and district levels, by and large considered the imparting of literacy as a techno-managerial and finance driven exercise towards the achievement of targets. Given the divergent and specialized 'departmental' thrusts of government, instances of government-led literacy campaigns which attempted a convergent developmental orientation to the literacy campaigns were an exception. Dhumka district (Kanjula in Karlekar ed., 2004: 270ff) which one visited in Jharkhand state and Roopnagar district in Punjab (Mahajan in Jena and Mathew eds., 2008: 17ff) were two such examples of government commitment which led to outstanding results. Government, by and large, considered the literacy campaigns as the territorial specialization of its Department of Education/Directorate of Adult Education extending its outreach into states and districts, with a responsibility to demonstrate literacy outcomes at a cost to process. The BGVS was, by and large, able to maintain the spirit of its principles in its interactions within the National Literacy Mission and with the Department of Adult Education (DAE) with respect to its own initiatives. However, with the growing tendency within the literacy campaigns after 1994–95 and especially after 1998 towards the latter set of values, the BGVS found itself increasingly alienated from and marginalized by the MHRD.

The keywords of the ideological perspective underlying the BGVS interventions over more than a decade, with their implicit values that were occasionally explicitly stated, were the following:

Equity and Self-Reliance: An ideological perspective based on equity was necessitated by the very inegalitarian contexts of the interventions. Access to literacy and basic education itself was seen as one access to equal opportunities. A perspective on self-reliance was especially required in a growing uni-polar context where a militarized superpower was exercising its hegemony and where other basic educational programmes were tending to be flooded with 'foreign aid'. This perspective also gained importance in a context where the dominant hegemony was increasingly being influenced by a perspective of liberalization and privatization of the economy in contexts of globalization, promoted by restructuring of economies and innovations in communication with implications for knowledge distribution.

A People's Movement Approach, Decentralized Democracy, Secularism and National Integration: The mobilization process and organizational structures for implementing the literacy campaigns emphasized these values. The very structure of village education committees was an operationalization of this principle where an attempt was made to put together major social forces such as the government, the voluntary organized and unorganized sectors and the teaching-learning community. Secularism and national integration were important in a context where dominant national hegemony was increasingly being influenced by sectarianism and communalism. It may be noted that the decade of the 1990s in the country was marked by events such as the Rath Yatras, the destruction of the Babri Masjid/Ram Janmabhoomi, communal violence, terrorism and disintegrative militancy.

Voluntarism and Scientific Awareness: The main body of the literacy campaigns worked on the principle of voluntarism. This involved at different times and for a period lasting over more than a decade, voluntary activists that might number over 10 million persons. Involving these persons in acting through popular, electronic and the print media in the spread of critical scientific awareness and literacy as a possible enabling skill to this end, was one of the important features of the literacy campaigns.

The foregoing may be seen as an ideological perspective emerging from civil society and the social developmental sector. This perspective may be interpreted from the interventions of the BGVS and in particular from a reiteration of an extract which was presented in chapter 2 on the BGVS and the literacy campaigns: "The crusade against illiteracy was a crusade against the conditions that maintained literacy, a crusade against disruptionists, a crusade against destabilization, a crusade against communalism, a crusade against dependence. It was seen as a second independence struggle for national integration and for self-reliance. It was a struggle to make democracy meaningful to the millions" (BGVS, 2001: 1).

A major issue of whether payments by way of honoraria should be made, at what level and for what purposes is closely related to the question of the spirit of voluntarism. The BGVS approach on the question has always conceded, and more appropriately asserted, that payments needed to be made to full-timers and that such personnel were needed at the national, state and district levels. Attempts were also made to cover the personal expenditures involved in activities such as travel for organizational activities. A significant contribution of the BGVS has been that it has largely succeeded in creating and sustaining a ground swell of community support for its programmes including the coverage of some of the costs. For example, it was estimated that for the 10-year period, 1990 to 2000, of the literacy campaigns as a whole the community contribution would work out to Rs 50,000 million by way of foregone honoraria to volunteer instructors which was earlier paid to instructors by the 1978 Adult Education Programme. On the other hand, the government and other agencies had spent around Rs 10,000 million for the same 10-year period (BGVS, 2003: 6). A detailed analysis by BGVS of the community contributions made during April 2004 to March 2007 suggests that for the approximately Rs 10 crore sanctioned by SDTT to the BGVS for various capacity-building and programmatic interventions, the local communities had effectively contributed Rs 41 crores; if all the labour, time and material contributions were to be converted to monetary value. This estimation of community contribution was made only for the activities related to basic education. Another estimate related to newly started GVVs and GVV inputs into existing schools arrives at a similar conclusion. Rs 22 crore had been spent or had been committed by local communities for 1,102 such schools till March, 2007, at an estimate of Rs 2 lakh per school for infrastructure. The real salary component foregone by the teachers worked out to an additional Rs 10 crore, while in fact the teachers were receiving only a nominal honorarium. As opposed to this, the BGVS had spent about Rs 1.5 crore in residential teacher training, material preparation and monitoring of GVV activities over a period of two years from support provided by the SDTT. The BGVS document draws attention to the fact that for every rupee invested by it, the community had invested over Rupees 20 (BGVS, March 2007:10). An important question still remains as regards how sustainable this would be in financial and motivational terms when the need for full-time personnel would be increased as a result of the creation of people's organizational forms and institutions at the gram panchayat level as part of the post-2006 strategy of convergence, concentration and decentralized academic resource support for nurturing the organizational forms for education for development.

Ideological and Organizational Tensions

The analysis of BGVS interventions suggests a series of interrelated organizational and ideological (value loaded) tensions/polarities:

- The scale of mass mobilizations, in relation to their sustainability through organization and institutionalization, and with retention of the quality of ensuing programmatic process.
- Scattered activities at wider national/state/district levels v/s the need for geographical concentration and the convergence of programmes for effective impact, considering holistic needs at micro individual/household/village community levels.
- The tension within the internal dynamics of the literacy campaigns between the need for relative spontaneity in mobilization v/s the need for discipline and nurturing of institutionalization towards sustainability of impact.
- The need to create an organization of development activists in the very act of engaging in the literacy campaigns, and the need to develop the capacities of these activists not only as mobilizers/campaigners but also as resource persons for development programmes.
- The need to translate the networked, mass organization of social development activists (the BGVS) into community-based, people's organizational forms. These people's organizations might serve as catalysts and as points of reference for decentralized democracy. It is not absolutely necessary, from a perspective of feasibility, to initiate as many people's organization forms as there are villages in the country; for these forms have a qualitative ripple and multiplier effect much like media of communication. They also serve to enhance and root sustainability.
- The BGVS's ideological perspective from a voluntary sector, civil society standpoint v/s the perspective of the state operationalized through government machineries with a relatively centralized, hierarchical, departmentally segregated standpoint.
- The ideological thrust of the BGVS which was largely moved by a spirit of voluntarism and the creation of a people's movement for social transformation v/s the ideology that was generally expressed by government adult education initiatives of an instrumental approach to the campaigns towards meeting prescribed targets of literacy outcomes.

- The tension between the need for literacy on a large scale as an enabling communicational skill and the need to contextualize this within the larger social developmental concerns and priorities of the non-literate population.
- Underlying all the foregoing concerns was the predicament that might be formulated in the following question: How does the social developmental agenda feed into the larger politico-economic agenda of social transformation?
- And related to the foregoing, the question of how does 'nirman'/construction through the social development sector relate to the need for 'sangarsh'/struggle on issues related to class, caste/tribe, gender and communal inequities in a highly polarized society?

ILLUSTRATION 10.5: *BGVS's Ideological and Organizational Tensions in Creative Resolution*

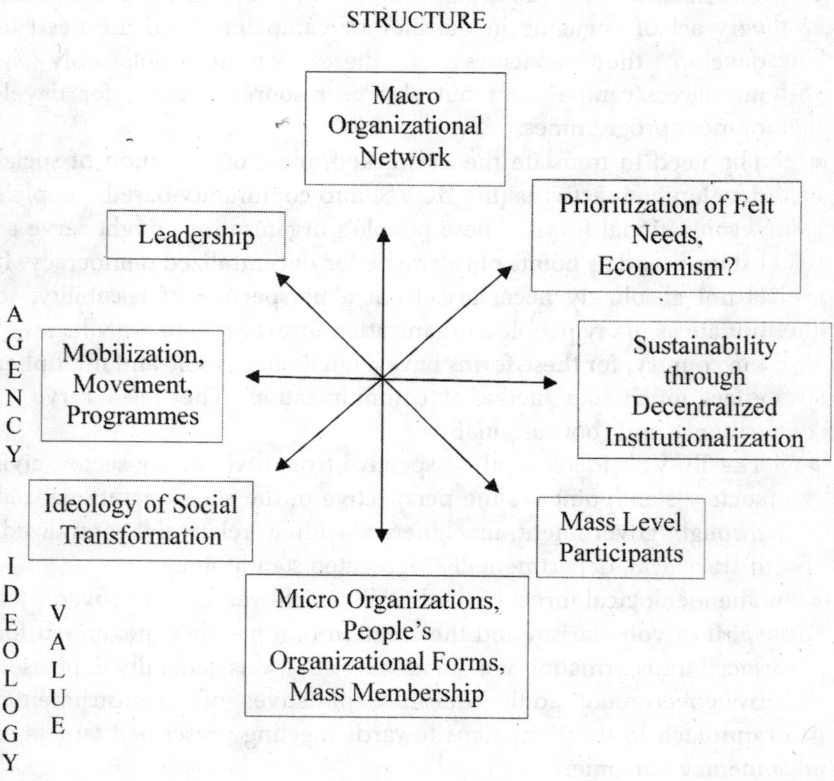

The documents of the BGVS suggest that the leadership was aware about these polarities in tension and was at pains to draw the attention of its educational activists to resolve them. The foregoing tensions which are only to be expected in a large scale social process, such as that initiated by the BGVS, might be represented in the following visualization:

Literacy for Social Transformation

How, if at all, can education and educational-developmental interventions like that of the BGVS contribute to structural change, despite the structural determination of education and the educational reproduction of structures? Such social transformatory processes arise, to some degree, from a redistribution of opportunities and to a more basic extent from the redistribution of resources. The question has sometimes been raised whether the participation of the BGVS in the literacy campaigns in collaboration with government has in effect resulted in silencing of the assertion of mass, democratic rights within civil society and a co-option by the state under the hegemony of socio-economically dominant forces. These questions have arisen from the long and contentious association with government lasting for 20 years, the relative concurrent run of the literacy campaigns with the new economic policies and the dominant hegemony of neo-liberalism from the early 1990s and the lack of change in the economic status of the India that was 'not shining'. This view gained some justification when the state had not hesitated to repress the social transformatory potential of the literacy campaigns. Some of the critical reflections during the early years of the literacy campaigns drew attention to the foregoing issues (Kumar, 1993; Banerjee, 1993; Saxena, 1993; S. Kumar, 1993; *EPW*, 1992; *Gyan Vigyan Sandesh*, 1994). In a strong critique of the literacy campaigns based on field experience in some districts, while conceding some of their positive features, Saxena points out some serious drawbacks in the policy and practice of the campaigns. These relate to the distorted analysis of social reality in some of the literacy texts, the disillusionment of the instructors towards the end of the campaigns and restrictions on critical discourse (Saxena in Kumar and Oesterheld eds., 2007).

It may be noted that in contrast with the techno-managerial approach of earlier programmes, the literacy campaigns have been a mass effort at addressing the problem of illiteracy through a state-initiated, participatory process that came close to being a cultural movement for literacy in some districts. This was undertaken within the constraints of a stagnant politico-economic context. A state-initiated, participatory people's process while appearing to be a contradiction in terms was necessary in a context of a lack of mass organizations capable of undertaking this task. Cultural mobilization and decentralized, participatory organizational forms within civil society was an attempt to counteract the negative intrusions of the state, especially in situations where there was repression of the transformatory potential of the campaigns (Saldanha, 1995: 1191). The BGVS-led initiatives and its growing mass base were in effect exploring the grey areas between literacy for 'liberation' and for 'domestication', as it constantly moved in the former direction resulting in a running tension with the state and at times in serious contradictions.

The history of the state-initiated, literacy campaigns and of the role of the BGVS in them, as discussed in the previous chapters, would have drawn attention to their contradictory character and to the fact of their internal tensions. The contradictions within civil society and in relation to the state were uncovered in the process of implementation as the Expert Group on Evaluation of Literacy Campaigns in India pointed out:

> "Mass literacy, on the other hand, because of the criticality of its size and pressure, may set off certain chain reactions on the socio-economic and political-administrative structures, the evidence of which we found in many areas. But it cannot by itself resolve the collective problem of mass scale impoverishment or widening inequalities in socio-economic conditions. In the absence of collective solutions to these problems, it is extremely difficult to stabilize newly acquired skills or set off the spiral movement for social development discussed above" (Expert Group, 1994: 33).

It goes on to add that there were several instances of not only 'organization for literacy' but also of 'literacy for organization' (Expert Group, 1994: 37).

Writing in the 1930s, Gramsci drew attention to the fact that literacy and education as part of larger cultural and ideological apparatuses are an area of contention between contradictory hegemonic forces (Gramsci, 1971: 242, 398; Saldanha, 2008 a and b). The double-edged political character of the process of literacy acquisition is confirmed by later writings:

> "Reading and writing, those apparently simple and fundamental acts, are in capitalism 'at one and the same time forms of regulation and exploitation and potential modes of resistance, celebration and

> solidarity'. This double movement echoes Caliban's cry: 'You taught me language; and my profit on it is, I know how to curse'. Our task as educators is to help the cursers find their collective voice" (Apple, drawing on Batsleer and others, in Lankshear and Lawler, 1987: xi).

In matters of literacy, the intentions of the dominant and those imparting literacy do not necessarily correspond to or get mechanically translated into the aspirations and the eventual discourse of the subaltern. Literacy can only be 'potential empowerment' (Gillette, 1987: 215). It is the process of literacy acquisition and the organizational forms towards that end, more than the contents of the literacy texts, that influence the social transformatory potential of literacy (Luke, 1993: 3; Gillette, 1987: 2006; Lankshear, 1993: 121–22; Arnove and Graff, 1987: 278–279).

It is in the light of the foregoing discussion that one arrives at the conclusion that people's organizational forms for literacy for development, as an expression of the aspirations of the most disempowered within civil society, are the crucial conditions for the possibility of the social transformatory potential of the literacy campaigns and for the very possibility of acquiring and sustaining literacy itself. It is also understandable that within the given politico-economic, structured context of civil society and in its relation to the state, 'organization for participation in development' – one of the objectives of the literacy campaigns – was one of the most neglected aspects of state initiatives. And despite several efforts on its part, it was only after 2005 that the BGVS was able to eventually achieve some sustainable forms of concentrated, people's organizations linked to its various literacy for development initiatives within clusters of gram panchayats as part of its 'strategy of convergence'. Organizations for development create the conditions for the possibility of socio-economic structural transformation and thus facilitate an environment conducive to the acquisition and sustaining of literacy. Literacy as an enabling skill can thus be translated into an entitlement and right within more equitous opportunity structures which thus provide a motivation for literacy, especially for adults.

An important question that sometimes arose from one's reflections on BGVS interventions and one's interactions with field level activists was: How does the social developmental perspective and strategy of the BGVS contribute to the ultimate goal and need for a politico-economic transformation? The BGVS intervention was primarily within the social developmental sector, generally considered as a sector with low political legitimacy and salience. The long-term perspective of the BGVS was to contribute to social transformation towards creating a society that would be equitous and self-reliant. Other potential arenas for a social transformatory role, beyond the BGVS's emphasis on social development, would be those based on the political economy of mass organizations (trade unions, peasant organizations) and agitational struggles on livelihood issues (land, access to other natural resources, wages and conditions of labour) and the political representational struggle of an electoral character. It is an irony of history that the potential of mass organizations on economic issues has remained relatively isolated from interventions on social developmental ones such as that of the BGVS and that electoral, party politics has generally been distorted by the corruption of power and by a transformation into what is largely a ritualization of consent through sectarian vote banks.

The experience of the last decade of BGVS interventions within the social developmental sector clearly suggests that the creation of a socially mobilized base does not and need not translate into electoral gains of any party political nature. Rather, advances within the social development sector should be seen in terms of the creation of a vast and growing basis of demand from below for equitable access to and control of a range of economic, social, cultural, and neglected institutional resources such as health and education. In the interest of sustainability, this basis of social demand could be further operationalized into people's organizational forms such as cultural groups, youth clubs, women's SHGs, cooperative forms of natural resource management, committees to oversee health and educational institutional resources such as elementary schools, CECs and village libraries. Further, and in terms of political significance understood in terms of the assertion of organized people's power, these decentralized organizations could serve as pressure groups for participation in and for staking claims on local self-governing bodies such as the gram sabhas and Panchayati Raj institutions. They could be networked into various federating structures in order to gain greater political leverage for demanding accountability and the right to information from elected representatives and the administration. The networked people's organizational forms, with a leadership that is sensitive to social issues, would then effectively be a process of the democratization of civil society from below. This then is the potential politico-economic significance of social developmental interventions such as those initiated by the BGVS.

The foregoing suggests a process similar to the 'agenda for cultural action' described by K.N. Pannikar (cited in BGVS, February 2002):

> "The purpose of cultural action is, therefore, to influence and change the character of the public discourse in civil society. It cannot be achieved through rejection, resistance and opposition alone. All the three are necessary, but not sufficient. What is required is the creation of a counter culture through constructive undertakings, which would alter the existing public discourse generated by globalization and communalism. This can be achieved only through the revitalization of indigenous cultural resources, remoulding them to face the contemporary challenges, at the same time without being obscurantist and revivalist. The formation of local communities with the ability to intimately intervene in the cultural life of the people is the necessary beginning for the creation of a counter culture."

11

Future Directions

On June 26, 2008, the NLM in collaboration with the National University for Educational Planning and Administration (NUEPA), held an important national level consultation on literacy to evolve future directions for an NLM strategy. BGVS activists at the central and state levels, present government officials responsible for the NLM and related development programmes and some officials who had participated in earlier literacy efforts took an active part in the consultation. One has participated in that process and is in basic agreement with the strategy document that emerged from that consultation (NLM, August 10, 2008). The document points out some of the major limitations based on past experience: gaps in the literacy, PL and CE phases due to delays in the production of teaching-learning materials, submission of accounts, fund flows and evaluation reports; lack of adequate mobilization and consequent shortcomings in the mission-mode management; indiscriminate expansion without adequate decentralization and civil society participation; the decline of political and administrative priority given to literacy after 1995; major deficiencies in the PL and CE phases; few and inadequately trained full-time staff; and inadequate capacities and systems for maintaining accounts (NUEPA, June 26, 2008 and NLM, August 10, 2008: 2–3).

Some of the proposed modifications in the strategy as discussed in the above-mentioned meeting which had earlier been suggested through studies, evaluation reports and advocacy notes but which were unfortunately largely ignored, were as follows: Viewing basic literacy, PL and CE as a single continuum of lifelong learning so that learners could move without a break from one phase to the other and within a particular district these phases could run concurrently, if necessary; the establishment of a basic literacy and life-long education centre, tentatively called a Lok Talim Centre, so as to provide a concrete presence for convergence of educational and development activities within each decentralized unit; the provision of basic literacy through a variety of contexts and individual/group specific approaches such as each-one-teach-one, volunteer instructors teaching about 10 persons, resident instructors in isolated regions, residential camps, the use of computer-assisted learning, etc.; strengthening the management and the academic resource support systems from the district level downwards and upwards to the state and national levels with adequately trained, full-time coordinators (NLM, August 10, 2008: 4ff).

It is appropriate that a variety of approaches to teaching-learning be adopted within a broad strategy of the literacy campaigns. The mobilizational process defines the character of the campaign approach and teaching-learning in pairs, within centres as groups or for a longer duration in one place as a residential camp are only modalities of conducting teaching-learning. These modalities could be selectively integrated into the campaign approach depending on context, human resources and needs. In fact, a residential camp has been found to greatly facilitate the learning of especially women. It takes them away from various responsibilities and oppressions, even though it may be for a short duration of say three weeks, to concentrate on learning and critical understanding of social issues; as for example in the Nirantar project in Uttar Pradesh and the Doosra Dashak project for the education of adolescents in Rajasthan (Saldanha, 2007). Besides intensive and continuous learning of a complex subject like literacy helps to strengthen the cognitive associations between phonetics, the script and object referents; without breaks, thus reducing the possibility of relapse. Based on a survey of acquiring literacy in western societies over five millennia from the invention of writing, Graff concludes that there can be no single route to achieve mass literacy (1986: 77). Agencies responsible for evolving a renewed strategy for the literacy campaigns would do well to refer to the benchmarks and indicators for adult education that have emerged from an extensive consultative process conducted by the Global Campaign for Education and ActionAid (November 2005, Archer, July 2007 and Saldanha, 2008c). The international benchmarks were offered as a guideline and a reference point for contextualizing adult education efforts, and not as a prescription.

The President of India, in her address to parliament on June 4, 2009, expressed the intention of government to focus on female literacy because, "Increased female literacy is expected to become a force multiplier for all our social development programmes". On September 8, 2009, the international literacy day, the Prime Minister announced a new thrust for the National Literacy Mission entitled 'Sakshar Bharat, Har Mahila Sakshar, Ham Sakshar' (Literate India, Every Woman Literate, We will be Literate). The programme visualized a coverage of 70 million adults in the age group of 15 years and above with a special focus on women, SCs, STs, minorities, other deprived groups and adolescents, especially in the low literacy states. Vocational training would be imparted to 140 million persons. It was hoped that the literacy rate would increase from 65 per cent in 2001 to 80 per cent in the five years till 2014.

As regards the future direction that the BGVS could take, the organization is in the best position to internally assess its history and provide correctives. This study can only make a small contribution to that process. The following are some summary, interrelated suggestions that emerge from this study and from a relatively external and independent perspective:

The sustainability of mobilizations, of educational and other developmental interventions lies in the creation of people's organizations interfaced with a national mass organization. This critical point has been discussed at length in the foregoing sections. The BGVS is not an NGO in the restricted sense of the term. It has not been a relatively middle class formation emerging from the voluntary sector, mediating between government and vulnerable sections of society with inputs of a welfarist or developmental or even a social activist or resource support character (see H. Sethi, 1984, for a depiction of this classification). It has also not been a mass organization in the traditional sense of the term; among workers, peasants, agricultural labourers or students, affiliated in some way to political parties. It has emerged as a result of initiatives from people's science activists who over a period of time developed a national level, mass organization of networked, social development activists. This in some ways constitutes a unique formation within civil society. The sustainability of the interventions of this formation whose membership was drawn largely from local communities depends to a great extent on creating people's organizations among the very vulnerable sections that it intends to involve. Chapter 8 suggests that this process is already underway from 2005, but this needs to be strengthened and expanded.

There is a need to visualize and operationalize all interventions into people's organizational forms. Some of these organizational forms, as related to BGVS and other development initiatives, may be Village

Education Committees (VECs), Watershed Committees, Bal Manch/Student Groups, Youth Groups, Women's Groups/Self-Help Groups, Health Committees and Gyan Vigyan Kendras. These formations need to be networked with resource support organizations and institutions such as CECs, NCECs, libraries, Jeevanshalas and GVVs, JSSs and SRCs. A federation of people's organizational forms can be actualized over a period of time as one has already observed with respect to MALAR in Kanyakumari district and Samata at the national level (Chapter 9, Section 3 and Chapter 4).

The people's organizational forms have the potential of participating in and acting as pressure groups on Panchayati Raj institutions. One has already observed this process, wherever such decentralized formations have been created by the BGVS. It needs to be recognized that the sustainability and effectiveness of interventions in terms of controlling and changing existing systems depend on their organizational capacity.

The NCECs and CECs may be operationalized as resource support organizations to people's organizational forms. It is clear that the capacities of participants within decentralized formations need to be enhanced. The existing structures of the government continuing education programme, such as NCECs and CECs, could be suitably modified and utilized as resource support institutions. Convergence of project initiatives, integration of TL-PL-CE with developmental interlinkages through CECs and concentration in clusters of gram panchayats appears to be the way ahead (Chapter 8). The CECs could be fruitfully utilized as nodal points for decentralized convergence and integration of social development inputs. One has observed that active CECs, such as in Mandi district, are already serving this purpose (Chapter 9, Section 1). The people's institutions and organizational formations, mentioned above, need to be nurtured over time. The dynamics of and the skills required for developmental interventions are different from the dynamics of mobilization. The BGVS might utilize its vast network of trained activists as catalysts for convergence, integration and interlinkage of initiatives with governing council members and state/district level activists playing a mentoring role to specific CECs.

There is a need for continued financial support for the BGVS from the government and other agencies. Linkages with government, despite the complexity of the relation, provide an opportunity for sustaining the scale of the activities. Support from the non-government sector might be seen as complementary and as promoting innovations within a wider programme. It is especially at this crucial stage when the wider developmental dimension of continuing education and the task of addressing the question of residual illiteracy are both a matter of national concern, that there is a need for an organizational network such as the BGVS that has been associated with government, at the initiative of the latter.

The interrelated process briefly depicted above would effectively be a strategy for the democratization of civil society. Power to the people might thus be seen as the creation of organized centres of people's power which would have the potential of serving as the basis of demand on the state for information, accountability, human rights and equitable distribution. In the aforementioned process of organized consolidation, the large scale cultural mobilizations from time to time on relevant issues need not be neglected. In fact, this has been the main strength of the BGVS right from 1989 and has been the condition for the possibility of its extensive network of state and district-wise participatory support. One sees the potential of this internal network, the consolidated organizational base, networked with other like-minded formations, emerging as a major force for advocacy with the state for relevant policy and practice, as seen post-2002 (Chapter 7).

While engaging in creating the socio-economic, the political and organizational basis for basic education – the conditions for the possibility for literacy – it is important that the BGVS does not sidestep the issue of the pedagogical discipline and creativity necessary for conducting teaching-learning for adult literacy. The secondary data for the last decade suggest that this was the case, despite engaging in activities more directly related to adult literacy like creating a cultural environment for the campaigns; setting in motion the organizational structures and the training of personnel; publications, conducting CECs and academic resource centres such as the SRCs and engaging in social awareness campaigns. The unfortunate irony of the literacy campaigns has been that civil society organizations have generally tended to move away from formal teaching-learning situations to concentrate on wider developmental inputs related to education; leaving the facilitation of adult literacy to the formally structured and target-bound programmes of the state. Another area of concern as seen during the course of our field visits is a tendency to concentrate on socio-economically more secure sections, at least during the initial stages of entry within particular rural communities, to the neglect of the most marginalized. This is partly due to the fact that the struggle for economic survival for some potential participants leaves very little time for investment in developmental processes and flows from the non-confrontationist approach of the campaigns. Another irony of developmental intervention is that those who have at least some resources tend to get even more, leaving out those who have almost none. This predicament needs to be addressed given that the non-literates are generally also those who are the most socio-economically disadvantaged.

It may be relevant to revert to the substantive issue of decentralized institutionalization through the formation of people's organizations in order to suggest what it might not be and what it could possibly be. It may be recognized that this complex issue gains added significance when discussing the activities of a major and unique formation such as BGVS with a presence in 22 states and 316 districts throughout the country by 2008. The mobilizations through cultural forms such as the kalajathas were repeated over time over the last 20 years. They were significantly extensive mobilizations interspersed with equally large expressions of popular solidarity through conventions held at different times. The programmes that ensued were consequently dispersed and covered a broad range largely within the social development sector. The capacity-building of state, district and sub-district level activists that emerged from the very process of mobilization was an equally challenging task and was largely addressed through a process of cascading training and orientation programmes. The sustainability of this massive human enterprise, apart from being socially constructed around the state and district level BGVS activists, needed a support system of the organization of the grassroots participants through various forms of people's organizations and institutions at the gram panchayat and even at the revenue village level.

The question of sustainability of a developmental process, in one's view, need not be reduced exclusively to the question of availability of finances; even though that would be of some significance within the context of institutionalizing relatively ephemeral social processes of mobilization. Apart from community contributions and the largely voluntary labour of its activists, the BGVS depended on finances from government during the period 1989 to 2002, state agencies and non-government agencies such as the Sir Dorabji Tata Trust from 2004 to 2008. The data for the district-wise coverage of BGVS, as discussed and illustrated in Chapter 10, Section 3 and the table and illustration in it, thus show a close relation between the availability of finances from these sources and especially the relative diminishing availability of finances during the period 1998–2004 that was compounded by an ideologically counter posed government in power at the centre. The latter period also demonstrates the strength and resilience of the voluntary basis of the organization to continue some programmes and mobilization efforts.

The process of institutionalization, as well, need not be reduced to issues of physical infrastructures, hierarchies and paid personnel, though such elements of creating 'institutional', academic resource formations did contribute towards the quality and sustainability of programmes at the field level. Examples would be the State Resource Centres (SRC) run by the BGVS in some states and the Basic Education Resource Centre (BERC) for elementary education in Bhopal, Madhya Pradesh.

Institutionalization may primarily be seen as a process of creating village level people's organizations which provides solidarity and continuity to process. It is also a matter of sustaining the quality of the process in terms of its ideology (vision, values and purposes) and the quality of social interactions within these processes. The large range of BGVS programmes and activities could be summarized and brought together under broadly three types of organizational forms relating to (1) livelihoods, (2) governance, and (3) cultural, educational and ideological communication.

The foregoing were some of one's concerns which were shared with the BGVS through review reports and earlier through the report entitled, The BGVS: Organization, Intervention and Perspectives in the Literacy Campaigns, dated March, 2003; of which this study is an edited, expanded ad updated version. It may be noted that the BGVS was self-critically aware of this issue right from 1995, as seen from reports of the secretary to the General Councils of 1995 and 1998 (Chapter 10, Section 3). Critically reflecting on its own experience, and in part responding to these reports, the BGVS undertook a major strategic orientation from 2006 onwards under the concept of 'convergence'. This is discussed in Chapter 8. The main elements of this strategy were:

1. A concentration of programmatic efforts and emerging people's organization forms within a nodal gram panchayat surrounded by four or five contiguous gram panchayats,
2. A convergence of organizational and human resource efforts within two or three such clusters in selected blocks of districts.
3. Capacity-building of about 8 to 10 village level, resource persons through training programmes within these clusters.

This approach serves as a relevant pointer to one of the future directions for BGVS. The other is the national level mobilizations, networking and advocacy for meaningful policy, as elaborated in Chapter 7.

The future strategy of BGVS could thus be a double-pronged one. On the other hand, the BGVS would need to consolidate its extensive national coverage and its diverse programmes by taking forward the approach it has adopted, especially over the last four years: concentrate on clusters of villages around nodal gram panchayats, converge programmes according to local needs and create human resource capacities to carry forward these activities of education linked to development. These decentralized centres of people's power through different organizational forms, democracy in its true sense, could serve as pressure groups on local self-governance for accountability. On the other hand, the second aspect of the strategy need not be neglected. The BGVS has over the last couple of decades, and especially since 2002 demonstrated its capacity to mobilize its mass base at district and sub-district levels for policy reform at the state and national levels. This has been achieved through cultural mobilization and awareness generation, networking and advocacy. The story of the BGVS over the last 20 years, as a networked social formation emerging from the social developmental sector adapting to different contexts, does provide one pointer to the possibility of civil society formations collaborating with, while holding the state accountable, thus creating the conditions for the possibility for more basic and equitable social transformations as dictated by the Constitution.

Appendices

Appendix 1
BGVS: A Chronology of Major Events

Source: Data Provided by BGVS and Gleaned from Various Documents

Year	*Major Events/Interventions/Programmes*
The Background, 1987–88:	
1987	The Kerala Sastra Sahitya Parishad (KSSP) formed in 1958, together with 25 People's Science Movements/Organizations (PSM) come together to organize the Bharat Jan Vigyan Jatha (BJVJ), 1987, to promote scientific awareness. The Jatha was sponsored by the Government of India (GoI), Department of Science and Technology. Apart from generating mass awareness, the Jatha also led to the formation of the All India People's Science Network (AIPSN).
1988	Ernakulam Literacy Campaign
Phase 1: Mobilizations for Literacy, 1989–93:	
1989	Formation of the Bharat Gyan Vigyan Samiti (BGVS) as a registered society at the request of the NLM; learning from the experience of BJVJ (1987), and the Ernakulam Literacy Campaign (1988) initiated by KSSP, in order to initially conduct the proposed 1990 Jatha.

1990	Bharat Gyan Vigyan Jatha to spread basic messages of literacy. Covered 40,000 villages in around 250 districts all over country.
March 1991–March 1992	Ernakulum Convention and national workshops On TLC : February 19–27, 1991 BGVS national workshop : July 1–4, 1991 BGVS national workshop and training programmes in TLCs : August 24–27, 1991 BGVS national workshop on post-literacy : November 10–14, 1991 BGVS second national workshop and extended executive meet : December 11–13, 1992 National Institute of Adult Education (NIAE)–BGVS workshop on literacy and gender equity : January 11–13, 1992 Literacy to health national workshop : January 23–25, 1992 Workshop on teachers retraining for UEE : January 27–February 5, 1992
April 1992–March 1993	TL/PL orientation workshops : 3–4 days Key resource persons training camp : 4–5 days BGVS perspective workshops : 2–3 days Post-literacy and related development workshops : 5–15 days TLC assessment/correction workshops : 4–5 days Teachers' exchange programme : September 6–13, 1992
Oct. 2–Nov. 14, 1992	Bharat Gyan Vigyan Jatha, 1992. The aim was to create a people's organization to speed up the literacy movement particularly in six low literacy states of Madhya Pradesh, Haryana, Uttar Pradesh, Orissa, Rajasthan and Bihar.
1992	Didi Bank in Dumka district of Bihar started during TLC. About 500 groups were formed out of which 200 were functioning well. Total collection was over Rs 9 lakh.
1992	Pudulakshni Programme in Nellore district of Andhra Pradesh. Around 400 self-help groups were functional. More than Rs 13

	crore had been collected till 1997. These groups had launched anti-arrack movement.
	Self-help groups were also formed in different parts of the country at different stages of the campaigns.
March–April, 1993	Samata Gyan Vigyan kalajathas for one month. Gyan Vigyan jatha of women for spreading messages of education and equality. Covered districts all over the country. April 8–9, 1993: Samata Akshar Mela in Jhansi. Four Samata jathas from four regions converged and a convention was held. More than a thousand kalajatha artists and women activists participated.
1993 onwards	Samata, a women's organization for literacy and empowerment:
	National resource persons' camp (Mandi, Himachal) : August 6–9, 1993
	Samata activists' meet (Bhopal) : May 7–12, 1995
	Northern region workshop : June 11–14, 1996
	Southern region workshop : August 1–4, 1996
	Samata national review : August 30–31, 1996

Phase 2: From Literacy to Development, 1994–97

Aug. 1993 to Feb. 1994	Hamara Desh (Our Country), a campaign for national unity and self-reliance. Balmelas (children festivals), Lok Sampark Andolan (mass contact programmes), Jansansads (people's parliaments) were held from the gram panchayat level to national level. A relay cycle yatra of thousands of neo-literates had been conducted during different components of the programme starting from January 1, 1994 from 14 corners of the country. The final batch of over 200 relay cyclists converged at Hyderabad on February 27, 1994. Week-long Vigyan Janotsava (people's science festival)
	Components of Hamara Desh programme:
	Mass Singing : October 2–November 14, 1993
	Lok Sampark : October 2–December 15, 1993
	Balmelas : August 15–December 30, 1993

	Train Contact : Aug. 15, Oct. 2, Nov. 14, 1993
	Train Contact : January 26, 1994
	Cycle Jatha : January 10–February 20, 1994
	Janotsav : February 21–February 28, 1994
	Jansansads : January 1–February 20, 1994
1993–97	Participatory Resource Mapping (PRM): A programme for community participation in the field of land and water management with the collaboration of other organizations at the panchayat level. The project on integrated drinking water and sanitation called WATSAN was started in four blocks:
	Mudukuluthur (Ramnathpuram) Tamil Nadu
	Ganjam — Orissa
	Kashipur (Purulia) — West Bengal
	Chainpur (Palamu) — Bihar
	Further spread in Kerala, Tripura, Madhya Pradesh, Karnataka, Maharashtra, Rajasthan. Total area of PRM done till March 31, 1997: 63,339 ha.
	National level orientation course (Palghat, Kerala) : September 30–October 5, 1993
	Block level orientation camp (Ramnathpuram, Tamil Nadu) : November, 1993
	Block level orientation camp (Bhanjnagar, Ganjam, Orissa) : November, 1993
	Block level orientation camp (Chainpur, Palamu, Bihar) : November, 1993
	Block level orientation camp (Kashipur, Purulia, West Bengal) : November, 1993
	Terminal workshop on Panchayat Resource Mapping (Coimbatore) : May 26–27, 1995
1994–95. (Extended to March 96)	Joy of Learning programme with the AIPSN.
	A series of children science festivals from village level to national level were organized to make learning joyful.
	National Joy of Learning Festival: November, 1994
	Delhi. Around 1,000 children participated. Around 10–15 lakh children and 35,000

	teachers were exposed to the programme at different levels in 250 districts.
	National level resource persons' workshop, New Delhi : July 13–15, 1994
February 2–12, 1994	Discussion on neo-literate books at the World Book Fair with National Book Trust.
March, 1994	Literacy to Health. In the first phase, 20 districts were undertaken. Emphasis was on health communication, participation, health surveys and local level planning. In the second phase, out of 20 districts, 10 were undertaken for deeper interventions including training of health activists, operationalizing of panchayat level action plans, local level monitoring and surveillance of health status and maternal and child health.
	First Phase: March 1994 to December 1996
	Health education campaign in 15 districts. Madhepura, Jehanabad, Nawadah, Begusarai and Jhabua in Bihar, Chamoli in Uttar Pradesh, Mandi in Himachal, Rohtak in Haryana, Bilaspur in Madhya Pradesh, Kurnool and Nellore in Andhra, Ganjam in Orissa, Ramnathpuram and North Arcot in Tamil Nadu, Bankura in West Bengal.
	Second Phase: January 1996 to December 1996
	Initiated and conducted health intervention in eight districts. In each district, 10 to 20 gram panchayats were undertaken. Nellore district, however, undertook a 400-village Arogya Deepam Programme.
	From January 1997 till date: Tamil Nadu and Bihar health programmes were continued.
	Literacy to health core group meeting and workshop : September 15–16, 1993
	Review workshop on literacy to health programme : February 9–11, 1995
	Literacy to health review-cum-planning workshop : January 14–18, 1997
Feb. 10–25, 1995	Bharat Gyan Vigyan Jatha, 1995. It was a motivation inducing jatha in Uttar Pradesh.

May 8–12, 1995	Rural Entrepreneurship Development Programme (REDP) workshop on PL strategies – REDP at Delhi.
Sep. 1995 to Jan. 1998	Watershed Development Programme (WDP): Protection, rational management, sustainable development and utilization of natural resources were important activities under this programme. It was started in 1995 with 20 to 25 clusters of villages in Tamil Nadu, Gujarat, Kerala, Bihar, Madhya Pradesh, Karnataka, Rajasthan and Orissa. Every year 20 to 25 clusters were taken under the programme for the next three years.
July 24–26, 1995	Workshop on watershed-based development (Hyderabad):
1995	Cosmic Voyage Programme.
	National level resource-cum-rehearsal camp for preparation of skits and songs for Cosmic Voyage Jatha : August 7–24, 1995
	Regional CV jatha rehearsal camp (Bikaner and Calcutta) : September 4–14, 1995
	Eight camps organized with eight regional resource persons in eight different parts of the country.
	Meghnath Saha Jatha from the Diamond Harbour of Calcutta. Covered 67 places in West Bengal, Bihar and Eastern Uttar Pradesh : September 16–October 10, 1995
	Chandra Shekhar Jatha from Bikaner. Covered 69 places in Rajasthan, Madhya Pradesh and Central Uttar Pradesh : September 16–October 10, 1995
	Both the jathas converged and explained the happenings of solar eclipse and other important activities in space. Allahabad : October 10–11, 1995.
	Safe watching arrangements were made at 30 points during the total solar eclipse : October 24, 1995
	Joy of Learning-Brahmand Melas : October 27–28, 1995.

May, 1996–99	Samata Vigyan Utsava, a programme to increase the knowledge base of women. It was taken up as a nation-wide programme. 7,000 utsavas were organized all over India. The focus was on the development of leadership among women at grassroots level. The issues discussed were: education, health, home-based production, women and science and technology, anti-arrack movement and violence in society. It basically comprised of Samata Vigyan Melas in different corners of the country on subjects related to their basic concerns, at the level of village, block, district, and state. Around 2,540 village level, 211 block level including 24 pilot melas and 176 district level including 86 pilot melas were held in two years (from 1995 to 1997) in Andhra Pradesh, Assam, Bihar, Haryana, Himachal Pradesh, Karnataka, Kerala, Madhya Pradesh, Maharashtra, Orissa, Pondicherry, Punjab, Rajasthan, Tamil Nadu, Tripura, Uttar Pradesh and West Bengal. In addition, 40 state level and 10 zone level workshops were also held to train women activists for organizing Samata Vigyan Utsavas.
1996	Rajasthan kalajatha for motivation.
March, 1996–2001	Jeevanshala (NFE/UEE): A different kind of non-formal education centre for children of 6–14 age group (never enrolled and drop outs) was started in Wyara block in Khamman district of Andhra Pradesh and Samhalkha block in Haryana. Eight other districts were included after some more ground work. Those are: Nawadah in Bihar, Shivkashi in Tamil Nadu, Kotkapura in Punjab, Lohwal in Assam, Unna in Himachal Pradesh, Phulbani in Orissa and Dhule in Maharashtra. NFE (Jevanshala II) in Nawada, Bihar, continued from March 1999 till 2003.
1996–97	Jan Vachan Andolan (PL programme), a country-wide people's reading campaign to

	create and spread the culture of book reading in the villages and then establish libraries under the villages library movement. Around eight lakh books/booklets meant for new readers were distributed/sold till 1997 and another eight lakh among children. Most of the children's books were published under children science series booklets.
	National review workshop on JVA in New Delhi : August 12–13, 1996
1996–1998	Desh ko Janein Desh ko Badlein:
	A programme with AIPSN to help ordinary people as well as activists to examine analytically and critically the process and product of 50 years' development after freedom. Three to four discussions groups of 50–60 persons in a village with the help of 10–15 activists in each gram panchayat. Nearly 10,000 gram panchayats were covered under the programme.
1996 to December 1997	Publications:
	The national centre of BGVS at Delhi published a number of low-cost books and manuals and also produced audio-videos. States have also brought out useful materials for various programmes. More than 1500 titles are with the library and central documentation centre. Almost 101 titles by the central unit and 16 by the Madhya Pradesh state unit are in Hindi, 16 in Telugu, 33 in Assamese, 6 in Malayalam, 5 in Kannada, 32 in Marathi, 57 in Oriya, 22 in Punjabi, 61 in Tamil, and 5 in Baglla by Tripura unit. A total of 9,27,080 books/booklets of 101 titles were published by central BGVS publication unit and 6,77,621 distributed in Bihar, Haryana, Himachal, Madhya Pradesh, Maharashtra, Rajasthan, Uttar Pradesh (East and West). The highest number was utilized by Bihar, i.e., 2,38,841.
	Some periodicals were also being published regularly: *Samata* (Hindi), *Gyan Vigyan Varta*

	(Hindi), *Gyan Vigyan Sandesh* (English), *Akshar Sainik* (Hindi).
1997	Efforts for developing alternative, sustainable and integrated village/GP level models of TL–PL–CE. All ongoing programmes like Samata, Jan Vachan Andolans started to integrate with village level TL–PL–CE programmes.
1997	National level Samata workshop in Topchachi, Dhanbad, Bihar, to understand different dimensions of movements during literacy campaigns like anti-arrak movement, grass-roots level enterprise, etc. Efforts were started to integrate Samata campaign with the TL–PL–CE programmes at different levels.
June, 1997	Preparation for pilot CE programme, i.e., training-orientation programme, identification of villages/GPs were completed. Actual implementation of the pilot CE programme was delayed due to delays in the release of funds.
1997–June 1998	(a) About 14 BGVS workshops and training camps organized at national level, 71 at state level, 312 at district level and 579 at block level. This achievement was well beyond the approved target and much before the closure of the project. (b) In all 69 Samata Mahila Utsavas were organized at state level, 279 at district level, 1,162 at block level and 4,639 at village level.

Phase 3: Continuing Education for Development with Scarce Resources, 1998–2001

1998 …	Pilot CE programme started. Literacy to Health programme extended to Maharashtra, Assam, Rajasthan, Tripura and Uttar Pradesh (West) Continued in the Jehanabd and Madhepura districts of Bihar and Raghunathpuram in Tamil Nadu. The village health registers became operational in these districts. Health programmes were initiated in Mathura, Agra, Unnao, Lucknow, Gonda, Gorakhpur,

	Jalaun, Hamirpur, Meerut, Bareli, Muzaffer Nagar, Bijnour, Chamoli, Haridwar, Pilibhit, Udhamsigh Nagar, Muradabad, Rampur, Rudra Prayag, Tehri Garwal, and Pauri Garwal of Uttar Pradesh.
January 1998	State level BGVS orientation programme in Guntur district of Andhra Pradesh. Around 110 activists participated.
	Impact of the media on children in collaboration with NISTAD.
January 23, 1998	PL–CE core group meeting at New Delhi
January–March, 1998	Centres in the low literacy states of Bihar, Rajasthan, Uttar Pradesh (West) undertook a series of programmes independently as well as in collaboration with the State Mass Education Directorates.
	The BGVS, Bihar unit continued to play a major role in the implementation of TL–PL programmes in the districts of Begusarai, Darbhanga, Dhanbad, Saharsa, Madhepura, Banka, Khagarias and Palamu, in particular.
	Organized training programmes in different districts to strengthen the TL-PL programme.
	Samata programme was also continued. Rajasthan unit undertook a number of training programmes in Baran, Alwar, Pali and Dholpur and also started the TL–programmes in the new panchayats.
	Uttar Pradesh (W and E) units continued with the efforts to establish village libraries with local resources under the Jan Vachan Andolan.
	A series of Samata Vigyanotsavas were organized in Andhra Pradesh, Assam, Bihar, Haryana, Karnataka, Maharashtra, Punjab, Rajasthan, Tamil Nadu, Tripura, Uttar Pradesh (W, E and C)
February 5–7, 1998	A national level workshop on Continuing Education (CE) at CVCD, Bangalore. Around 71 activists participated from various states.
	Modalities for implementing the new pilot CE programmes finalized. It was decided to start 160 NCECs and 1,440 CECS.

February 14–21, 1998	BGVS publications stall at World Book Fair in New Delhi.
February 17–20, 1998	Four-day national level workshop organized on primary education at Guwahati, Assam. Nearly 54 activists participated from Tripura, Assam, Orissa and Bihar.
February 17–20, 1998	Four-day national workshop on Continuing Education in Bhawanipura, Orissa. Around 70 activists participated from Orissa, Bihar and Madhya Pradesh.
February 18–19, 1998	Andhra Pradesh state level BGVS activists' discussion on policy issues.
	CE programme was discussed.
March, 1998	Women's week celebrated all over India
	State level Samata orientation programme in Nellore district. Around 25 activists participated. Close to 11 district level and 17 block level workshops were also held in Andhra Pradesh. An average of 60 activists participated in every workshop.
	10 village level Samata Vigyan Melas were organized in Andhra Pradesh. An average of 500–600 participants took part in each mela. 10–12 activity-based programmes were also organized.
March 4–12, 1998	Health kalajatha. Covered 23 Gram Panchayats of Amethi and Gauriganj districts in Uttar Pradesh.
March 15, 1998	Review meeting of Samata, eastern region at Patna.
March 15, 1998	Review meeting of BGVS, northern region in New Delhi.
	State coordinators of Haryana, Punjab, Rajasthan, Himachal, Uttar Pradesh participated. TL–PL–CE programmes and its coordination with Lok Chetna Kendra and Jan Vachnalayas were discussed.
March 21, 1998	Review meeting of BGVS, northern region in New Delhi.
April–June1998	A total of 53 titles were published in Assamese, Punjabi, Telugu, Bengali, Hindi, etc.

	National centre published six and others published 47 titles for neo-literates.
April 27, 1998	Review workshop of BGVS, southern region in Trissur (Kerala)
May 2–6, 1998	Review meeting of BGVS, eastern region in Bhubaneshwar, Orissa.
May 7–10, 1998	Four-day BGVS national workshop on TL–PL–CE and its linkage with gram panchayats in Dehradoon, Uttar Pradesh.
August 11, 1998	Review workshop on BGVS, northern region in Jaipur, Rajasthan. State coordinators of Haryana, Himachal, Rajasthan, Punjab, and Uttar Pradesh participated.
August 17–18, 1998	PL–CE Review workshop of BGVS eastern region. Around 40 activists from Assam, Bihar, Orissa, Madhya Pradesh and Tripura took part.
August 21–23, 1998	Northern region Samata workshop in Agra, Uttar Pradesh. Around 35 activists took part out of which 7 participants were from Kerala and Karnataka.
September 21, 1998	Review workshop on CEC and finance in Kottayam, Kerala.
September 25–26, 1998	Regional level core group meeting to discuss the ongoing TL–PL campaign. Strategy on CE prog- ramme and its linkage with Samata activities were discussed. About 30 activists participated from Assam, Bihar, Orissa and Tripura.
October 9, 1998	PL-CE northern regional coordination workshop in Jind (Haryana). Deep linkage established between the Lok Chetna Kendras and TL–PL–CE programmes in the northern states.
October 24, 1998	Review workshop of BGVS southern states in Nalgonda, Andhra Pradesh. After review, some decisions were taken.
October 25, 1998	National level workshop in Hyderabad to chalk out the strategy for the implementation of CE programme under the BGVS project for 1997–1998.
October 26–27, 1998	Review workshop of eastern region in Patna, Bihar.

	It was found that all the eastern states had achieved the set goals. Some regions like Assam had gone beyond expectation. Literacy campaigns and Samata Melas touched almost all the villages in the state.
	Jan Vachnalayas started in East and West Uttar Pradesh under the CE programme on a large scale with the cooperation of local communities.
	State units finalized the gram panchayats for pilot CE programme.
Oct.–Dec., 1998	Literacy to Health programmes that were already started were continued. Village health registers were operational in these villages.
	The village health sub-committees were formed in Maharashtra, Assam, Rajasthan, Tripura and Uttar Pradesh (West) with the linkage of pilot CE programme.
	Formation of district level literacy to health core groups, training, identification of villages, environment-building, health survey in selected villages, preparation of village health registers, awareness-building through health booklets, preparation and implementation of people's health plan were some of the highlights of the new and ongoing health programmes.
Oct.–Dec., 1998	The state centres of Bihar, Rajasthan, Uttar Pradesh (East and West) undertook a series of programmes to strengthen and initiate TL–PL programmes in the low literacy areas independently and also with the collaboration of State Mass Education Directorates.
	TLC started in Bongaigaon district of Assam.
Oct.–Dec., 1998	National centre published five books and state centres published 40 titles for neo-literates under people's library movement.
Oct.–Dec., 1998	One district level Samata workshop, seven block level workshops and 19 panchayat level workshops on Thrift and Credit Society organized in Assam.

	Around 25 state level Samata workshops, 62 district level Samata melas, 118 block level Samata melas and 213 village level activities were organized.
December 18–21, 1998	Around19 gram panchayat level workshops were organized on the Thrift and Credit Society in Assam. These were linked with TLC and PLC activities.
December, 1998	Watershed Project continued till December 1998 and then discontinued. It had been started in August 1995.
January, 1999	National workshop in Kanyakumari to understand the MALAR model. After this workshop Himachal, Kerala and Punjab started forming self-help groups on the lines of MALAR.
March 8–14, 1999	Women's week in Uttar Pradesh and release of the *Ummid-99* by Uttar Pradesh (E and C)
March 14–18, 1999	Sakshrata Kumbh in Haridwar, Uttar Pradesh. More than 600 participants from all corners of the country participated. A report was presented in the Kumbh saying that a total of 17,000 volunteers were active all over India.
April 25–28, 1999	Samata workshop in the Osiya village of Bighapur block in Unnao district of Uttar Pradesh
May 14–16, 1999	Three-day training camp in Aligarh Muslim University to launch literacy campaign in new areas of Aligarh. About 37 BGVS activists from five gram panchayats participated.
May 24, 1999	24 gram panchayats of three blocks of Barabanki district of Uttar Pradesh completed the health survey and entered into the second phase of the health programme, i.e., formation of village level health committees and established a dialogue with the present health service structures.
June 19, 1999	One-day orientation camp in Agra, Uttar Pradesh. Planning for the next three months was chalked out.
July 5, 1999	Jan Swasthya Samvad (mass health communication programme) organized by BGVS,

	Deoria in Junior High School, Bhataparani, Uttar Pradesh. Focus was on malnutrition.
July 11, 1999	Jan Swasthya Samvad in Aligarh district of Uttar Pradesh. Community Health Campaign was launched.
January 23, 1999	Samata eastern regional core group meeting in New Delhi.
	Plans were made to build up strong linkage with TL–PL and CE.
July 27–29, 1999	Workshop at Topchachi, Dhanbad. Concluded with decisions to strengthen linkages between the CE and Samata.
October, 1999	Super Cyclone Social Reconstruction in Orissa
October 29, 1999 ...	(a) Social mobilization drive in cyclone affected region of Jagatsinghpur with the financial support of ActionAid, India (Orissa).
February 15, 2000...	(b) First phase (immediate emergency phase) started: (Orissa)
	Major activities were: rescue of people and shifting to high ground, distribution of relief materials, identification of 'Nodal' NGOs for distribution of medicines, coordination of health teams in all nodes under Orissa Disaster Mitigation Mission. It covered 40,000 households.
	With the support of CRY–Calcutta, BGVS, Orissa sent health teams consisting of doctors, paramedical workers and volunteers to 10 severe cyclone affected areas.
	Supported the health team mobilized by CAPART and from 'Do Help' group from Warangal (Andhra Pradesh).
Mid-November–	(c) Second Phase started:
mid-December, 1999	Mobilized doctors and volunteers from other states through its all-India network. Conducted health camps in villages, provided support to the Nobel prize winning reputed organization 'Medicines Sans Frontiers' (MSF) to establish the weekly epidemiological surveillance system for 12 cyclone affected districts.

	Conducted 25 health camps in different areas with the help of AGRAGAMEE. District, block and village level volunteers delivered messages regarding simple first-aid treatment.
From mid-December, 1999 contd.	(d) Third phase started: Social mobilization and health activities for food, rehabilitation of orphans and destitute women and reconstruction were given top priority. ActionAid helped financially. The goals are: *Breaking passivity and promoting dignity and self-reliance *Micro-level planning for equity and substantial livelihood *Transparency and social audit to prevent corruption *Community-based trauma coping mechanism *Influencing government and development agencies *Active community participation
November 19–20, 1999	(e) Meeting on building up a civic society for the weak and deprived.
December 7–8, 1999	(f) In first phase: Orientation workshop. Almost 30 master volunteers from different districts participated. In second phase: 30 more volunteers were mobilized from the local block and districts.
Dec. 2–Dec. 24, 1999	(g) Food For Work (FFW): After the closure of the government-sponsored food for work, BGVS started the programme with financial help from other agencies to fulfil immediate food requirements.
December 8–10, 1999	National level workshop on CE. Around 45 activists participated representing almost all the states
February, 15, 2000 ...	(h) In third phase of cyclone intervention: All the volunteers were withdrawn from their respective nodes. Out of a total 60 volunteers, only eight volunteers trained as cluster coordinators. Eight node points were

	selected. Four assistant coordinators were selected at block level for community empowerment. One documentation officer was appointed to monitor and document the entire process of work/project properly and produce its report at regular intervals. One women empowerment officer to guide and coordinate as team leader on the problems of women was also appointed. Eight women cluster organizers were appointed in their respective clusters.
January, 2000	Literacy to Health programme continued with the planning to organize health meetings and discussions in at least 60,000 villages of the country by the end of the year. To gain an understanding about annual budget of the country, various discussions were organized in workshops and training camps under the title 'Budget-2001'. Special emphasis was laid on SHG, women and children's health and women's participation in panchayats by Samata activists.
January 25–31, 2000	National leadership development camp for women at Delhi. About 50 women participated. Issues were: Health, SHG, documentation and reporting, computer training, accounts keeping, personality development, reading materials, future planning, project designing, local management, qualities of a trainer, Samata and Continuing Education.
March, 2000	Special issue of Samata: *Ummid–2000*, a 100-page magazine on women and society was released by Uttar Pradesh, Samata. During the following months, several states held leadership development workshops for women.
May 16–22, 2000	Eastern region Samata leadership development workshop in Guwahati, Assam. Almost 55 activists and 11 resource persons participated from four states. The agenda was learning more about each other from each other. Six languages were used as a means of communication, i.e., Oriya, Bengali, Assamese,

	English, Hindi and Nagamese. It was proved once again that language is no bar.
June, 2000	(a) District and block level Samata committees were formed. (b) District and block level workshops and local level meetings were organized.
June–October 2000	(a) Kalajatha on health and local SHGs. (b) Discussion on health issues at different levels.
November, 2000	Health parliaments
November, 2000	Health assemblies at village level in several states.
Nov. 28–29, 2000	National health meet and march for Dhaka Health Meet scheduled on December 1–2, 2000.
January 6, 2001	Preparatory meeting for Gyan Vigyan Vidyalayas (GVV), BGVS office, New Delhi
January 10–11, 2001	Continuing Education (CE) meeting for the states of Uttar Pradesh, Bihar and Rajasthan, Sultanpur (UP)
Jan. 31–Feb. 6, 2001	Samata women's meeting, Palakkad and Calicut, Kerala
February 18–21, 2001	GVV workshop, Aligarh Muslim University
June 2001	Development and health planning at panchayat level, workshops

Phase 4: National Advocacy for Policy Related to Rights and the Convergence of Local Practice, 2002 ...

April 9, 2002	National Day of Action on Midday Meals undertaken by several BGVS state units as a follow-up to writ petition by People's Union for Civil Liberties, Rajasthan in April, 2001.
April 11–16, 2002	Samata SHG training of trainers, Bihar and Jharkhand, Nawada (Bihar)
May 16, 2002	National meeting for CE, BGVS National Office, New Delhi.
May 18, 2002	AIPSN–BGVS southern regional workshop for World Social Forum (WSF), Hyderabad, Andhra Pradesh
May 26–31, 2002	Samata national workshop, Jagatsinghpur
June 1–2, 2002	AIPSN–BGVS northern regional workshop for WSF, BGVS office, New Delhi

June 4–5, 2002	AIPSN–BGVS eastern regional workshop for WSF, Guwahati, Assam
June 15, 2002	AIPSN–BGVS mobilizing committee meeting for WSF, New Delhi
June 18, 2002	Review and planning meeting of Jeevanshala, BGVS office, New Delhi
June 30, 2002	Children's Festival, Brij Vihar, New Delhi
July 7, 2002	AIPSN–BGVS southern regional workshop for WSF, Trivandrum, Kerala
July 18–21, 2002	AIPSN–BGVS national workshop for WSF, Panchmarhi, Madhya Pradesh
September 15, 2002	AIPSN–BGVS meeting for WSF, Patna, Bihar
September 18, 2002	AIPSN–BGVS Coordination Committee meeting, Lucknow, Uttar Pradesh
September 23–24, 2002	Samata SHG training workshop, Barabanki, Uttar Pradesh
November 20, 2002	Women's Consultation and Core Group meeting for WSF, New Delhi
January 2–7, 2003	Asian Social Forum, Hyderabad
May 17, 2003	State level organizing committee meeting for kalajatha on Peace, Unity and Sovereignty, Bhopal, Madhya Pradesh.
July 6, 2003	Kalajatha meeting, Wardha, Maharashtra
July 7, 2003	Kalajatha meeting, Ahmedabad, Gujarat
July 8, 2003	Northern regional kalajatha coordination meeting, BGVS office, New Delhi
July 20, 2003	Kalajatha meeting, Bhopal, Madhya Pradesh
July 22, 2003	Rajasthan state level kalajatha meeting, Jaipur, Rajasthan
July 22–28, 2003	National kalajatha script production and material production workshop, Bhopal, Madhya Pradesh
July 26–27, 2003	Jan Swasthya Abhiyan (people's health movement) National Working Group Meeting, Bangalore.
September 8–October 2, 2003	Inauguration and initiation of kalajathas on Peace, Unity and Sovereignty in different states. This was also accompanied by kalajathas moving across states till October 4, 2003.

October 1–2, 2003	Culmination of kalajatha at Gandhi Maidan, Champaran (Mothihari), Bihar.
October 2, 2003	Culmination of Uttar Pradesh, Uttaranchal and Madhya Pradesh kalajatha programmes at various places in New Delhi.
October 2, 2003	Culmination of kalajatha programme, Gandhi Park, Dehradun, Uttaranchal.
October 2, 2003	Culmination of Punjab, Haryana, Himachal Pradesh and Rajasthan Kalajathas at Jalianwalan Bagh and Khatkar Kalan.
October 2, 2003	Culmination of Gujarat state level kalajatha at Sabarmati
October 4, 2003	Culmination of Uttar Pradesh and Uttaranchal state level programmes at Lucknow.
October 10–14, 2003	10th All India People's Science Congress, Shimla, Himachal Pradesh.
January 16–21, 2004	World Social Forum (WSF), Mumbai
April 14–16, 2004	National workshop of state coordinators and key activists on the modalities of the state planning for the Project on Empowerment Rights and Security, Aligarh, Uttar Pradesh.
May 18–27, 2004	National level Children's Science Festival, Alleppey, Kerala
May 24–June 3, 2004	Transit of Venus programmes held at Banaras, Barabanki, Meerut, Rae Bareilly, Muradabad, Rampur, Kanpur and Aligarh in Uttar Pradesh on sequential dates.
June 11–15, 2004	National convention and rally on Right to Food, Bhopal, Madhya Pradesh, with the participation of 500 persons.
July 12, 2004	Right to Food campaign meeting, New Delhi
September 2–4, 2004	National Education Assembly of BGVS activists on Right to Social Security, New Delhi, with participation of 4,000 persons.
September 19, 2004	National convention on Employment Guarantee and Right to Work, New Delhi.
October 30, 2004	Joy of Learning meeting, New Delhi

Nov. 27–29, 2004	Joy of Learning assembly, New Delhi, with participation of about 250 school children, teachers and resource persons.
December 19, 2004	Meeting on Employment Guarantee Act, New Delhi
December 21, 2004	People's Struggle for Employment Guarantee Act, New Delhi, with the participation of 100 persons.
January 10–14, 2005	Samata workshop, New Delhi
February 18–23, 2005	Cultural festival on 'Nature and the Environment', in collaboration with Ministry of Environment and Forest and cultural organizations, Malvankar Auditorium, New Delhi
April 2–3, 2005	Midday Meals guidebook preparation, Bhopal, Madhya Pradesh.
April 8–17, 2005	Jammu & Kashmir teachers' training, Srinagar, with the participation of 60 persons.
May 1–5, 2005	Employment Guarantee kalajatha workshop, Bhopal, Madhya Pradesh, with the participation of 30 persons.
May 13–June 29, 2005	Employment Guarantee jathas in different states
July 8–10, 2005	National Education Assembly, Kozhikode, Kerala
August, 2005	National Rural Employment Guarantee Act (NREGA) enacted
August 2–3, 2005	Right to Education meeting, New Delhi
October 2–3, 2005	Right to Education workshop involving representatives from several states. About 42 mass organizations and educational institutions working for education came together. Discussions focused on National Curriculum Framework and the Right to Education Bill. A campaign committee was formed.
October 10–11, 2005	SHG resource persons' training, Tikamgarh, Madhya Pradesh
October 10–11, 2005	Samata Vigyan Utsava orientation workshop, Jaunpur
October 12–19, 2005	Regional level workshops on the topic School Management and Quality Education, Bilaspur, Madhya Pradesh

October 24–30, 2005	CE prerak and NCEC prerak orientation workshop, Lucknow, Uttar Pradesh
November 18–20, 2005	Convention on the Right to Food and Work, Badu, West Bengal
December 2–9, 2005	Regional level workshops on the topic School Management and Quality Education, Surguja, Chattisgarh.
December 22–28, 2005	GVV teachers' training
January 5–11, 2006	Bal Mela training, Baran, Rajasthan
January 12–13, 2006	National level convention on Right to Education Bill and education policies, New Delhi.
January 28, 2006	Samata National Core Group meeting, New Delhi
February 2–5, 2006	Eleventh All India People's Science Congress held at Guwahati, Assam. About 7,000 state representatives of BGVS–AIPSN present.
February 9–13, 2006	Bal Mela training, Alwar
February 16–18, 2006	Basic Education Core Group meeting, Dhanbad, Jharkhand
February 18–23, 2006	Basic Education National Workshop, Bhopal
February 22, 2006	Right to Education Bill activists' meeting, Raipur, Chattisgarh
March 1–2, 2006	Right to Education workshop, New Delhi
April 6–7, 2006	Children's Right to Food Conference was held in Hyderabad, Andhra Pradesh. Issues related to midday meals were discussed.
August 6–7, 2006	Convention on Education for Decentralized Democracy and Development, New Delhi
August 21, 2006	Meeting on BGVS strategy for convergence involving state coordinators and executive committee members.
April 6–8, 2007	Convention on the Right to Food and Work, Bodhgaya, Bihar
May 4–6, 2007	Organizational camp on the future of BGVS, Jaipur. Around 125 BGVS activists participated.
June 7, 2007	Conference on Education for All coordinated by BGVS, Delhi
August 6–7, 2007	Launch of campaign for Education for Decentralized Democracy and Development.

September 1–October 8, 2007	Activists' Exchange Programme across states of BGVS coverage. About 550 activists participated.
Sept. 14–15, 2007	Meeting on Education for Decentralized Democracy and Development was organized. About 500 participants.
October 16–18, 2007	Review meeting on convergence strategy, Jaipur
November 3, 2007	Review meeting on convergence strategy, Koderma
November 18–19, 2007	Review meeting on convergence strategy, Katni and second phase convergence workshop, Pithoragarh.
November 20–25, 2007	Samata Workshop, Bhopal
Nov. 2007–Jan. 2008	Janadhikar Kalajathas (Cultural Caravan for People's Rights), with a focus on blocks and gram panchayat villages.
December 12–14, 2007	Planning meeting for convergence strategy, Bhopal
December 29–30, 2007	Review meeting on convergence strategy, Jaipur
January 1–3, 2008	National Experience Sharing Workshop on CE–Samata Convergence Strategy, Bhopal. About 70 participants
January 20–25, 2008	Workshop on convergence strategy, Bhind, Madhya Pradesh
March 12–14, 2008	Material preparation workshop for NREGA, G.B. Panth University, Allahabad.
April–October, 2008	Convergence training follow-up in states
June 27–July 1, 2008	Basic education national resource persons workshop, Bhopal
July 21–22, 2008	Seventh National General Council of BGVS, Tirupati, Andhra Pradesh.
September 11–30, 2008	Relief work for flood affected in Bihar.
December 20–23, 2008	12th All India People's Science Congress, Ranchi, Jharkhand with 800 participants.
December 29–30, 2008	Workshop on convergence strategy, Bhopal
Jan. 27–Feb. 1, 2009	BGVS members participated in Ninth World Social Forum, Belem, Brazil.
April 7, 2009	Meeting on Right to Food campaign. About 15 BGVS members from Rajasthan, Gujarat,

	Jharkhand, Assam, Bihar, Uttar Pradesh and West Bengal participated.
May 10, 2009	Meeting on the issues of convergence strategy involving state coordinators and executive committee members, BGVS National Centre, New Delhi.
June 19–25, 2009	Workshop of resource group for GVV, Bhopal Madhya Pradesh. Resource persons from Madhya Pradesh, Uttar Pradesh, Jharkhand, Orissa, Assam, Bihar and Gujarat participated.
July 20–22, 2009	Surya Grahan Utsava (festival of watching the solar eclipse), Patna, Bihar.

Appendix 2
BGVS: Some Publications
(January 1994–December 1996)

Joy of Learning Programme

I. Central Office

1. Night Sky Watching
2. Brahmand Yatra
3. Signs of the Zodiac
4. Akash Ki Or
5. Grahnotsav
6. Dharti Se Taro Tak
7. A Solar Eclipse Manual
8. Our Universe
9. Low Cost Science Experiments
10. Dhamakdham–Bal Songs
11. Bachcha Toli–Bal Songs
12. Sikhane Ka Maza (Guidebook)
13. Joy of Learning (Guidebook)
14. Mathematics
15. Jewels in the Sky
16. Grahan Ka Luka Chupi
17. Rashion Ke Chingh
18. The Story of our Universe
19. Chakmak (special issue)

II State Centres

A. Assam

1. Tangram
2. Origami
3. Science Experiment
4. Creativity and Imagination
5. Science Play
6. Songs and Stories
7. Riddles
8. Mathematics
9. Puppetry
10. Quiz
11. Nature Study
12. R.P's Hand Book

B. Bihar

13. JoL Guidebook
14. Akash Ki Maya
15. JoL Song
16. JoL Booklets

C. Gujarat

17. Toy Ba
18. Littler Science
19. Toy Treasure
20. Khel Khel Mein
21. Scientific Games
22. JoL Newsletter
23. JoL Training Hand Book-1

D. Himachal Pradesh

24. Brahmand Yatra

E. Karnataka

25. Chinara Mela
26. Meenu Huttiddu Hege
27. Nisarga Vigyan Samaja

F. Madhya Pradesh

28. Maze Maze Mein Sikha
29. JoL Activists Book
30. Cosmic Voyage
31. Siksha Main Maja

G. Maharashtra

32. JoL Booklet
33. JoL Songs
34. Zodiac in the Sky

H. Orissa

35. Guidebook
36. Children's Song
37. Ama Pila O'Ana School
38. Khusira Sikhiba

I. Punjab and Chandigarh

39. Khed Khed or Vich Vigyan
40. Sikhan Da Anand

41. Bal Goel
42. Puran Suraj Grehan
43. Sawal Jawab

J. Rajasthan

44. Bal Mela Guidebook
45. Porab Faiko Nayo Ujalo
46 Khuch Kahte Hai Khel
47 Grahan Ek Pariches

K. Tamil Nadu

48. Attam Pattam
49. Myalamilae
50. Karpanyium Kaithiranum
51. Origami
52. Namadhu Udal
53. Kannukam Irikkum
54. Pakkalil Oru Irravu

L. Uttar Pradesh

55. Bal Siksha
56. Pratyek Ke Liye Shiksha
57. Geet Aur Natak
58. Jan-Gyan I
59. Jan-Gyan II
60. Jan-Gyan III

(January 1997–September 2000)

I. Total Listeracy

1. Guidebook (English)
2. Guidebook (Hindi)
3. Training Curriculum (English)
4. Pathyakram (Hindi)
5. Training Strategy (English)
6. Prashikshan Ranniti (Hindi)
7. Marg Darshika (Hindi)
8. Saksharata Sarvekshan (Hindi)
9. Troubleshooting Dropouts (English)
10. Nitty Gritty Literacy Survey (English)
11. Troubleshooting Dropouts (Hindi)
12. Monitoring and Mulyankan

II. Post-Literacy

13. Keeping the Centres Interesting (English)
14. Grey Areas in Post-Literacy (English)
15. Emerging Concept in Post-Literacy (English)
16. PLC Modules 1,2,3 and 4

III. Resource Literacy

17. Handbook for Land Literacy

IV. Literacy to Health

18. Placing Health on Panchayat
19. Agenda Village Medical Kit
20. Women and Child
21. One Magical Morning
22. Between Living and Surviving
23. What Globalization does to

24. Whatever Happened to Health
25. Making Life Worth Living
26. A World Where We Matter
27. Confronting Commercialization of Health Care

V. Literacy and Gender Education

28. Unite We Sit–The Saving Movement
29. Meri Pahchan Part 1, 2, and 3

VI. Others

30. Sakshrta Ke Vividh Aayam
31. New World New India
32. Tomorrow Will be Too Late
33. Science for Nation
34. Nature, Society and Science

VII. Jan Vachan Andolan Series

A. In Hindi:

1. Idgah
2. Katha Sunder Lal Ki
3. Desh Bara Kab Hota Hai
4. Ja Sunio Hamari Kakare
5. Salama Ke Sawal
6. Hamare Gaon Ki Asha
7. Khoja Nasruddin Bharat Mein
8. Na Bara Na Chota
9. Bahano Ke Geet
10. Sarala Se Bani Sarala Ji
11. Bhai Chare Ka Itihas
12. Bulaki Baba
13. Chatur Champa
14. Aao Bat Karein
15. Ladu Bhoga Ki Kahani
16. Teen Betiyo Ki Maa
17. Auraton Ki Kavitaye
18. Jan Vachan Guidebook (Hindi)
19. Hamare Talab
20. Tap, Bap Aur Aap
21. Panipat Ki Hakko
22. Mulla Nasaruddin Ke Kisse
23. Raja Kaun
24. Satranj Ki Kahani
25. Polish Aur Hum
26. Dayan Va Anyakahaniyan
27. Sahi Aakar
28. Girgit Ka Sapna
29. Likhai Ke Kahani
30. Girgit
31. Manglu Yamraj Ke Darbar Main
32. Bazi
33. Kahkahi
34. Gulel Ka Khel
35. JVA Guidebook (English)
36. Ali Ka Nayay
37. Maa Ka Dudh
38. Gharelu Udyog
39. Do Goraiya
40. Bahino Ki Pirayen
41. Sapne Aur Sach
42. Hum Aur Hamara Akta
43. Gandhi Aise The
44. Iswar Ki Kahaniya
45 Aankh Ki Kahani
46. Duniya Ke Sabase Khoobsurat Aadmi
47. Kamgar Aurto Ka Haque
48. Jhun Jhuna
49. Sangharsh Katha
50. Akal Bari Ya Bahains
51. Maine Himmat Nahi Hari
52. Chuhe Aur Chuhe
53. Indra Ka Hathi
54. Dalu Das Ke Hath Kyon Kate
55. Kharidddar Ke Kanuni Haque

56. Yudh Se Lauta Pita Wa Anya
57. Barabari Ke Geet
58. Sukho Majari Ka Sandesh
59. Us Gaun Ke Larki
60. Ek Insan Ko Kitani Jamin Chahiye
61. Desh Ko Jano Desh Ko Badlo
62. Sau Shal Ka Cinema
63. Jisne Umeed Ke Veej Boye
64. Budget Ka Jhamela
65. Jungale Me School
66. Chinta Ki Char Bahine
67. Khet Me Ugi Machchliya
68. Meri Umma
69. Ninanve Ka Phere
70. Aurat Ki Kahani
71. Haraoti Ki Kahani
72. Baat Ki Baat
73. Himachal Jan Vidroh–1
74. Himachal Jan Vidroh–2
75. Himachal Jan Vidroh–3
76. Billiyon Ki Barat
77. Dani Ped
78. Ek Sham Jadugar Ke Sath
79. Akshar Chitra
80. Achcha School
81. Mishka Ka Daliya
82. Parmukh Ke Naam Patra
83. Hamari Nav Chali
84. Ikka Motor Tanga
85. Swarthi Rakshas
86. Phogge Ka Din
87. Vishwa Ki Kahani
88. Bachche Kaisa Bante Hai
89. Chippa Rahashya
90. Akhri Pata
91. Tota
92. Vigyan Ke Paryog
93. Khel Khel Main Shiksha
94. Anguthe Se Chitra
95. Rail Garhi
96. Grahan Main Bhi Surya Sunder
97. Bansi
98. Ganga Ram
99. Dukh Ka Mara Hand Pump Bechara
100. Jal Chakkar
101. Bahuroopiya
102. Vigyan Kya Hai
103. Sachcha Sathi Neem
104. Mai Nadi Anshu Bhari
105. Kisana
106. Hamara Pata
107. Larki Padhkar Karegi
108. Bhagirath
109. Nyare Lal
110. Mukti Ka Marg
111. Visarjan
112. Hirnauta
113. Nanhe Authar Ka Suraj
114. Bachche Aur Taraju
115. Mera Jadui School
116. Sadako Aur Kagaj Ke Pakshi
117. Bachche Darpan Aur Pratibimb
118. Bachche Aur Paryavaran
119. Bachche Aur Pani
120. Khushiyon Ka School
121. Aankhonki Chamak
122. George Washingaton Carvar
123. Bobak Bakara
124. Lui Brail
125. Nanhi Rajkumari Aur Chandrama
126. Murgi Ke Chuje
127. Ek Madhumakkhi Aur Ek Gulab
128. Wafadar Hathi
129. Fulon Ke Ummid
130. Jonathan Livinstone Seagull
131. Shin Ki Tipahiya Saikil
132. Hiroshima Ki Aag
133. Kuku Aur Bhuri
134. Khushal Bachche
135. Ande Se Chuja
136. Rimjhim Karati Barish Aai
137. Kura Kachara

138. Khatra School
139. Fardinend Ki Kahani*
140. Jauni Appalsid Ki Kahani*
141. Sanyukta Rastra Ke Tin Wade*
142. Binni Ke Janwar*
143. Larka Kya Hai Larki Kya Hai*
144. Padane Ka Maja*
145. Vigyan Ka Maja*
146. Prachin Aur Navin*
147. Panch Chini Bhai*
148. Prithawi Ke Rahasya*
149. Nilbag Ke David*
150. Meri Bahan Sun Nahin Sakati*
151. Madadgar Hath*
152. Whil Chair Hi Mere Pair Hai*
153. Ahilya Bai
154. Tentar
155. Mira Bai
156. Kyun Kyun Chori
157. Hawenl Nadi Ke Kinare
158. Ham Kaisi Duniya Chahte Hain
159. Charkhe Ka Sandesh
160. Sabke Liye Sawasthya
161. Sharab Ko Dor Bhagana Hain
162. Suchana Ka Adhikar

B. In Urdu

163. Hamare Talab
164. Gharelu Udyog
165. Hamare Gaon Ki Asha
166. Na Bara Na Chota
167. Bhai Chare Ka Itihas
168. Girgit Ka Sapna
169. Salama Ke Sawal
170. Bazi
171. Mulla Nasaruddin Ke Kisse
172. Likhai Ki Kahani
173. Ali Ka Nyay
174. Teen Vetiyo Ki Maa

C. In Telugu

175. Chivari Aaku
176. Amma Gudu
177. Gorinka Gudu
178. Paka Pakalu
179. Chebadulunaga
180. Kumari Narassaiah
181. Papam Vusarauelli
182. Unimmdi Gantala Bassu
183. Paudina Chettu
184. Kokolamma Katha
185. Mana Uri Aasa
186. Telusu Kundam
187. Uerribegula Vemaiah
188. Toka Chukka Katha
189. Usara Velli
190. Jeedimamidi Guttulu
191. Teta Teeequ
192. Vastu Sastriya Panselan
193. Pillipuranam
194. Aatala Sanadalo
195. Verribagula Veaya
196. Papam Vusaraueku

D. In Assamese

197. Udivid Jagat
198. Hamar Kheti Batir Katha
199. Pusharar Adhikar
200. Tehar Kahini
201. Darikonapparatimilor
202. Hathat Edinchiria Khanat
203. Shindu Upoittakar Soibhotha
204. Harishchandra Goswami

205. Pitha Aru Baidyajantrar Bihu
206. Baknor Kokar Sanchyar Sadhu
207. Barirchukat Swaisthya–1
208. Barirchukat Swaisthya–2
209. Barirchukat Swaisthya–3
210. Atitar Khel Dhemali
211. Bhut D211hangulai Ityadi
212. Likha Parha Kare Jeye
213. Grahak Sasetanata
214. Amar Paribesh Dushita Hoi Ahishe
215. Akhir Ka Kha
216. Akai Paki Dighala Kokai
217. Paniyei Pran
218. Mahakash Bijay
219. Lakshminath Bezbaroa
220. Makor Gakhir
221. Prithivir Sadhu
222. Jiva Gathanar Ekak Kosh
223. Saskya Surakshar Nirapad Upai
224. Katha Kuwakhel
225. A Sudden Day in The Zoo
226. Bakhor Kokar Sanchar Sadhu
227. Minar Hahi Based on Mina Smiles
228. Saksharta Abhijanat Putalanash

E. In Malayalam

229. Veettammayum Vaidyutiyum
230. Puthiya Vayana
231. Vanithakalum Kayikalokavum
232. Othupidichal
233. Ithu Sariyo
234. Veluthapakshiye

F. In Kannada

235. Girl Child is Born
236.Comets (Hale Bopp)
237.Bhagat Singh
238. Freedom Struggle
239. Folk Stories

G. In Marathi

240. Gharant
241. Ghondi Ram Mansataala
242. Dhoom Ketu
243. Sarda
244. Kalyantra
245. Samana Budhdhicha
246. Paej
247. Khel Budhdhbalacha
248. Aajicha Nyay
249. Merry Query
250. Shivrajchi Galol
251. Dr Rakhmabai
252. Tejli
253. Vigya Nache Khel
254. Garbar Ghotala
255. Sardyache Swapna
256. Teen Mulinchi Aai Trancreation
257. Aapali Aash Transcreation
258. Shyamchi Aai Madhil Goshthi
259. Jan Vachan Andolan
260. Transcreation
260. Setkyancha Shastragy Kawarhar
261. Surya Tughach Aahe–Transcreation
262. Shodhanchya Ganmati
263. Pandita Ramabai
264. Duniya Sarvanchi
265. Karmvir
266. Akashatil Lanpdav

267. Rumalathil Sasa
268. Soneri Anubhav
269. Katha Ganthichya
270. Kisshe Mulla Nasruddin
271. Sardi–Taap Yapasun Sutaka
272. Sagali Dharpakar
273. Shikanyasathi
273. Mavshicha Salla
274. Kuposnavar maat
275. Mangalu Yamrajachya Darwarat
276. Chamatkari Sakal
278. Dusit Pani Upay Kay
278. Khwaja Nasruddin Bhartat
279. Hum Aur Hamari Ekata
280. Bahano Ki Pirayen
281. Bhaichare Ka Itihas
282. Aurat Ki Kavitain
283. Desh Kab Bara Hota Hain
284. Maa Ka Doodh
285. Akkamai
286. Eka Vegalya Lagnachi Goshta
287. Manjarachi Varat
288. Denare Zhad

H. In Oriya

289. The Man Who Planted Trees
290. A Rich Bride
291. Our Sister in Search of Justice
292. What Is History
293. The Story of Onion
294. Return
295. The Voice of Books
296. Budha Sankhari
297. Andharua
298. Hunger
299. Julu's Adventure
300. The Genesis of Agriculture
301. When Daddy was a Little Boy
302. Call of Soil
303. Maguneera Sagada
304. George Washington
305. Shoka Sabha
306. Sikara
307. A Grain of Mustard Seed
308. Roots
309. How Apes Became Home Sapiens
310. Journey to the Solar World
311. Pebble and Mami
312. Stories About Zodiac Signs
313. Why the Sky is Blue
314. The Story of Our Hands
315. Pandita Ramabai
316. Panchanruta for Our Body
317. My Cow
318. Inspiration
319. The Story of Kuni
320. Tolstoy's Stories
321. Death of the Handsome Man
322. In the Search of Readers
323. Rats
324. Rebati
325. Pashu
326. Mansara Bilapa
327. Laxman Nayak Hanged
328. For Redeeming Our Indebted Future
329. Fifty Short Poems
330. JVA Songs
331. Folk Stories About Animals
332. Comet
333. The Book Friends of Gurujee
334. Dhulia Baba
335. A Gift of the Sky
336. Food Adulteration
337. A Letter From Wife
338. Leaf Zoo Part I
339. Leaf Zoo Part II
340. Children's Education in Foreign
341. Gapa Agapa
342. Life Story of Life
343. The Laughing Man

344. Dingura Sansar
345. Children's Folk Songs
346. Apes to Men
347. Bade Ghar ki Beti
348. A Grain of Musterd Seed
349. Biplab Bheri
350. Let Us Sing
351. A Sunrise in Kerala
352. Jonathan Livington Seagal
353. New India New World

I. In Punjabi

354. Mulla Nasir
355. Katha Sunder Lal
356. Ladoo Bhoga Di Kahani
357. Bhaichare Da Itihas
358. Balaki Baba
359. Rabb Nu Ate Hor Kahanian
360. Jaddo Haathan De Safai
361. Police Ate Asin
362. Panipat Di Hukku
363. Sade Pind De Asha
364. Khoja Nassiruddin Bharat Vich
365. Satranj De Kahani
366. Autan Diyan Kavitavan
367. Bikram Baital
368. Tin Dhian De Maa
369. Short Poem
370. Idgah
371. Desh Wada Kadou Hunda Hai
372. Raje Di Chon
373. Siyami Beero
374. Dyain Ate Hor Kalaniya
375. Beenwala
376. Gharelu Udyog
377. Do Gauraiya
378. Mangloo Yamraj De Darwar Vich
379. Maun Da Dudh
380. Keha Keha
381. Girgit Da Sapna
382. Sade Talab
383. Vadhai Di Chithi
384. Girgit
385. Sahi Aakar
386. Duniya De Sabh Ton Khubsurat
387. Asian Te Sadi Ekta
388. Gandhi Ajihe San
389. Auo Gal Kariye
390. Behno Ke Perian
391. Ishwar Diyan Kahaniyan
392. Baji
393. Salma De Sawal
394. Siani Beero
395. Bhai Anarath Karai
396. Nari Sansar
397. Billo
398. Jag Te Hor Kahanian
399. Vete Te Log
400. Faraj
401. Sada Aika Hunda Bad
402. Bure Da Ant Bura
403. Ranjhe De Panj Peer
404. Punjab De Pakhandi
405. Bachgiya Te Hor Kahaniya
406. Bhijriha Admi Te Hor Kahanian
407. Rishwat Te Hor Kahania
408. Kamani Dar Chakoo Tehorkahanian
409. Boolane He Paina
410. Ik Parvat Ik Kato
411. Kinna Bada Mullate Hor Kahanian
412. Tap Bhap Ate Tusin
413. Ali Da Mian
414. Kamkaji Aurat De Haq
415. Haroti Diyan Kahaniya
416. Ik Insan Noon Kini Jamin …
417. Bajat Da Jhamela

418. Khet Vich Ugi Machliya
419. Likhayi Di Kahani
420. Jangal Vich School
421. Akh Di Kahani
422. Angoothe Taun Chitar
423. Biliyan Di Barat
424. Meri Maa
425. Natak Suraj Grahin
426. Arjun
427. Do Hath
428. Pasa Palt Gaya
429. Alhar Kuri

J. In Tamil

430. Varthai Vyapar
431. Amma Anna Kappathunga
432. Azagiyum Kuthuvilakkum
433. Iravl Nagai
434. Mazhai Varudhu
435. Kadisi Ilai
436. Marumagal Vakku
437. Muthchi
438. Kulakulana Mundhirikka
439. Nam En Vatta Midukirom
440. Neeta
441. Ainthu Pengal Petra Avudaiappa
442. Anchu Roova
443. Kadhi Sollungal
444. Makkalukku Adhikaram
445. Melachathan
446. Asai Tosai
447. Kaycha Maram
448. Chinna Chinna Ettu Eduthu
449. Pey Mazhai
450. Kirukku Sanmugam
451. Rodu
452. Ettaray
453. Verum Nai
454. Verin Thudippu
455. Kaseem Maraikkayar
456. Kann Illatha Thambi
457. Verum Naay
458. Kaaycha Maram
459. Nallaghankal Kathai
460. Elumpillatha Naakku
461. Azhakiyum Kuthuvilakkam
462. Sandiran
463. Kannaki Kathai
464. Aaradi Nilam
465. Suthanthapporatta Varalar
466. Sooriyan
467. Kannaki Kathai
468. Kadumakappi
469. 1857 Ezhuch Muthal Viduthalmpor
470. Thikozhiyum Ammavum
471. Ezhai Pedum Padu
472. Kuttalam
473. Ekalvan Kathai
474. Thudiana
475. Kalatta Kuddumbam
476. Ezhuthalai Muraikal
477. Puthi Shli Penkal
478. Seeniammal Sarkkaraimammal
479. Jalianwala Bagh–Punjab Padukola
480. Ekalavyankathai
481. Thudiyana Samy
482. Galatta Kudumbam
483. A Guide To JVA in Bangla
484. Saksharata Kee Ken Kebhane
485. Mullyan Kee Ken Kebhane
486. Saksharata Karmasnchi Kee Ken
487. Shhutader Ambedkar
488. Padakhep
489. Natunjagat

Source: BGVS, Project Completion Report: January 1997–2000, New Delhi, 2001, Annexure–4).

References

Akash, A., "No to Liquor", in *Frontier*, January 16, 1993.

Anveshi, "Reworking Gender Relations, Redefining Politics: Nellore Village Women against Arrack", in *Economic and Political Weekly*, Vol. 28, January, 16–23, 1993.

Apple, M.W., "Foreword", in Lankshear, C. and Lawler, M. (eds.), *Literacy Schooling and Revolution*, London, The Falmer Press, 1987.

Archer, David, *The International Benchmarks on Adult Literacy*, Beijing, UNLD Conference, July, 2007.

Arnove, R.F. and Graff, M.J. (eds.), *National Literacy Campaigns: Historical and Comparative Perspectives*, New York, Plenum Press, 1987.

Athreya, V. and Chunkat, S., *Literacy and Empowerment*, New Delhi, Sage Publications, 1996.

Balagopal, K., "Slaying of a Spirituous Demon", in *Economic and Political Weekly*, November 14, 1992.

Banerjee, S., "Revisiting the National Literacy Mission", in *Economic and Political Weekly*, Vol. 28, June 19, 1993.

Baruah, A., *Dwitiya Saraighat: A Documentation on TLC of Assam Science Society*, Guwahati, Asom Siksha Bigyan Aru Kalar Sampad Kendra, December, 1996.

BGVS, *Bharat Gyan Vigyan Samiti*, New Delhi, 1990 (a leaflet).

—, *Preliminary Report on BGVJ and Proposals for the Future*, 1989–90, New Delhi, 1990.

—, *Guidelines for Implementation*, New Delhi, 1990.

—, *Report on Bharat Gyan Vigyan Jatha as on August 1, 1990*, New Delhi, 1990.

—, *Bharat Gyan Vigyan Jatha–1990: A Crusade Against Illiteracy*, New Delhi, 1990.

—, *Bharat Gyan Vigyan Jatha*, New Delhi, 1990.

—, *Report of the First General Council Meeting of NLMA: February 1991*, New Delhi, 1991.

—, *Achievements Under the Bharat Gyan Vigyan Jatha and the Paidal Jatha*, New Delhi, 1991.

—, *Report of the Bharat Gyan Vigyan Samiti (1991–92)*, New Delhi, 1992.

—, *Minutes of EC-NLMA Meeting: May 8, 1992,* New Delhi, 1992.

—, *The Bharat Gyan Vigyan Jatha–II*, New Delhi, 1992.

—, *Proposal for Support to Bharat Gyan Vigyan Samiti for 1994–95,* New Delhi, 1993.

—, *Bharat Gyan Vigyan Samiti: A Report 1989–93*, New Delhi, 1993.

—, *A Report of the Bharat Gyan Vigyan Jatha–1992 and Samata–1993*, New Delhi, 1993.

—, *Annual General Council Meet: July 9–10, 1994, Madras*, New Delhi, July, 1994.

—, *Joy of Learning*, New Delhi, July, 1994.

—, *Note on Perspective Programme of BGVS/AIPSN,* New Delhi, 1994.

—, *Gyan Vigyan Sandesh*, Vol. 1, Nos. 1–3, 1994.

—, *Report to the General Council Meeting: December 11–12, 1995, Hyderabad*, New Delhi, December, 1995.

—, *Joy of Learning–Project Completion Report*, New Delhi, 1995.

—, *Perspectives, Achievements, Tasks, … and Dreams*, New Delhi, 1995.

—, *Joy of Learning: Project Completion Report*, New Delhi, 1996

—, *Bharat Gyan Vigyan Samiti: Interim Report 1989–96*, New Delhi, 1996

—, *Minutes of EC–NLMA Meetings 1989–97*, New Delhi, 1997.

—, *Annual Report 1996–97*, New Delhi, 1997.

—, *Details of Grants-in-aid Received from MHRD–Project-wise (1989–1998)*, New Delhi, 1998.

—, *General Council Meeting: February 7–8, 1998, Bangalore*, New Delhi, February, 1998.

—, *Jeevanshala Update*, NFE CELL, Vol. 1, November, 1998, New Delhi, 1998.

—, *General Council Meeting: October 28–29, Bhubaneshwar,* New Delhi, October, 1999.

—, *Jeevanshala Update,* NFE CELL, New Delhi, 1999.

—, *Minutes of the BGVS General Council Meeting: October 28–29, 1999, Bhubaneshwar*, February, 2000.

—, *Jeevanshala: Ek Zalak*, presented at the National Workshop on Sharing Experiences of NGOs on Experimental and Innovative Projects under the MHRD Schemes, at NCERT, New Delhi, March 23–24, 2000.

—, *Project Completion Report: January 1997–September 2000*, New Delhi, 2001.

—, *Children's Participation for Realization of Their Rights–Bal Manch Report–2001*, Jaipur, 2001.

—, *Jeevanshala: Non-Formal Education of a Different Kind, Project: Wyra and Samalakha*, New Delhi, 2001.

—, *Impacts of Post-Literacy*, New Delhi, January, 2002.

—, *General Council Meeting: 16–17 February, 2002, Presentations and Papers*, Dhanbad, 2002.

—, *A Report on Continuing Education: Programme in Rajasthan*, Jaipur, 2002.

—, AIPSN, *Jatha for Peace, Unity and Sovereignty*, New Delhi, 2003 (a leaflet).

—, *Empowerment, Rights and Security, Three Year Programme*, 2003–2006, Proposal, New Delhi, 2003.

—, *Annual Report 2003–2004*, New Delhi, 2004.

—, *Annual Report 2004–2005*, New Delhi, 2005.

—, *Overview Report Submitted to SDTT*, New Delhi, April–November, 2005.

—, *General Council Meeting, Bhopal, December 28–29*, New Delhi, 2005.

—, *Annual Report 2005–2006*, New Delhi, 2006.

—, *Overview Report Submitted to SDTT*, August, 2006.

—, *Gyan Vigyan Vidyalayas for Democracy, Secularism, Equity and Scientific Temper*, New Delhi, March, 2007.

—, *Training Manual for Resource Persons at Gram Panchayat Level: Convergence Training*, New Delhi, August, 2007.

—, *SDTT Project, 2004–2008*, New Delhi, 2008.

—, *Review Report to Sir Dorabji Tata Trust*, New Delhi, January 2007–August 2008, 2008.

—, *General Council Meeting, Tirupati, Andhra Pradesh, July 21–22*, New Delhi, 2008.

—, *Gyan Vigyan Varta*, New Delhi, March, 2009.

Bhola, H.S., *Campaigning for Literacy*, Paris, UNESCO, 1984.

Chakrabarti, V., Patil, A. and Sudhakar, R., *Evaluation of Schemes of Total Literacy Campaign, Operation Restoration and Post-Literacy Programme of NLM (2008)*, Mumbai, SNDT Women's University, Department of Continuing and Adult Education and Extension Work, 2008.

Chandhoke, N., *State and Civil Society: Explorations in Political Theory*, New Delhi, Sage Publications, 1995.

—, "The 'Civil' and the 'Political' in Civil Society", in Elliott, C.M. (ed.), *Civil Society and Democracy: A Reader*, New Delhi, Oxford University Press, 2003.

—, *The Conceits of Civil Society*, New Delhi, Oxford University Press, 2003.

Chatterjee, B., "India, National Level NGO Influences Policy", in UNESCO, *Education for Rural Transformation*, Inruled, China, 2001.

Dighe, A., "A Postscript to Literacy as Liberation: The Nellore Experience", in Shukla, S. and Kaul, R. (eds.), *Education, Development and Underdevelopment*, New Delhi, Sage, 1998.

—, and others, *Campaigning for Literacy – The Experience of Bharat Gyan Vigyan Jatha: An Analytic Documentation Study*, New Delhi, BGVS, 1991.

Directorate of Adult Education, Status Report of Literacy and Post-Literacy Campaigns, New Delhi, 1994.

—, Ministry of Human Resource Development, Literacy and Post-Literacy Campaigns (Status as on March 1996), New Delhi, March 1996.

Economic and Political Weekly, "A Dangerous Thing", Editorial, Vol. 27, November 21, 1992.

Elliott, C.M., "Civil Society and Democracy: a Comparative Review Essay", in Elliott, C.M. (ed.), *Civil Society and Democracy: A Reader*, New Delhi, Oxford University Press, 2003.

Expert Group, *Evaluation of Literacy Campaigns in India*, New Delhi, Directorate of Adult Education, 1994.

Femia, J., "Civil Society and the Marxist Tradition", in Kaviraj, S. and Khilnani, S. (eds.), *Civil Society: History and Possibilities*, New Delhi, Foundation Books Pvt. Ltd., 2006.

Gillette, A., "The Experimental World Literacy Programme", in Arnove and Graff (eds.), *National Literacy Campaigns: Historical and Comparative Perspectives*, New York, Plenum Press, 1987.

Global Campaign for Education and ActionAid, *Writing the Wrongs: International Benchmarks on Adult Literacy*, November, 2005.

Graff, H.J., "The Legacies of Literacy: Continuities and Contradictions in Western Society and Culture", in Castell et al. (eds.), *Literacy, Society and Schooling*, Cambridge, Cambridge University Press, 1986.

Gramsci, A., *Selections from the Prison Notebooks*, in Hoare, Q. and Smith, G.N. (eds. and translators), New York, International Publications, 1971.

Ilaiah, K., "Andhra Pradesh's Anti-Liquor Movement", in *Economic and Political Weekly*, November 7, 1992.

Jena, V.K. and Mathew, A., *Leading the Way: New Initiatives in Adult Education*, Directorate of Adult Education, Ministry of Human Resource Development, Government of India, 2008.

Kanjula, S., "Total Literacy Campaign and its Links with Basic Education: Dumka, Jharkhand", in Karlekar, M. (ed.), *Paradigms of Learning: The Total Literacy Campaign in India*, New Delhi, Sage Publications, 2004.

Kanniyakumari District Literacy Committee, Arioliyakkam Functional Literacy Phase: An Intensive Programme for Functional Literacy and Institutionalization (June 1995 to May 1996), Kanniyakumari, May, 1995.

Karlekar, M., *Paradigms of Learning: The Total Literacy Campaign in India*, New Delhi, Sage Publications, 2004.

Kaviraj, S. and Khilnani, S. (eds.), *Civil Society: History and Possibilities*, New Delhi, Foundation Books Pvt. Ltd., 2006.

Kerala Sastra Sahitya Parishad (KSSP), *Science as Social Activism: Reports and Papers on the People's Science Movements in India*, Trivandrum, KSSP, 1984.

Kumar, K., "Market Economy and Mass Literacy: Revisiting India's Economics of Communication", in *Economic and Political Weekly*, Vol. 28, December 11, 1993.

Kumar, S., "Literacy Movement in Kerala: One Step Forward, Two Steps Backward", in *Economic and Political Weekly*, Vol. 28, October 9, 1993.

—, "Civil Society in Society", in *Economic and Political Weekly*, Vol. 35, No. 31, July 29, 2000.

Lankshear, C., "Adult Literacy in Nicaragua: 1979–90", in Freebody, P. and Welch, A.R. (eds.), *Knowledge, Culture and Power: International Perspectives on Literacy as Policy and Practice*, London, Falmer Press, 1993.

Luke, A., "Series Editor's Introduction", in Freebody, P. and Welch, A.R. (eds.), *Knowledge, Culture and Power: International Perspectives on Literacy as Policy and Practice*, London, Falmer Press, 1993.

Mahajan, V., "TLC in Roopnagar: A Campaign for Victory Over Illiteracy", in Jena, V. and Mathew, A. (eds.), *Leading the Way: New Initiatives in Adult Education*, New Delhi, Directorate of Adult Education, Ministry of Human Resource Development, Government of India, 2008.

Mahalir Association for Literacy, Awareness and Rights (MALAR) and Centre for Ecology and Rural Development, The Savings Movement–Guidebook, New Delhi, BGVS, January, 1999.

—, Awareness and Rights (MALAR), Annual Report presented in the 5th Annual District Conference held on July 28 and 29, 2000, Kanyakumari, 2000.

Mandi Saksharta Samiti, Project Proposal for Second Year on Continuing Education Programme, Mandi, June, 1999.

Mathew, A., *Indian Engagement with Adult Education and Literacy*, New Delhi, Ministry of Human Resource Development and National Institute of Educational Planning and Administration, April, 2000.

—, Role of NGOs in Basic Education and Literacy in India: Case of Bharat Gyan Vigyan Samiti, New Delhi, 1999 (unpublished).

—, and Handa, R., Bharat Gyan Vigyan Samiti: An Evaluation, New Delhi, 1999 (unpublished).

Ministry of Human Resource Development, Department of Education, National Literacy Mission, New Delhi, January, 1988.

Mishra, L., "National Literacy Mission: Past, Present, and Future", in Mukherjee, A. and Vasanta, D. (eds.), *Practice and Research in Literacy*, New Delhi, Sage Publications, 2002.

Mukherjee, A. and Vasanta, D., *Practice and Research in Literacy*, New Delhi, Sage Publications, 2002.

National Literacy Mission (NLM), National Literacy Mission, New Delhi, August 10, 2008.

—, Overview of the Literacy Programme, New Delhi, April 11, 2005.

—, Adult Education in India, New Delhi, August, 2008.

—, Strategies for Adult Education, New Delhi, August, 2009.

National University in Educational Planning and Administration (NUEPA), National Consultation on Literacy: Report, New Delhi, June 26, 2008.

Ong, Walter J., *Orality and Literacy: The Technologizing of the Word*, London, Methuen, 1982.

Pannikar, K.N., "Culture as a Site of Struggle", in *Economic and Political Weekly*, Vol. 44, No. 7, February 14, 2009.

Parameshvaram, "Vision on Futuristic Plan", in Report of BGVS General Council Meeting, Tirupati, Andhra Pradesh, July 21–22, 2008.

—, "A Great Leap Forward: To Bridge the Three Divides to be Liberated from the Three Curses", in Report of BGVS General Council Meeting, Tirupati, Andhra Pradesh, July 21–22, 2008.

Prem Chand, Status of Adult Literacy in India: A Data base for Literacy Programme, New Delhi, National Literacy Mission, Directorate of Adult Education, 2007.

—, "Eleventh Five Year Plan (2002–07) Quantitative Target for Literacy", in *Indian Journal of Adult Education*, Vol. 69, No. 2, April–June, 2008.

Rampal, A. and Manimala (eds.), *Nav Vikas La Sabjan Padbo*, Mussoorie, National Literacy Resource Centre and New Delhi, Books for Change, 2002.

Reddy, D.N. and Patnaik, A., "Anti-Arrack Agitation of Women in Andhra Pradesh", in *Economic and Political Weekly*, Vol. 28, May 22, 1993.

Robinson, M., "Civil Society and Ideological Contestation in India", in Elliott, C.M. (ed.), *Civil Society and Democracy: A Reader*, New Delhi, Oxford University Press, 2003.

Saldanha, D., "Socialization of Critical Thought: Responses to Illiteracy Among the Advasis in Thane District", in *Economic and Political Weekly, Review of Political Economy*, Vol. 24, No. 30, July 29, 1989; also published in Kumar, K., (ed.), *Democracy and Education in India*, New Delhi, Radiant Publishers, 1993.

—, "Cultural Communication in Literacy Campaigns: Social Relational Contexts, Processes and Hegemenic Organization", in *Economic and Political Weekly*, Vol. 28, No. 20, May 15, 1993.

—, "Literacy, Campaigns in Maharashtra and Goa: Issues, Trends and Direction", in *Economic and Political Weekly*, Vol. 30, No. 20, May 20, 1995.

—, "Literacy Campaigns and Basic Education: Status and Issues", in Desai, M., et al. (eds.), *Towards People-Centred Development*, Mumbai, TISS, 1998.

—, "Residual Illiteracy and Uneven Development", in *Economic and Political Weekly*, Vols. 34, 35, 36; Nos. 27, 28, 29; July 3, 10 and 17, 1999.

—, The Bharat Gyan Vigyan Samiti: Organization, Intervention and Perspectives in the Literacy Campaigns, Mumbai, TISS, March, 2003 (a monograph).

—, "Literacy-Communication, Urbanization-Development: Uneven Development in India", in Rogers, A. (ed.), *Urban Literacy: Communication, Identity and Learning in Development Contexts*, Hamburg, UNESCO Institute for Education, 2005.

—, *Education of Adolescents for Developments in India: The Case of Doosra Dashak*, Jaipur, Rawat Publications, 2007.

—, "Towards a Conceptualization of Social Action within Social Work: Teaching Social Action as a Dialogue between Theoretical Perspectives and between Theory and Practice", in *The Indian Journal of Social Work*, Vol. 69, Issue 2, April, 2008.

—, "Consciousness and Structure in the Gramscian Perspective: Conceptual Concerns", in *Contemporary Education Dialogue*, Vol. 6, No. 1, Monsoon 2008a.

—, "Consciousness and Structure in the Gramscian Perspective: Implications for Education", in *Contemporary Education Dialogue*, Vol. 6, No. 1, Monsoon 2008b.

—, "India: Contextualising the Benchmarks and Indicators for Adult Education", in *Adult Education and Development*, Vol. 71, 2008c.

Saldanha, D. et al., Evaluation Study of Reflect in Bangladesh: A Participatory, Collaborative Review, Dhaka, ActionAid, Bangladesh, August, 1999 (a monograph).

—, The Reflect Approach to Adult Education in India: Process and Policy Implications, Mumbai, TISS and DFID, May, 2000 (a monograph).

Saxena, S., "Limits and Consequences of Literacy Programmes", in *Economic and Political Weekly*, Vol. 28, February 20–27, 1993.

—, "Education of the Masses in India: A Critical Enquiry", in Kumar, Krishna and Oesterheld, J. (ed.), *Education and Social Change in South Asia*, New Delhi, Orient Longman Private Limited, 2007.

Sethi, H., "Groups in a New Politics of Transformation", in *Economic and Political Weekly*, Vol. 19, No. 7, February 18, 1984.

Shah, S.Y., *Indian Adult Education: A Historical Perspective*, New Delhi, Directorate of Adult Education, 1993.

Sharma, J., *A Gyan Vigyan Jatha of Women for Education, Equality and Peace*, New Delhi, BGVS, 1993.

Shatrugna, M., "Literacy and Arrack in Andhra", in *Economic and Political Weekly*, Vol. 27, November 28, 1992.

—, "Literacy as Liberation: The Nellore Experience", in Shukla, S. and Kaul, R. (eds), *Education, Development and Underdevelopment*, New Delhi, Sage Publications, 1998.

Street, B., *Literacy in Theory and Practice*, Cambridge, Cambridge University Press, 1984.

—, "Literacy and Development: Challenges to the Dominant Paradigm", in Mukherjee, A. and Vasanta, D. (eds.), *Practice and Research in Literacy*, New Delhi, Sage Publications, 2002.

Zachariah, M. and Soorya Moorthy, R., *Science for Social Revolution? Achievements and Dilemmas of a Development: The Kerala Sastra Sahitya Parishad*, New Delhi, Vistaar Publications, 1994.

Index